AMERICAN FORESTS

DEVELOPMENT OF WESTERN RESOURCES

The Development of Western Resources is an interdisciplinary series focusing on the use and misuse of resources in the American West. Written for a broad readership of humanists, social scientists, and resource specialists, the books in this series emphasize both historical and contemporary perspectives as they explore the interplay between resource exploitation and economic, social, and political experiences.

John G. Clark, University of Kansas, Founding Editor
Hal K. Rothman, University of Nevada, Las Vegas, Series Editor

AMERICAN FORESTS

Nature, Culture, and Politics

Edited by Char Miller

University Press of Kansas

Published by the University Press of Kansas (Lawrence, Kansas 66049), which was organized
by the Kansas Board of Regents and is operated and funded by Emporia State University, Fort
Hays State University, Kansas State University, Pittsburg State University, the University of
Kansas, and Wichita State University

Library of Congress Cataloging-in-Publication Data

American forests: nature, culture, and politics / edited by Char
   Miller.
      p.   cm.—(Development of western resources)
   Includes bibliographical references and index.
   ISBN 0-7006-0848-6 (alk. paper).—ISBN 0-7006-0849-4 (pbk.:
alk. paper)
      1. Forests and forestry—United States—History.   I. Miller,
   Char, 1951–   . II. Series.
   SD143.A596   1997
   333.75′0973′0904—dc21   97-14811

British Library Cataloguing in Publication Data is available.

Printed in the United States of America

10 9 8 7 6 5 4 3 2 1

The paper used in this publication meets the minimum requirements of the American
National Standard for Permanence of Paper for Printed Library Materials Z39.48-1984.

For Helen Hartnett Miller

CONTENTS

PREFACE

American Forests is an interdisciplinary collection of essays that explore the impact of forestry on natural and human landscapes since the mid-nineteenth century. It has two main goals: to present some of the most compelling arguments that have guided our understanding of the complex and evolving relationship between trees and people in the United States, and to point out those aspects of this tangled interaction that we have yet fully to understand or to articulate.

A reappraisal of a cultural idea and a scholarly field, *American Forests* follows forestry's chronological development, from its roots in the intellectual, scientific, and political debates of the latter half of the nineteenth century to the no less contested terrain in which the profession operates in the late twentieth century. Over that span of time, and with a particular reference to the USDA Forest Service, the volume assesses the shifting intersection of public policy and the environment, detailing changes in the assumptions that have defined and challenged the management of our nation's forested habitats. From these essays, one begins to recognize that forester Gifford Pinchot's famous assertion about what forestry offered the American people—"the greatest good, for the greatest number, for the longest time"—is not the simple, declarative statement it that appears to be.

American Forests has had its own complications, and I am grateful to several people in particular without whom it would not have gotten off the ground. Chief among them is Evelyn Luce, secretary in the History Department at Trinity University, whose tireless efforts, continued support, and good cheer helped in more ways than I can say. Ditto for Eunice Herrington, the department's senior secretary, who manages to keep me (and my colleagues) on an even keel. Maria McWilliams and her co-workers in Interlibrary Loan Services at the Elizabeth Coates Maddux Library worked diligently to secure articles for me during the early stages, as did Cheryl Oakes, of the Forest History Society, who also provided critical bibliographical help in the volume's final stages of production. This project has also benefited from the enthusiastic support of Ed Brannon and his dedicated staff at Grey Towers National Historic Landmark.

It is no less a pleasure to thank the anonymous reviewer of the manuscript, and Tom Cox, whose close analysis of the whole text was a stunning display of erudition and professional integrity, and the staff of the University Press of Kansas for its support. I am indeed fortunate to have gained the enthusiastic interest of Hal Rothman, editor of the Development of Western Resources series, and then to have had the opportunity to work closely with Mike Briggs, editor-in-chief, and Nancy Scott, acquisitions editor; they made what could have been an arduous editorial process a delight. As did the scholars whose work appears in these pages, and on whom I am only too happy to bestow the highest praise an editor can give: they beat every deadline.

Finally, my family, nuclear and extended, has always warmly encouraged my interests, prodded me when necessary, and then laughingly picked me up whenever I fell. The first to do all these nice things was my mother, Helen Hartnett Miller, and it is to her that *American Forests* is lovingly dedicated.

ACKNOWLEDGMENTS

Readers seeking fuller versions of the essays published in this volume can locate them through the following citations. We are grateful that the publishers granted permission to republish the articles:

Donald J. Pisani, "Forests and Conservation, 1865–1890," *Journal of American History,* September 1985, 340–59.

John F. Reiger, "Wildlife, Conservation, and the First Forest Reserve," in *The Origins of the National Forests,* ed. Harold K. Steen (Durham, N.C.: Forest History Society, 1992).

Harold K. Steen, *The Beginnings of the National Forest System,* FS-488 (Washington, D.C.: United States Department of Agriculture, Forest Service, 1991).

Richmond L. Clow, "Timber Users, Timber Savers: The Homestake Mining Company and the First Regulated Timber Harvest," *South Dakota History,* Fall 1992, 213–37.

Robert E. Wolf, "National Forest Timber Sales and the Legacy of Gifford Pinchot: Managing a Forest and Making It Pay," *University of Colorado Law Review* 60, (1989): 1037–78.

Hal K. Rothman, " 'A Regular Ding-Dong Fight': The Dynamics of Park Service–Forest Service Controversy During the 1920s and 1930s," *Western Historical Quarterly,* May 1989, 141–61.

Susan R. Schrepfer, "Establishing Administrative 'Standing': The Sierra Club and the Forest Service, 1897–1956," *Pacific Historical Review,* February 1989, 55–82.

Stephen W. Haycox, "Economic Development and Indian Land Rights in Modern Alaska: The 1947 Tongass Timber Act," *Western Historical Quarterly,* February 1990, 21–46.

Arnold W. Bolle, "The Bitterroot Revisited: 'A University [Re]View of the Forest Service,' " *Public Land Law Review* 10 (1989): 1–18.

Thomas G. Alexander, "From Rule-of-Thumb to Scientific Range Management: The Case of the Intermountain Region of the Forest Service," *Western Historical Quarterly,* October 1987, 409–26.

William G. Robbins, "The Social Context of Forestry: The Pacific Northwest in the Twentieth Century," *Western Historical Quarterly,* October 1985, 411–27.

David A. Clary, "What Price Sustained Yield? The Forest Service, Community Stability, and Timber Monopoly Under the 1944 Sustained-Yield Act," *Journal of Forest History,* January 1987, 4–18.

Dennis Roth, "The National Forests and the Campaign for Wilderness Legislation," *Journal of Forest History,* July 1987, 112–25.

Nancy Langston, "Forest Dreams, Forest Nightmares: An Environmental History of a Forest Health Crisis," an adaptation of her *Forest Dreams, Forest Nightmares: The Paradox of Old Growth in the Inland West* (Seattle: University of Washington Press, 1995).

CONTRIBUTORS

THOMAS G. ALEXANDER is Lemuel Hardison Redd, Jr., Professor of Western American History at Brigham Young University, and is a prolific scholar, having published more than twenty books and seventy articles on the history of Utah and the West, and on environmental history.

The late ARNOLD W. BOLLE was dean of the University of Montana School of Forestry. His chapter was orginally published as the keynote address of the eleventh annual Public Land Law Conference, held in Missoula, Montana, in April 1989.

Formerly chief historian of the Forest Service, DAVID A. CLARY now runs an environmental consulting firm in Bloomington, Indiana. He is the author of *Timber and the Forest Service.*

RICHMOND L. CLOW, who teaches in the Department of Native American Studies at the University of Montana, is co-author of *Tribal Government Today,* as well as other works on Native Americans.

STEPHEN W. HAYCOX is a professor of history at the University of Alaska in Anchorage. Specializing in the history of Alaska and federal Indian policy, he has published extensively on these issues. Current projects include studies of the Alaska Native Brotherhood and a new history of Alaska.

NANCY LANGSTON, an environmental historian and ecologist, is a visiting assistant professor at the Institute for Environmental Studies, University of Wisconsin, Madison. She is the author of *Forest Dreams, Forest Nightmares: The Paradox of Old Growth in the Inland West.*

CHAR MILLER is a member of the Department of History at Trinity University, in San Antonio. He is co-editor of *Out of the Woods: Essays in Environmental History,* and has completed a collection of essays on Gifford Pinchot.

DONALD J. PISANI is Merrick Professor of Western American History at the University of Oklahoma, and is a specialist in natural resources and the law in the American West.

JOHN F. REIGER, author of *American Sportsmen and the Origins of Conservation* and *Passing of the Great West,* and most recently of *Two Essays in Conservation History,* is a professor of history at Ohio University, Chillicothe.

WILLIAM G. ROBBINS is author and editor of six books, most recently *Colony and Empire: The Capitalist Transformation of the American West,* and teaches at Oregon State University.

An analyst for the United States Department of Agriculture, DENNIS ROTH is the author of *The Wilderness Movement and the National Forests.*

HAL K. ROTHMAN is associate professor of history at the University of Nevada, Las Vegas, where he edits *Environmental History.* The author of " 'I'll Never Fight Fire with My Bare Hands Again,' " *On Rims and Ridges,* and *Preserving Different Pasts,* he has also published numerous articles on environmental and western history.

SUSAN R. SCHREPFER, the author of *The Fight to Save the Redwoods,* is a member of the Department of History at Rutgers University. She is currently working on a history of environmentalism with a focus on the Sierra Club.

Longtime director of the Forest History Society, HAROLD K. (Pete) STEEN has written and co-edited numerous volumes on the history of forestry and conservation, including *The U.S. Forest Service: A History* and *The Origins of the National Forests.*

ROBERT E. WOLF served as assistant chief, Environment and Natural Resources Division, Congressional Research Service, between 1972 and 1984. A fellow of the Society of American Foresters, he was involved in the enactment of most conservation legislation from 1956 to 1984.

On Rewriting Forest History

Char Miller

Gifford Pinchot could not help himself. So essential was he to the establishment of the forestry and conservation movements in the United States and to the development of their scientific significance, political influence, and cultural impact that when it came time to write his autobiography, *Breaking New Ground,* he could conceive of his legacy only as an epic struggle—a struggle between good and evil, between foresters and conservationists who crusaded on behalf of the public good, and their enemies, the advocates of concentrated wealth. The Pinchot-led fight really had not been over forests so much as over America's soul.

This perception shaped the autobiography's Manichaean narrative as well as its author's take on how history ought to be written. On this subject, Pinchot had much to say and intriguingly opened *Breaking New Ground* with a set of prefatory comments about why *his* writing of history, "the story of an eyewitness," beats "documentary history all hollow." It does so because a "document may represent a fact, or it may represent the concealment of a fact"; it therefore may be "honest or it may be false." The only way for readers to distinguish between the two is through the kind of "personal recollection" that Pinchot proffered. After all, there "are many portions of the American story of Forestry and Conservation which will never be rightly understood unless the men who had a part in them supply the background of facts actually experienced," and their experience "alone can explain what the documents really mean." This interpretation left Pinchot in a delightful position: as the "only living witness" to much of the history he was to recount, as the writer of a memoir that need not be "decorated and delayed by references to authorities"—he was the authority—Pinchot compelled his audience to embrace his insights; as to the veracity "of nearly every statement" on *Breaking New Ground*'s more than 500 pages, he concluded, "you will have to take it or leave it on my say-so." History belongs to those who make it.[1]

Or does it belong to those who write about it? Certainly that is part of the historian's conceit, that we bring the past *to* life, that with the clarity only the passage of time can provide we are able to set another age in its appropriate and fullest context. This we claim even while we admit to being uncertain about the authoritativeness of our voices and wary of the various meanings

1

embedded in the documents through which we sift, a claim and its caveats that the great American forester dismissed as "pure nonsense." If "actions and events cannot be properly appraised until after generations have passed," he scolded, then nothing can "be understood until there is nobody left alive who knows the inside causes which produced them." A fair retort, but one that misses an equally important rejoinder—memory is itself a reconstruction of events through which we consciously or unconsciously reshape the past to suit present needs; what the eye once witnessed is not always the same thing that the "I" reports. Indeed, *Breaking New Ground* is itself a breathtaking example of this, a revisionist autobiography written by a number of authors.[2]

American Forests, a collection of chapters by many authors that explore the history of the profession that Gifford Pinchot did so much to create, has its own revisions to offer—starting with the beginnings of forestry in the United States. Pinchot, for example, dismissed most nineteenth-century discussions of forestry and conservation, including a book he considered "epoch-making," George Perkins Marsh's *Man and Nature: The Earth as Modified by Human Action* (1864), because such works and ideas had not yet influenced "the public mind." How did he know? Because his copy of the *New American Encyclopedia—A Popular Dictionary of General Knowledge* (1862) contained no references to forests or forestry. Never mind that the encyclopedia he leafed through in his library was published two years *before* Marsh's tome appeared, the facts as he wanted them to be understood were that there was no "widespread interest in the forest . . . until the early days of the present century," a result, one presumes, of his energetic leadership.[3]

About this he was wrong. He could not have secured the political support for the establishment of the Forest Service in 1905 had he not built on the energies and insights of many other individuals and plugged into the organizations they had created in the second half of the nineteenth century; he benefited from even as he used the very public opinion he would later indicate had not existed.

Just how fertile these roots of American forestry were emerges in the work of Donald Pisani, John F. Reiger, and Harold K. Steen, each of whom has recovered different aspects of its intellectual origins, as well as the scientific debates and political dilemmas in which it was embroiled. Tracking the published reports of forest devastation that followed in the wake of mid-nineteenth-century migration to the West has enabled Pisani, for example, to mark the steady increase in concern over cutover lands and the hyperexcited conclusions some reached that massive deforestation—a "timber famine"—was in the offing. Should it come to pass, it would signal a decline in America's spiritual force; our Edenic place in history was slipping away with each swing of an ax.

It was in the midst of this emerging set of cultural worries that Marsh's *Man and Nature* appeared. It quickly gained great popularity; its arguments about the clear and disturbing relationship between the present health of a nation's forested estate and the society's future prospects were published widely in national magazines and regional newspapers, in part because they spoke to a preexisting and brooding sentiment. Marsh seemed a prophetic voice because his audience was already attuned to his jeremiad.

This interplay between popular sentiment and intellectual argument during the post–Civil War years unfolded especially in the sporting press, a niche market that included *Forest and Stream,* the *American Sportsmen,* and *American Angler,* among other periodicals. Their editorial content blended what Reiger has called "the sportsman's code" with a growing awareness of depredations on what was once considered the illitimable western landscape. Hunters and anglers read regularly of the struggles to preserve such landmarks as Yellowstone, the battles to set aside portions of the Adirondacks, and the innumerable attempts to protect local habitats from the ravages of an industrializing world. Linking these various issues, according to George Bird Grinnell, editor of *Forest and Stream,* was a conservation primer that made the "proper and sensible management of woodlands" central to the debate: "No woods, no game; no woods, no water; and no water, no fish"— this, ten years before Pinchot entered the fray.

And fray it already was. Concerned sportsmen and the sporting press launched lobbying campaigns to establish some form of government regulation of public lands. Grinnell's Boone and Crockett Club, with its decidedly patrician cast, proved particularly effective in exerting pressure on federal officials, including Secretary of the Interior John W. Noble, to respond to its demand for the protection of Yellowstone and, later, the passage of enabling legislation for national forests generally. Whatever these successes—and there were plenty of failures, too—the connection between an emerging politics of conservation and the enactment of law was tentative, and it was made more so because of the slow and often convoluted legislative process.

Just how complex this process could become is evident in Steen's synthetic account of the passage of Section 24 of the Forest Reserve Act of 1891, which authorized the president "to set apart trust reserves where, to preserve timber, he shall deem it advisable." This wording seems straightforward enough, but the history that underlay this section's directive language, and the legacy of congressional debate on which it rested, is complicated almost beyond description. By drawing on the scholarship of Ron Arnold, Sally Fairfax, Joseph Miller, and others, Steen lays out this debate's rich record. It began with a series of failed forestry initiatives in the 1870s and early 1880s, continued with the emergence of executive branch interest in the passage of such legislation with the establishment of the Division (later Bureau) of Forestry in the Department of Agriculture in 1881, and concluded with the development of links between the division's professional staff and other federal scientists, the American Forestry Association and like-minded public-interest groups, and interested members of Congress. In combination and individually, they slowly stitched together the requisite legislative coalition that in time created (barely) enough momentum to enact the Forest Reserve Act, which at once gave the president the power to delineate what would become national forests, and thereby sanctioned the federal government's active management of these public lands.

The act offered no guidance, however, on how these lands' boundaries were to be established, the degree to which the land within them would be managed, or what "management" might entail. Some of these concerns would be resolved through legislative initiatives and legal measures, such as the Organic Act of 1897, which directed the secretary of the interior "to make rules and regulations for the protection of the reserves," a mandate that was subsequently reinforced through a series of landmark Supreme Court decisions in the early twentieth century. Others would be developed on the ground, as was Timber Case No. 1, Homestake Mining Corporation's bid in 1898 for the right to log under government regulation in the newly created Black Hills Forest Reserve. The bid was as controversial as it was revealing of the nature of early government control of lumbering in public forests, as Richmond L. Clow observes. For years, Homestake had clear-cut vast stretches of the western forests of South Dakota without payment, at times resorting to fraudulent land claims to do so. This despoliation sparked a number of federal lawsuits that were terminated when the company relinquished its illegal claims and legitimately applied for timber-cutting rights within the reserve. After submitting a plan that adhered to Pinchot's conception of selective harvesting and that was to be overseen by inspectors of the General Land Office, Homestake initially acted as it had in previous years: subsequent inspection of this first timber sale revealed that the company had high-graded the forest, had left few seedlings, and had not followed safe fire-prevention practices. The government's compensation? A meager $1 per 1,000 board feet.[4]

Although Homestake's compliance would improve over the lifetime of this particular sale, the cost of public forest timber remained low, as Robert E. Wolf notes in his examination of the history of federal timber sales. Prices remained low despite Pinchot's assurance to Congress, shortly after the Forest Service was established in 1905 and was given the power to regulate use on the newly named national forests, that his infant agency would manage the forests and make them pay. Pinchot's was a bold claim, one that was never fulfilled during his five-year tenure as head of the Forest Service and, as Wolf's analysis of financial data over the twentieth century suggests, has never been fulfilled. During the early years of the Forest Service, there was a recognition that some forests in the system were so badly cutover, or so inaccessible, that they might never turn a profit. Others might have paid dividends, but did not because below-cost timber sales could not possibly recoup the high costs of management; by 1919 operating costs totaled roughly $58 million, and receipts totaled $34 million, a deficit of $24 million that did not include the millions of dollars spent on improvements to the national forests and expenses associated with running the Forest Service's office in Washington. Over the years, the agency has hidden these imbalances and discrepancies from both Congress and the public through increasingly sophisticated forms of creative accounting and the development of a budgetary category called "net public benefits," which the service has acknowledged it cannot quantify but which it asserts must nonetheless be factored into the annual budget. At the end of the twentieth century, in Wolf's telling, Pinchot's optimistic vision of making the national forests pay "still haunts the agency."

The Forest Service is haunted, too, by other kinds of controversies that have formed its political identity and cultural standing and have influenced its ability to pursue the practice of forestry itself. Perhaps most notable of these is the odd triangular and conflicted relationship that has emerged among it, the National Park Service, and the Sierra Club. As Hal K. Rothman and Susan R. Schrepfer argue, these institutions have cooperated as often as they have fought, and their interactions have gone a long way toward defining, then redefining, how Americans regard public lands and the federal agencies devoted to their welfare.

It was definitions of that welfare, in fact, that stimulated the competition: shortly after the National Park Service was created in 1916, and in an effort to secure a wider influence over the public domain, its leaders, Stephen Mather and Horace Albright, crafted a political campaign to wrest from the Forest Service portions of national forest lands, touting the new agency's primary commitment to aesthetic and cultural values. They apparently were more consistent with those of the motoring American tourists who filled the nation's roadways in the prosperous 1920s than were the values of the Forest Service. A remarkably aggressive public advertising campaign was coupled with equally effective backroom congressional lobbying, and the result was the expansion of the national park system, most of the land for which was transferred from the Forest Service's holdings.

Different value systems accounted for some of these triumphs: the Forest Service could no longer claim to be the only, or even leading, voice for conservation within the federal government. Some were a result of the Forest Service's inability to alter its internal culture and political strategies to meet the new challenge; although it articulated new policies to blunt Park Service advances—especially in the development of recreation and wilderness areas—they would not emerge centrally until after World War II. It was more successful, by contrast, in local negotiations with conservation organizations such as the Sierra Club; through fostering personal contacts, serving in community organizations, and sharing pertinent information and advice on how best to manage particular forests, each of which helped bolster its requests for political support in its battles with Mather and later with the even more acquisitive Harold Ickes, the Forest Service periodically forestalled the Park Service's expansionist fervor. For the agency, cultivating what Schrepfer calls "a clientele relationship" paid dividends.

The Sierra Club benefited from these exchanges as well. By maintaining close working relationships with both federal agencies, it was often able to mold public policy in keeping with its perspectives, gaining more land designated as wilderness in California's national forests, for instance, even as it endorsed the transfer of that state's Kings Canyon from the Forest Service to the Park Service. The context that allowed for this kind of delicate maneuvering collapsed in the mid-1950s, however, as the Forest Service shifted from its longtime custodial mode to a far more intense management of and harvesting within its forests, a policy that was met with increasingly sharp rebuttals from the Sierra Club. With the demise of the previously close cooperation came an age of disaffection and dispute that has transformed the character of political discourse among conservationists; no longer a given, consensus is not necessarily even a desired end.[5]

As these institutional battles unfolded through the middle years of the twentieth century, other defining struggles loomed to highlight the complex of forces then influencing the practice of forestry on the nation's lands. President Truman's signing of the Tongass Timber Act of 1947 is a case in point: originally designed "to protect Indian rights in Alaska," the bill in its final form did nothing of the kind, instead encouraging the Forest Service to sell timber leases that both undercut Indian ancestral claims to land in southeastern Alaska and gave a critical boost to the region's infant pulp industry. Piecing together this complicated story, Stephen W. Haycox muses that modern capitalist development took precedence over the preservation of the Tlingit's and Haida's rights, a trade-off that many white Alaskans, Forest Service officials, and members of Congress readily accepted: for them, the Tongass Timber Act was an important first stage in the final drive to Alaska statehood. Cutting trees would mean more jobs; more jobs would expand the territory's human population, which then would lead to a greater infusion of wealth into the treasury to support the fledgling state. Forestry was a form of patriotism.

This equation made more sense in the late 1940s than it would in the late 1960s when some of its social and environmental consequences became evident. In response to the dramatic boom in demand for housing after World War II, and encouraged by political forces and its own inclinations, the Forest Service first experimented with extensive clear-cuts in western forests, salvaging timber damaged in a beetle epidemic. This new harvesting practice signaled the arrival of what Arnold W. Bolle calls the agency's "Hard Hat" era and its stress on clear-cutting as a method "good for the nation, the land, and the forests." Timber had become the Forest Service's mission.

This mission would engender growing opposition in localities such as Montana's Bitterroot Valley: in the early 1960s, angered by the deleterious impact of clear-cuts on wildlife populations, soil erosion, and landscape aesthetics, and disturbed by what they perceived to be the agency's contempt for their concerns, a group of citizens began to agitate for congressional hearings on the Forest Service's policies. Seven years later, this agitation resulted in the Bitterroot Report, the finding of a Senate-sponsored investigation that Bolle headed and that especially analyzed the practice of clear-cutting and the policy of timber supremacy on which it depended. This heavily publicized report opened the door for further critiques such as the Church Guidelines, which stipulated the limitations on clear-cutting, including the identification of those lands on which it could not be practiced—a congressional reminder to the Forest Service that its charge was to protect the "health of the resource," not simply and blindly pursue "commodity production." In this sense, the Bitterroot and subsequent Monongahela controversies in the late 1960s and early 1970s offered a direct challenge to the developmental focus of the Tongass Timber Act.

To cut or not to cut: that was not the only question. Public foresters were continually confronted with other pressures on the land that subtly and not so subtly determined their professional activities. Grazing, for instance, had long been a prime use of national forest land; the evolution of range-management practices had been one of the most important markers of the agency's ability to adapt to new situations. What has made this adaptive process in the agency's Region 4 so compelling, Thomas G. Alexander has noted, is the sheer length of time it took to graft the results of scientific research onto regulations governing the use of the range. Simply establishing a scientific basis for determining the carrying capacity of a particular range was hard enough—not until the 1920s was it possible to decide roughly how many sheep or cattle could graze and bed down on a plot of land without damaging it. Add to that delay in the gathering of knowledge the fact that members of the agency often discounted the significance of these research findings and that the findings were frequently met with outright skepticism from affected ranchers, and it is no surprise that range management proved so contentious both inside and outside the agency.

Securing the precedence of science over "rule-of-thumb" management was as complicated on the range as it was in the forests, and it was not accomplished, Alexander believes, until the late 1950s or early 1960s. One consequence of this transformation of managerial strategy was that it helped fend off ongoing and intense efforts to reassert "user control of federal grazing lands," efforts that were manifest as well in timber production. But conditions were more dire in the woods than on the range during the post–World War II years, for the pressures for accelerated harvests were felt not just on the forests themselves but in the communities that depended on them. Indeed, as William G. Robbins and David A. Clary have found, there is a tangled relationship among lumber companies, the Forest Service, and these forest-dependent communities, a relationship embedded in an economic structure and "cultural world that encouraged plunder of both humans and the environment." This economic culture, Robbins argues, has made it nearly impossible to avoid the boom-and-bust cycles so inimical to community stability.

That at least has been the experience of towns in the forested regions of the Pacific Northwest throughout the twentieth century, especially since the 1980s, when the once seemingly endless private forestlands were rapidly denuded in response to market forces. These forces also overpowered any alternative proposals for timber harvesting, including one that the Forest Service had first advocated for the region in the late 1930s. Well aware that the timber industry's cut-and-run philosophy would leave bankrupt economies and ruined communities in its wake, the Forest Service had tried to develop a forest-management policy to stabilize forest industries and the people who depended on them. But after the passage of the law that apparently accomplished these ends—the Sustained-Yield Act of 1944—the Forest Service became concerned that the act would not provide the leverage needed to control lumber companies' activities. Then came the disaster: announcing that it had agreed to a 100-year contract to produce 100 million board feet of lumber with a logging company in Shelton, Washington—a length of time and size of cut that surely fit within the parameters of sustained yield—the Forest Service was ill-prepared for the raucous protests the news generated. To the protestors, it appeared as though the agency favored monopolistic practices, and the furor this perception unleashed was so great that it forced the Forest Service to back away from the arrangement, as it eventually would do with negotiated deals in other parts of the country. Sustained yield as a philosophical response to corporate capitalism had failed.

More alive, curiously, was an idea that had even more radical implications for management of the national forests—the possibility of no management. That is the net effect of the concept of wilderness areas, large regions of scenic or unspoiled landscapes within the national forest system that are preserved as they are. But preservation of this sort clashed with the Forest Service's mission of regulating for the wise use of resources—unless, of course, the definition of "use" was expanded to include recreation and aesthetic values, a transition in cultural appreciation that Dennis Roth captures in his discussion of the enactment of the Wilderness Act of 1964.

That the Forest Service played a role in the bill's passage is a result in part of its past. Three of the major proponents of the idea of wilderness—Aldo Leopold, Arthur Carhart, and Robert Marshall—worked in the service in the 1920s and 1930s and were able to convince the agency to establish wilderness or primitive areas in a number of western forests. The Forest Service also responded to the wilderness concept because it could not afford to lag behind in the unending interagency competition with the Park Service; designating lands as wilderness may have been a strategic bulwark against continued Park Service appropriation of Forest Service lands. Moreover, in the custodial age before World War II, there was no reason not to leave some lands pristine.

These economic and political incentives changed in the postwar logging boom, threatening many of the early wilderness designations of national forestland. But these changes would be met, and subsequently matched, by a set of countervailing influences: the increasing number of recreational visitors to the national forests, the emergence of an increasingly sophisticated environmental movement, and a Congress that by the mid-1960s was positioned to support an ultimately modest but significant piece of legislation—the Wilderness Act of 1964—that reconceived how Americans thought of public landscapes.

The impact of this legislation on the conception of the profession of forestry was manifold. Since the passage of the Wilderness Act, a steady stream of congressional legislation and judicial decisions has begun to manage the managers of national forests, attempting to regulate their activities, scrutinize their policy procedures, and assess their budgetary commitments. What the Endangered Species Acts (1966, 1973), National Wild and Scenic Rivers Act (1968), National Trails Act (1968), National Environmental Policy Act (1969), National Forest Management Act (1976), and a host of other initiatives amount to is an amazing, turbulent, and constant reappraisal of professional forestry and foresters. Some of these regulatory demands are at odds with one another, frustrating the Forest Service as well as the many and varied users of the national forests, and thus they have served as convenient examples of the mindless bureaucracy so reviled in late-twentieth-century American political culture.[6]

Yet it is also true that many of these laws and acts were passed with the consent of (if not written by) the agency in hopes of maintaining its ability to determine its fate; it has been caught in a web of its own making. Figuring out how to maneuver within this ever-changing context, and therefore how America's public foresters ought to do their jobs, has produced a spate of new perspectives. One of these, "New Forestry," was the brainchild of ecologist Jerry Franklin, whose work (though not included in this collection) marked a critical intellectual turning point: his land-management research is considered unique because it explicitly rejected the agency's policy of high-level timber production, and asserted instead the primacy of biodiversity, ecosystem complexity, and aesthetic values. Nature, not nurture, would determine the extent to which, or even if, public forestlands are to be managed.[7]

Promising a more eclectic form of management, "New Forestry" seemed to provide the language by which to resolve the tension between those who favor continuing timber production and those who advocate expanding wilderness areas. Or so it appeared in 1989 when Franklin began to publish his pathbreaking work. Since then, the debates and squabbles have ratcheted up, especially in the Pacific Northwest, in response to lawsuits over endangered species and conflicts about riparian legislation and clean air and water regulations. A good portion of these controversies actually turn on the question of forest health—what it means, how it is defined and achieved—a matter of considerable consequence in the Blue Mountains of eastern Oregon and Washington where once-extraordinary forests of ponderosa pine have evolved into stands of sickly and fire-prone fir and lodgepole pine. The array of forces that brought about this disturbing transformation are the subject of Nancy Langston's interdisciplinary research. In it she weaves together the cultural, ecological, political, and economic influences that guided foresters in their quest to perfect the Blues' "general riot of natural forest," making it by turns "efficient, orderly, and useful." This dream produced instead a nightmare, a tragic testament to the way in which "decent people with the best of intentions ended up destroying what they cared for most." Nothing can restore the ponderosa-draped Blue Mountains, but Langston believes that by altering the human demand for efficiency and maximized production, by learning to live on the land "by paying attention to the land," the region's biota might regain some of its former complexity.

There is a lesson here for historians. Most scholarship on forest history has focused on the human perspective, on the economic structures, social institutions, and political strategies that people have developed to exploit this well-wooded terrain, an emphasis that *American Forests* necessarily reflects. Shifting that vantage point just a bit to incorporate the land and its biota, as well as the disturbances, natural and introduced, that affect its evolution, will complicate our research yet enrich its insights. Moving out of the library and into the woods will have another reward: the crafting of a form of eyewitness history that Gifford Pinchot once asserted historians could never write.

NOTES

1. Gifford Pinchot, "On Writing History," *Breaking New Ground* (New York: Harcourt, Brace, 1947), xxii–xxiv.

2. Pinchot cites those who wrote and edited the text with and for him (ibid., xxiv and acknowledgments), confirmation of which appears in M. B. Dickerman, oral-history interview, in *View from the Top: Forest Service Research,* ed. Harold K. Steen (Durham, N.C.: Forest History Society, 1994), 105–6.

3. Pinchot, *Breaking New Ground,* xxiii.

4. On the significance of the Organic Act, see Harold K. Steen, *The U.S. Forest Service: A History* (Seattle: University of Washington Press, 1976), 34–37.

5. The remarkable degree to which the Sierra Club has shifted away from its clientele relationship with the Forest Service of the mid-twentieth century is evident in its attacks on the agency's Ecosystem Management policies (Paul Rauber, "Ecosystem Management," *Sierra,* April 1995, 44–52, 70, 72) and in the club membership's

spring 1996 vote to demand the end of all logging on federal lands (Mike Tharp, "Woodman, Spare That Tree," *U.S. News & World Report,* 13 May 1996, 36).

6. See Paul W. Hirt, *A Conspiracy of Optimism: Management of the National Forests Since World War Two* (Lincoln: University of Nebraska Press, 1994), chap. 10.

7. Jerry Franklin, "Toward a New Forestry," *American Forests,* December 1989, 37–40.

Part One

ROOTS OF FORESTRY

Forests and Conservation, 1865–1890

Donald J. Pisani

Historians who have examined such important subjects as post–Civil War American attitudes toward nature and the wilderness, federal land policies, the national parks idea, the crusade to create national forests, and fish and wildlife protection usually assess these concerns over the abuse of natural resources as legacies of "Progressivism."[1] Much of the popular scientific thought concerning land use in the nineteenth century has been overlooked, particularly the ideas espoused by those who worried about the nation's forests. Their persistent fear of timber famine after the Civil War and basic assumptions regarding the value of woodlands demonstrate that a conservation "ethic"—if not a unified, coherent movement—existed long before Progressive reformers popularized conservation. That ethic derived from the fear that abuse of the land threatened the future of American civilization. Late-nineteenth-century conservationists were as often moralists and philosophers as scientists, and in many ways their beliefs differed from the ideology preached by such men as Theodore Roosevelt, Gifford Pinchot, W. J. McGee, Frederick Haynes Newell, Richard T. Ely, and Charles R. Van Hise. But they also anticipated the later conservationists, especially in exploring the interrelationship of different natural resources and their uses.

In the nineteenth century, legislative interest in conserving the nation's forests was limited. Not until 1878, in the ill-conceived Timber and Stone Act, did the national government provide for sales of woodlands separate from agricultural and mineral lands, and initially that law applied only to California, Oregon, Washington, and Nevada. At both the state and the federal levels, many bills were considered during the 1870s and 1880s to protect forests from fires, foraging livestock, lumbermen, farmers, miners, manufacturers, and other wood users. Some measures called for the creation of state or national forests, but outside New York and Pennsylvania, those proposals enjoyed little success.[2]

That should not suggest that the public or the scientific community lacked interest in the woodlands. Concern for the future of American forests antedated the Civil War. For example, in both *The Pioneers* (1823) and *The*

Prairie (1827), James Fenimore Cooper lamented the destruction of trees. In *The Pioneers,* Judge Temple, who personifies reason and social responsibility, warns that Americans are "felling the forests as if no end could be found to their treasures, nor any limits to their extent. If we go on this way, twenty years hence we shall want fuel." And François André Michaux, who in 1819 published in French the first systematic study of American forests (revised and issued in English in 1849 as *Northern American Sylva*), noted an "alarming destruction of the trees . . . which will continue to increase in proportion to the increase in population. The effect is already felt in a very lively manner in the great cities, where they complain more and more every year, not only of the excessive dearness of firewood, but even of the difficulty of procuring timber for the various kinds of building and public works."[3] Michael Williams asserts that "in 1840 probably 95 percent of America's energy requirements for heating, lighting, and motive power were supplied by wood; coal hardly entered into the picture at this time." Cities along the eastern seaboard grew dramatically during the early decades of the nineteenth century, and farmers—particularly in New York and New England—supplemented their incomes by cutting cordwood for urbanites. The increasing use of steam power by riverboats and railroads also drove up the demand for wood; in 1850 a typical 400-ton boat burned 660 cords on an eleven-day round trip between Louisville and New Orleans. In some places, particularly in New York and northern Ohio, forests were burned to produce ashes used in the production of potash and pearl ash; that industry often went hand in hand with clearing land for agriculture or grazing.[4]

The first extended warning of timber famine came from Frederick Starr, Jr., whose essay "American Forests: Their Destruction and Preservation" appeared in the *Report of the Commissioner of Agriculture for the Year 1865.* Starr alerted his readers to "an impending national danger, beyond the power of figures to estimate, and beyond the province of words to express." He calculated that from 1850 to 1860 about 30 million acres of heavily forested land had been stripped to produce new farms. If the nation's population continued to grow at the rate of the 1850s, more than 100 million additional forested acres would be cleared during the 1860s and each succeeding decade for farming alone—an area roughly the size of California. The danger extended far beyond the timber supply. Starr observed that "there is no one thing in our land which has more certainly caused the present high rates of labor than the high price of fuel for all domestic and manufacturing purposes, the high rents for the industrial classes, and the high price of the raw material upon which nearly one-half million of our industrious, intelligent mechanics labor for their bread." Economic prosperity depended on "cheap bread, cheap houses, cheap fuel and cheap transportation for passengers and freights." Since the forests of New England and the Middle Atlantic states had been severely depleted, the cost of transporting lumber from even greater distances was as significant as the total quantity of timber available. As the price of building materials rose, the urban poor enjoyed less and less hope of escaping crowded tenements for homes of their own. Starr implied that since most republican virtues and values depended on widespread property ownership, the foundation of the Republic was threatened.[5]

Starr recognized that a significant turning point in the nation's use of timber had been reached as settlers poured onto the Great Plains. The population of Kansas grew by 240 percent during the 1860s and by 173 percent during the 1870s, while Nebraska's increased by 355 percent and by 268 percent during the same decades. The absence of timber on the plains was a major reason the pine forests surrounding the Great Lakes were opened to logging. Communities along the eastern seaboard had been built close to timber supplies—unlike the farms and cities of the plains, which were located on the edge of what had long been known as the Great American Desert.[6]

The nation's rapidly expanding rail network also contributed to the destruction of forests. Not only did new lines expose previously inaccessible tracts of land to the ax and the plow, but many railroads owned and operated lumber companies. The railroads consumed enormous quantities of wood for cars, stations, fuel, fences, and especially cross ties. One historian has calculated that from the late 1870s to about 1900, the railroads used 20 to 25 percent of the "annual timber product." In 1890 *Scientific American* estimated that 73 million ties were needed each year to construct new roads and to maintain old ones. (Before chemical treatment for insect damage became common, ties had to be replaced every five to eight years.) Additional demands came from rapidly expanding cities and industries, especially as factories converted from water to steam power.[7]

Forest fires also endangered the timber supply. Farmers had always used fire to clear forests and to burn dead grass to improve pasturage. But the opening of the arid West to mining and stock raising in the 1860s and 1870s resulted in the invasion of virgin forests by grass fires touched off by sparks from locomotives, campfires of careless hunters, and fires purposely set by sheepmen.

The destruction of timber appeared particularly rapid around the Great Lakes, in the Rocky Mountains of Colorado, and in California. In 1866 the commissioner of the General Land Office observed that the dwindling forests of the Great Lakes were a "serious concern," an alarm echoed by the United States commissioner of mining's statistics for the Rocky Mountain forests in 1870. California was particularly vulnerable. The mining industry used enormous quantities of wood for ore reduction and shaft timbers, and the rapid growth of San Francisco, Oakland, Sacramento, and other communities kept the demand for building materials high. Since most Sierra Nevada forests remained inaccessible until the 1880s and 1890s, the lumber industry was for several decades restricted largely to a few heavily logged counties along the coast from Eureka to Monterey. In the late 1860s, the California State Board of Agriculture predicted that one-third of the state's timber had already been cut and that at the current rate the state's entire supply would disappear within forty years. The United States commissioner of agriculture was even more pessimistic. In 1872 he warned that "requirements of the State for forest products will be at least ten times greater for the next twenty-two years." As the decade wore on, estimates became gloomier. In 1874 a writer in the *Overland Monthly* stated that within twenty years California would be importing most of its wood from Alaska; and in an 1878 editorial titled "The Abuse of Nature and Its Penalties," the *Sacramento Daily Union* cautioned that at the current rate of logging, "the exhaustion of the forest growth of the Sierra is only a question of some ten years, and . . . if the rate of consumption is increased the catastrophe will occur considerably sooner." Those fears continued well into the 1890s.[8]

Estimates of the nation's timber supply were equally alarming. They varied enormously because students of forestry differed as to what constituted accessible timber, especially given the rapid construction of railroads. They also disagreed about units of measurement and about what species of trees were usable or desirable for factories, houses, furniture, fuel, and other needs. In his report for 1877, Secretary of the Interior Carl Schurz warned that at the existing rate of consumption, within twenty years the supply would "fall considerably short of our home necessities." For the first time, the census of 1880 contained a survey of the nation's forests. Charles Sprague Sargent, professor of arboriculture at Harvard University, compiled the report largely from published documents, statements of timberland owners, and information provided by state land agents. Such important western species as Douglas fir and ponderosa pine were not considered. In an article in *North American Review*, Sargent reassured readers that the forests were "still capable of yielding a large amount of material, and of continuing to do so for many years." His census report, however, predicted that the most common source of sawtimber, the white pine, would be used up in about eight years and that the most likely substitute, California redwood, would disappear soon thereafter. The report prompted *Forest and Stream*—the most prominent popular forestry journal in the country—to forecast a twenty-five-year overall supply. Later in the decade Bernhard E. Fernow, chief of the Forestry Division of the United States Department of Agriculture, estimated a fifty-year supply. But in 1889 Schurz warned that "men whose hair is already gray will see the day when in the United States from Maine to California and from the Mexican Gulf to Puget Sound there will be no forest left worthy of the name."[9]

Passionate warnings of timber famine reflected a fear deeper than that of the overuse of an essential natural resource. Schurz, and many others, worried that Americans had violated fundamental laws of nature and faced dire consequences. Ironically, arguments against deforestation assumed that while nature operated according to immutable, relentless laws, man had a profound effect on nature. Human beings were not just prey to forces beyond their control; because natural laws were so predictable, man could often mold the environment to his advantage.

The foundation of that thinking was the assumption that, under "normal" conditions, the environment was humid and wooded; grasslands and deserts were "abnormal." *Forest and Stream* explained in 1873: "That all these arid plains, thousands of years ago, were covered with trees seems to be highly probable. From their laying flat, the forests, once on fire, were consumed to the very last tree." Fernow suggested that the entire earth would have been covered with forests, "save only a few localities," had man and other animals not interfered with nature's norm. The Great Plains had been turned to vast, barren prairies by forest and grass fires; the devastation was completed by herds of hungry, tramping buffalo that destroyed new seedlings. "You must remember," Fernow told a reporter in 1891, "that the entire earth is a potential forest." As late as 1899 Charles E. Bessey, a professor at the University of Nebraska, suggested in a paper presented to the American Association for the Advancement of Science that, where not impeded by towns or fields, pine trees had spread across Nebraska and parts of the Black Hills of South Dakota "with a good deal of rapidity."[10]

Not only were forests considered the norm, so was abundant year-round rainfall; and the two went hand in hand. Years before the Civil War, writers observed that deforestation rendered the local climate more severe, subject to greater extremes of heat and cold. Noah Webster noted in 1799 that in the wake of extensive logging in New England's forests during the eighteenth century, the "warm weather of autumn extends into the winter months, and winter into summer months." Farm journals in New England readily accepted the idea that forests influenced climate and made it almost commonplace by the Civil War.[11]

The corollary that forests produced or at least increased rainfall also antedated the Civil War, but it held little relevance for residents of the humid half of the nation. Not until settlers reached the semiarid plains did the idea gain wide currency. Then it won the endorsement not just of land speculators—who never tired of painting the Great Plains as a potential Garden of Eden—but also of respected scientists ranging from geologist Ferdinand V. Hayden, head of the United States Geographical and Geological Survey, to the nation's foremost student of the forests during the 1870s and 1880s, Franklin B. Hough. In 1874 the *Pacific Rural Press*, California's leading farm journal, bluntly declared that "the fact that forests have a beneficial effect on the surrounding country, by producing an increase of rain, is indisputable." *Scientific American* confidently proclaimed in 1888 that the correlation between forests and rainfall was "thoroughly well established." Nor was the influence restricted to the forested area. In 1885 *Nature* observed that "forests exercise an influence on climate which does not cease on their borders, but extends over a larger or smaller adjacent region according to the size, kind, and position of the forest." The editor of *Science* concluded in 1888 that "so often has it been asserted that the growth of forests promotes rainfall, that it has almost become an axiom in science as well as among the people."[12]

Many theories were offered to explain how forests stimulated rainfall. One held that tree roots tapped groundwater and released it into the atmosphere through leaves or needles. This moisture, added to that carried by passing clouds, produced precipitation. Another explanation was that forests served as vast canopies to prevent or to reduce the escape of radiant heat from the soil. The lower temperature in or near forests encouraged atmospheric condensation and lowered the dew point. A third hypothesis was that winds moved much faster over open ground than over trees. In effect, forests provided more resistance to air, so that rain clouds backed up over the trees, concentrating the moisture. Another argument maintained that forests caused upward wind drafts, compressing the air above the trees until it became saturated with water, which fell as rain or snow. Because trees were pointed, and often bore pointed needles, some scientists assumed that forests were nature's assembled lightning rods and attracted thunderstorms much better than did flat or round objects. Clouds were positively charged with electricity, and trees carried a negative charge; hence forests could force rain clouds to alter their course and to congregate above the trees.[13]

Some scientists denied that forests had any significant effect on rainfall or on the climate generally.[14] But other forest influences were more widely accepted. The relationship of forest to farmland had long been of interest to farmers, and not just because trees had to be cleared before crops could be planted. Forests offered a hospitable habitat to a richer variety of game than either the grasslands or the deserts of the West. They also produced rich soils. In 1885 *Forest and Stream* editorialized:

> Forests are . . . on certain soils an essential preliminary to agriculture, and of essential benefit on all soils. Their function is to elaborate the organic elements in compounds readily assimilable by plants, which cannot draw them directly from the atmosphere; and to decompose certain insoluble forms of lime and potash into soluble salts, the presence of which in the cereals is necessary to the support of man and beast.

In short, soil, no less than climate, depended on the forest.[15]

Trees were as important to city dwellers as to farmers. Before the Civil War, the issue of whether forests were healthful or dangerous generated considerable debate. The prevalence of malaria, chills, and a wide variety of fevers prompted Americans to consider the cause and transmission of disease. Malaria was assumed to derive from a toxic gas, or "miasma," that issued from moist, decaying animal and vegetable matter. In an address to the American Philosophical Society in 1700, Hugh Williamson stated that forests preserved swamps and marshes, blocked the purifying rays of the sun, and exuded an atmosphere "constantly charged with gross putrescent fluid." Jeremy Belknap, in his *History of New Hampshire* (1792), acknowledged that "whilst one condemns the air of woodland as destructive to life and health, another celebrates it as containing *nutritive* particles." Belknap himself believed that forest air was "remarkably pure." The forest absorbed "noxious vapors" and contributed to the transmission of healthful breezes while a "profusion of effluvia from the resinous trees imparts to the air a balsamic quality which is extremely favourable to health." Nevertheless, many frontiersmen noted that once the forests had been cut and burned, and the marshes drained or filled, the incidence of fevers dropped sharply.[16]

Those who worried about the pernicious effects of the forests did not disappear after the Civil War, but their voices were all but drowned out by those who promised great therapeutic benefits. For example, in California the Southern Pacific Railroad introduced the fast-growing *Eucalyptus globulus*, or blue gum, from Australia. It was expected to curb malaria epidemics in the swampy Central Valley as well as to provide lumber (particularly for railroad ties), fuel, and windbreaks. The slim, stately trees would slow the winds that carried "disease gases." They would also absorb moisture from the soil, retarding the process of vegetative decay. The eucalyptus leaves contained a volatile oil whose strong odor was thought to disinfect the air—as well as the ground once the leaves fell. The eucalyptus had unique health-giving qualities, but all trees were assumed to absorb dangerous gases and to screen or to filter fungi and bacteria from the air. The forests themselves did not produce disease gases. "Since cholera, typhus, yellow fever and malaria are soil diseases of miasmatic origin," explained Fernow,

> the forest soil becomes important. . . . The vegetable matter in the forest soil is deficient in albuminoids, potash, phosphates and nitrates, and is therefore less nutritive for bacteria than field, garden or city soil. Temperature and moisture conditions in the forest soil are also different and less favorable to microbe life, which thrives best with certain temperatures and an alternation of dry and wet as is found in unshaded fields.

The forests prevented such bacteria from entering the atmosphere because the ground did not dry out and turn to dust—which was easily carried by the wind—as did open fields. Fernow favored the creation of large urban parks as well as the preservation of the forests. The parks would reduce disease by bringing forest influences to the city.[17]

Everyone, moreover, had a stake in the forests' alleged ability to conserve water. Forests captured water in the spongelike humus as well as underground.

Their shade and equable temperatures helped prevent evaporation. Forests also retarded the melting snow in the spring, limited erosion in the mountains, and prevented flooding in the valleys and plains below. And since they released water at a gradual rate, rather than in torrents, they served as natural reservoirs for farmers who irrigated arid lands. J. B. Harrison, secretary of the American Forestry Association, warned in 1889:

> If forest-conditions are destroyed on the mountains . . . evil and destructive forces which no human power can control will be liberated and set in motion. The soil will be carried down from the mountain slopes. . . . The streams will be ruinous torrents for a short time each year . . . and their channels will be dusty chasms during the season when water is most needed. The air will be filled with dust from the perpetual erosion of the hills. . . . The laws and forces of nature will not make exceptions in our favor, though we are a great country.

Sargent was one of the staunchest critics of the idea that forests changed the climate, but he agreed that Americans faced "great disasters . . . unless the safeguards which nature has furnished are respected and preserved."[18]

Those "disasters" were severe indeed. In 1876 *Scientific American,* in an editorial titled "Timber Waste a National Suicide," predicted that "a period, so near as to be practically tomorrow . . . is at hand when our existence as a nation will end." Americans, so critics charged, had behaved as spendthrifts, squandering resources accumulated over centuries. The obsession with short-term profit blinded them to the truth that the essence of civilization was its debt to future generations. "A people can only justify its claim to be called civilized," wrote Charles Eliot Norton, "by so using the free gifts which it has received from Nature and its own predecessors as to transmit them undiminished and improved to its successors."[19]

Just as nature's laws were held to be immutable and predictable, so were the social and economic consequences of violating those laws. Victorian Americans were fascinated with the contrast between civilization and savagery. And as the pace of industrialization and urbanization increased—especially given the simultaneous subjugation of the nation's last "savages," the Indians of the Great Plains—the contrast became even more stark. Since civilization required an active process to sustain itself, human societies had a tendency to regress to more primitive institutional forms. Evolution did not ensure the continued success of an "advanced" society any more than it ensured the continued dominance of one species of animal over its competitors. Once deforestation passed a certain critical point, the process of decay was irreversible, much as a fatal disease. Most of the humans and wild animals, subjected to extremes of heat and cold, drought and flood, would flee the ravished land. Those remaining, deprived of the basic building materials of civilized communities, would revert to barbarism. Poverty would replace plenty; the "survivors" would become a society of nomads subject to a pastoral economy. The religious overtones to that grim view of the future are obvious: the American forests were pictured as a latter-day Garden of Eden. Just as man had paid a stern price for neglecting his earlier trust, careless stewardship of God's gifts promised divine retribution.[20]

The authors of those jeremiads thought history had provided abundant precedents to confirm their dire predictions. The high priest of forests and natural law was George Perkins Marsh, whose epochal *Man and Nature: The Earth as Modified by Human Action* was published originally in 1864. The book was an immediate success. Many of the articles cited in this chapter were directly or indirectly inspired by Marsh's monumental work. Late in his life, Sargent complained to Robert Underwood Johnson, a leading conservationist, that the Progressives had forgotten Marsh's contribution. "No account of the movement of forest preservation in this country," Sargent wrote in 1908, "should overlook the value of this remarkable book. I, at least, owe my interest in forests and forest preservation to it almost entirely. The younger generation apparently know nothing about it."[21]

Marsh may not have been well-known in 1908, but late-twentieth-century historians have "discovered" him such that his basic ideas are very familiar to contemporary students of natural resources.[22] But his were revolutionary ideas (if not entirely original) in the 1860s. He challenged the prevailing nineteenth-century assumption that resources were inexhaustible and demonstrated that the use of one natural resource often had profound effects on other resources. He showed that man was part of nature, not independent and above it. He revealed the importance of ecological balances in nature:

> Nature left undisturbed, so fashions her territory as to give it almost unchanging permanence of form, outline, and proportion, except when shattered by geologic convulsions; and in these comparatively rare cases of derangement, she sets herself at once to repair the superficial damage, and to restore, as nearly as practicable, the former aspect of her dominion.

Marsh considered the land as the one stable force in human life. The wise use of nature's bounty would provide man with permanent, fixed values in a changing world, not just prevent waste. "All human institutions . . . have their instability, their want of fixedness, not in form only, but even in spirit," he noted. "It is time for some abatement in the restless love of change which characterizes us, and makes us almost a nomad rather than sedentary people."[23]

The lack of "fixedness" in human institutions had been driven home to Marsh as he pondered the landscape and ruins of ancient civilizations. As minister to Italy, he became convinced that the destruction of forests surrounding the Mediterranean had played a large part in the fall of the Roman

Empire. Over one-half of the lands that had been part of that dominion, he noted, were

> either deserted by civilized man and surrendered to hopeless desolation, or at least greatly reduced in both productiveness and population. Vast forests have disappeared from mountain spurs and ridges; the vegetable earth accumulated beneath the trees by the decay of leaves and fallen trunks, the soil of the alpine pastures which skirted and indented the woods, and the mould of the upland fields, are washed away.[24]

American scientists and popular writers quickly picked up the fall-of-nations theme. In his essay "American Forests," which appeared less than two years after Marsh's *Man and Nature,* Starr quoted extensively from Marsh's work and concluded: "Palestine and Syria, Egypt and Italy, France and Spain, have seen some of their most populous regions turned into forsaken wilderness, and their most fertile lands into arid, sandy deserts. The danger to our land is near at hand." Such gloomy litanies became very common during the last three decades of the nineteenth century. Many thoughtful Americans might have arrived at Marsh's conclusions had *Man and Nature* never been published; the book was as much a digest and synthesis as a work of original research and thought. But few books have found a more receptive audience or elicited more discussion.[25]

Popular writers did not merely echo Marsh, but found new examples of the law of "desertification" all around them. In 1877 *Forest and Stream* reprinted an article from the *London Economist* reporting that following the discovery of gold in California, Chilean peasants burned large forests in the lower Cordillera mountains to raise wheat to supply the new market. That, the journal concluded, had—in fewer than thirty years—dramatically reduced precipitation and threatened the country with "sterility." Another writer told how the Turkish provinces south of the Balkan Mountains in present-day Bulgaria once enjoyed "abundant crops" and "comparative prosperity" until the Ottoman navy exhausted local forests to build ships. Since that time, drought and famine had plagued the region.[26]

In the United States, deforestation in the Adirondack Mountains was blamed for destroying navigation on the Hudson River and threatening the economic prosperity of New York State. The deserts of the Southwest were even more alarming. Most observers believed that evidence of ancient civilizations in the region indicated that it had once been heavily forested. Deforestation had touched off the inevitable process of desertification, and the deserts of the Southwest were spreading like a malignant tumor. "In the Gila valley the improvidence of a prehistoric race has already begun to Africanize our compact continent," Felix L. Oswald wrote, "and if the same agencies continue to modify the climate of the Atlantic slope, our cotton states will, in fifty years from now, be reduced to the necessity of raising their crops by the aid of irrigation. The locust will ravage the plains of the Gulf coast."[27]

The fear that abuse of the forests would inevitably destroy the United States crested in the 1870s and 1880s: the severe Great Plains drought of the late 1880s and early 1890s discredited the idea that trees or human habitation had increased the water supply, and low farm prices during the years 1893 to 1897 drove many farmers off the land. In the 1890s and after, Great Plains residents became interested in irrigation and in rain-making experiments using various chemicals, explosives, and cannons. For the most part, however, they turned to dry farming as the answer to aridity. That the opening of the plains to settlement had stimulated much of the writing about "forest influences" was reflected in the dramatic decline in public interest in the forests after 1893. In 1897 Sargent, as editor of *Garden and Forest,* announced the demise of his journal, lamenting that "there are not persons enough in the United States interested in the subjects which have been presented . . . to make a journal of its class and character self-supporting."[28]

At about the same time, technological changes reduced the nation's dependence on wood. Railroads began to treat cross ties with zinc chloride and, later, with creosote, and by the 1960s ties provided thirty-five to fifty years of service rather than the five to ten years during the 1870s or 1880s. Once chemical treatment began, hemlock, tamarack, and red oak, in addition to the more insect-resistant white oak and cedar, could be used for ties. And not only were coal and petroleum increasingly substituted for wood as energy sources, but wood also gave way to brick, stone, cement, iron, and steel in many buildings, ships, bridges, freight cars, farm implements, and even desks and filing cabinets. Per capita consumption of wood declined sharply after 1905, while the use of cement increased from 20 million barrels in 1901 to 90 million in 1913. By the second decade of the twentieth century, competition from new materials had driven down prices and prompted lumber trade associations to launch an advertising campaign to show the benefits of wood over substitutes. With supply exceeding demand, fears of a timber famine all but disappeared, and estimates of the remaining lumber supply became much more optimistic. In 1911, following the most comprehensive survey ever made of the nation's forests, the Bureau of Corporations declared that at existing rates of use the supply of timber would last for fifty-five years. That was a far cry from the bleak estimates of Schurz and Sargent in the 1870s and 1880s, and the estimate—which did not include new growth—was double that contained in the census of 1900.[29]

Perhaps the best way to assess the significance of nineteenth-century attitudes toward forests and conservation is to compare post–Civil War conservationists with those who followed them in the early twentieth century. Although the postwar intellectual elite ranged from philosophers to journalists to ministers, most of its leaders were scientists (including Sargent, Hough, and Fernow). The same was true of the Progressives, though once in power they assigned much of their practical work to engineers. Equally important, a "multiple use," or "multiple purpose," concept of natural-resource development linked the two groups. Usually that idea has been attributed to twentieth-century water-resource planners, specifically their discovery that water is one resource with many related uses, such as navigation, irrigation, and power.[30] The forest literature of the Gilded Age, wrong as it was in many of its assumptions and conclusions, did the same thing. The farmer, shipper, hunter, merchant, and banker all had as much stake in the woodlands as did the lumbermen. The destruction of forests represented more than greed, waste, and poor planning: it altered stream flow, dried out the land, drove off birds and game animals, contributed to massive soil erosion, and ultimately undermined the foundations of society itself. The idea that nature operated according to clearly defined, predictable natural laws served as the intellectual foundation for the dictum that the various uses of each resource be carefully integrated and coordinated.

A persistent moralism also connected the two groups. Most conservationists saw the way natural resources were used as a barometer of the health of American society. In his brilliant *Conservation and the Gospel of Efficiency: The Progressive Conservation Movement, 1890-1920*, Samuel P. Hays places so much emphasis on science, efficiency, and federal planning that he obscures the "soft" side of early-twentieth-century conservation. A prime example of Progressive moralism was the crusade for federal reclamation that culminated in the Newlands Act of 1902. Proponents of that measure saw an America gone wrong. They worried about urban crowding and poverty, strikes, a return of the depression of the 1890s, the rapid growth of cities, land monopoly, and a relative decline in the nation's rural population. They had many immediate, practical, selfish motives for favoring federal reclamation, but they sold the policy to the public as a program to salvage the "wasted," barren lives of homeless city dwellers and to arrest a perceived decay of republican ideals and civic virtue. Here was an opportunity to make a landless, volatile, working class into an army of yeoman farmers who would build a dryland empire. In the West, property ownership would serve as a ballast to the old ways and ideals. The reclamation crusade, unlike many other Progressive conservation policies, began as an attempt to restore a lost balance to American society, just as nineteenth-century forest conservationists sought to teach Americans to respect balances in nature.[31]

Sharp differences separated the two groups of conservationists, however. The moral strain in early-twentieth-century conservation did not extend to forests. A handful of conservationists raised the specter of timber famine well into the new century, but the idea that such a famine would lead to desertification or that it symbolized a fatal flaw in American society disappeared. No longer did conservationists brood about the decline of American civilization, and the jeremiad quality in earlier writings faded away.[32] The change occurred in part because the post–Civil War conservationists could better remember a more predictable agricultural society and economy. They had a harder time accepting the new industrial order, with its rapacious hunger for natural resources, than did the twentieth-century conservationists, who were born later and who accepted bigness (if not monopoly) as inevitable. Then, too, those who wrote about forests after the Civil War *appear* more pessimistic than their intellectual descendants because they lacked the skills to measure or to quantify man's impact on nature. Both groups of conservationists consisted of scientists, but such academic disciplines as silviculture, hydraulic engineering, and agrology did not exist in the 1860s, 1870s, and 1880s. Determining the nation's timber supply depended not just on finding reliable units of measurement, but also on understanding the rates of growth of different species of trees and whether tree cultivation on a large scale was feasible. That knowledge, in turn, depended on understanding soils, water, and weather. The conservationist of 1910 was the legatee of great advances in science and technology.

Given the gravity of their message, why did the forest conservationists fail to attract greater public attention during the 1870s and 1880s? "It is only a short time since a large proportion of the public appeared to think that forests were useful only as supplying lumber and firewood," *Forest and Stream* editorialized in 1884, "but this ignorance has now been replaced in many minds by a more intelligent comprehension of the nature of woodlands." That comprehension was not so widespread as *Forest and Stream* suggested; outside California and the Great Plains states, it did not exist in the West. In most of the trans-Mississippi region, the pioneer ethic of "cut and run" prevailed in 1890 as it had in 1860. Conservation during the early decades of the twentieth century was not a "mass movement," but it certainly received more publicity than did conservation efforts during the nineteenth century. Marsh's intellectual heirs never constituted a unified "movement," nor did they have clear objectives and carefully drawn policies. Many Progressives embraced a new federalism and centralization, but post–Civil War conservationists regarded government with deep suspicion. They balked at any dramatic increase in federal power, unable to decide whether woodlands ought to be protected as public or as private land, or by what level of government, if any. They could not decide, as a group, between two fundamental choices: whether to increase the wood supply by encouraging tree planting or to preserve the existing supply by enacting laws to protect the forests from fires and wasteful logging. And since neither Congress nor late-nineteenth-century presidents solicited their advice on a large scale, they had little opportunity—let alone incentive—to translate their ideals into policies. The resulting detachment from the give-and-take of practical politics reinforced a natural scholarly "aloofness." The scientists and humanists who wrote about the forests had the luxury and liability of observing nature from the easy chair.[33]

The unifying force behind forest conservation was a pessimistic view of the future. Roderick Nash and many others have distinguished between aesthetic conservationists and utilitarian conservationists.[34] Each group held a very different view of nature. However, a third group ought to be added: those who supported conservation, not so much out of a sense of beauty or even a desire to promote the greatest good for the greatest number, but out of a fear of nature's ultimate dominance over man. The post–Civil War conservation ethic extended beyond the forests. Any new synthesis of conservation in the period from 1865 to 1890 will have to look at land and water use, and perhaps at wildlife, as well as at woodlands, and it will have to consider attitudes toward the use of natural resources throughout the nation, not just in the West.[35] It will have to explain why, in an age generally characterized as optimistic—an era imbued with faith in progress—a significant number of conservationists found the fall-of-nations theme so compelling. Not until the 1960s did such a somber view of the future reappear in the United States. Naïve as they were, those nineteenth-century Cassandras seem surprisingly modern.

NOTES

1. Samuel P. Hays, *Conservation and the Gospel of Efficiency: The Progressive Conservation Movement, 1890–1920* (Cambridge, Mass.: Harvard University Press, 1959); Donald C. Swain, *Federal Conservation Policy, 1921–1933* (Berkeley: University of California Press, 1963); A. L. Riesch Owen, *Conservation Under F.D.R.* (New York: Praeger, 1983). See also J. Leonard Bates, "Fulfilling American Democracy: The Conservation Movement, 1907 to 1921," *Mississippi Valley Historical Review,* June 1957, 29–57; Gordon B. Dodds, "The Historiography of American Conservation: Past and Prospects," *Pacific Northwest Quarterly,* April 1965, 75–81; Gordon B. Dodds, ed., "Conservation and Reclamation in the Trans-Mississippi West: A Critical Bibliography," *Arizona and the West* 13 (Summer 1971): 143–71; Thomas LeDuc, "The Historiography of Conservation," *Forest History,* October 1965, 23–28; Timothy O'Riordan, "The Third American Conservation Movement: New Implications for Public Policy," *Journal of American Studies,* August 1971, 155–71; Donald Fleming, "Roots of the New Conservation Movement," *Perspectives in American History* 6 (1972): 5–91; James L. Penick, Jr., "The Resource Revolution," in *Technology in Western Civilization,* ed. Melvin Kranzberg and Carroll W. Pursell, Jr., 2 vols. (New York: Oxford University Press, 1967), 2:431–48; Robert O. Beatty, "The Conservation Movement," *Annals of the American Academy of Political and Social Science,* May 1952, 10–19; Grant McConnell, "The Conservation Movement—Past and Present," *Western Political Quarterly,* September 1954, 463–78; and Lawrence Rakestraw, "Conservation Historiography: An Assessment," *Pacific Historical Review,* August 1972, 271–88. Hans Huth, *Nature and the American: Three Cen-*

turies of Changing Attitudes (Berkeley: University of California Press, 1957); Arthur A. Ekirch, Jr., *Man and Nature in America* (New York: Columbia University Press, 1963); Alfred Runte, *National Parks: The American Experience* (Lincoln: University of Nebraska Press, 1979); John F. Reiger, *American Sportsmen and the Origins of Conservation* (Norman: University of Oklahoma Press, 1986); James B. Trefethen, *An American Crusade for Wildlife* (New York: Winchester Press, 1975); Roderick Nash, *Wilderness and the American Mind* (New Haven, Conn.: Yale University Press, 1967); Donald Worster, ed., *American Environmentalism: The Formative Period, 1860–1915* (New York: Wiley, 1973); Donald Worster, *Nature's Economy: The Roots of Ecology* (San Francisco: Sierra Club Books, 1977); Roy Robbins, *Our Landed Heritage: The Public Domain, 1776–1936* (Princeton, N.J.: Princeton University Press, 1942); Paul W. Gates and Robert W. Swenson, *History of Public Land Law Development* (Washington, D.C.: Government Printing Office, 1968). Ekirch concludes: "Conservation did not become an important American ideology until the 1900's" because the United States was "too much a land of plenty to be worried over alleged or impending scarcities. . . . Only the so-called closing of the frontier—at least in the sense of free and easy exploitation of the West—made conservation the serious concern of some Americans" (*Man and Nature in America*, 81–99, esp. 81–82).

2. Andrew Denny Rodgers III, *Bernhard Edward Fernow: A Story of North American Forestry* (Princeton, N.J.: Princeton University Press, 1951), 9, 42, 100, 154–58, 206–26; Gates and Swenson, *History of Public Land Law Development*, 550–52, 565–70. Hans L. Trefousse, *Carl Schurz: A Biography* (Knoxville: University of Tennessee Press, 1982), 241–42, devotes only one paragraph to Schurz's pathbreaking forest and conservation policies. For the arguments of the scientists and popular writers, see John Ise, *The United States Forest Policy* (New Haven, Conn.: Yale University Press, 1920), 42–44, 52–53, 55–78, 112–18, 120–29, 141–42; and Jenks Cameron, *The Development of Governmental Forest Control in the United States* (Baltimore: Johns Hopkins University Press, New American Library, 1928), 201–10.

3. James Fenimore Cooper, *The Pioneers* (New York: New American Library, 1964), 20, 100, 103, 218–19; James Fenimore Cooper, *The Prairie* (New York: New American Library, 1964), 19, 24–25, 69, 122, 206; Gilbert Chinard, "The American Philosophical Society and the Early History of Forestry in America," *Proceedings of the American Philosophical Society*, July 1945, 469; Samuel Trask Dana, *Forest and Range Policy: Its Development in the United States* (New York: McGraw-Hill, 1956), 74–75; Ise, *United States Forest Policy*, 26–27. On James Fenimore Cooper, see Lee Clark Mitchell, *Witnesses to a Vanishing America: The Nineteenth-Century Response* (Princeton, N.J.: Princeton University Press, 1981), 42–47.

4. Michael Williams, "Products of the Forest: Mapping the Census of 1840," *Forest History*, January 1980, 6, 10, 14–15.

5. Frederick Starr, Jr., "American Forests; Their Destruction and Preservation," in *Report of the Commissioner of Agriculture for the Year 1865* (Washington, D.C.: Government Printing Office, 1866), 210–34, maintained that because Americans had little respect for public property, the creation of state or national forests would do little to avert the famine. He favored, instead, inducements to cultivate trees on cutover lands closer to the cities.

6. Ibid., 212; Bureau of the Census, *Abstract of the Twelfth Census of the United States, 1900* (Washington, D.C.: Government Printing Office, 1902), 34–35; James

Elliott Defebaugh, *History of the Lumber Industry of America,* 2 vols. (Chicago: The American Lumberman, 1906–1907).

7. Sherry Hessler Olson, "Commerce and Conservation: The Railroad Experience," *Forest History,* January 1966, 3; Sherry Hessler Olson, *The Depletion Myth: A History of Railroad Use of Timber* (Cambridge, Mass.: Harvard University Press, 1971), 8–29; "The Rapid Destruction of Our Forests," *Scientific Monthly,* December 1887, 225–26.

8. Ise, *Unites States Forest Policy,* 31–32; J. M. Tuttle, "The Minnesota Pineries," *Harper's Magazine,* March 1868, 409–23; *Report of the State Board of Agriculture for 1868 and 1869* (Sacramento, Calif.: State Printing Office, 1870), 28; *Biennial Report of the State Board of Agriculture for the Years 1870 and 1871* (Sacramento, Calif.: State Printing Office, 1872), 21; *Report of the Commissioner of Agriculture for the Year 1872* (Washington, D.C.: Government Printing Office, 1874), 442; A. W. Chase, "Timber Belts of the Pacific Coast," *Overland Monthly,* September 1874, 249; *Sacramento Daily Union,* 19 June 1878; *Garden and Forest,* 4 December 1895, 490; "Destruction of Forests in California," *Scientific American,* 14 December 1895, 377. See also *Sacramento Daily Union,* 25 November 1869; *Sacramento Daily Union,* 1 February 1870; *Pacific Rural Press,* 26 August 1871, 118; *Report of the Commissioner of Agriculture for the Year 1883* (Washington, D.C.: Government Printing Office, 1883), 448.

9. U.S. Congress, House, *Report of the Secretary of the Interior,* House Reports, 45th Cong., 2nd sess., no. 1, 1 November 1877, 2 vols. (Washington, D.C.: Government Printing Office, 1877), 1:xvi; U.S. Congress, House, *Report of the Secretary of the Interior,* House Reports, 45th Cong., 3rd sess., no. 1, 1878, 2 vols. (Washington, D.C.: Government Printing Office, 1878), 1:xii; Charles S. Sargent, *Report on the Forests of North America (Exclusive of Mexico)* (Washington, D.C.: Government Printing Office, 1884); Charles S. Sargent, "The Protection of Forests," *North American Review,* October 1882, 386–401; *Forest and Stream,* 13 April 1882, 223; *Forest and Stream,* 31 January 1884, 2; *Forest and Stream,* 25 December 1884, 422; *Forest and Stream,* 15 Jan. 1885, 482; "The Forest Census," *Nation,* 2 April 1885, 284–85; Fernow, "Our Forestry-Problem," 231; "United States Division of Forestry," *Popular Science Monthly,* September 1891, 714; Frederic Bancroft, ed., *Speeches, Correspondence and Political Papers of Carl Schurz* (New York: G. P. Putnam Sons, 1913), 5:24. In 1903 Bernhard E. Fernow predicted that the nation's forests would be exhausted within thirty years, "and . . . most important coniferous supplies in a very much shorter time" ("Outlook of the Timber Supply in the United States," *Forestry and Irrigation,* May 1903, 230). Martha A. Dietz, "A Review of the Estimates of Sawtimber Stand in the United States, 1880–1946," *Journal of Forestry,* December 1947, 865–74.

10. *Forest and Stream,* 25 September 1873, 104; "Forests," *Scientific American,* 19 September 1891, 181; "A Forest 3,000 Miles Long by 1,700 Miles Wide," *Scientific American,* 2 March 1895, 139; Charles E. Bessey, "Are the Trees Advancing or Retreating upon the Nebraska Plains?" *Science,* 24 November 1899, 768–70.

11. Noah Webster, Jr., "On the Effects of Evergreens on Climate," *Transactions of the New York Agricultural Society, 1799* (New York, 1799), 51–52; Howard W. Lull, "Forest Influences: Growth of a Concept," *Journal of Forestry,* September 1949, 700–705.

12. U.S. Congress, House, *Report of the Secretary of the Interior, Part I,* House Reports, 40th Cong., 2nd sess., no. 1, 18 November 1867 (Washington, D.C.: Gov-

ernment Printing Office, 1867), 159–60; Franklin B. Hough, "On the Preservation of Forests and the Planting of Timber," in U.S. Congress, House, *Cultivation of Timber and the Preservation of Forests,* House Reports, 43rd Cong., 1st sess., no. 259, 17 March 1874 (Washington, D.C.: Government Printing Office, 1874), 90–101; *Pacific Rural Press,* 13 June 1874, 376; "Influence of Forests on Climate," *Nature,* 4 June 1885, 115; *Science,* 23 November 1888, 241. For overviews of the influence of forests on rainfall, see Henry Nash Smith, "Rain Follows the Plow: The Notion of Increased Rainfall for the Great Plains, 1844–1880," *Huntington Library Quarterly,* February 1947, 169–93; David M. Emmons, "American Myth: Desert to Eden; Theories of Increased Rainfall and the Timber Culture Act of 1873," *Forest History,* October 1971, 6–14; and Charles R. Kutzleb, "American Myth: Desert to Eden; Can Forests Bring Rain to the Plains?" *Forest History,* October 1971, 14–21.

13. *Biennial Report of the Board of Agriculture of the State Agricultural Society for the Years 1866 and 1867* (Sacramento, Calif.: State Printing Office, 1868), 13, 14; "Forests and Rainfall," *Popular Science Monthly,* 8 (November 1875), 111–12; "How Woods Preserve Moisture," *ibid.,* 28 (January 1886), 429–30; "Forests and Climate," *ibid.,* 47 (May 1895), 139; Fernow, "Our Forestry-Problem," 229; *Forest and Stream,* 19 August 1875, 21; Abbot Kinney, "The Forest: Forestry in California— IV," *Garden and Forest,* 17 October 1888, 405–6; B. E. Fernow, "Climatic Influence of Forests," *Garden and Forest,* 29 March 1893, 148–49; Bernhard E. Fernow, "The Influence of Forests on the Quantity and Frequency of Rainfall: Mr. Gannett's Paper," *Science,* 23 November 1888, 242–44; *Science,* 5 June 1891, 313–14.

14. John Wesley Powell, director of the United States Geological Survey (USGS); Henry Gannett, chief geographer of the USGS; and Charles S. Sargent doubted that forests promoted rainfall: J. W. Powell, *Report on the Lands of the Arid Region of the United States with a More Detailed Account of the Lands of Utah. With Maps* (Washington, D.C.: Government Printing Office, 1878), 1–4, 14–19, 71–73; Henry Gannett, "Do Forests Influence Rainfall?" *Science,* 2 March 1888, 99–100; Gannett, "Influence of Forests on the Quantity and Frequency of Rainfall," 242–44; Charles S. Sargent, "The Rainfall on the Plains," *Garden and Forest,* 6 June 1888, 169; Sargent, "Protection of Forests," 386; "American Forestry," *Nation,* January 1879, 87–88; Daniel Draper, "Has Our Climate Changed?" *Popular Science Monthly,* October 1872, 665–74; "Relation of Elevation and Exposure to Rainfall," *Popular Science Monthly,* March 1881, 714–15; "The Laws of Rain-Fall," *Popular Science Monthly,* July 1882, 423; "Forests and Climate," *Popular Science Monthly,* August 1882, 562; George E. Curtiss, "The Rainfall on the Plains," *Garden and Forest,* 24 October 1888, 411–12; *Forest and Stream,* 11 November 1875, 212; *Forest and Stream,* 2 October 1884, 183.

15. *Forest and Stream,* 1 January 1885, 441; "Forestry," *Popular Science Monthly,* September 1876, 632; "The Preservation of Forests," *Scientific American,* 8 March 1879, 145. See also the memorial to the state legislatures adopted by the American Association for the Advancement of Science at its August 30, 1880, meeting, in Franklin B. Hough, *Report on Forestry, Submitted to Congress by the Commissioner of Agriculture* (Washington, D.C.: Government Printing Office, 1882), 59–60.

16. Chinard, "American Philosophical Society and the Early History of Forestry in America," 453; Jeremy Belknap, *The History of New Hampshire,* 3 vols. (Dover, N.H.: O. Crosby and J. Vanney, 1812), 3:171–72.

17. Kenneth Thompson, "The Australian Fever Tree in California: Eucalyptus and Malaria Prophylaxis," *Annals of the Association of American Geographers,* June 1970, 230–44; *Forest and Stream,* 24 September 1874, 101; "Trees and Health," *Popular Science Monthly,* April 1878, 758; "Sanitary and Climatic Influence of Forests," *Popular Science Monthly,* January 1894, 426; "The Sanitary Value of Trees," *Scientific American,* 12 June 1886, 375; B. E. Fernow, "The Forest: Hygienic Significance of Forest Air and Forest Soil," *Garden and Forest,* 18 January 1893, 34–35.

18. *Forest and Stream,* 13 April 1882, 204; *Forest and Stream,* 17 April 1884, 221; "Influence of Forests on Climatic Conditions," 118; F. L. Oswald, "The Climatic Influence of Vegetation—A Plea for Our Forests," *Popular Science Monthly,* August 1877, 385–90; "The Forest," *Popular Science Monthly,* November 1890, 143–44; J. B. Harrison, "Forests and Civilization: The North Woods—VII," *Garden and Forest,* 11 September 1889, 442; [C. S. Sargent], "Forests and Floods," *Garden and Forest,* 4 November 1896, 441. The influence of forests on stream flow—almost an article of religious faith in the 1870s and 1880s—became a hot issue during the early years of the twentieth century. See Gordon B. Dodds, "The Stream-Flow Controversy: A Conservation Turning Point," *Journal of American History,* June 1969, 59–69.

19. "Waste Land and Forest Culture," *Scientific American,* 13 March 1875, 161; "Timber Waste a National Suicide," *Scientific American,* 12 February 1876, 97; "Forests and Civilization," *Garden and Forest,* 19 December 1888, 505; C. E. Norton, "Forests and Civilization," *Garden and Forest,* 10 July 1889, 333.

20. Sylvester Baxter, "The Forestry Work of the Tenth Census," *Atlantic Monthly,* November 1881, 682; *Forest and Stream,* 21 August 1873, 26; *Forest and Stream,* 25 December 1884, 442; William Hammond Hall, "Influence of Parks and Pleasure-Grounds," *Overland Monthly,* December 1873, 527; Egleston, "What We Owe to the Trees," 686; *Pacific Rural Press,* 19 April 1884, 380.

21. George Perkins Marsh, *Man and Nature: The Earth as Modified by Human Action* (New York: C. Scribner, 1864); Charles Sprague Sargent to Robert Underwood Johnson, 25 November 1908, box 6, "Incoming Correspondence," Robert Underwood Johnson Collection, Bancroft Library, University of California, Berkeley.

22. David Lowenthal, *George Perkins Marsh: Versatile Vermonter* (New York: Columbia University Press, 1958). See also Jane Curtis, Will Curtis, and Frank Lieberman, *The World of George Perkins Marsh, America's First Conservationist and Environmentalist* (Woodstock, Vt.: Countryman Press, 1982); Ekirch, *Man and Nature in America,* 70–80; and Charles E. Randall, "George Perkins Marsh: Conservation's Forgotten Man," *American Forests,* April 1965, 20–23.

23. Marsh, *Man and Nature,* 29, 279–80; Charles Darwin, *On the Origin of Species by Means of Natural Selection; or, The Preservation of Favored Races in the Struggle for Life* (London: John Murray, 1859).

24. Marsh, *Man and Nature,* 9. Two modern writers essentially agree with Marsh's man-centered judgment: J. Donald Hughes, *Ecology in Ancient Civilizations* (Albuquerque: University of New Mexico Press, 1975), 128; J. V. Thirgood, *Man and the Mediterranean Forest: A History of Resource Depletion* (London: Academic Press, 1981), 158–62.

25. Starr, "American Forest," 225–26; *Report of the State Board of Agriculture*

for 1868 and 1869, 32; Oswald, "Climatic Influence of Vegetation," 386–87; "Tree Waste and Its Sequence," *Scientific American,* 30 March 1878, 193; *Forest and Stream,* 7 September 1876, 73–74; Egleston, "What We Owe to the Trees," 683–84; *Pacific Rural Press,* 20 September 1884, 241; *Pacific Rural Press,* 7 March 1885, 230; Francis Parkman, "The Forests and the Census," *Atlantic Monthly,* June 1885, 835–39; John Muir, "The American Forest," *Atlantic Monthly,* August 1897, 155; "Observations in the Sahara," *Popular Science Monthly,* September 1885, 715; Abbot Kinney, "Our Forests," *Overland Monthly,* December 1886, 619; *Third Biennial Report of the State Board of Horticulture of the State of California for the Thirty-eighth and Thirty-ninth Fiscal Years* (Sacramento, Calif.: State Printing Office, 1889), 118. Sargent did not agree with Marsh's view that human actions were mainly responsible for the conversion of once fair lands to deserts. See Sargent, "Protection of Forests," 395. See also J. D. Whitney, "Are We Drying Up?" *American Naturalist,* September 1876, 513–20.

26. *Forest and Stream,* 12 April 1877, 146; Oswald, "Preservation of Forests," 36. See also "Forests and Drought," *Scientific American,* 18 January 1873, 14; *San Francisco Evening Bulletin,* 5 January 1878; "Deforestation and Floods in China," *Popular Science Monthly,* November 1883, 142–43; and "Forest Devastation in Japan," *Popular Science Monthly,* September 1886, 714–15.

27. *Forest and Stream,* 7 September 1882, 102; *Forest and Stream,* 13 December 1883, 381; *Forest and Stream,* 31 January 1884, 1; Felix L. Oswald, "Changes in the Climate of North America," *North American Review,* April 1884, 365; Henry Michelson, "Forests in Their Relation to Irrigation," *Forester,* January 1899, 9–10; J. Blatchford Collins, "The Relation of Forest Preservation to the Public Welfare," *Forester,* June 1899, 127–29.

28. *Garden and Forest,* 29 December 1897, 518. On rainmaking experiments, see Clark C. Spence, *The Rainmakers: American "Pluviculture" to World War II* (Lincoln: University of Nebraska Press, 1980). For dry farming, see Mary Wilma M. Hargreaves, *Dry Farming in the Northern Great Plains, 1900–1925* (Cambridge, Mass.: Harvard University Press, 1957).

29. Olson, "Commerce and Conservation," 13–14; Paul F. Sharp, "The War of the Substitutes: The Reaction of the Forest Industries to the Competition of Wood Substitutes," *Agricultural History,* October 1949, 274–79; U.S. Congress, Senate, *The Lumber Industry: Message from the President of the United States,* Senate Reports, 61st Cong., 3rd sess., no. 818, 14 February 1911 (Washington, D.C.: Government Printing Office, 1911), 15.

30. For the "multiple-purpose" concept, see Hays, *Conservation and the Gospel of Efficiency,* 100–105. Fish culture, not scientific forestry, contributed the idea of "sustained yield," or "continuous yield," to the conservation of renewable natural resources. See Norman G. Benson, ed., *A Century of Fisheries in North America* (Washington, D.C.: American Fisheries Society, 1970); Donald J. Pisani, "Fish Culture and the Dawn of Concern over Water Pollution," *Environmental Review* 8 (Summer 1984): 117–31; Dean C. Allard, Jr., "Spencer Fullerton Baird and the U.S. Fish Commission: A Study in the History of American Science" (Ph.D. diss., George Washington University, 1967); and Reiger, *American Sportsmen and the Origins of Conservation,* 52–56.

31. Donald J. Pisani, "Reclamation and Social Engineering in the Progressive Era,"

Agricultural History, January 1983, 46–63; Hays, *Conservation and the Gospel of Efficiency.*

32. *Forestry and Irrigation,* one of the leading conservation journals during the first decade of the twentieth century, warned of impending timber shortages: Raphael Zon, "The World's Demand for Timber and the Supply," *Forestry and Irrigation,* February 1901, 41–44; "Our Waning Forests," *Forestry and Irrigation,* June 1901, 142; B. E. Fernow, "Outlook of the Timber Supply in the United States," *Forestry and Irrigation,* February and May 1903, 74–78, 226–29; "Ostriches vs. Wise Men," *Forestry and Irrigation,* February 1908, 61–62; "The Woods We have," *Forestry and Irrigation,* May 1908, 249–50; W. J. Wallace, "Startling Words of Timber Expert," *Forestry and Irrigation,* May 1908, 255–56.

33. *Forest and Stream,* 31 January 1884, 1; Ekirch, *Man and Nature in America,* 71.

34. Nash, *Wilderness and the American Mind,* 129–30, 135–40; Hays, *Conservation and the Gospel of Efficiency,* 122–98; Swain, *Federal Conservation Policy,* 6–7, 124–25.

35. On the post–Civil War "land question," see Gates and Swenson, *History of Public Land Law Development;* Paul W. Gates, *Agriculture and the Civil War* (New York: Knopf, 1965); Fred A. Shannon, *The Farmer's Last Frontier: Agriculture, 1860–1897* (New York: Farrar and Rinehart, 1945); and Gilbert C. Fite, *The Farmers' Frontier: 1865–1900* (New York: Holt, Rinehart, and Winston, 1966).

Wildlife, Conservation, and the First Forest Reserve

John F. Reiger

While their first concern was always wildlife, sportsmen-conservationists of the late nineteenth century quickly perceived that their many efforts on behalf of game mammals, birds, and fishes were a solution to only half the problem. It would do little good to conserve wildlife if its habitat continued to shrink, for eventually both would be gone. That part of the environment most immediately threatened was the forest.[1]

Possessing an Old World code,[2] sportsmen of the upper classes saw forests not as a challenge to the American mission of progress, but as one of the essential settings for that important activity called sport. Free from the prejudices of the frontiersman, farmer, and logger, sportsmen viewed trees as something more than a hiding place for Indians, an obstacle to plowing, or a source of financial gain. Woodlands were both the home of their quarry and the aesthetic backdrop for that avocation which many considered more rewarding—in a noneconomic sense—than their vocation.

As in the case of wildlife depletion, the appearance in the early 1870s of the first national sporting periodicals, *American Sportsman, Forest and Stream,* and *Field and Stream,* helped focus sportsmen's anger over woodland eradication and unite them against it.[3] When *American Angler* appeared early in the next decade, another voice for forest conservation was added to the sporting press. Like the other journals, *American Angler* endeavored to keep its readers informed of the most up-to-date information on "natural history," and that included the disastrous effects of unregulated logging and pulp-mill discharge into rivers and on fish and game. In addition to attacks on water pollution, the paper also explained in detail how uncontrolled lumbering ruined fishing waters by causing such habitat changes as bank erosion and higher water temperatures.[4] Like the other periodicals, *American Angler* illustrated a remarkable understanding of ecological principles.

Of the four major publications, *American Sportsman* and *Forest and Stream* proved to be the most concerned with forest conservation. Founded in 1871, the former journal repeatedly lamented the extent and ramifications of woodland destruction, and as a solution to the problem, it suggested that European forestry techniques be adapted to American timberlands.[5]

When *Forest and Stream* was founded in 1873, it quickly proved that it was even more dedicated to forest conservation than its predecessor. Editor Charles Hallock stated every week in *Forest and Stream*'s subtitle that his paper was "Devoted to . . . Preservation of Forests," and he lived up to that claim by frequently calling attention to the depletion of timberlands and the need for their protection.[6] Hallock's interest in this issue may have been spawned, in part at least, by George Bird Grinnell. Although Grinnell did not join the paper's staff until 1876, he was associated closely with it from the beginning as a writer, financial supporter, and natural history adviser. Since his graduation from Yale in 1870, he had also kept in touch with scientific developments through his close association with Othniel C. Marsh, a sportsman and paleontologist who was then one of the university's most prominent faculty members. Grinnell assisted Marsh on his 1870 fossil-collecting expedition to the Far West, entered Yale's Sheffield Scientific School in early 1874, and received a Ph.D. under Marsh in 1880.[7]

After becoming *Forest and Stream*'s editor and owner in 1880, Grinnell concentrated on defining "sportsmanship" and conserving wildlife. It did not take long, however, for him to understand that more was needed. In April 1882, therefore, he began his editorial drive to transform the nation's orientation toward its woodlands. Years earlier, Hallock had pointed the way by drawing attention to how rapidly the timberlands were being depleted and by suggesting Europe's system of managed forests as an alternative to the wasteful methods of American lumbering. But Grinnell went far beyond his predecessor in publicizing the European science of forestry.

In "Spare the Trees," the opening editorial of his campaign on behalf of the forests, he manifested awareness of the interrelationship of all natural resources. "If we have the most perfect code of game and fish laws which it is possible to devise," he wrote, "and have them ever so thoroughly enforced, what will they avail if there is no cover for game nor water for fish?" Employing the ideology of the business-farm community, he called for Americans to use their "proverbial thriftiness and forecast" to achieve "the proper and sensible management of woodlands." The forests must be seen as a "crop . . . which is slow in coming to the harvest, but it is a sure one, and is every year becoming a more paying one." In addition, "it breaks the fierceness of the winds, and keeps the springs from drying up, and is a comfort to the eye. . . . Under its protecting arms live and breed the grouse, the quail and the hare, and in its shadowed riles swim the trout." Although the lesson was a simple one, it had not yet been learned by the American people: "No woods, no game; no woods, no water; and no water, no fish."[8]

Ever since the early days of *Forest and Stream,* the weekly's editors had been interested in the possible applicability to American conditions of Euro-

pean developments in sport, natural history, and science. Particularly significant in this regard was the Europeans' attitude toward their woodlands. In
an 1883 editorial, "Forestry," Grinnell reported: "In parts of Europe forestry
is a science, and officers are appointed by the governments to supervise the
forests; and only judicious thinning of young trees and cutting of those which
[have] attained their growth is allowed."[9]

He pointed out that the system was used not only on government lands
but on private holdings as well, "the theory being that the individual will
pass away, but the forest must remain forever." He contrasted the Continental emphasis on continual resource management with the situation existing in America, where the sovereignty of private ownership allowed an
individual to "buy a tract of land in the great water producing region of the
State and for his own pecuniary benefit render it forever sterile." Grinnell
suggested that laws regulating forest use, like those already existing in
Europe, should be immediately passed in the United States. As in the case of
game legislation, he believed that statutes protecting the forests would have
democratic results and "work well for the people at large."[10]

In 1884 *Forest and Stream* stepped up its campaign to educate the American people in the principles and methods of forestry. In March, Grinnell used
the recent floods of the Ohio and Mississippi Rivers as illustrations of "the
terrible effects of our criminal waste of woodlands." He asked for massive
reforestation along the rivers' banks and the creation of state and federal
forestry commissions. Later that spring, he went further and demanded that
the national government immediately appoint "a Competent Forestry Officer," a "trained professional" to lead in "the inauguration of a system of forest conservancy." In the five-part series "Forests and Forestry" (1884–1885),
Grinnell consistently used almost the entire front page of his weekly to explain the fundamentals of the European science. He argued that forestry's
concepts were applicable to every country. While American trees and soils
were not exactly like those in Germany and France, the Continent's expert
foresters were "capable of adapting general principles to changed conditions." And "pending the theoretical and practical training of young Americans," these foreign professionals should staff the forestry bureau. Under
their direction, it could become an animated, functioning department.[11]

At the same time that Grinnell, through *Forest and Stream,* was beating
the drum for general forest conservation, he was also leading a campaign that
aimed, first, to define the meaning of Yellowstone Park for the American people and, second, to establish for it an effective administration. The 1872 act
creating the reservation had for its object the protection of a natural
"museum" of "wonders"—geysers, hot springs, and canyons. The park was
not preserved to be either a wilderness or a game refuge. The only concern of
those few interested in the area was that the "curiosities" be made available to
tourists as soon as possible. Instead of believing that the park should remain

in a pristine state, most of these individuals assumed that it would soon be "improved" by a multitude of hotels, roads, and other conveniences.[12]

During the rest of the 1870s and the very early 1880s, most of Congress, as well as the general public, virtually forgot about the park. Because of its inaccessibility, there was at first little danger to it outside of the depredations of commercial hunters, who were killing the reserve's big game for the money their hides would bring in markets to the east.

But by 1881, the tracks of the Northern Pacific Railroad had approached the vicinity of the reservation. "Soon after," Grinnell recalled in his autobiography, Henry Villard, the railroad's president, "took out a special train carrying a number of guests—railroad men, capitalists, and scientific men—to show the public the country traversed by his road." And "among those who then visited the Park were some . . . who saw its possibilities as a pleasure resort, and realized that the privileges offered to lessees through the Act establishing the Park would have a money value to those who might secure them."[13] Soon these men would begin their efforts to exploit the reserve, inspiring Grinnell to launch a campaign aimed at protecting the park by clarifying its status.

In large measure, Grinnell's crusade was the outgrowth of his experience in the West. Because the boundaries of Yellowstone Park were drawn with little real knowledge of the terrain, a number of expeditions were sent into the region to see exactly what Congress had, in fact, set aside. One of these was an 1875 reconnaissance led by engineer William Ludlow. As the expedition's official naturalist, Grinnell became thoroughly familiar with the park and its problems, the most obvious of which was hide hunting.[14]

Although all species of big game were being systematically slaughtered, he was most alarmed by the destruction of the buffalo in this, their last stronghold. For seventy years, the dream of western expansion had fed on buffalo meat, and the animal had become the symbol of the new land, the game Old World aristocrats and New World patricians—Grinnell and Theodore Roosevelt among them—had to shoot, as a kind of initiation rite into frontier Americanism. Now, with the establishment of Yellowstone National Park, there appeared to be a possibility that the bison might be preserved, though the founders of the park had not conceived of it as a game refuge.[15]

Although Grinnell's conception of the national park as a wildlife preserve was articulated as early as 1877,[16] it took several years for him to realize that if his idea were to become a reality, something more was required than sporadic protests. On December 14, 1882, he provided that "something more" by launching a crusade in Forest and Stream to define the status of Yellowstone National Park and protect it from commercialization.

The first editorial, "Their Last Refuge," was both a plea for the buffalo and a detailed analysis of the deficiencies in the act creating the reserve. He pointed out that the statute put the destiny of the reservation completely in the hands of the secretary of the interior. This official had the power to grant leases to private persons and corporations for the purpose of building roads, hotels, and other facilities, and to decide what regulations should be devised for the park. With regard to wildlife, only their "wanton destruction" with "the purpose of merchandise or profit" was specified as one of the offenses the secretary was to "provide against."[17]

Grinnell's editorial made it clear that the vagueness of the act subjected it to a number of interpretations and left loopholes for those who sought to use the reserve for their own profit. An example was the section on wildlife, which seemed to suggest that individuals or corporations could kill all the game they wished, just as long as they were not "wanton." The greatest deficiency, of course, was that the act provided no machinery for carrying out any regulations the secretary of the interior might promulgate. As Grinnell later recalled, the secretary's rules "soon came to be regarded as a dead letter. Anyone was at liberty to cut down the forest, kill the game or carry away natural curiosities, and all these things were constantly done."[18]

He cogently summed up the problem in the 1882 editorial: "This 'great and glorious government' has again stultified itself by enacting laws without supplying the means to enforce them. The Park is overrun by skin-hunters, who slaughter the game for the hides, and laugh defiance at the government." In fact, "the curse of politics has entered into the management of the reservation," with "the little money appropriated for its maintenance" being "wasted by incompetent and ignorant officials. It is leased to private parties, who desire to make a peep show of its wonders."[19]

Grinnell would soon have aid in his efforts on behalf of American forests in general and Yellowstone Park in particular. The establishment of the Boone and Crockett Club, named after two of America's most famous hunters, would be that help. After Grinnell became friends with Theodore Roosevelt in the mid-1880s, he emphasized to him the need for an effective sportsmen's society, to do for the larger mammals what the Audubon Society—founded by Grinnell in 1886—was doing for birds. Roosevelt agreed. Accordingly, in December 1887, he invited a number of his big-game-hunting friends and relatives to a dinner party in Manhattan at which the Boone and Crockett Club was born.[20]

It was probably Grinnell who first pointed out that some provision should be made for club membership for those who were not big-game hunters but who had worked for wildlife preservation. Examples were his two friends geologist Arnold Hague and Supreme Court lawyer William Hallett Phillips; the latter was also an enthusiastic angler. They had labored for Yellowstone Park, which entitled them to membership, even though neither man had killed any big game. After some consideration, it was decided that non-hunters could be elected to associate or honorary membership. In time, the club's members would include many of the most famous and respected men in America, individuals like Henry L. Stimson, Henry Cabot Lodge, Elihu Root, Owen Wister, Wade Hampton, Gifford Pinchot, and many from the American patrician class. As a result, the organization's influence would prove far in excess of that of any ordinary association of similar size. In fact, the Boone and Crockett Club—and *not* the Sierra Club—was the first private organization to deal effectively with conservation issues of national scope.[21]

As is usually the case, the work of the organization was accomplished by only a small number of members, the rest being content merely to attend the annual dinner. Of these active members, Grinnell was the most influential. He formulated almost every idea the club came to stand for; he did a great part of the work on the Boone and Crockett book series on hunting and conservation, and effectively used *Forest and Stream* as the "natural mouthpiece of the Club."[22] A subsequent director of the society, the noted explorer and naturalist of Alaska, Charles Sheldon, went so far as to declare: "The Boone and Crockett Club . . . has been *George Bird Grinnell* from its founding. All its books, its work, its soundness, have been due to his unflagging work and interest and knowledge."[23] As Sheldon understood, some of the most important figures in the first conservation movement—including its two future leaders, Roosevelt and Pinchot—were members of the club. "When Theodore Roosevelt became President," former Secretary of the Interior Stewart Udall has pointed out, "the Boone and Crockett wildlife creed . . . became national policy." Forests and water could be included in that "creed," for in time the club took as its basic approach Grinnell's idea that all renewable resources benefited from continual, efficient administration.[24]

The club's interest in the conservation of big game naturally turned it toward Yellowstone National Park. Describing his early relationship with Roosevelt, Grinnell later recalled that "the original attempt by a certain group of men to secure for their own profit control of all the important attractions of the park had been defeated before I knew him well, but as soon as he understood about the conditions in Yellowstone Park, he gave time and thought to considering its protection."[25] It would not be long before Roosevelt joined Grinnell, Phillips, and Hague in actively working to establish a "government" for the park that would adequately protect its wildlife and forests.

By 1891, the leaders of the Boone and Crockett Club were ready for a major effort on behalf of the Yellowstone. The club's annual dinner was to be held on January 14 at the Metropolitan Club in Washington, D.C. Roosevelt wanted to use the occasion to emphasize to government officials the need for action, and he invited a gallery of notables—seated on his left was Secretary of War Redfield Proctor, and on his right, Speaker of the House Thomas B. Reed. Grinnell sat opposite Roosevelt, with Secretary of the Interior John W. Noble on one side and Samuel Pierpont Langley, physicist and secretary of the Smithsonian Institution, on the other. A few members of Congress, including Henry Cabot Lodge, as well as Arnold Hague and William Hallett Phillips also attended.[26]

At a business meeting beforehand, Grinnell and Roosevelt had drawn up a series of resolutions that were read at the dinner

> *Resolved,* That the Boone and Crockett Club, speaking for itself and hundreds of [sportsmen's] clubs and associations throughout the country, urges the immediate passage by the House of Representatives of the Senate bill for protection and maintenance of the Yellowstone National Park. *Resolved,* That this Club declares itself emphatically opposed to the granting of a right of way to the Montana Mineral Railroad or to any other railroad through the Yellowstone National Park.

A third resolution endorsed "the efforts now being made to preserve the groves of big trees [giant sequoias] in California" and thanked "the Secretary of the Interior for his interest in this matter."[27]

After Roosevelt and Phillips made short speeches on the requirements of the reservation, one of the congressmen asked a number of questions that were answered by Hague and Roosevelt.[28] "We then got to the subject of . . . large game," Grinnell reported to his friend Archibald Rogers, "and Langley, in response to a request from Roosevelt, said that he believed from what he had heard, that the large game of the Continent would be practically exterminated except in such preserves as the Yellowstone National Park, within the life of the present generation of men."

After Langley had made his comment, "Roosevelt . . . asked me to say something of the way in which game had disappeared in my time," Grinnell continued in his letter to Rogers, "and I told them a few 'lies' about buffalo, elk, and other large game in the old days." Clearly, Grinnell's long and varied experience in the primitive West had entitled him to Roosevelt's esteem. When he finished his description of "the old days," a general conversation followed until about eleven o'clock, when the group broke up.[29]

Grinnell felt that the dinner had been a success, because "we excited a real interest," and he was now "more hopeful than . . . for two or three years." Despite his optimism, the railroad lobby proved successful in keeping the House from considering the Senate bill before the end of the session.[30]

In *A Brief History of the Boone and Crockett Club* (1910), Grinnell explains that "the attempt to exploit the Yellowstone National Park for private gain in a way led up to the United States forest reserve system as it stands to-day," because "as a natural sequence to the work that they [the club's leaders] had been doing" in regard to Yellowstone Park "came the impulse to attempt to preserve western forests generally." Since their original concern had been the park, it might seem odd that concrete results on the forestry question were obtained three years before the passage of the

1894 Yellowstone Park Protection Act. The reason for this was simply that the battle over the park took place in a public arena against determined western opposition, while the results in forestry were achieved by circumventing the popular forum. Nevertheless, the interrelationship between the two issues is shown by the fact that the first forest reserve President Benjamin Harrison chose to set aside in 1891 was the Yellowstone National Park Timberland Reserve, adjacent to the national preserve. "In essence," says one observer, "the Yellowstone became the birthplace for both the national parks and national forests." He might have added that the systems for managing both were created largely by members of the Boone and Crockett Club.[31]

As in the case of Yellowstone National Park, Grinnell led the club on the forestry issue. The editorial effort he began in 1882 to transform the nation's orientation toward its woodlands continued unabated through the decade. The central thrust of his sophisticated but simply stated proposition was that "the Federal government must husband its resources and place them under systematic management," the purpose of which was exploitation without waste. Grinnell emphasized, in fact, that not to use resources was in itself wasteful: "The proposal to lock up the forests and prevent all further utilization of their products is one that cannot be entertained." The latter statement was made in 1888 and matches exactly the policy that would be established in future years by two other Boone and Crockett members, Gifford Pinchot and Theodore Roosevelt. While Grinnell was acting in his usual capacity as the instigator of public opinion, the Supreme Court lawyer William Hallett Phillips was busy in his customary role as a behind-the-scenes negotiator. Like others in the Boone and Crockett Club, he had arrived at his interest in forestry via his involvement in the crusade over the Yellowstone:

> In 1887 Phillips . . . had succeeded in interesting Mr. [Lucius Q. C.] Lamar, Secretary of the Interior, and a number of Congressmen, in the forests, and gradually all these persons began to work together. At the close of the first Cleveland Administration, while no legislation had been secured looking toward forest protection, a number of men in Washington had come to feel an interest in the subject.[32]

In 1889 President Harrison appointed John W. Noble of Missouri as secretary of the interior. As in the case of his predecessors, Noble received the "treatment" from the directors of the Boone and Crockett Club as soon as he entered office. This consisted of personal visits from Phillips, Hague, and Roosevelt, and invitations to the club's dinners. But the one all-important difference was that Noble, unlike his forerunners, was highly receptive to the organization's expression of concern for the forests.

Why this should be true is not entirely clear. Although Noble was later an associate member of the Boone and Crockett Club, it is not known whether he ever hunted for recreation or accepted the environmental obligation inherent in the code of the sportsman. But it is known that he believed field sports helped individuals who pursued them to make a success of their lives,[33] and this, of course, is one of the basic themes of the sporting tradition.

Noble, in any event, enjoyed the attentions of the prestigious Boone and Crockett Club, and he was in close touch with at least two of its members, Phillips and Grinnell, by 1889. In fact, the latter believed that it was Phillips, who was already a good friend of the secretary of the interior, who was most responsible for involving Noble in the effort to preserve western forests.[34] *Forest and Stream*'s editor probably knew what he was talking about, as he worked with both men to accomplish the same end.

Grinnell's relationship with Noble began in the spring of 1889 when Grinnell, who was a champion of the Native American, sought to oust an Indian agent who was exploiting the Blackfeet of northwestern Montana and succeeded only when the new secretary of the interior interceded personally in the affair after being alerted by Phillips. From that time to the end of Noble's term in office, the secretary and *Forest and Stream*'s editor were in frequent communication on conservation matters and Indian affairs.[35]

Following the position advocated earlier by *Forest and Stream,* Noble came to agree that to save the timberlands, they would have to be withdrawn from the public domain. The means for accomplishing this end were provided on March 3, 1891, when "An Act to Repeal Timber Culture Laws and for other Purposes." was signed by President Harrison. Pushed through at the close of the Fifty-first Congress, the legislation was an effort to revise the land laws of the United States. Those who lobbied hardest among the members of Congress to have the bill approved were Bernhard Fernow, chief of the Division of Forestry, and, to a lesser degree, Hague and Phillips.[36]

The granting of power to the president to set aside timberlands was the last of the bill's twenty-four sections, being "inserted in [the] Conference Committee in the last hour of Congress by the insistence of Mr. Noble, that he would not allow the bill to be signed by the President unless the clause was added."[37] Soon after the passage of the bill, Hague "saw Secretary Noble and [suggested] . . . the setting aside of the Yellowstone Park Forest Reserve adjoining the Park." His aim, as Grinnell explained at the time, was "protection for the territory south and east of the Park, which it has so long been hoped might be added to the reservation." Noble liked Hague's idea, but before acting, he wanted to be sure there were no legal pitfalls. To resolve this question, Hague returned the next day with William Hallett Phillips, Noble's friend and adviser, and all three discussed the legal question. After dismissing all doubts, Noble carried the project to the president, who promised to give the order. The dimensions of the proposed tract were discussed in several conferences between Noble and Hague, and, finally, on March 30, 1891, President Harrison issued the proclamation setting aside the first forest reserve. Calling the tract the Yellowstone National Park Timberland Reserve, Harrison defined its boundaries in *exactly* the same language Hague had used in his proposal to Noble.[38]

Though this land would be administered differently than the national park, it eventually obtained real protection when the Forest Service eliminated wasteful logging and uncontrolled fires, the two factors that had previously threatened its existence. At the same time, crucial wildlife habitat was preserved and hide hunting eliminated. In one sense, therefore, Harrison's proclamation was the culmination of the effort Grinnell had begun in 1882 to have Yellowstone Park extended on the east and south, an effort that Phillips and Hague had later taken up.

The Yellowstone reserve contained 1,239,040 acres, all in Wyoming, and was the inauguration of the national forest system, which today totals about 191 million acres. Shortly after its establishment, Roosevelt, representing the Boone and Crockett Club, endorsed the action and commended Harrison and Noble. Grinnell did the same in *Forest and Stream* and urged the public to accept the reserve and the policy it represented. Some years later, Noble would gratefully acknowledge the aid Grinnell and "his very popular and influential paper" had given him, before and after the forest reserve system was initiated.[39]

Though historians have only recently begun to pay attention to the role of sportsmen and their allies in the making of the original conservation movement, the members of the Boone and Crockett Club, whose immediate goal was the conservation of wildlife, especially big game, proved central to the establishment of the first forest reserve.

NOTES

1. In 1975, the writer published *American Sportsmen and the Origins of Conservation,* which argued that upper-class "sportsmen"—those who hunted and fished for recreation rather than commerce or necessity—were the spearhead of a conservation *movement* originating in the 1870s; the University of Oklahoma Press republished the book in 1986, and this chapter is an amended version of one small part of that monograph.

2. John F. Reiger, *American Sportsmen and the Origins of Conservation* (Norman: University of Oklahoma Press, 1986), chap. 1.

3. "Game—Its Extinction: The Cause, and the Remedy," *Chicago Field* [later name of *Field and Stream*], 3 August 1878, 392; "Why the Prairies Are Treeless," *Chicago Field,* 29 January 1881, 394; "Tree Planting," *American Field* [later name of *Field and Stream*], 21 July 1883, 49; "A Public Park," *American Field,* 22 December 1883, 577; "State School of Forestry," *American Field,* 16 July 1884, 49; "Nurseries for Game," *American Field,* 24 October 1885, 385.

4. *American Angler,* 17 May 1884, 310; *American Angler,* 24 May 1884, 328;

American Angler, 20 December 1884, 386; "Destruction of the Trout and Trout Streams of Central New York," *American Angler,* 1 January 1887, 8–9; "How Shall We Preserve Our Water Supply?" *American Angler,* 5 March 1887, 145–46.

5. "Forest Legislation," *American Sportsman,* 25 October 1873, 56; "Foreign Sporting Notes," *American Sportsman,* 7 March 1874, 361; "Wood and Forest," *American Sportsman,* 21 November 1874, 120; *American Sportsman,* 13 March 1875, 377; "Our Trees," *American Sportsman,* 20 March 1875, 392; "Forest Preservation in Europe," *Rod and the Gun* [later name of *American Sportsman*], 10 July 1875, 231; A. S. Collins, "Decrease of Brook Trout in the United States," *Rod and the Gun,* 7 August 1875, 280; "Waste Land and Forest Culture," *Rod and the Gun,* 18 March 1876, 390; "Are We Drying Up?" *Rod and the Gun,* 20 January 1877, 246.

6. The very first issue of the paper (August 14, 1873) stated: "For the preservation of our rapidly diminishing forests we shall continually do battle. Our great interests are in jeopardy . . . from the depletion of our timber lands by fire and axe." For some other examples of Hallock's interest in the subject, see "Woodman Spare That Tree," *Forest and Stream,* 21 August 1873, 26; "The Preservation of Our Forests," *Forest and Stream,* 4 September 1873, 56; "The Adirondack Park," *Forest and Stream,* 11 September 1873, 73; "What the Germans Say About Wood Cutting," *Forest and Stream,* 18 September 1873, 89.

7. For a detailed discussion of Grinnell's early career, see John F. Reiger, ed., *The Passing of the Great West: Selected Papers of George Bird Grinnell* (Norman: University of Oklahoma Press, 1985).

8. *Forest and Stream,* 13 April 1882, 204.

9. *Forest and Stream,* 19 July 1883, 481.

10. Ibid.

11. "Unheeded Lessons,"*Forest and Stream,* 27 March 1884, 161; "Forests and Forestry V," *Forest and Stream,* 22 January 1885, 502.

12. Roderick Nash, *Wilderness and the American Mind* (New Haven, Conn.: Yale University Press, 1982), 108–13; "The Yellowstone National Park," *Scribner's Monthly,* May 1872, 121, cited in Nash, 113.

13. George Bird Grinnell, "Memoirs," 94, George Bird Grinnell Papers, Yale University, New Haven, Conn.

14. John Ise, *Our National Park Policy: A Critical History* (Baltimore: Johns Hopkins University Press, 1961), 21–22. Reiger, ed., *Passing of the Great West,* 117–19.

15. For Grinnell's buffalo hunting, see Reiger, ed., *Passing of the Great West,* 58–72; see also George Bird Grinnell, "Last of the Buffalo," *Scribner's Magazine,* September 1892, 267–86. On Roosevelt's hunting, see James B. Trefethen, *Crusade for Wildlife: Highlights in Conservation Progress* (Harrisburg, Pa.: Stackpole, 1961), 2.

16. Reiger, *American Sportsmen and the Origins of Conservation,* 99–100.

17. *Forest and Stream,* 14 December 1882, 382.

18. Ibid., 382–83; Grinnell, "Memoirs," 95.

19. *Forest and Stream,* 14 December 1882, 382–83.

20. Reiger, *American Sportsmen and the Origins of Conservation,* 118–20; George Bird Grinnell to T. E. Hofer, 15 January 1919, Letter Book, 269, Grinnell Papers.

21. Grinnell to W. H. Phillips, 5 June 1889, Letter Book, 354; Grinnell to Arnold Hague, 22 February 1888, Letter Book, 297. Phillips was "a resident of Washington

[D.C.], a Supreme Court lawyer, with a large acquaintance there" (*Forest and Stream,* 15 May 1897, 381); Grinnell to N. P. Langford, 25 July 1905, Letter Book, 742–43. Besides being Grinnell's close friend, he was also his lawyer; Grinnell to W. H. Phillips, 3 September 1888, Letter Book, 476–77.

22. George Bird Grinnell, ed., *A Brief History of the Boone and Crockett Club With Officers, Constitution and List of Members for the Year 1910* (New York: Forest and Stream, 1910), 20; John P. Holman, "A Tribute to George Bird Grinnell," in "Boone and Crockett Club Officers, By-Laws, Treasurer's Report and List of Members for the Years 1938–1939" (July 1939), 29–30, Boone and Crockett Club Papers, Club Headquarters, Missoula, Mont.

23. Charles Sheldon to W. Redmond Cross, 3 May 1926, Boone and Crockett Club Papers.

24. Stewart Udall, *The Quiet Crisis* (New York: Avon, 1967), 161.

25. George Bird Grinnell, "Introduction," *The Works of Theodore Roosevelt,* national ed. (New York: C. Scribner's Sons, 1926), 1:xxiii.

26. "Boone and Crockett Club Meeting," *Forest and Stream,* 22 January 1891, 3.

27. Ibid.

28. Grinnell to Archibald Rogers, 17 January 1891, Letter Book, 186–87.

29. Roosevelt's regard for Grinnell is evident in his desire to have Grinnell be his hunting partner: Grinnell to James Willard Schultz, 24 May 1888, Letter Book, 361; Grinnell to Archibald Rogers, 8 August 1888, Letter Book, 444.

30. Grinnell to Rogers, 17 January 1891, Letter Book, 187; "The National Park Bill," *Forest and Stream,* 12 March 1891, 145.

31. Grinnell, *Brief History of the Boone and Crockett Club,* 21, 23; Ernest F. Swift, *The Public's Land: Our Heritage and Opportunity* (Washington D.C.: National Wildlife Federation, 1969), 7.

32. "Utilize the Streams," *Forest and Stream,* 11 August 1887, 41; "Forests of the Rocky Mountains I," *Forest and Stream,* 25 October 1888, 261–62; "Forests of the Rocky Mountains II," *Forest and Stream,* 1 November 1888, 282–83; "Forests of the Rocky Mountains III," *Forest and Stream,* 8 November 1888, 301–2; "Popular Forestry Instruction," *Forest and Stream,* 6 December 1888, 381; "Practical Forest Restoration I," *Forest and Stream,* 28 February 1889, 105; "Practical Forest Restoration II," *Forest and Stream,* 14 March 1889, 149; "Practical Forest Restoration III," *Forest and Stream,* 21 March 1889, 169; "Practical Forest Restoration IV," *Forest and Stream,* 28 March 1889, 189; Grinnell, *Brief History of the Boone and Crockett Club,* 23.

33. Reiger, *American Sportsmen and the Origins of Conservation,* 45.

34. Grinnell went so far as to claim that it was "through the influence of William Hallett Phillips [that] . . . a few lines inserted in an act passed by Congress March 3, 1891, permitted the establishment of forest reserves." ("Big-Game Refuges," in *American Big Game in Its Haunts,* ed. George Bird Grinnell [New York: Forest and Stream, 1904], 443). For other interpretations of who was responsible for inserting these crucial lines, see Harold K. Steen, "The Beginning of the National Forest System" [this volume]; and Ron Arnold, "Congressman William Holden of Indiana: Unknown Founder of the National Forests," in *The Origins of the National Forest,* ed. Harold K. Steen (Durham, N.C.: Forest History Society, 1992). For an example of Phillips's early dedication to the forests of the Yellowstone, see *Forest and Stream,* 11 Febru-

ary 1886, 41. In "Secretary Noble's Monument," *Forest and Stream,* 9 March 1893, 203, Grinnell wrote: "It will be remembered that *beginning* [my emphasis] with the Yellowstone National Park, which was brought to the notice of Mr. Noble early in his administration, he has given much attention to the question of our parks and timber reservation[s]"; this statement undoubtedly refers mainly to Phillips. For examples of the close working relationship between Phillips and Noble, see Grinnell to W. H. Phillips, 25 May 1889, Letter Book, 322; Grinnell to John Noble, 25 May 1889, Letter Book, 321; Grinnell to Phillips, 28 May 1889, Letter Book, 329; Grinnell to Phillips, 5 June 1889, Letter Book, 354; Grinnell to Phillips, 7 November 1889, Letter Book, 453–55; Grinnell to Phillips, 4 December 1889, Letter Book, 16; and Grinnell to Phillips, 24 April 1891, Letter Book, 383. For the fact that Noble is usually credited with obtaining the insertion of the important lines in the 1891 act, see John Ise, *The United States Forest Policy* (New Haven, Conn.: Yale University Press, 1920), 115. Although he admits that the history of this issue is extremely vague, Ise accepts Bernhard E. Fernow's later claim that he and Edward A. Bowers, of the American Forestry Association, "had educated Noble up to the point" of demanding the insertion of the forest-reserve clause. While Fernow and Bowers deserve credit for exerting some influence, Phillips was probably easily as important—despite the fact that, unlike Fernow, he left no readily accessible documentation of his role. Like many other patrician pioneers of conservation, "he labored long and earnestly for the public good [but] . . . preferred that his efforts should not be known, and that others should receive the credit for what he did" ("William Hallett Phillips," *Forest and Stream,* 15 May 1897, 381). This citation refers to an unsigned obituary of Phillips written by Grinnell; the former had drowned near Washington, D.C., on May 9.

35. Grinnell to Phillips, 25 May 1889, Letter Book, 322; Grinnell to Noble, 25 May 1889, Letter Book, 321; Grinnell to Phillips, 28 May 1889, Letter Book, 329; "Secretary Noble and the Indians," *Forest and Stream,* 30 May 1889, 373; Grinnell to Phillips, 5 June 1889, Letter Book, 354; Grinnell to Noble, 19 June 1889, Letter Book, 380–81. For some examples of Grinnell's efforts to get the Indian agent removed, see Grinnell to Commissioner of Indian Affairs, 20 November 1888, Letter Book, 497–502; Grinnell to Commissioner of Indian Affairs, 30 November 1888, Letter Book, 39–66; Grinnell to J. W. Schultz, 4 December 1888, Letter Book, 7–9; Grinnell to L. H. North, 13 December 1888, Letter Book, 34–35.

36. Arnold Hague to Grinnell, 11 April 1910, Grinnell Papers.

37. Bernhard E. Fernow to Grinnell, 12 April 1910, Grinnell Papers; see also Steen, "Beginning of the National Forest Service."

38. Hague to Grinnell, 11 April 1910; *Forest and Stream,* 9 April 1891, 225; Hague to Grinnell, 11 April 1910.

39. A copy of this resolution, dated April 8, 1891, is in the Boone and Crockett Club Papers; *Forest and Stream,* 9 April 1891, 225; *Forest and Stream,* 22 October 1891, 265; *Forest and Stream,* 3 December 1891, 385; John Noble to Grinnell, 11 March 1910, Boone and Crockett Club Papers; Noble to Grinnell, 15 March 1910, Grinnell Papers.

The Beginning of the National
Forest System

Harold K. Steen

The setting aside of the very first American national forest, although effective and long-lasting, was not hitch-free. The record does not reveal just how he felt about it—whether or not he was embarrassed—but the president felt compelled to issue a correction: "I, Benjamin Harrison, President of the United States, for the purpose of removing any doubt and making the boundaries of said reservation more definite" is language included in a September 10, 1891, proclamation. The president was referring to his earlier action on March 30 of that year, which was intended to establish the boundaries of a forest reserve adjacent to Yellowstone National Park. But the hastily prepared first proclamation was defective, and nearly a half-year later, he issued a corrected version.[1]

Arnold Hague of the United States Geological Survey was author of the defective proclamation, and he noticed the error almost immediately after the president had issued it. It was not clear from the initial legal descriptions precisely where the boundaries were. Also, the traverse did not close; that is, if a surveyor ran the boundary lines as described in the proclamation, he would not end where he started. But, Hague wrote to his friend and associate George B. Grinnell, "nobody but yourself will notice anything wrong in the proclamation." However, someone did notice, and in July Thomas H. Carter, commissioner of the General Land Office, reported to Secretary of the Interior John Noble that he had examined the March 30 proclamation and found it deficient. Carter went on to explain that he knew what the president had intended and would work up a correct description. Not all that auspicious a beginning for a process that would initiate the reservation of 8 percent of the nation's land.

The presidential action of March 30, 1891, had been authorized by a bill that Harrison had signed into law less than a month earlier, on March 3. That law, which historians now call the Forest Reserve Act of 1891, followed two decades of congressional debate over the nation's forests. The debate did not end in 1891, however, and Congress would continue to wrestle with the issue until June 4, 1897, when President William McKinley signed the National Forest Management Act, also know as the Organic Act. This 1897 act determined

49

the purposes for which the national forests could be created, primarily to ensure predictable supplies of water and timber. Not until the 1960s and 1970s would Congress, and the courts, take another look at those purposes.

It would be the Civil War, with all its tragic disruptions, that would trigger concern over western public lands. Thus the national forest story really begins in the 1860s with the opening of the West. In 1862 Congress passed and President Lincoln signed land-grant legislation to encourage construction of a railroad to the West Coast and to offer homesteads free to those who would build homes and live on the virgin land. There were also grants to states to support colleges of agriculture and mechanical arts, and the Department of Agriculture was established; this latter action created a department that would directly involve the government in land management and that would ultimately house a federal forestry agency.

These public land statutes of the Civil War were just four in a long sequence of land laws. Beginning with the Ordinance of 1785 under the Articles of Confederation, the new nation had decided that its western lands were to be surveyed and transferred from public to private ownership. Sales of these lands would generate substantial revenue to support government programs, and settling the land would ensure sovereignty over it. By 1880 there would be more than 3,000 federal statutes concerning public lands, and in those days before income tax, revenue from land sales provided major support of the federal budget.

Major indeed: during the nineteenth century, fully one-half of the nation was transferred into private ownership—largely in 160- or 640-acre pieces—through transactions recorded by dipping a goose-quill pen into an inkwell and committing the legal description to paper. And the Civil War statutes accelerated the process; grants to railroads and settlers would eventually account for a full quarter of the nation's land area.

Land-grant statistics, as awesome as they are, do not fully capture their impact on western development. Vast railroad checkerboard grants stretched from the Mississippi River to the Pacific Ocean. Twenty-two percent of Montana, for example, was granted to the Northern Pacific Railway. Settlers—homesteaders—followed the tracks, riding the trains west to settle and shipping their produce east by rail. Settlers and railroaders found themselves locked in an uneasy symbiotic relationship: settlers were "freight" to the railroaders, and railroads were to the settlers the key to the marketplace. As migration increased territorial populations, Westerners petitioned for statehood, and as these new states entered the Union, the center of political gravity in Congress shifted westward as well. More and more people were trying to earn a living on these former public lands, and their elected representatives brought new perceptions and priorities to Congress. This process was aided by appointing Westerners to committees on agriculture and public lands, the infrastructure that would initiate and review bills of interest to the West.

Between 1871 and 1897, Congress would consider nearly 200 bills that were concerned in some way with forests on the western public lands. Most of these were read once, ordered printed, and dropped from view. A few passed one house but not the other, while some had great staying power, being introduced year after year. The two most famous acts that jumped all the legislative hurdles and were signed into law—the Forest Reserve Act of 1891 and the Organic Act of 1897—were in fact amendments to other statutes. In other words, the early history of legislation regarding forest reserves is both voluminous and complex, and tracing a particular thread requires great patience and more than a little detective skill.

The first forestry bill of national significance was introduced in the House of Representatives in 1872. H.R. 2197, to encourage the planting of trees and the preservation of forests on the public domain, was read a first and second time, ordered printed, and referred to the House Committee on Agriculture. The committee reported favorably, but when the House of Representatives considered the bill, it failed to pass by a narrow margin of 81 to 87.

Debate on H.R. 2197 was typical of that which would follow for the next several decades. Its sponsor spoke at length about treeless prairies needing afforestation and the debilitation that deforestation had brought to the Mediterranean region. Forests were reported to reduce floods while increasing rainfall, attributes of interest to those involved in river-based commerce and farmers in the arid West. But opponents feared loss of options for those settling the land who needed easy access to wood supplies and also needed to be able to clear forests for agriculture, mining, town development, and all the activities common to the westward movement of the American population.

When forest advocates spoke in Congress, they invariably included gruesome descriptions of barren land—usually somewhere in Europe or Asia—descriptions often in the form of direct quotes from a growing body of scientific literature that was sounding the alarm about deforestation. In fact, scientists both reported and advocated; the scientific impulse would have a significant impact on forestry legislation. None more so than George Perkins Marsh, whose *Man and Nature: The Earth as Modified by Human Action* would be cited almost immediately in executive reports, such as the annual report of the commissioner of agriculture; in speeches on the floor of Congress and in committee reports; by other scientists; and eventually by land managers. With good reason: *Man and Nature* painted a sad picture of human excess in Europe, Asia, and Africa where land had for millennia been abused and misused. Marsh proposed the notion of responsible stewardship—use the land and its resources but in such a way that it would retain its fecundity—thus forecasting such modern concepts as sustained yield, sustainable development, and a land ethic.

There was a also scientist of another kind who would alter the trajectory of the history of American public land, Franklin B. Hough, a physician from

Lowville, New York. As a statistician for the federal census in 1860 and 1870, Hough noticed a shift during the decade that resulted in fewer sawmills in the eastern part of New York State and more in the western. He also saw shifts in population that were at the very least coincidental with this relocating industry. Intrigued, he traveled to Washington, D.C., and read everything he could find on forests at the Library of Congress. His concern for the status and condition of forests grew, and he began to craft a paper for presentation at the 1873 annual meeting of the American Association for the Advancement of Science.

Hough's paper, "On the Duty of Governments in the Preservation of Forests," was well received. In fact, Hough and Harvard botanist George Emerson headed a committee with instructions to write a petition asking Congress to address the issue. In Washington, Hough met Minnesota congressman Mark Dunnell, who became his champion. He had also met with President Ulysses S. Grant, who, with the encouragement of Interior Secretary Columbus Delano, agreed to send the AAAS memorial to Congress with his recommendation that it be implemented. One outgrowth was H.R. 2497, an 1874 bill that would authorize "appointment of a commission for inquiry into the destruction of forests" and that was referred to the Committee on Public Lands. The accompanying committee report reprinted President Grant's letter transmitting the AAAS memorial and another of the secretary of the interior urging Congress to act favorably. It also summarized scientific concern for forests. The Senate Committee on Public Lands issued a similar report, but no bill would appear in that chamber.

Dunnell helped Hough through the congressional maze, but prospects seemed bleak. The House Public Lands Committee failed to act on the memorial. In desperation, Dunnell had a rider attached to the 1876 agriculture appropriations measure calling for a man "of scientific attainments" to be appointed to "report on forestry." The rider was retained, and the proposals in the AAAS memorial were thus brought to fruition, although the appointment was in the Department of Agriculture and not Interior, as originally anticipated; years later, much would be made of the logic of having "forestry" in Agriculture, but the location was due much more to last-minute parliamentary strategy than to logic.

It was no surprise when Commissioner of Agriculture Frederick Watts named Hough to be the federal forestry agent. In this capacity, Hough compiled three *Reports Upon Forestry*, published in 1877, 1880, and 1882. (A fourth and final report by Nathaniel Egleston would appear in 1884.) In them, Hough discussed land laws, tree planting, soil types, uses of wood, dangers from insects and fire, relations of forests to climate, and the forests of other nations. He saw that America's tradition of private property rights prevented public intervention in many destructive practices. He recommended that public timber be withdrawn from sale or entry, or use, protected from fire, and cut under lease similar to the Canadian system. Congress was impressed enough to upgrade Hough's "forestry agent" operation and establish the Forestry Division in 1881, making it a permanent bureau of the Department of Agriculture in 1886.

At the same time that Hough was laboring to have Congress establish federal forestry activity, another physician was making his mark on American forest history. John Aston Warder was also concerned about forest conditions, and in 1875 he called a small group to meet in Cincinnati. The resulting exchange of ideas was so fruitful that the group decided to meet subsequently and formalized the process by forming the American Forestry Association (AFA). The AFA became a widely respected voice calling for responsible stewardship of forestlands. It used memorials and in other ways sought to influence congressional decisions; essentially all significant forest legislation during the next century would reflect the AFA's influence.

During the 1880s, Congress kept considering, sifting, and referring forestry legislation, but in the American legislative system, with burden of proof on the advocates, forestry proponents were too tentative to carry the day. Ohio senator John Sherman is a case in point; in 1882 he introduced S. 1826, for the "preservation of the woods and forests of the national domain adjacent to the sources of the navigable rivers and their affluents [sic]." He stated that the American Forestry Association supported it and that it was as "important as any subject which can receive the consideration of the Congress." But, he added, the forests would be protected by the army and "does not involve any expense." No expense, indeed, for one of the most important subjects that Congress might consider! The bill was referred to the Committee on Agriculture; a companion measure was introduced in the House and referred to its Agriculture Committee. Nothing more happened.

Although the stream of forestry bills continued in both the House and the Senate during the 1880s, one of the two dozen bills that went into the hopper during 1888 deserves scrutiny because it contained language that three years later would authorize the beginning of the national forest system. Designated S. 1779, and sponsored by Eugene Hale of Maine, this bill "for the Protection and administration of the Forest on the Public Domain" was a major measure that had been drafted by Bernhard Fernow, chief of the Division of Forestry and secretary of the American Forestry Association. It called for the withdrawal and classification of forestland and authorized the president to designate certain of these lands as "permanent forest reserves." A new bureau in the Department of the Interior would administer the reserves. A year earlier, General Land Office agent Edward A. Bowers had submitted a report to his secretary that contained some of the same points. It is reasonable to assume that Bowers's thoughtful report had influenced Fernow, whom Bowers would in all likelihood have consulted anyway. S. 1779 was sent to committee, where it stayed. In the House, its counterpart suffered a similar fate. It and other forestry measures were replaced by H.R. 7901.

Indiana congressman William S. Holman, chairman of the Public Lands Committee, reported on H.R. 7901 on February 20 "to secure to actual settlers the public lands adapted to agriculture, to protect the forests on the public domain, and for other purposes." The bill was offered as a substitute for twenty-nine others that the committee had been considering. Subsequent debate and discussion would fill many pages of the *Congressional Record,* showing what the forestry concerns and issues were in 1888. Highest on this list were the need to prevent land, water, or mineral monopolies and to ensure that the "actual" settler had ready access to the land made available under the Homestead Act or other public land laws.

Six out of its twenty-nine sections dealt with timber. Section 4 stated that timber could be sold, Section 5 explained how the sale would be advertised and the receipts accounted for, and Section 6 described the purchasers' rights and obligations; Section 7 detailed administrative infrastructure; Section 8, conceptually similar to the Hale bill, authorized the president to reserve certain forestlands from entry, "on which the trees and undergrowth shall be protected from waste or injury." The secretary of the interior could call on the army to provide the protection, a practice only recently inaugurated in Yellowstone National Park. Finally, the intent of Section 9 is hazy, but under it land surveyors would record commercial forest stands down to forty-acre units, and it would be up to the commissioner of the General Land Office to prescribe rules for these lands.

Holman continued to advocate H.R. 7901, referring to it as "the homestead bill," but others were less than sanguine. Haggling over procedure filled pages of the *Record,* and at times the substance of the bill seemed almost incidental. Congressman Thomas McRae of Arkansas joined with Holman to explain the sections to those who were skeptical. Should timber be sold separately from the land? Should there be more protection against monopolists? Should there be more protection of the settlers' needs for wood? Amendments were offered and either accepted or challenged, but the substance of Sections 4 through 7 remained intact.

Sections 8 and 9 were offered together, and what little debate there was on them concerned the need to strengthen the language to protect the rights of "actual" settlers, as opposed to speculators or monopolists. There was no amendment offered that was acceptable to the House, and the clerk continued with readings of Section 10 and on to the end of the bill. Following major debate and compromise on sections concerning coal lands, the bill passed the House on June 27. In the Senate, it was referred to the Committee on Public Lands but not reported out. The bill seemed dead, but at least a portion of it was to survive when, two years later, a portion of it was incorporated into Section 24 of the Forest Reserve Act of 1891.

Since 1886, federal forestry efforts in the Department of Agriculture had statutory permanence, so the Division of Forestry no longer needed to be renewed each year at appropriations time. Chief Fernow was a major player in the American Forestry Association, and the Hale bill, which he had authored, would prove to be an important stepping-stone in the creation of the national forests. Fernow was also active in the American Association for the Advancement of Science. In early 1890, the AAAS sent a memorial to President Harrison, urging the "proper administration of the remaining timber lands in the hands of the Governments of the United States and Canada." The AAAS understood that it was difficult to devise a workable plan to administer the public forestlands, and its Forestry Committee recommended the appointment of a House–Senate committee to consider legislative options. During the interim, forestlands should be withdrawn from entry and protected from fire. In a parallel effort, individual members of the Forestry Committee had been consulting with legislators. One such effort saw Fernow working with Congressman Dunnell, who introduced H.R. 7026, for the "Reservation and preservation of forestlands on the Public Domain and to establish a commission to examine into the condition of said lands, and to report a plan for their management." Fernow repeatedly appeared before Dunnell's committee and was assured of its "interest and full appreciation." But the Public Lands Committee felt that more general legislation was needed before forestry issues could receive its full attention.

Harrison sent the AAAS memorial on to Congress: "I very earnestly recommend that adequate legislation . . . be provided, to the end that the rapid and needless destruction of our great forest areas may be prevented." Much of the memorial's rationale centered on the need to protect western watersheds from destruction by fire and indiscriminate logging. Only the federal government had the ability to manage such lands for the broader public benefit, which exceeded local needs.

Although the public lands were largely in the West, events back east helped explain an abstract concept like conservation. In New York, proponents of a forest reserve in the state's Adirondack Mountains worked to set aside a large, nonfederal watershed to protect water supplies for the Erie Canal. The debate had lasted for decades, but the preserve was created in 1885, followed in 1894 by an amendment to the state's constitution to ensure the permanent protection of basic resource values. What is important here is that the preserve and the debate surrounding it received much attention in the press, in reports of the Division of Forestry, and on the floor of Congress. Obviously, not everybody was watching the Adirondack situation, but those involved in setting aside federal forest reserves from the public domain were, and proponents were both intrigued and encouraged by this state action. The effect is difficult to measure, but the creation of the Adirondack preserve helped make its federal counterparts a reality.

There is still another line of events to pursue to understand congressional action in 1891, authorizing the president to set aside forest reserves, and that is the impact of the establishment of Yellowstone National Park in 1872. The park is large, it would turn out to be the largest in the nation, but its supporters believed that it should be even larger. One of those was Arnold Hague, a geologist with the United States Geological Survey. Hague had been assigned to survey the park and its natural wonders, and he became convinced that to protect and expand the park, Congress would need an economic rationale; protection of forested watersheds seemed to hold promise. He boldly proposed expanding Yellowstone by moving the original park boundary nine miles south and twenty-five miles east. Hague found a willing sponsor in Missouri senator George Vest, who in 1884 introduced a bill to expand the park according to Hague's model. The bill passed the Senate, but failed in the House. Four years later, they were still at it, and as Hague observed to an associate, "It is a very [difficult] matter to get any legislation accomplished which does not affect any congressional district. The Park is of interest to the nation, but there is no Congressman who feels that he has a large constituency behind him demanding the passage of the bill."

One strategy was to develop a constituency for the park, which turned out to be a hunting organization called the Boone and Crockett Club. In 1889, the club sent letters asking for support of Vest's bill to enlarge the park: "The Boone and Crockett Club, from the interest which it has taken in this matter, is in a position to know the sentiment and desires of kindred associations throughout the United States. Thousands of letters through out the country testify to the widespread interest in the better preservation and maintenance of the Park." This bill died, new ones would be introduced, and months and years passed. But as with the public debate over the Adirondack preserve, those over Yellowstone set the framework for subsequent discussions over public land management generally, in particular the Forest Reserve Act of 1891.

It should not be surprising that during a century of passing more than 3,000 statutes concerning public lands, those Congress enacted included a few that did not work as planned. In 1890 Congress took on a housekeeping task to repeal and amend existing legislation until the major public land problems were satisfactorily resolved. Various degrees of fraud and encouragement of speculation were only two defects charged against certain statutes, such as the Desert Land Act and Preemption Acts. But it would be a bill to repeal the Timber Culture Act "and for other purposes" that would become a vehicle for reform, and incidentally apparently a means to expand Yellowstone National Park.

The Timber Culture Act itself, largely an aside to this narrative, had been passed in 1873. It was a variation of the Homestead Act that addressed the special needs of settling in the plains states. If one would plant a certain number of trees, then the 160-acre parcel of public domain would be his. It sounded good on paper; the trees would provide fuel, fence posts, lumber, shade, and it was thought at the same time increase rainfall—all scarce items in large portions of the West. But the law had also opened the way for a great deal of land fraud, and its repeal had been advocated for years by many, including the commissioner of the General Land Office.

On March 18, 1890, the House of Representatives began its examination of H.R. 7254, which had been referred to the Committee on Public Lands. Congressman Dunnell had sponsored the Timber Culture Act of 1873, which he alone in the House felt obliged to defend. He also suggested that his sponsorship of the effort that had created the position of federal forestry agent in 1876 showed his strong interest in forestry matters. But, he added, forestry legislation was pending in other committees that had the support of the Division of Forestry and the American Forestry Association; before the Timber Culture Act was repealed, a forest-management law should be in place.

Holman was unsympathetic. He attacked the Timber Culture Act, claiming that it had been "a source of dishonesty from the beginning." Other members saw the law as mainly providing opportunities for speculation. Dunnell tried valiantly to delay a vote, but his objections were swept aside by an impatient House. In just four days, the bill passed and was sent to the Senate.

The senators busied themselves amending the House bill, which had looked largely at repealing the Timber Culture Act. In addition to public lands in Alaska and town sites carved from the public domain, senatorial interest in water was reflected in several amendments; one section treated reservoir sites, and four sections discussed canal rights-of-way. There was little debate, except over the right to manufacture lumber out of timber cut from mineral lands.

The Senate approved the amended bill on September 16; it was back on the floor of the House on September 25 with a request for a conference. As the clerk began to read the bill, bickering broke out over whether or not it should be heard or referred to the Public Lands Committee to analyze the Senate amendments. Holman held for continuation of the reading but was voted down; the bill went to committee. On September 30, the House clerk read aloud: "Your committee have had under consideration House bill 7254, to repeal the timber-culture law, and for other purposes, and recommend that the House non-concur in all Senate amendments and agree to a conference."

When Lewis Edwin Payson moved for nonconcurrence on September 30, he was asked whether there would be an agreement that year. He responded: "I will say to the gentleman, if I may properly do so in advance, that unless the Senate recede from their entire amendment and pass the repeal of the timber culture law as the House passed it, no agreement will be reached at this session." The motion was then agreed to, and the Speaker appointed Congressmen Payson, Holman, and John A. Pickler of South Dakota to serve as conferees. Nearly five months later, on February 28, 1891, the conference committee reported back. It would be significant that only three days remained before the Fifty-first Congress would adjourn its second session.

In the Senate, Preston B. Plumb of Kansas reported that "after full and free conference" the committee recommended that both houses of Congress adopt a bill containing twenty-four sections. Going into conference, the bill had included only twenty-three sections, and a quirk of history has made the basic bill subordinate to the added Section 24: "A bill to repeal the Timber Culture Act" is remembered as the Forest Reserve Act of 1891.

Senator Plumb pushed his colleagues hard to ratify the amended bill without waiting for it to be printed, insisting that "every line of it has been in one shape or another passed, I think, by the Senate heretofore." Besides, time was short, and the Senate had other matters to consider before adjournment. Senator Wilkinson Call of Florida challenged: "It seems to me [if] this bill is of so much importance that it would be well for us to know exactly what is in the report . . . although I do not desire to delay it a moment."

Plumb restated: "There is nothing in the report on any subject whatever that has not already undergone the scrutiny of this body, and passed by this body." For good measure he added, "[A]t this period of the session there has got to be something taken for granted or else the public business can not go forward as it should." Call wanted the record to show that he opposed any measure that would "prevent a single acre of the public domain from being set apart and reserved for homes for the people of the United States who shall live upon and cultivate them."

In response, Plumb pulled out the rhetorical stops and assured Call that "no bill has passed this body or any other legislative body that more thoroughly consecrates the public domain to actual settlers and home-owners than does the bill in the report just read. That is the central idea of the bill." Not fully convinced, Call cautiously responded, "[I]f that is true, then it meets my approval." The presiding officer then called for the vote, and the conference report was accepted. It was now up to the House, which was considering the amended H.R. 7254 concurrently with the Senate.

As a member of the conference committee, Congressman Payson led off by asking to have the clerk read the bill, but first to read a synopsis of the various sections. The summary seems accurate enough; Section 24 "authorizes the President to set apart trust reserves where, to preserve timber, he shall deem it advisable." Acknowledging that one section had not previously passed the House, Payson then asked that the reading of the "long" bill be dispensed with.

Dunnell complained that the bill's title suggested that repealing the Timber Culture Act was its purpose, when in fact "every kind of legislation imaginable finds itself included in this omnibus bill." Robert Adams of Pennsylvania was more to the point, asking Payson which section had been added. "That is the forestry reservation," Payson responded. "We have made a provision in this bill authorizing the President . . . whenever in his judgment he deems it proper to do so, to make a reservation of the timber lands, principally applying it to the watersheds of the West, so that the water supply in that country may be preserved from entry and until legislation shall have passed Congress whereby these lands shall be opened." (These "temporary" reserves would remain in place until 1976 when Congress, through the National Forest Management Act, gave permanence to the lands reserved by presidential proclamation.)

Congressman McRae of Arkansas, who would subsequently be seen as a strong advocate of forest reserves, thought that Section 24 should be eliminated: "This is an experiment which may prove beneficial to that part of our country, and may assist in its development, or it may not; but I do believe, Mr. Speaker, that the power granted to the President by section 24 is an extraordinary and dangerous power to grant over the public domain." He went on to explain that the reservation of forested watersheds in the West was not a problem, but the president would also have the authority to reserve public lands of agricultural quality, and that was unwise.

Holman, who had been the author of the 1888 bill with similar language on presidential proclamations, explained that the intent now "in regard to the withdrawal of forestland is exactly the same as the bill passed last session, after very careful consideration." McRae reminded Holman that he had been opposed to such presidential authority during the previous session, and he remained so. Dunnell chimed in with support for McRae's position: "This is a vast power to give the President." Congressional debate over just how and for what the reserves were to be managed would continue until 1897.

And then things got petty. Dunnell rightly challenged the effort to keep the bill from being read in full, and Holman agreed. But Payson dug in his heels and accused Dunnell of engaging in innuendo against the conference committee: "I am almost expecting the gentleman [Dunnell] to intimate that there has been an immense lobby around the corridors here in order to force passage of this bill." Payson made it personal by stating that "the gentleman from Minnesota . . . is ignorant of the provisions of this bill [and] has not yet got out of the primary school of ordinary statesmanship [laughter]."

Tactics were clear. If the bill was to be printed in full, the delay would cause its defeat, because all would have to focus instead on the pending appropriations measure, which obviously took precedence. It had to go through that evening or be held over. Some members cried, "Vote, vote," and Payson turned up the heat. The bill was "perhaps the last one I shall ever be connected with in the public service." He was proud of his ten years in Congress and was going to retire. He and Holman had labored "night after night" to craft a bill that provided for "homes for the poor and the reclamation of the desert." He told Dunnell that he took "great pride" in this "fitting termination" of his public service. More bickering and more innuendo and some parliamentary slight of hand, and objections to the conference committee report were overcome; the House approved the bill on February 28. There was a final reading on March 2 but no discussion, and the bill went to the executive mansion for President Harrison's signature on March 3, 1891.

Generations of scholars have looked at the 1891 act—that is, Section 24— and speculated on its origins. That it was added in conference committee and adopted without referral to both houses of Congress is mentioned almost without fail, even though the practice was not all that unusual in those times. Several scholars have pointed to the similarity of language between Section 8 of the 1888 bill and Section 24 of the 1891 act, suggesting that Congressman Holman, who was also a member of the 1890/1891 conference committee, got Section 24 added. Of course, if it is the concept rather than the detail of presidential proclamation that is significant, then Fernow's authorship of the 1888 Hale bill would make him "father" of the national forest system.

Historians generally have offered a similar lament that the record is not complete enough to state with certainty what happened in the conference committee when Section 24 was added. Contemporaries give different accounts: South Dakota senator Richard Pettigrew says that he did it; publisher Robert Underwood Johnson says that he did it; Fernow says that Secretary Noble did it because Noble modestly implied that he had; and some say that Bowers of the General Land Office was the key. Pettigrew and Johnson "remembered" their role much later, and it was some time after 1891 that Noble told Fernow that it maybe would be proper for him to get some credit. Fernow's correspondence during late February and early March 1891 fairly clearly shows that he was not even aware of the law until two weeks after Harrison signed it. Finally, according to Hague's account, it was he who brought the news to Noble's attention, and so it goes.

Arcane debates aside, it is clear that Holman has not received his due from forest historians. A close comparison of Section 8 (1888) and Section 24 (1891) offers convincing evidence that one led to the other; the law as adopted in 1891 is in capital letters laid over the 1888 language:

THAT THE PRESIDENT OF THE UNITED STATES MAY FROM TIME TO TIME SET APART AND RESERVE, IN ANY STATE OR TERRITORY HAVING PUBLIC LANDS BEARING FORESTS, [in] ANY PART OF THE PUBLIC LANDS designated in the act as timber lands, or any lands WHOLLY OR IN PART COVERED WITH TIMBER OR UNDERGROWTH, WHETHER OF COMMERCIAL VALUE OR NOT, AS PUBLIC RESERVATIONS, on which the trees and undergrowth shall be protected from waste or injury, under the charge of the Secretary of the Interior; AND THE PRESIDENT SHALL, BY PUBLIC PROCLAMATION, DECLARE THE ESTABLISHMENT OF SUCH RESERVATIONS AND THE LIMITS THEREOF[.] and may employ such portion of the military forces as may be necessary.[2]

This comparison offers mute testimony as to why Section 24 has such cumbersome syntax and is in fact an incomplete sentence. Hasty editing of the conveniently handy Section 8 explains the awkwardness, and lack of anything approaching a consensus on forest reserve purposes and management infrastructure explains what was omitted. As we know now, it would take six additional years to agree on purposes, and that agreement would barely squeak by even then.

As a member of the 1891 conference committee, Holman was positioned to provide the language for Section 24, and common sense insists that he did. The most valuable result of this belated discovery of Holman's contribution is that it gives a better look at congressional intent, because the 1888 bill was accompanied by a committee report that provides context for Section 8, which helps explain what happened when the 1891 statute was implemented. The committee report clearly acknowledges the intent to establish forest reserves to protect water supplies, a key point that is not at all apparent in the actual statute.

As it turned out, the rationale for the first reserve to be established under the new procedure provides little insight into the creation of the reserve system as a whole, but let us begin by watching the initial proclamation take shape.

The Geological Survey's Arnold Hague had been monitoring congressional activity in hopes that the bill to expand Yellowstone Park would pass. On March 16 he wrote to an associate that many bills, including the park bill, failed to pass because Congress was distracted by debate over a proposed telegraph cable to Hawaii. But he saw the opportunity offered by Section 24 of the March 3 act, and he asked the chief clerk in the Department of the Interior for "such forms as you may have in you office for the setting aside of reservations from the public lands." He went on, "I am very anxious to adjust the matter of the lands adjoining the Yellowstone Park which the Secretary has signified his desire to reserve."

The very next day, Interior clerk E. M. Davidson wrote to Hague: "I enclose herewith a copy of the form of letters usually written by the Secretary in recommending the reservation of lands for public purposes together with the endorsement of the President. The paper is returned to the Department by the President and then referred to the General Land Office where record is made which completes the reservation."

Form in hand, Hague wrote to Secretary Noble on March 25:

As requested by you during our interview last week with regard to the reservation of forest lands near the headwaters of the Yellowstone River, we take pleasure in enclosing for your consideration, a draft of a proclamation, setting apart, by order of the President a tract of country situated to the south and east of the present boundaries of the Yellowstone National Park.

He assured Noble that the tract was "identical" to that proposed in the Vest bill to enlarge the park, and he reminded him that the bill had passed the Senate "four times" but had failed in the House: "In all the Rocky Mountain country there are few areas, if any, of equal extent [that are] better adapted for a National Forest Reservation, and none which surpass it in any way for its advantage as a natural reservoir for the storage of water." He added that the southern portion provided breeding places for elk and deer, and the animals needed to be protected from the growing number of hunters. President Harrison obliged on March 30, and the Yellowstone Park Timberland Reserve was on the books; on July 1, 1908, the reserve was renamed the Shoshone National Forest.

A week later, Hague wrote to several associates explaining what had happened. He had seen the Bill to Repeal the Timber Culture Act as a means to salvage the intent of the failed Vest bill, he had brought the matter to the attention of Secretary Noble, and he had drafted the presidential proclamation. He saw that the proclamation was defective because of vague and incomplete boundary descriptions, such as not stating that the eastern and southern park boundaries doubled as reserve boundaries, but he thought that "nobody" would notice. As it turned out, the defects were noticed and corrected months later.

Meanwhile, officials were quickly gearing up to implement the newly granted proclamation authority. On May 15, 1891, the commissioner of the General Land Office sent a circular to all field agents instructing them to gather information on tracts suitable for forest reserves. The instructions contained two main points: the reserves were to protect watersheds, and those who would be affected by the reservation would be given an opportunity to state their opinions.

The notice was placed in local newspapers and posted where the public would see it. The response was prompt, substantial, and thoughtful. It is obvious that the language of the notice influenced the letter writers, who often referred specifically to the official request for information and included statements about timber and water supplies. Some letters were short and general, but others gave lengthy rationales for the creation of a particular forest reserve and a few even contained legal descriptions. Authors included settlers, those in business, law firms, water districts, livestock associations, and banks, and generally represented the full range of people living on or near potential forest reserves.

A broad cross section favored reserves; opposition was more narrowly focused on the mining industry's concern that its freedom to act might somehow be curtailed. Others, such as Colorado senator Henry M. Teller, urged caution, lest settlers suffer needless hardship brought on by a callous government in distant Washington, D.C. This point would be much emphasized during congressional debate over the next half decade, and indeed when the president in 1897 appeared to ignore it, the reserve system itself was placed in extreme jeopardy.

Congress turned almost immediately to the task of determining the purposes of the forest reserves, for under the vague terms of the 1891 proclamation, they functioned as quasi-parks. But the reserves were withdrawn from entry under land laws, and while they could not be settled, they could not yet be managed; they sat for six years waiting for Congress to decide, during which time about 40 million acres would be reserved.

In 1892 Representative Thomas McRae introduced H.R. 10101, "To protect forest reservations." His bill did not get very far, but the committee report that accompanied H.R. 10101 contained language that became the unofficial theme of the forest reserve system:

It becomes, therefore, necessary, also, to prescribe the manner and methods by which the timber growing thereon [in the reserves], the mineral contained therein, the water powers furnished by them, and the pasturage within the same shall be used, so as not to injure or destroy the primary objects for which these reservations have been made, namely, to secure such forest conditions as are necessary to preserve an even water flow.

Use but don't abuse; clearly the reserves were not to be "locked up."

These and other sections of the committee report emphasize a point that is not all that well understood today—the primary driving force behind forest reserve legislation at that early time was protection and enhancement of water supplies, including flood protection. Representative McRae made this point early on: "The objects for which these reservations are made or are to be made . . . are represented to be protection of the forest growth against destruction by fire and ax and preservation of forest conditions upon which water conditions and water flow are said to be dependent." Said to be dependent by whom? By the scientists in the Division of Forestry, General Land Office, Geological Survey, Irrigation Survey, and broader-based American Association for the Advancement of Science and National Academy of Science who had been speaking and writing about the tight relationship between forests and water supply—quantity and quality—and the need to provide for responsible management of one in order to ensure the other. Since 1872 Congress had translated this scientific concern into a series of bills to protect forests at the headwaters of streams and "for other purposes." As a result, it would have been more accurate to label the reserves "water reserves," but forests were the most visible component, so forest reserves they became.

When trying to determine what Congress was intending, regarding the purposes of forest reserves, one can learn much by looking at a variety of alternatives contained in bills considered. Congress examined a range of options: states' rights versus federal responsibilities, use versus preservation of resources, and detailed prescriptive statutes versus delegation of broad administrative authority to an executive agency. The final product, signed into law on June 4, 1897, means much more when seen for what it might have been but was not.

In 1893 McRae introduced H.R. 119, "to protect forest reservations," which contained the basis for the statute enacted in 1897. The "purposes" clause by 1893 had taken on essentially its final form: "That no public forest reservation shall be established except to improve and protect the forest within the reservation or for the purpose of securing favorable conditions of water flow and continuous supplies of timber to the people." This statement had impressive staying power; Congress tinkered with other sections, but the "purposes" language stayed much the same.

Everyone seemed to agree that those who lived on or near the reserves would not be unduly inconvenienced—they would have full access to resources, but they had to operate under the permit system. Thus the administrative agency was obliged to grant rights of way, for example, but not to the detriment of the purposes for which the reserves had been established.

Timber sales were a touchy matter, even for those who favored them. There was the usual concern about monopoly, and there was substantial sentiment that no timber should be cut. Instead, the reserves should be dedicated to the protection of watersheds. This ambivalence may explain why the timber sale section of the bill is so detailed and so specific, in comparison with sections dealing with other matters. To be sold, timber had to be "marked and designated," appraised and sold at least at that price, and the sale needed to be properly advertised so all could take advantage of it.

H.R. 119 and similar bills made some progress toward passage, but something—probably too little support rather than too much opposition—prevented any one of them from clearing all the hurdles on the way to the president's desk. Seeking a breakthrough, at the urging of Bernhard Fernow and others, Secretary of the Interior Hoke Smith asked National Academy of Sciences president Wolcott Gibbs to appoint a committee to study the question of forest reserves and make recommendations on their creation and management. In 1896 Gibbs appointed Alexander Agassiz of Harvard, army engineer Henry L. Abbott, Geological Survey geologist Arnold Hague, Harvard botanist Charles S. Sargent, and Gifford Pinchot. Sargent was named chairman, and Pinchot, a young and energetic forester and the only commissioner not a member of the academy, was named secretary. Armed with a $25,000 appropriation to cover expenses, the commission headed west to examine existing and potential reserves, and to develop its recommendations.

The commission's goal was ambitious. Areas already reserved or to be reserved were by definition rather remote and poorly documented. The commissioners traveled in the western mountains by train, by buggy, and on horseback. They lodged in hotels when they could and camped out when they could not. For part of their journey, they had the benefit of the company of southern California's forest reserve advocate Abbot Kinney and the Sierra Club's John Muir. After several months accumulating all the information they could by direct observation and the reports of others, the commissioners returned to the East. Chairman Sargent asked Pinchot and Hague to write the report for consideration by the whole body.

When asking NAS president Gibbs to appoint a forest reserve committee, Secretary Smith had included three questions: Is it practical to establish and protect forest reserves? Is the influence of forests on climate, soil, and water conditions adequate to justify reserve creation? What sort of legislation is needed? The sixty-page report went far beyond the original charges.

The report began with the obligatory survey of undesirable forest conditions in Europe and Asia as a rationale for not letting that happen in the United States. There were descriptions of existing and proposed reserves, and a lengthy section on the preferred administrative agency. Appendixes included sample bills. But as events unfolded, by the time the official report was published in late May 1897, it was moot.

The report was already late in February 1897, but Secretary Smith told President Grover Cleveland that the basic information on which reserves should be created was at hand. The reasons remain unclear, but with less than a month remaining in office, Cleveland decided to proclaim the 21 million acres of forest reserves as recommended by the NAS commission, and proclamations dated February 22—Washington's Birthday—seemed an appropriate remembrance for the first president. Thus without prior consultation with those who would be directly affected or with their representatives in Congress, the forest reserve system was more than doubled in size with a few strokes of the presidential pen.

It is difficult to sort out political hyperbole from justifiable outrage, but by any measure the reaction was severe. Of the critics, Fernow was perhaps the most gentle by labeling the presidential action "injudicious." He added that the proclamation had "stirred up such an antagonism as we have never had before." Congressional opponents of the proclamations, and there were many, attached a rider to the appropriations measure that repealed Cleveland's action. In his very last legislative act, the president vetoed the appropriations bill, with its onerous amendment, and then took part in his last ceremonial act, accompanying William McKinley to his inauguration.

The new president began his term by calling a special session of Congress; his predecessor's veto had left the McKinley administration without appropriations. Also, his broader agenda included a deteriorating situation in Cuba, and he needed to keep congressional support for the pending declaration of war against Spain. McKinley met with Pinchot (who by now was eclipsing Fernow as the nation's most influential forester) and others, assuring them that he was in favor of saving the forest reserves, but he would not take any overt action that might jeopardize his larger interests.

Getting a forestry measure through was going to be tricky, because even before Cleveland's provocative act, McRae's H.R. 119 and similar measures had not been able to gather anything approaching momentum. And now, opponents could appear reasonable and insist that it was inappropriate to consider anything other than appropriations during this special session. Opponents with less concern about the appearance of reasonableness could make speeches on the floor that castigated the former president and his act: "I do not think there is a man on earth who is such a blunderhead that he can make even a thousandth part of the mistakes that President Cleveland made. [Laughter and applause.]" The NAS commissioners themselves fared little better, being accused of making recommendations for forest reserves based on information that reserve opponents characterized as having been gathered only in cozy western drawing rooms.

Reserve proponents had a steep hill to climb before they could save Cleveland's proclamations and also gain passage of a statute that defined the purposes for which reserves could be established. The first reserve had been proclaimed in the spring of 1891, and now it was the spring of 1897 and still the purposes had not been agreed on, even though 40 million or so acres had been set aside. Fernow, Pinchot, Hague, Charles Walcott from the Geological Survey, and others worked the congressional cloakrooms to find a rallying point.

As with so much of this story, accounts vary as to just how the hostility was tempered. What is clear is that Senator Pettigrew, chairman of the Public Lands Committee, withdrew his early opposition to the reserves and became a supporter. Walcott is generally credited for swinging him around. It seems a bit strange that the opponents agreed to compromise, since they had the high moral ground—Cleveland had in fact proclaimed reserves without prior consultation, an essential ingredient since 1891. But compromise they did, and the focus of the compromise was a nine-month suspension of Cleveland's reserves and allowing settlers who were already on the proclaimed land an opportunity through the so-called lieu land clause to swap their holdings without penalty for public land outside the reserve. After nine months, Congress would take another look at the reserves to determine whether they would be reinstated.

In the House, McRae made one last attempt to substitute language from his earlier bills that "nothing shall prohibit the use of water" instead of the more favored "all waters may be used." He ultimately failed, and the appropriations measure for the Geological Survey was amended to provide for survey of the reserves, suspension of Cleveland's reserves for nine months, and definition of purpose: reserves were to be established for timber and water supplies; settlers had a right of access; mature timber could be marked and designated, appraised, and sold at auction; all water could be used under state and federal law; and substantial administrative latitude was granted to the executive administering agency. Since the amendment applied to all reserves created under the 1891 act, the Yellowstone reserve was included. Finally, during the nine-month suspension period there were occasional references to the approaching deadline, but it passed without notice and Cleveland's reserves were fully restored.

The new law gave management of the tracts to the General Land Office. In 1902 that agency would establish Division R to carry out this mandate, and the division's foresters could use a newly minted *Forest Reserve Manual* for guidance. Since 1897 *Rules and Regulations Governing Forest Reserves* had served as a basis for management and protection, but the new manual reflected the existence of a forestry agency. In 1905, as part of the broader conservation movement, the reserves and the work of Division R were transferred to the Bureau of Forestry in the Department of Agriculture. In 1907 Congress, always sensitive to its prerogatives, rescinded the president's authority to proclaim forest reserves in six western states, in practical terms achieving what had come within a whisker of happening in 1897.

The 1897 appropriations measure is now called the Organic Act, the Forest Management Act, or sometimes the Pettigrew Amendment. Coupled with the 1891 act, the 1897 amendment served well until 1960, when Congress considered and then passed the Multiple Use–Sustained Yield Act, which was determined to be "supplemental to, but not in derogation of, the purposes for which the national forests were established as set forth in the Act of June 4, 1897." In the 1970s there would be significant court challenges regarding both timber and water sections, but whatever limitations are obvious in retrospect, the two statutes (or amendments to statutes) provided the means for a grand experiment in public land and resource management that even critics grudgingly pay their respects to. That the 1970s saw greatly increased federal involvement in a broad spectrum of environmental issues, and Congress at the same time reversed itself and enacted prescriptive forestry legislation to replace earlier broad mandates, should not be seen as criticism of the original effort. Even the Constitution is amended from time to time; specific statutes cannot be expected to do better.

NOTES

1. This synthetic account was originally published as *The Beginnings of the National Forest System,* FS-488 (Washington, D.C.: United States Department of Agriculture, Forest Service, 1991), and was published without footnotes. We have kept this format, but the author wishes to acknowledge his debt to the following scholars and their arguments: Ron Arnold, "Stepchild of America," in *People of the Tongass: Alaska Forestry Under Attack,* ed. K. A. Soderberg and Jackie DuRette (Bellevue, Wash.: Free Enterprise Press, 1988); Samuel T. Dana, *Forest and Range Policy* (New York: McGraw-Hill, 1956); Sally K. Fairfax and A. Dan Tarlock, "No Water for the

Woods: A Critical Analysis of *United States v. New Mexico*," *Idaho Law Review* 15 (1979): 509–54; Joseph A. Miller, "Congress and the Origins of Conservation: Natural Resource Policies, 1865–1900" (Ph.D. diss., University of Minnesota, 1973); Harold K. Steen, *The U.S. Forest Service: A History* (Seattle: University of Washington Press, 1976).

2. See Ron Arnold, "Congressman William Holden of Indiana: Unknown Founder of the National Forests," in *The Origins of the National Forests,* ed. Harold K. Steen (Durham, N.C.: Forest History Society, 1992), 301–13.

Part Two

FIRST CUTS

Timber Users, Timber Savers:
The Homestake Mining Company and
the First Regulated Timber Harvest

Richmond L. Clow

The Progressive Era has emerged as a period crucial to the success of the late-nineteenth-century conservation crusade. During this optimistic era of social reform, with its faith in technology and efficiency, demands for a halt to the destruction and waste of the nation's natural resources became established federal policy. Many studies have examined the varied themes of the conservation movement, from the aesthetic importance of the environment to the fear that the depletion of resources, such as timber, threatened the very existence of American society.[1] These studies have most often defined the users of resources as the despoilers of the environment. Such an approach, however, ignores the role that industry played in defining conservation.

An illustration of the importance of resource users to the conservation story can be found in the Black Hills of South Dakota, where the Homestake Mining Company had been the largest consumer of trees from the region's public lands. The company's logging operations passed through three phases corresponding to changes in popular attitude and national policy regarding resource conservation. From just after the beginning of the Black Hills gold rush in 1876 until the creation of the Black Hills Forest Reserve in 1897, Homestake loggers destroyed large portions of the forest with the aid of legislation that encouraged the unlimited use of the nation's apparently inexhaustible timber resources. With the beginning of the shift in federal policy toward conservation and the advent of the forest reserve, the company initiated fraudulent mining claims to keep on cutting trees from the restricted land. Finally, once the leadership of Homestake understood the Progressive foundation of the movement to save resources and realized that conservation was in its best long-term interest, the mining company not only accepted forest conservation but also played an active role in shaping modern forestry. Embracing the new conservation policy, Homestake initiated Timber Case No. 1, the first regulated timber harvest from a public forest reserve.

Largely through the efforts of Gifford Pinchot, the leadership of Homestake Mining Company came to understand the movement's philosophical foundation and promote forest conservation. Pinchot, a young, energetic eastern forester who eventually became the first head of the United States Forest Service, championed the cause of scientific management of the nation's forests. Under the system he espoused, foresters, not politicians or lumbermen, would guide lumber operations. For Progressives like Pinchot and his followers, "conservation" meant the proper management of forests for the production of a steady and ongoing supply of lumber for the nation's industries. Proponents of "preservation," on the contrary, stressed the perpetuation of the wilderness in a state of nonuse. No compromise existed between these competing views, as the public split in 1897 between Pinchot and John Muir, the country's leading preservationist, illustrated. When confronted with these two alternatives, Homestake supported conservation, whose emphasis on wise use of the forests would ensure a continual lumber supply for the company's gold-mining operations.[2]

A critical relationship existed between nineteenth-century gold mining and lumbering. Trees provided cordwood for fuel, boards for building construction, and shoring for mine tunnels, all of which were essential to the recovery of gold. Thus the commercial exploitation of the Black Hills forest had begun with the gold rush of 1876. In that year, entrepreneurs shipped several small sawmills to the Black Hills to supply rough boards for the fledgling gold-mining industry as well as local building construction.[3] Congress further helped western mining operations obtain lumber by passing the Free Timber Act of 1878, authorizing miners to take for mining purposes "any timber or trees growing or being on the public [mineral lands] . . . subject to such rules and regulations as the Secretary of the Interior may prescribe for the protection of the timber."[4] The secretary's office established regulations prohibiting the cutting of any tree less than eight inches in diameter and requiring that brush and treetops be disposed of in a manner that would prevent the spread of forest fires. Largely unenforced, these regulations did nothing to halt the quick destruction of the yellow, or ponderosa, pine forests in the Black Hills. Together, town builders and miners logged 1.5 billion board feet from 1876 until 1898.[5]

A small, isolated mountain range, the Black Hills lie along the South Dakota–Wyoming border between the Belle Fourche River and the south fork of the Cheyenne River. About 120 miles long and 40 miles wide, the range rises up to 4,000 feet above the surrounding short-grass prairie and, because of the higher elevation, receives more rainfall than the adjacent grassland.[6] Accessible and well timbered, the mountains permitted easy exploitation, a fact that was not lost on miners. Henry M. Chance, a mining engineer who had traveled the region, wrote in 1891 that large tracts of the pine forest in the northern Black Hills had "been cut on a large scale for use at the

Homestake and other mines . . . [because the trees are] of inestimable value in the development of their mineral resources, furnishing a good, cheap mine-timber." The southern Black Hills, which offered limited mining opportunities and therefore retained its trees, presented a much different landscape. "It is impossible," Chance observed, "to travel through the Black Hills, especially through their southern portion, without being charmed by the beauty of the country."[7]

In the first years of logging, when timber was plentiful, only the best trees were taken. When timber became scarce and the second cuttings began, lumbermen took the remaining trees, leaving large clear-cut areas. Often only 50 percent of each tree was used and the rest discarded as waste. Competition between mining companies contributed to the squandering of timber; lumbermen sometimes cut logs only to prevent another mining company from getting them. Surplus logs often rotted at mining operations that had been abandoned. Henry S. Graves, a professional forester, noted that in the northern Black Hills, the center of the region's mining industry, timber was "almost entirely cut within a radius of 8 miles from Deadwood," leaving the hillsides barren of trees.[8]

While these wasteful lumbering practices altered the Black Hills landscape, logging was not solely responsible for transforming the environment. Periodic natural fires also thinned the pine stands. As a result, the forest covering the Black Hills was not extremely dense, and miners did not set fires to clear the land in order to conduct prospecting activities, as they did in many parts of the Rocky Mountains. Instead, train engines throwing sparks and burning sawdust piles at local lumber mills were the main causes of man-made forest fires in the Black Hills. In the early years, once a fire started, it often burned uncontrolled for weeks because no fire-protection program existed.[9]

The years of unregulated cutting and unchecked burning did not go unnoticed. In 1892, Per Axel Rydberg, a field agent for the United States Department of Agriculture, compiled an inventory of Black Hills flora. He described the region as having been "one large pine forest; but now large tracts are made bare by the ravages of lumbermen, mining companies, fire, and cyclones." Rydberg observed that only "stumps, fallen logs, and the underbrush" remained, and he predicted that "it will be no wonder if in a short time the dark pine forest is gone and the name 'Black Hills' has become meaningless."[10]

Taken together, commercial cutting, man-caused fires, and natural fires destroyed the pine forest and in the process created a new, less commercially valuable, plant community. Instead of pine, bur oak took hold at the lower elevations, and aspen and white birch began growing at the higher elevations; neither had any immediate commercial value. In time, pine would again replace the aspen and birch as the forest community changed in an orderly succession. The uncontrolled commercial exploitation of the yellow pine accelerated these natural changes in the forest's landscape, threatening its value to industry for decades to come.[11]

Many individuals and corporations shared responsibility for depleting the Black Hills forests between 1875 and 1890, but as the largest consumer of the region's timber, Homestake Mining Company was the most visible violator of the few regulations that governed the cutting of trees on public lands. The company constructed its own narrow-gauge railroad in 1881 to haul timber to Lead, the location of its gold-milling operation. Named the Black Hills & Fort Pierre, it eventually extended to the small community of Piedmont on the east-central edge of the Black Hills. In addition to the railroad, the company operated lumbering camps throughout the northern Black Hills where loggers converted free trees into the cordwood, building materials, and mine timbers essential to Homestake's profitable gold operation.[12]

Eventually, Homestake's lumbering practices brought the company to court because its loggers violated the secretary of the interior's regulation forbidding the cutting from public lands of trees under eight inches in diameter. The United States attorney filed charges against the company in 1894, claiming that it had illegally cut 6,828,160 trees from public land and seeking $688,804 in damages plus interest. Attorneys for the plaintiffs asked to move the trial from Deadwood to Sioux Falls, in the eastern part of the state. They cited the impossibility of obtaining a fair trial in the Black Hills, where a large number of the residents had themselves engaged in unlawfully cutting timber at one time or another. The attempt to move the trial failed, and the case was heard in Deadwood. Four years later, Judge John Carland ruled that the Homestake Mining Company had to pay $75,000 in damages—a small penalty when one considers the value of the timber. Investigators for the General Land Office, which administered the nation's forest resources at the time, estimated the value of timber that the company had taken illegally at between $2 million and $3 million.[13] This early timber-cutting case served only as a prelude to further government intervention as the conservation movement gathered momentum during the Progressive Era.

Scientists, who had been among the first advocates of land ethics, made up the vanguard of the conservation movement. George Perkins Marsh published *Man and Nature*, his classic study warning of environmental destruction, in 1864. A decade later, Franklin B. Hough, another scientist, advocated the conservation practices of the forestry profession, then in its infancy in the United States, to save the forests and their associated resources. Initially, the efforts of the scientific community did not sway Congress. That situation began to change in 1896, when Secretary of the Interior Hoke Smith requested the National Academy of Sciences to prepare a report outlining a "rational forest policy" for the United States. Wolcott Gibbs, president of the academy, appointed a National Forestry Commission and directed that group to locate sites for future forest reserves on the public timberlands and recommend that the United States assume a stronger administrative posture over the proposed reserves.[14]

Several members of the National Forestry Commission visited the Black Hills and other public lands throughout the West in the summer of 1896. Later the full commission reported, "It is evident that without Government protection these forests [of the Black Hills], so far as their productive capacity is concerned, will disappear at the end of a few years, and . . . their destruction will entail serious injury and loss to the agricultural and mining population of western North and South Dakota."[15] President Grover Cleveland followed part of the commission's recommendations and on February 22, 1897, created thirteen new forest reserves. Among them was the Black Hills Forest Reserve, which consisted of 967,680 acres of timbered lands. Cleveland based his action on an 1891 law that authorized the president to create forest reserves and to establish a permit system regulating the cutting of trees on public lands.[16]

Because no provisions for the regulated cutting of timber on the restricted land accompanied Cleveland's order, his proclamation in effect removed from public use all land and timber within the Black Hills reserve and the twelve other reserves created under the measure. Gifford Pinchot, a commission member who represented the new era of efficient, scientific exploitation of the nation's public forests, had misgivings over the direction Cleveland's proclamation had taken. Pinchot favored the European system of management for continual production, in which old timber was cut in order to encourage the growth of desired species.[17]

Pinchot was not alone. Black Hills residents openly opposed the new reserve and wanted Cleveland's proclamation reversed, fearing that it would disrupt both the local mining industry and the region's general economy. In addition, the local populace believed that the existence of the reserve denied individuals their right to use the public lands in fulfillment of the American dream. The Homestake Mining Company, a model of industrial success and one of North America's largest mining operations, also opposed the creation of the reserve. Cleveland's order would stop Homestake from cutting free, timber by such quick and profitable, but wasteful, practices as clear-cutting, which had enabled the company to maintain its dividend-paying operation.[18]

The omission of any provisions for the regulated use of the new reserves created a storm of protest across the West. In the face of pressure to abolish the reserve system altogether, Congress passed the Forest Management Act of June 1897, assuring lumber consumers currently logging on public lands that the newly created reserves would continue to supply timber for their future needs. The legislation authorized the creation of forest reserves not only to improve and protect timber resources and water flow but also "to furnish a continuous supply of timber for the use and necessities of citizens."[19]

With the passage of the Forest Management Act, Pinchot's philosophy of forest management prevailed. Instead of being preserved or "locked up," the yellow pine of the Black Hills would continue to be exploited in a modified form. The law empowered the secretary of the interior to draft regulations under which local domestic and industrial consumers, including mining, lumbering, and grazing interests, could use the forest. Congress authorized the secretary of the interior to sell the dead or mature trees found within the reserve. The General Land Office advertised the event, marked the trees for sale, and supervised the harvest. Anyone who illegally cut or destroyed timber inside a reserve would receive a maximum fine of $500 or twelve months in prison or both. In short, government supervision replaced the logger's choice. Instead of allowing indiscriminate cutting, government officials selected timber for harvest.[20]

Unfortunately, the solution was not going to be that simple. Gifford Pinchot, visiting the Black Hills in the fall of 1897 as special forest agent for Secretary of the Interior Cornelius N. Bliss, described the landscape between Deadwood and Englewood in the northern hills as a cutover and burned forest. In Bear Gulch near Spearfish, however, he discovered "a beautiful and vigorous forest, of great potential value. But it is now full of locations for mining claims, which appear on the trees. . . . [The] common report in the Hills ascribes these claims to men working for the Homestake."[21] These fraudulent mining claims, which failed to display the requisite "discovery holes," had been filed to circumvent the new cutting restrictions. Economic historians Gary D. Libecap and Ronald N. Johnson assert in an article in the *Journal of Economic History* that restrictive laws in the Pacific Northwest forced timber consumers to resort to fraud in order to obtain the timber necessary for profitable logging. Confronting a similar situation, Homestake eluded the law because the profits from doing so were greater than the cost of litigation and punishment.[22]

In an attempt to curtail this practice without alienating company officials, Gifford Pinchot, working for Secretary Bliss, presented Homestake Mining Company superintendent Thomas J. Grier and company attorney Gideon C. Moody with a regulated harvest plan on November 3, 1897. This opportunity was Pinchot's chance to advance scientific forest management through winning the support of a large gold-mining operation that was also a large timber user. During a three-hour meeting, he convinced Homestake to send an application to the secretary of the interior asking permission to purchase timber from the United States at a minimal cost under the terms of the 1897 Forest Management Act, even though it did not officially take effect until March 1, 1898. Upon approval of the application, the company could legally cut trees on the reserve instead of obtaining lumber through fraudulent means. Grier and Moody informed Pinchot that they supported, in principle, the concept of the forest reserve and that the company would also help to fight forest fires. Homestake even offered to fund a government mechanism for selling timber, since none existed at the time.[23] Once company officials understood Pinchot's concept of conservation, they endorsed his plan. Neither litigation nor the threat of penalties had swayed Homestake in the past. Rather, the company came to support conservation because it ensured continual use of the public forests at minimal cost. In short, conservation was in the company's best interest.

From this discussion between Pinchot and Homestake management arose Timber Case No. 1, the first government-regulated timber cut on a public forest reserve and the beginning of modern regulated forestry practices in the United States. Important for Pinchot personally was the fact that his scientific forestry methods were on trial. The Timber Case No. 1 experiment involved the Homestake Mining Company purchasing standing trees on the Black Hills Forest Reserve and then cutting those trees under the supervision of a government forester. As Pinchot noted in a later report, "There is no other forest in the United States in which practical forestry is more urgently needed, or in which results of such importance may be more easily achieved." He concluded, upon "its preservation depends the timber to supply a great and rapidly growing mining industry."[24]

Conditions were right for success: Pinchot was working with a mining company that required timber to maintain its dividend-paying operation and a badly abused public forest that required efficient management of the remaining trees to sustain gold mining in the future. In addition, the project provided future foresters with valuable experience. William B. Greeley, later chief of the United States Forest Service, wrote that the Black Hills provided "the enthusiastic young foresters in Gifford Pinchot's bureau . . . an immediate chance to do real business in selective logging. Here the needs of the Homestake . . . required large sales of ponderosa pine, carefully marked and remarked to cut only mature trees and leave all the promising striplings."[25]

In early February 1898, Homestake Mining Company began to formulate its proposal for cutting trees on the Black Hills reserve based on Pinchot's principles of forest management. Homestake superintendent Thomas Grier took the next step toward putting the company's logging operation under government regulation when he relinquished the fraudulent mining claims that Homestake had filed in the Black Hills reserve. On April 8, 1898, Grier submitted the company's formal application for the cutting of timber in the reserve to the secretary of the interior. The application described the size and number of trees to be logged, the location of the cut (eight sections of land along the tracks of the company railroad about four miles southwest of Nemo in the east-central Black Hills), and the amount of timber to be taken annually (measured in both linear and board feet). While Homestake's application was complete and detailed, the boundaries of the proposed logging area followed the grid survey lines of townships and ranges instead of following the terrain's natural contours, a process that would have ensured minimum damage to the soil. Despite the environmental problems the application posed, the mining company had established the groundwork for the first regulated timber cut from a forest reserve.[26]

Unfortunately, the Department of the Interior's General Land Office, which was charged with overseeing all timber operations, had no experience in regulating timber harvest. This situation created undue delay and hardship for Homestake. The General Land Office dispatched Special Agent C. W. Greene in early May 1898 to report on the condition of the trees in the proposed cut area. Not until August 1898, however, did the land office appoint a supervisor, H. G. Hamaker, for the Black Hills Forest Reserve and instruct him to investigate the area. The agency's acting commissioner ordered Hamaker to "bear in mind the forest reservation policy of this office to supply present and future needs for timber within the state by providing for the use of timber which can be cut without detriment to the reservation." The commissioner further informed Hamaker not to overvalue the lumber because the government was not interested in deriving "a revenue therefrom, but to meet local demand . . . for the legitimate purposes of trade." The minimum price was placed at $1 per 1,000 board feet. Hamaker's duties also included supervising the disposal of treetops and other waste and ensuring that only mature trees were cut, but without stripping the forest of all future seed trees.[27]

Hamaker surveyed Homestake's proposed logging area in the fall of 1898 and suggested that the mining company be permitted to cut only on the burned areas of the Black Hills reserve. The General Land Office forest supervisor, C. W. Garbutt, dismissed that proposal, probably because Homestake protested. The company cited the high cost of selectively logging dead trees and maintained that dead lumber was not strong enough for mining purposes. R. O. Robinson, head of Homestake's lumber operation, informed Hamaker: "In our timber business . . . we will be unable to make use of anything but the saw timber and the timber that will make . . . 11 and 6 in flatts [the large timbers used underground]." In addition, the company was converting to coal at the time the reserve was created and claimed it had no use for cordwood. Robinson stated that the company would cut it and dispose of the treetops but only because the law so required.[28]

Hamaker submitted his first written report on the pending timber cut in late April 1899, and it reflected Homestake's position on cordwood. His superior, William A. Richards of the General Land Office, ordered Hamaker to resubmit the report, demanding that Homestake pay for the cut cordwood even though the company claimed that it would not be used because of declining need. In his amended report, Hamaker noted that he wanted "the Government to get full pay for all timber sold from this reserve," but that Homestake still refused to pay for cordwood and would instead pile it with the brush rather than haul it from the logging area.[29] Concerned with making the reserve defray the operating expenses, Hamaker wrote that he would make the company "pay for every cord they cut."[30] Eventually, Homestake purchased the cordwood.

In making his amended report, Hamaker created another delay when he suggested that the proposed cut be open to bidders, permitting other lumber users an opportunity to get the timber. From early August to October 1899, the General Land Office printed notices in local newspapers advertising the timber sale and soliciting bids even though it was obvious that the cut would go to the Homestake. The area was the same one the company had made application for in April 1898 and was near its railroad line.[31]

In October 1899, Homestake officials submitted their bid at the original price of $1 per 1,000 board feet for all the timber in the proposed Nemo cut. Because of a serious wood shortage at the Lead stamp mills, the company had asked permission to begin cutting on reserve land in September 1899. That request was denied. Homestake would be able to cut trees sixty days after the end of the advertising date, but that prospect was subject to a change if a higher bid came from another operator. Predictably, however, the General Land Office awarded the bid to Homestake, and the company deposited over $5,000 with the receiver of the General Land Office in Rapid City for the timber to be logged near Nemo. Thus more than a year and a half after Homestake submitted its application to cut timber in the Black Hills Forest Reserve, Timber Case No. 1 was finally under way. The experiment in regulated logging in the Black Hills had begun, and the rest of the nation's lumber users watched.[32]

On November 5, 1899, General Land Office forest superintendent C. W. Garbutt directed J. F. Clark, the land office forest ranger at Englewood, to mark trees eight inches in diameter and larger for cutting. In addition, Garbutt ordered Clark to inform Homestake loggers that the company could not remove any logs until the ranger had measured the timber to ensure that trees suitable for sawing into large-dimension mine timbers would not be used for cordwood. Further, the Homestake loggers were to stack treetops and other waste into piles for burning.[33]

Supervisors' instructions did not translate into working practices, however. The new forest managers were perplexed when it came to the problem of disposing of the dead and down timber that was found throughout the Hills. Homestake officials claimed that the price the government charged for timber should not include "dead and down" or "dead and standing" timber because it was worthless for mining purposes. After visiting the Nemo cut, land office inspector C. W. Greene agreed that most of the dead timber was worthless and the prices charged were too high. He maintained, however, that the rate of $1 per 1,000 board feet of green pine was fair. While at the logging site, Greene noticed another problem: thick windfalls, which he feared would burn and destroy the live timber. In order to protect the forest from potential fires, Greene recommended that Homestake receive the dead timber free for taking it out of the logging site. Forest Superintendent Garbutt disagreed, contending that fifteen cents a cord for dead-and-down trees and fifty cents a cord for dead-and-standing timber was incentive enough to encourage Homestake to take the dead timber.[34] Garbutt's view prevailed, and the company lost the free-dead-timber issue.

Obviously, differences of opinion existed between employees in the General Land Office over what constituted proper forestry practices. Much of the disagreement among the individual foresters who reviewed Homestake's compliance with the stipulations of Timber Case No. 1 arose from the fact that the regulations governing logging practices on forest reserves were in their infancy. The vague requirements translated into impractical enforcement and questionable results. On occasion, this situation may have encouraged Homestake to violate the spirit of the new Progressive Era conservation practices. When General Land Office Forest Inspector I. A. Macrum examined the Nemo cut in late August 1900, he reported that brush and debris were not piled for burning and that the trees left to seed future stands of timber were inferior specimens. In addition, Homestake lumbermen had removed trees under eight inches in diameter and left the hard-to-cut trees standing in ravines. Contributing to this neglect of good lumbering practices, the forest ranger assigned to oversee the logging spent his summer on fire patrol and was absent from his management duties at the Nemo cut. Frank Lytle, the new ranger, deflected all of the inspector's complaints and praised the Homestake Mining Company.[35]

Macrum's criticism of Homestake reached company superintendent Thomas Grier, who denied the inspector's accusations. According to Grier, the company had "thoroughly complied with all requirements relating to cutting and removing of such timber, and at all times will hold itself ready to comply with whatever is desired by the parties in charge of the Forest Reserve." The superintendent added that Homestake would continue to "contribute to the preservation of the forest or the successful carrying out of the rules and regulations established" to cut trees on the public lands. Forest Supervisor H. G. Hamaker concurred with Grier after inspecting the Nemo logging operation and wrote in Homestake's defense, "The instructions have been as fully complied with as it has been possible for the Company to do." Secretary of the Interior Ethan Allen Hitchcock appointed Seth Bullock to the position of forest supervisor of the Black Hills reserve at the turn of the century. Bullock agreed with his predecessor's assessment that the Homestake Mining Company had continually cooperated with forestry officials to the point of acting promptly "upon any suggestions made as to [the] care of the young timber, [and] the proper cleaning of the slash."[36]

Forest Inspector Macrum did not retract his first comments against Homestake, but when he returned to the cutting location in September 1901, he reported that the company was properly taking timber from the logging area and "leaving the territory in good shape." He added that there was "a marked improvement in the manner of doing the work on this purchase over that of my last inspection." Despite these early administrative problems, Carl A. Newport, a forester and student of forest policy, later wrote, "The Homestake Mining Company led the way for the lumber industry [of the Black Hills] by purchasing timber and meeting the necessary regulations."[37]

After numerous requests for extensions, Homestake Mining Company completed Timber Case No. 1 in 1908. Under the contract, Homestake cut nearly 15 million board feet of lumber and 5,100 cords of wood. The transfer of forestry duties from the General Land Office to the Forest Service under the Department of Agriculture in 1905 created no new hardships for Homestake, which was bound to follow the regulations that had been drafted for Timber Case No. 1. During the years the contract was in effect, both forestry personnel and timber users gained an understanding of how a regulated cut should operate on public forestland. It would be inaccurate to describe this first regulated cut as good forestry because it was essentially a clear-cut. For example, the average number of seed trees left standing after the company completed logging Case No. 1 was just two per acre, or 482 board feet of timber; by comparison, the Forest Service required 2,611 board feet per acre for seed purposes following a 1937 Black Hills harvest.[38]

Even though it could not be cited as a model of modern forestry practices, Timber Case No. 1 inaugurated an era of government regulation over tree harvests on the public lands that was essential to the conservation of the resource. The advent of government control forced timber users like Homestake to become more selective in their exploitation of the timber on the public domain. Such users came to support the new logging regulations upon recognizing that the destructive cutting practices of the past jeopardized the timber supply they depended on to fill their present and future needs. Efficient management could ensure the continued supply of the forest products essential for maintaining the industry. Homestake, the company of waste during times of free timber, became a company of frugality. In fact, the fear of a timber shortage in the Black Hills and the threat of having to purchase higher-priced lumber imported from outside the region made local mining companies even more possessive and protective of the region's timber. Shortly after the creation of the Black Hills reserve, the local mining industry secured an embargo prohibiting the shipment of green cut timber from the national forest out of South Dakota. The embargo ended in 1912, the year Homestake completed its conversion to electricity.[39]

Companies like Homestake hoped for other returns on their conservation investment. Thomas Grier, addressing the second American Forest Congress in 1905, claimed that "far-seeing" mining companies had demonstrated public

responsibility by making long-range plans that ensured the continued exploitation of mineral deposits and the employment of workers. Because of the industry's civic value, Grier argued, miners should be entitled to the same privileges
that nonlumbering enterprises possessed in the forest reserves. He criticized
the government's practice of granting permanent rights-of-way through
reserves to irrigation and transportation companies while giving mining companies only temporary permits. According to Grier, the mining companies had
demonstrated their civic responsibility in the conservation of public forests,
and the removal of this imposition "would not open the door to reckless
waste of forest resources."[40]

The mantle of "civic obligation" and the threat of exhausting the resource
did not guarantee the best use of timber resources, however. Over the years,
more federal regulations emerged to govern the harvest of trees on public
lands. The mining industry's early destructive lumbering practices, such as
high grading—that is, taking only the best trees and leaving the diseased and
disfigured—had left their imprint on the Black Hills forest, particularly the
northern one-third. As late as 1928, 100,000 acres of forestlands were non-
productive because of the unregulated cutting and damaging fires that had
occurred near the mining centers of Lead and Deadwood.[41]

The mining companies of the Progressive Era have been described as anti-
conservationist because they opposed the establishment of forest reserves.
The Homestake experience reveals another facet of both the industry and
the conservation movement. Company officials worked with Gifford Pinchot
to turn conservation into an economic asset. In fact, that alliance was relatively easy to accomplish because the Black Hills Forest Reserve had been
created essentially to enhance economic interests through the efficient management of limited resources. Thoughtless timber practices had the same
effect on the company's lumber supply as closing the forest to all logging;
without free lumber, mining costs increased and the stockholders received
smaller dividends. Company management, once they understood the intent
of the 1897 Black Hills Forest Reserve, supported the concept of a forest
reserve and the conservation of timber resources through government regulation and efficient planning.[42]

Lost in the process of establishing the forestry theories behind Timber
Case No. 1 was the possibility of maintaining the Black Hills forest as
untouched wilderness.[43] Conservation, not preservation, was the hallmark
of the Progressive Era. Both Homestake Mining Company officials and the
men trained in forestry practices advocated resource conservation for the
same end—enhancing the local economy. That alliance, which became the
backbone of the nation's modern conservation era, began in the Black Hills.
Instead of fighting the inevitable regulation imposed on the public forests,
Homestake played an integral and understandably self-serving role in supporting modern forestry practices.

NOTES

1. Samuel P. Hays, *Conservation and the Gospel of Efficiency: The Progressive Conservation Movement, 1890–1920* (Cambridge, Mass.: Harvard University Press, 1959), 1–3. In "Forests and Conservation, 1865–1890," *Journal of American History,* September 1985, 340–59, Donald J. Pisani asserts that a conservation "ethic" existed for several decades before Progressive reformers popularized the cause. While scientists led the later movement, its leaders in the post–Civil War years were as often "moralists and philosophers" who anticipated modern conservationists in their understanding of the interrelatedness of natural resources. For more on the late-nineteenth-century fears of timber famine that helped to spur the conservation movement, see David A. Clary, *Timber and the Forest Service* (Lawrence: University Press of Kansas, 1986); and Sherry H. Olson, *The Depletion Myth: A History of Railroad Use of Timber* (Cambridge, Mass.: Harvard University Press, 1971).

2. Roderick Nash, *Wilderness and the American Mind,* rev. ed. (New Haven, Conn.: Yale University Press, 1973), 134–38.

3. U.S. Department of Agriculture, Forest Service, *The Black Hills National Forest 50th Anniversary* (Washington, D.C.: Government Printing Office, 1948), 1–2.

4. *United States Statutes at Large,* 20:88, Act of 3 June 1878.

5. Samuel Trask Dana, *Forest and Range Policy: Its Development in the United States* (New York: McGraw-Hill, 1956), 63–64; Darrell Hevenor Smith, *The Forest Service: Its History, Activities and Organization* (Washington, D.C.: Brookings Institution, 1930), 15; Forest Service, *Black Hills National Forest 50th Anniversary,* 7.

6. Henry S. Graves, "Black Hills Forest Reserve (South Dakota and Wyoming)," in U.S. Department of the Interior, *Nineteenth Annual Report of the United States Geological Survey,* pt. 5, *Forest Reserves* (Washington, D.C.: Government Printing Office, 1899), 68–69.

7. H. M. Chance, "The Resources of the Black Hills and Big Horn Country, Wyoming," *Transactions of the American Institute of Mining Engineers* 19 (1891): 50, 58.

8. Graves, "Black Hills Forest Reserve," 88–90. Graves became the first dean of the Yale School of Forestry, which the Pinchot family endowed. He later replaced Gifford Pinchot as chief of the United States Forest Service.

9. Ibid., 81–85. Stephen J. Pyne discusses fire and man's efforts to both use and prevent it in *Fire in America: A Cultural History of Wildland and Rural Fire* (Princeton, N.J.: Princeton University Press, 1982).

10. P. A. Rydberg, "Flora of the Black Hills of South Dakota," in U.S. Department of Agriculture, Division of Botany, contributions from the *U.S. National Herbarium* 3, no. 8 (13 June 1896): 476–77.

11. Graves, "Black Hills Forest Reserve," 77. For more information on fire as an ecological tool, see Eugene P. Odum, *Fundamentals of Ecology,* 3rd ed. (Philadelphia: Saunders, 1971), 131–37. For a discussion of plant succession and climax habitat, see Robert E. Ricklefs, *Ecology* (Portland, Ore.: Chiron Press, 1973), 752–58, 764.

12. Graves, "Black Hills Forest Reserve," 88–91; Mildred Fielder, *The Treasure of Homestake Gold* (Aberdeen, S.D.: North Plains Press, 1970), 106–7, 130.

13. National Academy of Sciences, *Report of the National Academy of Sciences for the Year 1897* (Washington, D.C.: Government Printing Office, 1898), 57–58;

U.S. Circuit Court, District of South Dakota, Western Division, Deadwood, S.D., *United States of America v. Homestake Mining Company,* Law Case Files, 1890–1938, Box 12, USDC–South Dakota, Case no. 139, Records of District Courts of the United States, Record Group 21, Federal Archives and Records Center, Kansas City, Mo.

14. Harold K. Steen, *The U.S. Forest Service: A History* (Seattle: University of Washington Press, 1976), 8–20; National Academy of Sciences, *Report of the National Academy of Sciences for the Year 1896* (Washington D.C.: Government Printing Office, 1897), 12–16; Frederick W. True, ed., *A History of the First Half-Century of the National Academy of Sciences, 1863–1913* (Washington, D.C.: [National Academy of Sciences], 1913), 314–23. President Theodore Roosevelt implemented the essence of the academy's report in 1905 when he established the United States Forest Service, a separate bureau for the supervision of forest reserves. True, *History of the First Half-Century,* 318–19; Steen, *U.S. Forest Service,* 148.

15. National Academy of Sciences, *Report for the Year 1897,* 19.

16. *United States Statutes at Large,* 26:1093–1103, Act of 3 March 1891; Jenks Cameron, *The Development of Governmental Forest Control in the United States* (Baltimore: Johns Hopkins University Press, 1928), 204–5; Gifford Pinchot, *Breaking New Ground* (New York: Harcourt, Brace, 1947), 107–8.

17. Pinchot, *Breaking New Ground,* 1, 93–97.

18. *Deadwood Independent,* 1 March 1897. Pinchot was determined to broaden the use of the reserves, as both his commission work and his public statements indicate. In 1898, he told members of the American Institute of Mining Engineers assembled at Atlantic City for their annual meeting that the new forest reserves would continue to supply timber for the mining companies. See Pinchot, *Breaking New Ground,* 105–9; *Transactions of the American Institute of Mining Engineers* 28 (1899): 339–46.

19. *United States Statutes at Large,* 30:35, Act of 4 June 1897. This vital piece of forestry legislation, sometimes called the Pettigrew Amendment, formed the basis of forest reserve management for the next six decades. Senator Richard F. Pettigrew of South Dakota sponsored the amendment to the Sundry Civil Appropriations Bill, which won western tolerance of the reserve system by unlocking reserve resources. See Steen, *U.S. Forest Service,* 34–36.

20. *United States Statutes at Large,* 30:35, and 25:166, Act of 4 June 1888; Pinchot, *Breaking New Ground,* 114; Nash, *Wilderness and the American Mind,* 137.

21. Gifford Pinchot diary, 1 November 1897, Gifford Pinchot Papers, Library of Congress, Washington, D.C.

22. Gary D. Libecap and Ronald N. Johnson, "Property Rights, Nineteenth-Century Federal Timber Policy, and the Conservation Movement," *Journal of Economic History,* March 1979, 129–42. Under the Mining Act of 1872, an individual could control the use of all resources on a claim by spending $100 on development each year or by obtaining a patent. Thus much of the land claimed under the act was more valuable for other purposes (i.e. timber cutting) than for the mining of any mineral it might contain. See *United States Statutes at Large,* 17:91, Act of 10 May 1872; and Dana, *Forest and Range Policy,* 290–91.

23. Pinchot diary, 3 November 1897.

24. Gifford Pinchot, *Report of the Forester for 1901,* in U.S. Department of Agri-

culture, *Annual Report of the Department of Agriculture for the Year 1901* (Washington, D.C.: Government Printing Office, 1901), 329.

25. William B. Greeley, *Forests and Men* (Garden City, N.Y.: Doubleday, 1951), 59–60.

26. Gideon Moody to Binger Hermann, 15 February 1898, Miscellaneous Letters Received, Records of the Bureau of Land Management, Record Group 49, National Archives, Washington, D.C.; Thomas Grier to Cornelius N. Bliss, 8 April 1898, Records Relating to the Timber Sales in the Black Hills National Forest, 1898–1912, Homestake Mining Company, Case No. 1, Records of the Forest Service, Record Group 95, National Archives, Washington, D.C. [this set of records is hereafter cited as Case No. 1].

27. Acting Commissioner of the General Land Office to H. G. Hamaker, "System of Timber Cutting Within Reserve," September 1898, Lands and Railroads Division, Letters Received, 1807–1897, Records of the Office of the Secretary of the Interior, Record Group 48, National Archives, Washington, D.C.

28. Binger Hermann to H. G. Hamaker, 2 November 1898, and R. O. Robinson to Hamaker, 17 February 1899, both in Case No. 1.

29. H. G. Hamaker to Commissioner of the General Land Office, 25 April 1899, and Williams A. Richards to Hamaker, 6 June 1899, both in Case No. 1.

30. Hamaker to Commissioner of the General Land Office, 28 June 1899, Case No. 1.

31. Hamaker to Commissioner of the General Land Office, 12 June 1900, Case No. 1.

32. Thomas J. Grier to Commissioner of the General Land Office, 20 October 1899; H. G. Hamaker to Commissioner of the General Land Office [telegram], 30 August 1899; W. A. Richards to Hamaker [telegram], 31 August 1899; and W. S. Warner to Commissioner of the General Land Office, 4 November 1899, all in Case No. 1. A 1902 decision of the Eighth Circuit Court of Appeals provides another example of the land office's difficulties in administering the forest reserve expeditiously. The United States had charged Homestake with trespass in the cutting of trees between September 1898 and May 1899 under an expired verbal agreement with the secretary of the interior. Regarding the government's charge that Homestake should have submitted a formal application for the cutting of the timber, the court referred to the length of time the Timber Case No. 1 agreement had taken to negotiate and upheld Homestake's cutting of the timber that was necessary to maintain its operation. See Pinchot, *Breaking New Ground*, 116; and *Deadwood Daily Pioneer-Times*, 17, 18 September 1902.

33. C. W. Garbutt to J. F. Clark, 5 November [1899] [copy], Case No. 1.

34. C. W. Greene to Commissioner of the General Land Office, 12 December 1899, and C. W. Garbutt to Commissioner of the General Land Office, 11 January 1900, both in Case No. 1.

35. I. A. Macrum to Commissioner of the General Land Office, 31 August 1900, and Frank Lytle to H. G. Hamaker, 19 October 1900, both in Case No. 1.

36. Thomas J. Grier to W. A. Richards, 19 October 1900; H. G. Hamaker to Commissioner of the General Land Office, 23 October 1900; and Seth Bullock to Commissioner of the General Land Office, 29 August 1901, all in Case No. 1.

37. I. A. Macrum to Commissioner of the General Land Office, 9 September 1901,

Case No. 1; Carl A. Newport, "Forest Service Policies as They Affect the Lumber Industry: A Case Study of the Black Hills," *Journal of Forestry,* January 1956, 18. For more information on the poor regulations and weak administration surrounding the early timber cuts, see Dana, *Forest and Range Policy,* 110–18.

38. Forest Service, *Black Hills National Forest 50th Anniversary,* 8–10.

39. George A. Duthie, "Timber, an Economic Resource of the Black Hills," *Black Hills Engineer,* March 1928, 105; *Pierre Capital-Journal,* 26 April 1912.

40. T. J. Grier, "Mining and Forestry in the Black Hills," *Engineering and Mining Journal,* 2 March 1905, 409. For a discussion of the 1905 American Forest Congress, sponsored by the American Forestry Society, see Michael Frome, *Whose Woods These Are: The Story of the National Forests* (Garden City, N.Y.: Doubleday, 1962), 57–58.

41. Duthie, "Timber," 104.

42. G. Michael McCarthy, *Hour of Trial: The Conservation Conflict in Colorado and the West, 1891–1907* (Norman: University of Oklahoma Press, 1977), 24–25; Paul D. Kelleter, "The National Forests of the Black Hills," *Pahasapa Quarterly,* June 1913, 9–12.

National Forest Timber Sales and the Legacy of Gifford Pinchot: Managing a Forest and Making It Pay

Robert E. Wolf

Late in his life, Gifford Pinchot recalled the words of Professor Lucien Boppe of the French Forest School, with whom Pinchot had studied in 1890: "When you get home to America you must manage a forest and make it pay." Pinchot said he "never lost sight of [that] advice," and made good on that claim when in late 1890, in an address to the American Economic Association, the young forester declared of the Zurich City Forest that "its production in wood and money was almost beyond belief." Forestry could be profitable.[1]

His historic commitment of the Forest Service to this concept has been ignored. Instead, after years of paying lip service to Pinchot's ideal of the profitable forest, the Forest Service contends that the real measure of a forest's value lies in its social "benefits," most of which it admittedly cannot quantify. This contention forms the crux of the debate over national forest timber sales that emerged in the mid-1970s and continues to engulf them.[2]

This chapter will examine the concept of financially profitable public forestry in the thinking of early agency leaders and its impact on the Forest Service's management of the national forests throughout the twentieth-century. In so doing, it will also explore the problems that have emerged as a result of the agency's attempt to maintain the illusion of profitability.

It is useful when tracing the history of this aspect of forestry to recall that timber sales, which began on the federal forest reserves in 1898, started with substantial annual losses to the government. Data from the Interior Department's General Land Office and the Agriculture Department's Bureau of Forestry show that through 1904 costs were $1,605,700 and revenue was $203,100.[3] This was one lever Pinchot used to get the reserves transferred to the Department of Agriculture. Managing them through the Bureau of Forestry—he became its fourth chief in 1898—would also permit the reserves to demonstrate the financial common sense of forestry to private owners.[4]

For the next six years, that is just what he believed his agency was accomplishing. In 1901, for instance, Pinchot claimed his division's study of a private

Arkansas forest demonstrated how present lumbering methods could be modified "without encroaching too far upon *present* [and] will hasten the production of a second crop upon the lumbered area." A private New England forest was said to show that cutting the "stunted . . . malformed trees . . . pay[s]." Scientific management on a private Tennessee holding was claimed to have "left the forest in a good condition and yielded a profit at least equal to that usually earned by ordinary lumbering under similar conditions in that neighborhood."[5]

President McKinley's death in 1901 elevated Theodore Roosevelt to president and provided Pinchot with the political fulcrum for moving the forest reserves from the Interior Department to Agriculture, though this would not occur until Roosevelt won a term in his own right. After extended legislative negotiations, a transfer bill passed the House in December 1904. The Senate added four significant sections to the bill; of special interest is Section 5: "That all money received from the sale of any products or the use of any lands or resources of said forest reserves shall be . . . available . . . for the protection, administration, improvement, and extension of the Federal forest reserves."[6] This gave Pinchot the unusual authority to generate operating investment revenue through the sale of resources and fees to defray costs of operation, outside presidential or congressional control. There is no hearing record on this major, last-minute, and unusual grant to spend receipts. Pinchot's subsequent testimony before the House Appropriations and Expenditures Committees makes clear, however, that he engineered this change. Congress assented because Pinchot promised to operate the reserves at a profit within five years. The House–Senate conference committee accepted most of the Senate amendments but placed a five-year cap on Forest Service use of receipts to cover costs. Roosevelt signed the measure into law on February 1, 1905, merging Pinchot's Bureau of Forestry into the newly created Forest Service, and transferring the forest reserves from the Department of the Interior. Pinchot now had an opportunity to deliver on his promises of public forestry's profitability.[7]

Chief Pinchot's appearances before congressional committees were consistently marked with claims that the national forests either were on their way to showing profits or were, in fact, profitable. Further, many of the hearings, often prompted by Pinchot's claims, focused on the topic of costs and receipts. Despite his optimism and glowing projections, however, Pinchot's claims could not withstand scrutiny. He used selective cost data and juggled his authority to spend timber sale receipts. A hard look at the Forest Service under Pinchot reveals that the agency and the timber program continued to lose money, something even he tacitly acknowledged in the last years of his Forest Service tenure when he sought to shift the focus away from pure monetary profit.

In early 1906, just after assuming management responsibilities, Pinchot contended: "We have . . . a very careful cost-keeping system and can tell you exactly what any part of the work actually costs and how cost compares with actual work." Later that year, testifying for funds for the next fiscal year, Pinchot stressed how useful it had been to be able to spend receipts. He declared that within three to five years the service would be self-supporting, and spoke of his dual mission—"to handle the reserves better, and to make them pay for themselves."[8]

Pinchot presented Congress with specific financial projections that portrayed profits as almost within reach, projections that continually excluded important Forest Service costs. When in January 1907 the chairman of the House Agriculture Committee asked for a report on receipts, Pinchot responded that the transfer had, in effect, changed the previous year's loss to a profit, leaving him with "$400,000, as a nest egg."[9]

He arrived at this inaccurate conclusion by claiming unspent receipts as income, and ignoring the substantial congressional appropriation for that year.[10] When questioned about his logic, Pinchot admitted he had not stated the situation as he should have. He confessed to spending "very much more money," part of which was income from the reserves. Later, and to divert attention from his prior misstatement, Pinchot revised his remarks, claiming that he expected to add $500,000 more to receipts this year and to keep on doing this "simply by the prosecution of the work as now planned."[11]

At his January 1907 budget hearing, Pinchot planned to request a $5 million loan, but sensing congressional resistance, he cut his original request to a $2 million direct appropriation in the form of a loan. He stated that there was "one very serious obstacle" to achieving his goal of timber sale profits— there was "absolutely no capital" for development. He likened his situation to a farmer without tools.[12]

He promised repayment, with interest, at $500,000 annually beginning in 1917. Asked if the working-capital request was to put the forests "on a business, income-producing basis," Pinchot responded, "That is it exactly." Congress dealt Pinchot a harsh blow, granting only a $500,000 direct annual appropriation and canceling the privilege to use revenues to cover agency costs.[13]

Appearing later in 1907 before the House Committee on Expenditures of the Department of Agriculture, Pinchot forecast his receipts and costs through fiscal year 1917, depicting the by-now-traditional stairway to financial paradise. Over the next decade, he forecast that receipts would rise faster than costs, producing a cumulative profit of over $5 million by 1917. Scrutiny of his forecast, however, exposes key elements that distorted the true financial picture.

First, for the years 1906 to 1909 Pinchot included appropriations as both a "receipt" and an "expenditure," shrinking each year so that after 1910 the Forest Service would no longer depend on appropriations. Second, his figures also added in a $500,000 request for working capital in 1908. Third, the forecast failed to break out program cost categories. Without information on planned expenditures, congressional evaluation of his plans was difficult at best.[14] The greatest flaw in Pinchot's projections was his grossly optimistic receipt predictions. Despite the lack of specific cost data in his forecast, actual costs rose approximately as projected. Receipts, however, fell far short of his estimates, resulting in steady program losses, not profits.[15] This has continued to be the case over the decades—costs outstripping receipts amid claims that imply gross receipts are financial profits. The methods the service has used to display program costs and receipts have not permitted evaluation of program relationships. Moreover, agency data have never clearly set out the total receipt–cost picture, annually or over time.

Pinchot was equally inventive when he gave Congress purported cost data. His display of Forest Service results for fiscal years 1906 to 1908, the first three full years he served as chief, illustrates this point nicely. Pinchot claimed profits of over $100,000 for fiscal 1907, but only by excluding the required payments of 10 percent of receipts to the counties and improvement costs. The latter were not defined by the service but presumably were capital expenditures. In addition, this estimate of income excluded the mounting expenditures for "general forestry," the former Bureau of Forestry's research and promotion work. Since Pinchot had claimed earlier that he would cover all costs within five years, exclusion of these expenditures hardly presented an accurate view of Forest Service finances. Even with such costs excluded, however, data from 1906 through 1908 showed annual losses.[16]

Pinchot also attempted to divert congressional attention from the Forest Service's bottom line by claiming that the national forests were rapidly increasing in value. He contended that growth in the land area managed had only moderately increased costs.[17]

In testimony for fiscal year 1909 funds on January 23, 1908, Pinchot, still contending he had already fulfilled his promise to make the forests self-supporting, sought to shift the emphasis from the profitability of public forestry to improving private land management. He asked to be considered free of the obligation "to get every cent we can out of the national forests in order to make them self-supporting." The basis for this change in emphasis, he said, was that a timber famine would arrive in less than thirty years. He now wanted the ability "to do the best thing for the forests and the best thing for the country at large, instead of fixing my main attention on revenue." To encourage timber management and production on private forestland, Pinchot stressed that Congress should fund forest colleges and the agency's effort to develop private forest plans.[18]

After less than three years of natural forest management, Pinchot boasted of profitable operations plus a precise cost-accounting system. His capital-fund request, seeking a delayed-payment loan, demonstrated his desire to avoid diluting the profit picture he was painting. Pinchot's rhetoric proclaimed short-term, cash-flow profit. The fiscal data show that the financial reality was "red ink."

In January 1910 William Howard Taft fired Pinchot for insubordination, and appointed Henry S. Graves as the second chief of the Forest Service. Graves, an early Pinchot associate, was then dean of the School of Forestry at Yale, which the Pinchot family had endowed. He set to work to regain the political ground the service had lost in the controversy surrounding Taft's dismissal of Pinchot and the bitter congressional investigation that followed. He expanded timber sales using long-term, remote-area-development contracts. He also touted forest-level cost control and resource sale profits. During his tenure, however, came a rare agency admission—few forests broke even, and some of the agency's 172 million acres of federal land, only half of which was forested, might never yield profitable timber sales. Undaunted, Graves downplayed this admission amid typical accounting ploys and overoptimism.

The December 1910 budget hearing opened with the Budget Committee chairman listing the complaints made in the House about the previous Forest Service budget. Graves responded that he now had "the actual cost in the field of conducting timber sales."[19] Criticism intensified during the December 1911 budget hearing, with renewed attacks against the Forest Service budget made on the House floor. The chairman, calling some of these attacks ridiculous, urged Graves to explain why costs, which had been only $350,000 when Interior did the job in 1904, had skyrocketed from $1 million in 1907 to $5.5 million in 1912. Graves gave no explanation, but merely affirmed once again that his policy was "making the receipts . . . meet the expenses."[20]

In the hearing on the fiscal 1914 budget, Graves outlined an aggressive plan to find applicants for large sales to build logging railroads to cut timber in remote areas. He claimed applications for 9 billion board feet in new sales, and estimated that he could sell 5 billion board feet, which would bring in $700,000 yearly in new revenue. This was a stark policy shift. Earlier, Pinchot had contended that a private stumpage glut had caused low lumber prices, private timber liquidation, and plant migration. His timber sale policy had been to sell timber only to meet proven needs. Graves did not address the logic of expanded sales in a weak market, which would exacerbate the glut and drop private timber values. Although some key Forest Service officials continued to express Pinchot's previous deep concern about the rapid, nationwide consumption of timber, the waste of the forest, and the effects of wildfire, railroad-caused fire, and carelessness with the forest, Chief Graves sought increased timber sales. This was deemed logical because sales were not only well below projected levels, but also well below biologically sustainable levels.[21]

But of even greater significance was Graves's plan to secure a positive cash flow on every national forest believed to have such a potential—a proposal that included the revealing recognition that some forests would always cost more to operate than they would return to the Treasury in hard cash. Graves continued to adhere, however, to the original Pinchot view that total receipts would be enough to make the agency financially self-sufficient.

Contributing to the Forest Service claim that timber sales were profitable was a provision added in the fiscal year 1913 Appropriations Act. It allowed the sale of mature, dead, and down timber, without advertisement, "at cost" to farmers for their own use.[22] Chief Graves described the "at cost" pricing system as "practical." Individual sale costs were not to be determined. Instead, the prior year's sale cost, standardized by region, was used to set current year prices. Typically, the prices charged for "at-cost" sales were about one-third of the prices paid for commercial sales.[23]

Clearly, the Forest Service estimated that timber sale costs were very low. Since, in fact, it lacked an effective measurement system for all costs, the "at-cost" pricing system did not truly measure cost. The service's failure to disclose true costs imbedded in the mind of Congress and the public the idea that commercial timber sales, which brought prices three to four times higher than the "at-cost" sales, more than covered all agency costs, when they did not.[24]

The fiscal year 1915 budget hearing marks the high point of service claims of profitability for individual forests. Graves touted his much lower per-acre forest management costs, as compared with those in Prussia, as well as the promise held by an accelerated sales program. His most comprehensive statement during the hearing on his approach to timber sale profitability described Forest Service "policy to work toward a self-supporting basis—not only for the individual forests but for all of the expenditures of the entire Forest Service. We have the resources and we are ultimately going to be able to meet our expenses." Graves supported this statement with detailed fiscal year 1913 data maps that showed how far he had yet to go toward achieving profitability; nationally, revenue did not even cover what Graves termed the "local operating cost" of managing the individual national forests. He tried to explain this situation with a map showing the distribution of profitable and unprofitable forests, estimating, for example, that by 1923 over 130 forests would capture their "local operating costs." Yet he conceded that eighteen forests, due to past depredations or other factors, would *never* reach a state of timber sale profitability. On this basis, Graves extrapolated that by 1928 total receipts would cover all costs, including Forest Service operations that were not profit oriented and the unprofitable forests that were managed mainly for protection.[25]

In sum, the first fifteen years of Forest Service timber sales were years of optimism, an optimism powerful enough to obscure mounting evidence of widespread unprofitability. In budget hearings for fiscal year 1920, for example, the service produced a ten-year untotaled display of receipts and appropriations for the years 1909 to 1919. When examined, this showed that expenditures exceeded receipts by $28.5 million for the decade. The annual reports emphasized gross revenue, while avoiding presentation of a full financial picture. They set forth profit as either a promise for the future or an increase in gross receipts—the agency's persistent erroneous definition of this term.[26]

Between 1920 and 1950, the Forest Service employed a two-pronged approach to bolster its claim that the timber program was profitable. First, it continued to compare total revenues and partial costs, avoiding revenue–cost displays by program. Second, the agency began to contend that unquantified, nonmonetary benefits resulting from timber sales were in addition to any money received. The implication was that cash losses were overcome by good things that would flow from the cut forest and the grazed range.

William B. Greeley, who replaced Graves in 1920, developed this argument in his first annual report, which continued the oft-repeated theme about Forest Service profits, but which now added nonmonetary benefits as part of the equation. Revenues were claimed to exceed management and administration costs, although expenditures for fire protection, road construction, and other capital improvements were excluded.[27] Future timber supplies, water, and recreation were mentioned as benefits, but not quantified in terms of either output or dollars. Greeley assumed that all such benefits would increase along with monetary income. Returns in the form of "public benefits" were said to deserve weight, even though these benefits were not measurable in dollars. If dollars alone were entered on the ledger, the Forest Service claimed, its goals could not be achieved. While the agency still maintained that forestry was profitable, it constantly stressed nonmonetary benefits.

That is what it emphasized in the years immediately before and during the Great Depression. In 1927, the service curbed new national forest timber sales and extended existing contracts on a no-cost basis, saying that this would ensure that national forest timber would not further depress private timber prices. During the Depression, sales almost stopped completely, agency attention shifted to unemployment relief work, and cost accounting became the focus. A new accounting system was introduced that would allegedly separate costs and income associated with revenue-producing programs from those that did not yield revenue. The 1931 annual report, outlining the new system, said true costs, including overhead and depreciation on investments, would cover every function. The cost–benefit relation would become clear, facilitating informed and discriminating decisions. Two years later, the new system was claimed to be "recognized by outside experts" as going beyond the best that private business had worked out" and "a decided forward step in cost control." Furthermore, the 1933 report indicated, all "stand-improvement work for timber production on the national forests will be confined to work which is expected to yield a financial profit on the investment." This statement presumed, of course, that costs were known and that long-term-profit forecasts could be made. Later, the 1942 report referred to unspecified revisions in the accounting system allegedly made to improve the correlation of budget and accounting needs.[28]

World War II and the following years marked an explosive increase in timber sales. The Forest Service returned to the theme that many forests paid their own way in the 1948 annual report, claiming an excess of local cash income over local operating costs. The report acknowledged, however, as had Chief Graves earlier, that some forests would never pay their own way. These forests encompassed vital watersheds, with high costs and low incomes, such as those in southern California.[29]

Yet the 1948 report also cautioned that despite expected growth in receipts, total forest costs might not be covered. Now, the objectives of national forest operations were declared to be service and public benefits, not profit. Benefits such as community stability, water, and recreation were considered difficult to value. At the same time, the report inconsistently claimed that each dollar spent on timber management returned several dollars to the Treasury and, of greater note, that timber salvage and thinnings more than paid their way.[30]

This complication was amplified when the 1951 annual report asserted that total Treasury returns exceeded all agency costs, as well as that many individual forests' receipts exceeded operating costs. The report reiterated, however, that it would be "impossible and unwise" to assign to nonrevenue-producing uses a monetary value. The 1952 report's financial claims went further, asserting that forests with low cash income would eventually yield larger returns from new timber growth and that roads returned more in timber than their cost. Neither claim was documented, nor was that included in the 1958 report, which heralded the fact that cumulative receipts since 1905 had passed the $1 billion mark as "hard cash proof" that multiple-use management and protection "is paying off." The era of asserting that "receipts" meant "profits" was in full bloom.[31]

The debate over the Multiple Use–Sustained Yield Act of 1960 nearly changed all that. When the Forest Service sought enactment of the act,[32] several matters were settled quietly behind closed doors. As a consequence, the timber industry ironically has avoided having to operate under a substitute it proposed, which, had it passed, would have elevated profit maximization on government timber sales to the Forest Service's primary goal.

In a meeting on the administration version of the bill, Deputy Forest Service Chief Edward C. Crafts told Senator Phil Hart of Michigan that the service did not want to define the key terms "multiple use" and "sustained yield" in the law. Hart, however, secured agreement from Senate Agriculture Committee chairman Allen Ellender that the bill would not move in the Senate until the service defined the terms. Meanwhile, in testimony before the House Committee on Agriculture on March 18, 1960, Ralph Hodges, executive vice president of the National Lumber Manufacturer's Association (now American Forest Products Association), presented an industry substitute bill. The industry substitute gave timber top billing and made earning dollar profits a basic agency goal. Section 2 of the industry bill said in part: "In the administration of the national forests due consideration shall be given to the relative values of the various resources in particular areas so that the national forests shall be made financially self-supporting insofar as possible." Hodges contended:

> [The national forests] are capable of producing a return to the Federal Government of many millions of dollars annually over and above operating costs when placed under intensive forest management. . . . [O]ur national forests are operating at only about one-third of their known potential capacity. Costs of protection and management exceed returns by more than $40 million annually. . . . [T]he national forests could produce goods and services on a multiple use and sustained yield basis, and at the same time return substantial sums to the Treasury.[33]

The Forest Service then set to work in the House to provide definitions for the bill's key terms, while overcoming the industry arguments. The service's definition of multiple use went into law without debate. It provided that it was not necessary to secure "the combination of uses that will give the greatest dollar return or greatest unit output." This language rebuffed the industry effort to force the service to obtain maximum financial profit. Some now warp these fifteen words, claiming that they authorize the service to ignore financial considerations completely and place no controls on monetary losses. In fact, the words say only that dollar profit and use yields need not be the "greatest." The 1960 act is not a license to lose money.[34]

Had the industry profit test prevailed, current sale levels would be far lower. Ironically, the agency currently uses the act's language to justify belowcost sales, from which industry has profited considerably. Industry long ago dropped its view that the national forests should be run for profit under Pinchot's "businesslike" idea.

The 1960s and 1970s were decades of intensified optimism for the timber sales program. As usual, this optimism colored the financial presentation by using gross receipts and the deceptive concept of the "value" of timber sold. The agency's 1966 annual report, for instance, trumpeted the earning of its second $1 billion from timber receipts, noting that it took fifty-three years to get the first $1 billion but only seven years to get the second $1 billion. These figures presented an incomplete picture. Neither the gross nor the net fiscal situation was specified at either benchmark. In the 1970s, as nominal stumpage rates rose, the Forest Service again distorted receipt information when it reported that the reported "value" of timber sold yearly rose from $700 million to almost $2 billion; receipts never matched the bids. Nevertheless, Forest Service annual reports would say, for example, "11.3 billion board feet were actually sold at a value of $1,962 million," implying that sold "value" represented net income after costs. Furthermore, the Forest Service did not, and still does not, display the value of uncut timber under contract—timber "sold" but not yet cut and paid for. It also fails to show adjustments in uncut volume and value due to normal factors such as volume errors, changes in value, and defaults. Receipts from timber actually cut were only about two-thirds of that estimated as the value "sold" in the twelve-year period from 1976 through 1987. The figure for the value of timber sold not only represented hoped-for future receipts, but also ignored that a substantial part of the anticipated receipts would be consumed in reforesting the lands harvested, and the real net income would have to consider operating and investment costs and 25 percent county payments.[35]

At least as misleading as the discrepancy between cut and sold report "receipts" and true fiscal receipts has been the Forest Service insinuation that increased sales are the route to increased profits. For example, the 1986 annual report claimed that "in 1986, timber brought $757 million into the treasury—almost exactly $200 million more than sales garnered in FY 1985." Again, to refer to money coming "into the treasury" and being "garnered" gives the impression that the money received is profit to the treasury. Time after time, gross receipts have been set forth without costs. The program that generates the largest portion of receipts and incurs the largest portion of costs lacks even a rudimentary display of these accounting fundamentals in the text of each annual report.

A 1980 study by the Natural Resources Defense Council concluded that on many national forests, timber sale program costs exceeded receipts, an analysis the Forest Service dismissed.[36] By 1983, faced with declining Forest Service receipts and a reduced timber cut, Congress became concerned. In an era of mounting budget deficits, timber sales have sparked widespread public debate. In the aftermath of a timber recession in the early 1980s, during which industry secured relief from over $2 billion worth of existing contracts, pressure for meaningful cost accounting and more attention to profitable operation developed. When industry, for example, drastically reduced public forest timber cutting, especially avoiding cutting sales with high-bid stumpage rates, it sought and received no-cost extensions of existing contracts.[37] This massive industry relief fueled doubts about the financial wisdom of the Forest Service selling timber when its costs exceeded the net revenue that the Treasury would realize. The agency's failure to provide timber program financial accounts intensified congressional interest in a full-cost accounting system.

In March 1983, the House Appropriations Committee's Interior and Related Agencies Subcommittee asked the Forest Service to lay out all timber program costs and revenue for fiscal year 1982, on a cash-flow basis, forest by forest.[38] Despite its length, the agency's fifteen-page answer avoided the meaningful analytical responses the committee sought, and omitted state, regional, and national totals. Only forest-level costs to prepare and administer sales, timber sale support, and Knutson-Vandenberg (KV) reforestation costs were compared with receipts placed in the National Forest and KV Funds. The Forest Service left out significant costs, such as appropriated funds needed to reforest logged lands, general administration, road engineering and construction costs, and payments to counties. It also left out the symmetrical "receipts" and costs for timber cut to cover a number of agency operating and investment-type timber activities. Despite these significant omitted costs, the Forest Service data showed that eighty-six forests with 50 percent of the cut had a $90,272,000 negative cash flow before counting county payments.[39]

The House Appropriations subcommittee was unhappy with the answers provided by the Forest Service. The subcommittee chairman, Sidney Yates, took two actions: he asked the committee's Surveys and Investigations staff to examine the agency Timber Sale Program;[40] and he requested that the Congressional Research Service (CRS) analyze the material the agency had submitted and make suggestions regarding a better accounting of receipts and costs. The agency's work was to be independent of, and not in consultation with, the Forest Service.[41]

In addition, independently and without the knowledge of the CRS or the House investigations staff, the Wilderness Society did a timber sale study,[42] as did the General Accounting Office (GAO).[43] Were these four analyses not enough, the Forest Service, on its own initiative, incorporated into its 1983 annual report an analysis by region that purported to show timber sale costs and the "sold value" of timber for fiscal year 1983.[44] All these documents were issued in early 1984 and confirmed the widespread existence of "below-cost" timber sales. Thus there were five independent analyses of timber program receipts and costs on the scene when the House Appropriations Committee undertook hearings on the Forest Service budget on April 3, 1984.

Notwithstanding that these five independent analyses of timber program receipts and costs employed Forest Service data, when the House Appropriations Committee's Interior Subcommittee held hearings on the Forest Service budget, the subcommittee and agency officials disagreed about their accuracy. They clashed over the validity of the conclusions in the Wilderness Society's report, and over accounting procedures. The result was direction from the Appropriations Committee that the Forest Service develop a timber sale accounting system.[45]

Three years later, the Forest Service sent to Congress its accounting proposal, styled the Timber Sale Program Information Reporting System (TSPIRS). The TSPIRS methodology contained three reporting mechanisms: Report 1 was a Financial Account; Report 2, an Economic Account; and Report 3, an Employment, Income and Program Level Account. The GAO, at the request of the House Appropriations Committee, analyzed and endorsed the concepts of TSPIRS Report 1 and gave support to what it termed an "end-results approach."[46] When the Forest Service and GAO appeared before the committee on April 14, 1988, the committee members' questions suggested reservations about many of the changes, but a willingness for the agency to continue the fieldwork then in progress.

The House report on the fiscal year 1988 budget not only recited agency efforts to date on the TSPIRS concept and congressional concern about where it was heading, but also turned down the Forest Service plea (which GAO had supported) for greater expenditure flexibility and the use of gross indicators to define goals. The committee's two-page reaction showed strong skepticism about the usefulness of proposed TSPIRS Report 2 (Economic Account) and Report 3 (Employment, Income and Program Level), neither of which it had sought. It directed the Forest Service to concentrate its energies on Report 1, the Financial Account. It gave the service two years to compile and perfect the Financial Account. At this point, the service had not yet sent 1987 test results to the committee, although GAO had run some partial checks. The conference report agreed that Report 1 should be implemented and work should continue "to develop more precise and useful information for reports 2 and 3."[47]

The Forest Service proceeded with the agencywide test of TSPIRS, and in December 1988, it published the first TSPIRS series for each national forest.[48] Its release brought mixed reviews. Conservation groups, such as the Wilderness Society, were generally critical. Timber-industry spokespersons claimed that these groups were distorting the figures. Randal O'Toole of Cascade Holistic Economic Consultants labeled TSPIRS an "Accounting System that can't count," and claimed the Forest Service designed it to justify uneconomic timber sales by the jobs they support.[49]

The TSPIRS National Summary itself opened with the glow of self-praise: "Dear National Forest User: Good News! The timber sale program on the National Forests shows that receipts exceed costs by $540,076,000 during fiscal year 1987 based upon generally accepted accounting principles." This prefatory enthusiasm was overdone. One must look at the fine print in TSPIRS Test Table 1, for example, to realize that the Forest Service net gain was $267,486,000—half the amount claimed by the chief.[50] There is no accounting principle that justifies this unqualified claim of profits double those the report contains, but this is only the beginning of the agency's obfuscation.

The forest-level reports permit seeing TSPIRS's weaknesses, but only after painstakingly dissecting and reassembling Forest Service data. The results were assembled by grouping forests according to "profit" or "loss," aggregating them by region and nationwide. This forest data omitted, however, $384,505,000 of costs: $66,909,000 of regional office costs plus $44,006,000 of Washington office costs and $273,590,000 in county payments.

Beyond the misleading nature of the overview in the National Summary, there are major omissions in portrayals of costs at the forest and regional levels. In addition, TSPIRS discrepancies with administrative and fiscal data and structure adds to cross-checking problems. Even one steeped in these vagaries of Forest Service data is quickly enveloped in a numerical morass. TSPIRS does not handle receipts in the same way as do agency fiscal reports, and timber-cut figures differ from data in "cut and sold" reports. Cross-checks yield different results. An examination of the service's raw TSPIRS data shows eighty-one forests with negative cash flows, not the sixty-eight forests that TSPIRS implies.[51] The chief's claim of profits of $540 billion is followed by the statement that the new accounting work will enable the service to reduce costs and increase revenues, and the assurance that in reading the report you will find "a sincere effort to improve our accountability in the timber sale program." A hard look at the figures, however, shakes one's confidence. A document aimed at improving management would deal with losses more frankly than in an oblique one-sentence reference buried in the report. O'Toole details the wide variation in actual "growth pool" expenses in the TSPIRS results by forest as he traces how "$400 million simply disappeared into a black hole." He uses forest examples as well as showing that twenty-three of the sixty-four forests on which he had actual data charged none of their actual expenses to the "investment" pool. In addition, he explains how costs ignored in Report 2—because in theory they "have already been accounted for" in the Financial Report—have simply disappeared.[52] When one recalls Graves's 1913 forecast of profitability, TSPIRS takes on an aura of déjà vu.

An equally serious problem has been the agency's use of multicentury write-off periods. Before the release of TSPIRS, the Wilderness Society questioned the soundness of road-cost amortization in the Tongass National Forest.[53] The Forest Service shrank road investment costs through depreciation amounting to 1,810 years on one forest; the average was 235 years for the twelve forests in the Rocky Mountain Region.[54] The effect was to reduce admitted losses in the regions that lose money and to inflate profits on forests in the Pacific Northwest. Write-offs that extend beyond the useful life or replacement period, if used by a business, would ensure plant deterioration. In addition, the Forest Service failed to pick up all costs for earlier investments or to consider replacement costs, the effects of inflation, and road life and route changes. The TSPIRS data also showed that in 1987, 65 percent of the road program was reconstruction.[55] The facts clearly suggest that road life is not as long as timber rotations.

The chief also contended that "timber harvesting contributes greatly to jobs and income." Profitable private timber, of course, provides as many jobs and as much labor income as will subsidized public timber. The service ignored the fact that forests that provide timber at a profit are more efficient providers than those that lose money. The agency did not provide any evidence that it lost $102 million on the 3.9 billion board feet it cut on eighty-one forests in 1987, or that it lost another $90 million cutting 3.6 billion board feet in 1988.[56] Furthermore, the service did not document its view that these sales are the most cost-effective way to meet the nation's timber needs, or that a smaller subsidy to private owners might yield the same cut at a lower outlay. TSPIRS, as has been the case with earlier "accountings," purposely understates the costs and presents a picture that justifies the money-losing timber program. However, this most recent accounting effort, with all its flaws, has shown that at least one-third of the timber program fails to recapture costs; in reality, the entire program's costs exceeded receipts.[57]

The goal of making public forestry pay remains elusive. As a 1985 Society of American Foresters' task force observed: "No accepted method yet exists for identifying and quantifying nonmarket benefits for comparative analysis, and adequate techniques do not exist for allocating joint costs to several different resource programs."[58] Gifford Pinchot's unmet challenge— to manage the national forests and make them pay—still haunts the agency.

NOTES

1. Gifford Pinchot, *Breaking New Ground* (New York: Harcourt, Brace, 1947), 10, 11, 15; Harold Pinkett, *Gifford Pinchot, Private and Public Forester* (Urbana: University of Illinois Press, 1970), 20.

2. See U.S. Department of Agriculture, Forest Service, *1987 Timber Sale Program Information Reporting System, Final Report to Congress* (Washington, D.C.: Government Printing Office, 1988), 11 [hereafter cited as *1987 Report to Congress*].

3. For information on early data for managing the forest reserves from 1899 to 1904, see *Hearings on Estimates of Appropriations for the Fiscal Year Ending June 30, 1909, Before the House Committee on Agriculture*, 60th Cong., 1st sess., 1908, 290 [hereafter cited as *Hearings on Estimates, 1909*].

4. Pinchot, *Breaking New Ground*, 105–87.

5. Gifford Pinchot, *Report of the Chief of the Division of Forestry*, H. Doc. 6, 57th Cong., 1st sess., 1901, 327–28.

6. S. Rep. 2954, 58th Cong., 3rd sess., 1905.

7. *Hearings on Expenditures in the Department of Agriculture Before the House Committee on Agriculture*, 59th Cong., 2nd sess., 1907, 791–883 [hereafter cited as *Hearings on Expenditures, 1907*]. Pinchot went so far as to assure committee members that after five years he would not even need the $1 million annual appropriation for general forestry; *Congressional Record*, 58th Cong., 3rd sess., 1905, 964, 1369–70, 1397; H. Rep. 3975, 58th Cong., 3rd sess., 1905; Act of 1 February 1905, 33 Stat 628.

8. *Hearings on the Estimates of Appropriations for the Department of Agriculture for the Fiscal Year Ending June 30, 1907; Also of Members of Congress and Other Interested Persons on Bills Relating to the Department of Agriculture Before the House Committee on Agriculture*, 59th Cong., 1st sess., 1906, 258 [hereafter cited as *Hearings on Estimates, 1907*]. Later in the same hearing, Pinchot assured the committee that "the forest reserves will be practically self-supporting this year" (255–76).

9. *Hearings on Estimates of Appropriations for the Fiscal Year Ending June 30,*

1908, Before the House Committee on Agriculture, 59th Cong., 2nd sess., 1907, 145 [hereafter cited as *Hearings on Estimates, 1908*].

10. *Hearings on Estimates, 1909,* 290.

11. *Hearings on Estimates, 1908,* 146, 152.

12. Ibid., 144–71.

13. Ibid., 157–60, 162–63, 169.

14. U.S. Department of Agriculture, Forest Service, *Report of the Forester for the Fiscal Year Ending June 30, 1912* (Washington, D.C.: Government Printing Office), 30; U.S. Department of Agriculture, Forest Service, *Report of the Forester for the Fiscal Year Ending June 30, 1917* (Washington, D.C.: Government Printing Office), 2 [hereafter cited as *1917 Annual Report*].

15. *1917 Annual Report,* 2. This report merely recites a few selected figures and gives very little data on costs. It does say operating costs were $4 million, but does not clearly show substantial expenditures for road and other investments. The data show that receipts were well under estimates, while costs had risen about as projected.

16. *Hearings on Estimates, 1909,* 290.

17. As early as 1906, Pinchot contended that the value of the reserves was easily $300 million and that the yearly cost to administer them was less than one-third of 1 percent of this value. He also contended that this was a very conservative estimate of value as he assigned the timber a price of $1 per 1,000 board feet, and that the value was rising at a rate of 10 percent per year. See *Hearings on Estimates, 1907,* 258; and *Hearings on Expenditures, 1907,* 792. In 1907 testimony, Pinchot said that the acres managed had risen from 58 million to 127 million, while expenditures had climbed from $800,000 to almost $2 billion. He then stated that he was managing to double the area, with more than a doubling of agency work, at a cost that was only $100,000 more than that experienced three years before with half of the area and less than half the work. He attributed this to "increased returns" (*Hearings on Expenditures, 1907,* 878). Even a cursory look at Pinchot's figures shows he was wrong; both absolute and preacre management costs had climbed substantially.

18. *Hearings on Estimates, 1909,* 292, 297–98.

19. *Hearings on Estimates of Appropriations for the Fiscal Year Ending June 30, 1912, Before the House Committee on Agriculture,* 61st Cong., 3rd sess., 1911, 126 [hereafter cited as *Hearings on Estimates, 1912*].

20. *Hearings on Estimates of Appropriations for the Fiscal Year Ending June 30, 1913, Before the House Committee on Agriculture,* 62nd Cong., 2nd sess., 1912, 161, 180–81.

21. *Hearings on Estimates of Appropriations for the Fiscal Year Ending June 30, 1914, Before the House Committee on Agriculture,* 62nd Cong., 3rd sess., 1913, 131–57, 178 [hereafter cited as *Hearings on Estimates, 1914*]. The term "biologically sustainable levels" represents a forester's view of how much timber could be cut on a biological, not a financial, basis. Simultaneously, however, a glut in the market in 1913 had depressed lumber prices. See H. Steer, *Lumber Production in the United States, 1799–1946,* Miscellaneous Publication 669 (Washington, D.C.: Department of Agriculture, 1948), 7–9.

22. Act of 10 August 1912, 37 Stat. 269, 287. In 1962, after fifty years of use, it was repealed at the request of the service on the grounds that keeping track of who was qualified was too difficult and that times had changed, rendering at-cost sales

inappropriate (Act of 23 October 1962, § 5, 76 Stat. 1157; see also H. Rep. 2377, 87th Cong., 2nd sess., 1962, 36).

23. *Hearings on Estimates, 1914*, 167; U.S. Department of Agriculture, Forest Service, *Regulation S-22 for At-Cost Sales (Use Book,* 1915). For data revealing the relation between "commercial" and "at-cost" timber sale prices, see U.S. Department of Agriculture, Forest Service, *Report of the Forester*, 1916, 8; U.S. Department of Agriculture, Forest Service, *Report of the Forester*, 1931, 41; U.S. Department of Agriculture, Forest Service, *Report of the Forester*, 1942, 5.

24. Section 14(h) of the National Forest Management Act (NFMA), 16 U.S.C. § 472a(h), 1982. Timber salvage sales revisited the 1912 "at-cost" act by specifying that advertised rates must capture certain minimum sale costs.

25. *Hearings on Estimates of Appropriations for the Fiscal Year Ending June 30, 1915, Before the House Committee on Agriculture*, 63rd Cong., 2nd sess., 1914, 239–311 [hereafter cited as *Hearings on Estimates, 1915*]. Expenditures in U.S. national forests were less than 2.5 cents per acre, compared to Prussian costs of over $2 per acre (*Hearings on Estimates, 1915*, 253). For data on receipts and costs, see *Hearings on Estimates, 1915*, 283–85. Within fifteen years, total receipts were to cover all Forest Service expenses, including aid in the form of fire assistance, reforestation of trees, and timber management advice to private landowners, as well as overhead costs.

26. *Hearings on Estimates of Appropriations for the Fiscal Year Ending June 30, 1920, Before the House Committee on Agriculture*, 65th Cong., 3rd sess., 315; see also U.S. Department of Agriculture, Forest Service, *Reports of the Forester*, 1905–1920.

27. U.S. Department of Agriculture, Forest Service, *Report of the Forester*, 1920, 1–2, 4–5.

28. *Senate Committee on Interior and Insular Affairs, Review of National Forest Timber Sales in Three Western Regions* (Comm. Print 1958, 2) [hereafter cited as *Review of Timber Sales*]; U.S. Department of Agriculture, Forest Service, *Report of the Forester*, 1929, 12–13, 19; U.S. Department of Agriculture, Forest Service, *Report of the Forester*, 1931; U.S. Department of Agriculture, Forest Service, *Report of the Forester*, 1933, 5, 6, 21; U.S. Department of Agriculture, Forest Service, *Forestry in Wartime, Report of the Forest Service*, 1942, 23.

29. *Review of Timber Sales*, 2; U.S. Department of Agriculture, Forest Service, *Report of the Forester*, 1948, 15–16.

30. U.S. Department of Agriculture, Forest Service, *Report of the Forester*, 1948, 5, 16, 22, 24.

31. U.S. Department of Agriculture, Forest Service, *Report of the Forester*, 1951, 37–38; U.S. Department of Agriculture, Forest Service, *Report of the Chief of the Forest Service*, 1958, 2.

32. 16 U.S.C. §§ 528-31, 1982.

33. *National Forests—Multiple-Use Sustained Yield, 1960: Hearings on H.R. 10572 Before the Subcommittee on Forests of the House Committee on Agriculture*, 86th Cong., 2nd sess., 1960, 63–66 (statement of Ralph D. Hodges, director, Forest Division, National Lumber Manufacturers' Association).

34. 16 U.S.C. § 531(a), 1982; C. C. Miniclier, "Timber Sales Spark Cheers, Jeers," *Denver Post*, 14 December 1988, 1B.

35. U.S. Department of Agriculture, Forest Service, *Report of the Chief of the Forest Service*, 1966, 2; U.S. Department of Agriculture, Forest Service, *Report of the Chief of the Forest Service*, 1979, 79. Analysis of the cut and sold data from the Forest Service's annual reports from 1976 through 1987 reveals the Forest Service sold 131,846,434,000 board feet of standing timber at a bid value of $13,222,592,032,000 or $100.29 per million board feet. During this same period, some contracts were canceled and there was a massive 1984 bailout that returned 9,748,000,000 board feet originally bid at over $2.5 billion upon payment of only $170 million. An unknown quantity was resold, about 3 billion board feet. Despite these returns, 123,109,374,000 board feet were cut in these twelve years, 6.6 percent less and 8,737,060,000 board feet less than the total volume reported "sold." However, timber management records show that only $8,980,337,823,000 was paid for this timber. The price paid of $72.95 per million board feet is $27.34 per million board feet less than the bid value. The Forest Service has not provided a reconciliation of volume and value of timber activity.

36. Thomas Barlow, Gloria Helfand, Blair Orr, and Thomas Stoel, *Giving Away the National Forests* (Washington, D.C.: Natural Resources Defense Council, 1980), 29; *Department of the Interior and Related Agencies Appropriations for 1985: Hearings Before the Subcommittee of the House Committee on Appropriations*, 98th Cong., 2nd sess., 1984, 239–308.

37. *Federal Timber Contract Payment Modification Act*, 16 U.S.C. § 618 (1982). Prices for national forest timber cut peaked in fiscal year 1979, fell in 1980, rebounded in 1981, and then plummeted in 1982. Bid rates followed a generally similar pattern, but at a plateau through 1981, well above prices actually paid for timber cut. The volume of cut timber fell as the market collapsed, but the Forest Service continued a high level of sales despite drastic declines in the cut and prices. See memorandum from Robert E. Wolf, assistant chief, Environment and Natural Resources Division, Congressional Research Service, to Sidney Yates, chairman, Subcommittee on Interior Appropriations, House Appropriations Committee, 7 March 1984, 2 [hereafter cited as *Wolf/Yates Memorandum*].

38. *Department of the Interior and Related Agencies, Appropriations for 1984: Hearings Before the Subcommittee of the House Committee on Appropriations*, 98th Cong., 1st sess., 1983, 326–29, 330–342 [hereafter cited as *Hearings on Appropriations, 1984*].

39. *Hearings on Appropriations, 1984*. Although 1982 was a poor revenue year, the negative cash flows for some forests were high enough to suggest that negative flows were normal for these forests.

40. Surveys and Investigations Staff, *Report to the House Committee on Appropriations, Timber Sales Programs of the U.S. Forest Service*, 1984. This report reviewed Regions 5 and 6 for fiscal years 1982 and 1983, and found fourteen of eighteen Region 5 (California) forests and four of nineteen Region 6 (Oregon and Washington) forests had costs greater than timber receipts. It also determined that the Forest Service had failed to include all relevant costs.

41. *Wolf/Yates Memorandum*. The Congressional Research Service (CRS) review responded to specific committee concerns about deficiencies in the Forest Service data submitted for fiscal year 1982. To sharpen the focus on 119 forests, CRS displayed data by thirty-nine states. From Forest Service annual reports, it developed the volume and value of timber sold and cut, using the latter to lay out three price scenarios to com-

pare against the costs the service displayed for fiscal year 1982. Because CRS used substantially greater receipts than those the Forest Service had listed, a lower level of negative cash flows emerged. The CRS work not only confirmed significant negative cash flow situations but outlined an approach to measuring receipts and costs.

42. V. Alric Sample, *Below Cost Timber Sales on the National Forests* (Washington, D.C.: The Wilderness Society, 1984), examined fiscal years 1978, 1982, and 1983 and concluded that five of nine regions consistently had net losses. These five regions were estimated to have cash-flow losses totaling $443 million for the three study years.

43. *General Accounting Office, U.S. Comptroller General, Congress Needs Better Information on Forest Service's Below-Cost Timber Sales,* 1984 [hereafter cited as *GAO Report*]. The GAO examined 3,244 timber sales in four regions for the years 1981–1982. Overall, receipts for these sales were estimated to be $712 million over costs, but in 1981 below-cost sales had receipt shortfalls of $64 million and in 1982 the estimate was $92 million.

44. U.S. Department of Agriculture, Forest Service, *Report of the Chief of the Forest Service,* 1983, 21–25, 91. The Forest Service's fiscal year 1983 report confirmed the widespread existence of "below-cost" timber sales. In this analysis, the service said that 37 percent of the timber volume sold in 1983 would not recover costs. In this presentation, the Forest Service used a different cost base than it had used in the 1982 data presented to the House Appropriations Committee. It also substituted the anticipated receipts from timber sold for actual receipts used in the earlier presentation. It is noteworthy that in the text and table of the 1983 display, the service contended it was measuring "sales cost."

45. *Department of the Interior and Related Agencies, Appropriations for 1985: Hearings Before the Subcommittee of the House Committee on Appropriations,* 98th Cong., 2nd sess., 1984, 193–674.

46. *Department of the Interior and Related Agencies, Appropriations for 1989: Hearings Before the Subbcommittee of the House Committee on Appropriations,* 100th Cong., 2nd sess., 1988, 792–818 [hereafter cited as *Hearings on Appropriations, 1989*].

47. H. Rep. 171, 100th Cong., 1st sess., 1988, 65–67; *Hearings on Appropriations, 1989,* 769–1080; H.R.J. Res. 395, 100th Cong., 1st sess., 1988, 902.

48. This is a three-part document consisting of: (1) U.S. Department of Agriculture, Forest Service, *Timber Sale Program Annual Report, Fiscal Year 1987 Test, National Summary;* (2) U.S. Department of Agriculture, Forest Service, *Timber Sale Program Annual Report, Fiscal Year 1987 Test, Forest Level Information;* (3) U.S. Department of Agriculture, Forest Service, *Timber Sale Program Annual Report, Fiscal Year 1987 Test, State Level Information* (Washington, D.C.: Timber Management, 1988) [hereafter cited as *1987 National Summary*].

49. C. C. Miniclier, "Timber Sales Spark Cheers, Jeers," *Denver Post,* 14 December 1988, 1B; Randal O'Toole, "The Case of the Missing $400 Million," *Forest Watch 9,* 3 (December 1988): 6–13.

50. *1987 National Summary,* 1, 6; *Hearings on Appropriations, 1989,* 793, 797–832.

51. Data from the *1987 National Forest Level Information Summary,* reveals that TSPIRS allocates regional and Washington office costs to forests in proportion to vol-

ume cut. A different picture emerges than the service implies—forest cash flows shrink, reported negative cash flows are actually worse, and claimed profits fall.

52. *1987 National Summary,* 1; O'Toole, "The Case of the Missing $400 Million," 9.

53. The Wilderness Society contends that less than 1 percent of the 1986 engineering and road construction expenditures were included in the TSPIRS cost pool, likening this to a 200-year road amortization plan. The organization also alleges that the cost pool has grown at a rate of 8 to 10 percent since 1977, thus more than doubling. See The Wilderness Society, *GAO Tongass Report* (18 April 1988).

54. The Wilderness Society, *1988 Timber Receipts and Expenditures on the National Forests, by Forest Service Region* (Washington, D.C.: The Wilderness Society, 1989).

55. *1987 National Summary,* appendix C (employment, income, and program level account for the forest road program). In its 1989 report, the House Appropriations Committee instructed the GAO and the Forest Service to review the amortization of road costs (H. Rep. 120, 101st Cong., 1st sess., 1989, 79–80).

56. *1987 National Summary,* 1. Letter from author to Sidney Yates, chairman, Subcommittee on Appropriations for the Department of Interior and Related Agencies, House Appropriations Committee, 30 March 1989 [hereafter cited as *Letter to Yates*]. See also Tom Kuhnle, *The Forest Service Timber Sale Information Reporting System* (Washington, D.C.: National Defense Council, 1989); W. Shands, T. Waddell, and G. Reyes, *Below-Cost Timber Sales in the Broad Context of National Forest Management* (Washington, D.C.: The Conservation Foundation, 1988).

57. *Letter to Yates,* attachment 2, comparing timber receipts. The figures during this time were as follows: total costs, $8.86 billion; total receipts, $6.19 billion; net loss, $2.67 billion, exclusive of interest. If interest at the rate of 8.62 percent were included, the total loss would increase to $4.3 billion (all figures in nominal dollars).

58. Society of American Foresters, *Report of the Below-Cost Timber Sales Task Force, Fiscal and Social Responsibility in National Forest Management,* 1986, vi. A September 1995 GAO cash flow report (RCED-95-237FS) for 1992–1995 revealed that 103 forests lost $1,179,800,000 cutting 13.653 billion board feet, a loss of $486.42 per million board feet, or $660 per acre. Only 15 forests showed a profit; the total net loss for the 118 forests was $995.4 million. In July 1996, the U.S. Department of Agriculture's inspector general declared that the Forest Service's "financial statements do not present fairly, in conformity with applicable government accounting principles," their financial position. The audit identified pervasive errors, material misstatements, and departures from accounting principles affecting seven basic operating systems at the field and Washington office levels (source: 08401-4-AT, 18 July 1996).

Part Three

AT LOGGERHEADS

"A Regular Ding-Dong Fight": The Dynamics of Park Service–Forest Service Controversy During the 1920s and 1930s

Hal K. Rothman

As the primary manager of land in the American West, the federal government has played a significant role in the development of the region. Often vested with vast power over land and resources, federal administrators remain one of the most important groups in shaping both the growth of the region and its direction.

This power often engenders internecine rivalry. Many of the federal agencies with holdings, influence, or desires in the West have grappled with one another. In some cases, different agencies have sought the implementation of conflicting programs and policies to the same tract of land, such as the rancorous battle between the National Park Service (NPS) and the United States Department of Agriculture Forest Service during the 1920s and 1930s. The two agencies competed over land, primarily in the West, and sought to impose differing value systems on it. They operated in a largely closed environment, with an advantage to one side necessarily resulting in a loss for the other. As a result, the squabbles between the two agencies often seemed petty, motivated by little more than bureaucratic intransigence and a degree of territoriality rivaled only by medieval despots. One participant accurately described the nature of the conflict when he referred to a specific acquisition battle as "a regular ding-dong fight."[1]

In fact, the conflict between the two agencies revealed a clash between the dominant value systems of different eras in the twentieth century. The older of the two agencies, the Forest Service, grew out of the emphasis on scientific conservation that Theodore Roosevelt articulated during his administration. Founded in 1905 as a result of the efforts of Gifford Pinchot, the first scientifically trained forester from the United States, the Forest Service embodied the doctrine of wise use of resources. Pinchot shaped his agency to promote the idea of wise use—the greatest good for the greatest number of people through scientific management. His successors, especially William B. Greeley, expanded this to emphasize the needs of local industries.

During the 1920s, the dominant current in the United States Forest Service remained the same as it had been in the first decade of its existence. Although Aldo Leopold, Robert Marshall, and Arthur Carhart began to stress the preservation of wilderness as an important objective for the agency and some Forest Service regions began to develop recreational programs, such efforts were the work of individuals within the agency rather than a concerted effort by foresters to accommodate uses that did not involve the development of marketable resources. The Forest Service remained true to the tenets of Gifford Pinchot and his peers: it sought to promote the use of natural resources through a network of regional management that encouraged foresters to have considerable sensitivity to local concerns.[2]

Many factors helped create this local emphasis. The division of management of the agency into regions, its policies of recruitment and promotion from within, its early emphasis on enforcement of federal rules and regulations, and the lonely nature of the life of early foresters—to say nothing of political necessity—all contributed to a decentralized hierarchy that responded to the needs of ranchers, farmers, and timber concerns.

The division of the Forest Service into regional jurisdictions had roots that preceded the agency's founding. Bernhard Fernow advocated decentralization of federal forest activities in the 1880s, and twelve years later, Pinchot followed with similar plans. By 1905, the forest reserves were divided into three jurisdictions; in 1907, Pinchot recast the three into six regional offices. Although the foresters moved freely from one region to another, they paid attention to the differing needs of their various constituencies. In the words of one scholar, this autonomy "gave forest officers far from the Washington, D.C., headquarters a status rare in federal bureaus."[3] It also removed the real decision makers of the Forest Service from the terms of national debate. Located in the individual national forests and in the regions, these men focused on the issues of their areas.

The Forest Service *Use Book* served as the link between the Washington office of the agency and rangers in distant national forests. Initially designed to fit in a forester's pocket, this book of regulations and instructions spelled out the scope of the responsibilities of the agency for field personnel. Foresters in the field could rely on it to remind them of the tenets of their agency: managing to create a perpetual supply of timber, preserving watersheds, and protecting local industry from unfair competition.[4]

Autonomy in the field led to the substitution of the *Use Book* for policy. With Pinchot's pressure to make decisions in the field—to solve the problems of each national forest at the forest level—and with an administrative document that focused exclusively on wise use and regulation, many western rangers implemented the doctrines of their agency in a parochial fashion. Overworked, foresters solved the problems posed to them often without looking at the implications for agencywide policy.

The men who became foresters also influenced the evolution of the Forest Service. "The aim was to select competent woodsmen for rangers—men who could shoot straight, handle horses, travel with a pack outfit in the hills, and generally take care of themselves outdoors," Elers Koch, one of the first Forest Service men, recalled much later. Initially, most of these men came from the areas that contained national forestland; the law that transferred the national forests from the Department of the Interior to the Department of Agriculture in 1905 dictated that foresters had to come from the state in which the national forest was located. Supervisors like Koch selected the best men they could find for ranger positions, and the ones they chose were of a piece with the homesteaders and timbermen with whom they had to work. Local men with an understanding of local concerns helped the Forest Service make an impact in remote corners of the West.[5]

On the heels of the initial cadre came a second generation, trained in scientific forestry at eastern universities. These men were the living embodiment of progressive conservation, trained in science and dedicated to wise use through management. Science provided the answer to difficult questions, according to the doctrines of the Progressive Era, and these new foresters saw their management decisions as having the force of the most important values of their era.

Many of the early leaders of the agency rose through the ranks, and by the 1920s, some attained positions of significance in the agency. Major Robert Y. Stuart, who became chief of the Forest Service in 1928, was an agency inspector in 1907. In the fall of 1908, District 1 in Missoula, Montana, included two future chief foresters: Ferdinand A. Silcox, who succeeded Stuart in 1933, was associate forester to district forester William B. Greeley, himself the chief from 1920 to 1928. Earle H. Clapp, Richard H. Rutledge, Leon F. Kneipp, Arthur Ringland, and many others rose through the ranks to positions of responsibility. Rutledge, who old-time forester Clarence Swim decided in 1909 was "a likely looking lumberjack who . . . would make good foreman material," became a regional forester in Region 4 and, by 1930, had begun to develop recreational programs for the Dixie National Forest. In 1938, he moved to the Department of the Interior as chief of the Division of Grazing. Clapp became acting chief in 1939, reverting to associate chief in 1943 when Lyle F. Watts received the top position. Kneipp, who also served as a general inspector, became assistant forester. Ringland served in numerous policy-making positions. From 1915 well into the 1940s, this first generation of foresters shaped the decision-making process in this decentralized agency.[6]

Their experiences during the early years of the century influenced their view of the obligations of the Forest Service. Initially, foresters found much resistance to the idea of conservation. They spent their time surveying large expanses of open land, disputing illegal land claims, fighting fires, and performing duties that required direct management of land. There were few forest rangers in the field, and millions of acres for which they were responsible. Most worked alone or in pairs. They had to be "self-reliant and self-sustaining," determined to carry out regulations that vocal parts of their constituencies did not understand, want, or appreciate.[7] The men who were selected for the Forest Service were tested for skills, but more important for the kind of individualism that characterized westward pioneers. These men had to fend for themselves in a dangerous physical world often teeming with people hostile to their objectives.

They also believed that what they did and the way they did it was intrinsically right. In the words of one scholar, the Forest Service became "something more like a religion," its officials convinced that their policies answered the pertinent questions.[8] The *Use Book* became the bible of the Forest Service, its generalized procedures and regulations serving as the text from which foresters made local decisions.

As they ascended to positions of greater responsibility, the foresters brought the values that their experience had taught. What had shaped their character as foresters—the battles over fraudulent homestead claims, the ever-present danger of forest fire, the desire to survey wild land, and the necessity of working with local constituencies—dominated the consciousness of these men as they made policy for their agency. They were not insensitive to aesthetic, cultural, and recreational concerns; to them, such issues were simply not as important as the original mission of the Forest Service.

The values that dominated the agency during the 1920s and early 1930s, in short, were a combination of individualist spirit and progressive ethos, part of nineteenth-century America and equally of the regulatory world that succeeded it. Often living as wilderness men on the fringes of established society, foresters embodied order. They determined the legality of land claims and uses, and usually had the character to enforce their decisions. As such, foresters were an odd combination of scientists who understood the language of conservation and frontiersmen who could communicate with the most remote of homesteaders.

In contrast, the National Park Service was a creature of the twentieth century. From its inception, the NPS hungrily sought a national constituency. A promotional wizard, Stephen T. Mather, became its first director. Previously he had created a national market for 20 Mule Team Borax, and later went into business with a partner and made a sizable fortune. Like many social and business leaders of his era, Mather then sought to channel his energy to civic projects. In 1914, when Secretary of the Interior Franklin K. Lane received an irate letter from Mather about conditions in the national parks, the secretary found the man he sought to manage the national parks and monuments.

Mather had excellent conservation credentials and came from the right social circle in which to promote the parks. He belonged to dozens of fraternal and civic organizations, including the Sierra Club, and was a lifelong advocate of Sigma Chi Fraternity. In 1912, he joined Theodore Roosevelt's "Bull Moose" third-party run for the presidency. Mather had friends throughout the business community and the world of journalism, and he was no stranger to the political arena of Washington, D.C. A driven man with compulsive tendencies, Mather often assumed too much responsibility. In 1904, he had a serious nervous breakdown, a recurring condition that three times interrupted his career in the Park Service. Nevertheless, he accepted the challenges of the national parks with typical vigor.[9]

Mather brought an unparalleled enthusiasm to the national parks. Immediately after becoming assistant to the secretary of the interior in charge of national parks, he began to implement programs to attract attention to the park system. Lane gave him an assistant, Horace M. Albright, a young Californian, and together the two furthered legislation to establish the National Park Service. When Congress authorized a bureau to manage the national parks in 1916, Mather and Albright began to market parks in the same manner that Mather had sold borax to the American public. Mather lobbied his friends in Congress, taking important legislators and influential citizens on catered tours of western national parks. Mather's friend from their days at the *New York Sun,* Robert Sterling Yard, then the Sunday editor at the *New York Herald,* went to Washington to orchestrate publicity for the national parks.

Together, Mather and Albright developed an extraordinary promotional program. Between 1917 and 1919, 1,050 magazine articles about the national parks graced the pages of American publications. In 1917, Yard gave away 250,000 park booklets and 83,000 auto maps, and circulated 348,000 feet of motion-picture film to organizations interested in the parks. At Mather's behest, western railroad companies financed the publication of *The National Parks Portfolio,* an exhilarating collection of photos of the most dramatic scenery in the national park system. The Park Service sent more than 275,000 of them to selected members of the public. The national parks message spread.[10]

Although Pinchot had campaigned aggressively for forestry at the turn of the century, in the late 1910s and the 1920s the Forest Service did not counter the Park Service with a widespread promotion of its own. Foresters were content to work with their primary constituencies, and as a result, their agency's campaigns generally focused on the people who already composed their audience.[11] Much of the effort of the Forest Service centered on education in conservation forestry, a practice that paled in comparison with professional marketing efforts that featured the spectacular scenery of Yellowstone and Yosemite.

Albright quickly developed into a force in the back rooms of Congress, and he furthered the Park Service cause with land acquisition programs and astute management of the few resources that the agency had available. His refusal to be bested at anything and his extraordinary knack for developing interdependent relationships served the NPS well. While Mather worked the public, Albright became the man behind the scenes, the liaison to Congress who made the deals that allowed the system to grow. The two proved a formidable team.[12]

By the early 1920s, the National Park Service had taken major steps to ensure its survival. Early on, Mather recognized the importance of the automobile to his agency, and providing roads and facilities for auto tourists topped NPS objectives. Mather also decided that the park system must include the most spectacular scenery on the continent. The Forest Service consented to the transfer of the Grand Canyon National Monument and its reclassification as a national park in 1919. Other park areas that fit the agenda that Mather and Albright developed also became national parks—Mukuntuweap National Monument became Zion National Park, and Sieur de Monts National Monument became Lafayette National Park (later renamed Acadia National Park)—and the two men developed a clear conception of the parks to sell to the public. They began a program to link the western national parks with a "park-to-park highway," acquired new national monuments to break up the long stretches between existing national parks, and received a congressional allotment for road building in the national parks.[13]

The National Park Service tapped the pulse of the Jazz Age. It sold Americans leisure and grandeur at a time when, in the aftermath of World War I, outdoor recreation increased beyond the significance that Progressive America had assigned it; the outdoors connoted appreciation for American values as well as for the physical strength of its people. The innovative techniques that Mather had developed in the business world proved useful in selling the parks to a willing public and in making many friends for the Park Service. Mather's flamboyant style of broadening the sphere of NPS influence contrasted with the understated efforts of the Forest Service to serve an identified but limited constituency. When the inevitable happened—when the Park Service and the Forest Service became engaged in a fight for the role of lead federal conservation agency—the Park Service had a wider constituency with an urban base, better promotional materials, a national focus, and an aggressive campaign for acquisitions.

The terms of the battle between the two agencies cast the Park Service as the aggressor, and by 1925, Mather and Albright were poised to attack. The Forest Service controlled a sizable percentage of federal land in the West, including many national monuments. Believing that it was better suited to manage such areas than the Forest Service, the Park Service began to pressure the Forest Service for control of scenic lands or tracts that contained significant or historical features.

Prior to 1925, the Park Service had only peripherally challenged the Forest Service. Mather and Albright were busy building the Park Service from within—changing some of the more scenic national monuments to national parks and fending off attempts to establish inappropriate parks, such as Secretary of the Interior Albert B. Fall's proposed All-Year National Park near his ranch in southern New Mexico—and did not yet have the strength and support to challenge the Forest Service directly.[14]

Yet points of contention already existed. Many in the Forest Service had opposed the creation of the Park Service, believing that their agency could manage recreation in the parks along with its other responsibilities. They did not feel that the nation needed another conservation-oriented agency, particularly if it fell to the Department of the Interior. By the early 1920s, streamlining the federal government had become an issue, and talk of combining the Forest Service and the Park Service in either the Department of the Interior or the Department of Agriculture gained credence. This ruffled both sides and led to a climate where mistrust grew. Little incidents had repercussions that far outweighed their significance; the Forest Service published a map of California that left the national parks as blank spaces, inspiring a complaint from an offended Stephen Mather. In 1921, Arthur H. Carhart, a landscape architect with the Forest Service, brought agency recreational programs to the fore at a national state parks conference. Mather responded, a local newspaper published an account of the difference in opinion, and a rift developed. Interagency relations continued to deteriorate despite the peacekeeping efforts of Greeley and others. In 1924, Mather and Greeley were on speaking terms, but few others in either agency felt warmly toward their counterparts.[15]

The mid-1920s were the beginning of a period of transition for the Forest Service. Under Greeley, a pragmatic leader and an astute politician, the Forest Service and the timber industry worked closely to increase the harvest of timber on national forest lands. Timber sales increased throughout the first half of the decade, peaking in 1926. A fifteen-year downward spiral in demand followed, forcing foresters to reassess many of their policies.[16] The agency also faced an increasingly powerful and determined adversary in the Park Service.

By 1924, the Park Service had achieved a sort of "power-parity" with the Forest Service. Mather's lobbying had produced significant results. Many congressmen considered themselves staunch national park advocates, and appropriations for the agency grew each year. Even the prolonged conflict with Ralph Henry Cameron, United States Senator from Arizona, over his claims in the Grand Canyon, strengthened the Park Service. Cameron's blanket opposition to anything Mather proposed rallied park advocates both in and out of Congress. Increasingly widespread ownership of the automobile, federal expenditures for western roads, and increasing leisure time and affluence boded well for the Park Service. It had become the political equal of the Forest Service, and the cultural climate in the United States augmented the

Park Service's influence. From Mather's and Albright's point of view, this was the time to challenge the Forest Service.

Stephen T. Mather fired the first salvo in 1925. That February, Secretary of the Interior Hubert Work created the Coordinating Committee on National Parks and Forests (CCNPF) to monitor the growing feud, which Mather only intensified when he proposed the establishment or enlargement of twelve park areas, including Yellowstone, Sequoia, Grand Canyon, Crater Lake, Mount Rainier, and Rocky Mountain national parks, as well as the creation of a 300,000-acre national park out of the Forest Service's Bandelier National Monument and Santa Fe National Forest.[17]

The members of the committee played important roles in American conservation. Representative Henry W. Temple of Pennsylvania, a staunch conservationist and a frequent supporter of the Park Service, chaired the committee. Charles Sheldon of the Boone and Crockett Club, a well-known conservation organization founded in 1887 by George Bird Grinnell and Theodore Roosevelt, and Major William A. Welch of Palisades Interstate Park Commission rounded out the committee. Mather and Greeley also held seats. In reality, each of the members had myriad obligations, and they often sent representatives in their stead. Some of the representatives did more to complicate issues than to resolve them.[18]

The creation of the CCNPF revealed much about the rivalry between the two agencies. Its existence indicated that relations had deteriorated so badly that the two sides could not be counted on to resolve their differences. A higher authority to rule on Park Service–Forest Service disputes had become necessary. It also suggested that Congress had become too partisan an arena for resolution of these issues. Each agency had its advocates and detractors on Capitol Hill, and in the heady days of the 1920s, advocacy often overwhelmed merit.

Mather's proposals revealed the new confidence of the Park Service. By articulating a clear-cut agenda, he cast the terms of the battle for the next decade. The Park Service targeted specific areas of national forests because of the values they contained, and began a program to pursue the inclusion of these places in the park system. This aggressiveness itself was not new, but its orchestrated character was different, suggesting that the Park Service recognized it was working from a new position of strength.

That is when relations between the two sides disintegrated, of which the dispute over the area surrounding the Bandelier National Monument in New Mexico offers compelling testimony. Established in 1916, Bandelier belonged to the Forest Service by virtue of the gentlemen's agreement that accompanied the passage of the Antiquities Act of 1906; this meant that the Departments of the Interior and Agriculture continued to administer national monuments created from their respective domains. In 1916, with a number of proposals to create a national park in the region on the floor of Congress,

Secretary of Agriculture David F. Houston sent foresters Arthur Ringland and Will Barnes to inspect the area. The men decided that the region lacked national park characteristics and would make a better national monument.

After the establishment of the monument, the Park Service continued to pursue the idea of a park. A park effort failed in 1919, but a proposal gathered momentum during 1923 and 1924. Mather's agenda included a 300,000-acre national park that encompassed the 22,000 acres of Bandelier and much more. The two agencies prepared to face off once again, and the CCNPF planned a fact-finding visit to New Mexico.

In public hearings in New Mexico, the Park Service and the Forest Service went after each other with uncharacteristic viciousness. In Santa Fe, the Forest Service constituency lambasted Jesse L. Nusbaum, the superintendent of Mesa Verde National Park, who represented Mather on the tour. Nusbaum did not successfully defend himself or his agency from the attack. In a nineteen-page diatribe he subsequently sent to Mather, he claimed that A. J. Connell, a former forester who ran the Los Alamos Ranch School about seven miles from Bandelier, insisted that the NPS would prevent local residents from using the natural resources of the area and would force tourists to ride in "the shrieking yellow busses of the transportation monopolies." Nusbaum believed that Connell's accusations reflected the secret goal of the Forest Service to thwart the park through innuendo. He contended that the actions of Barrington Moore, Sheldon's representative to the hearings and a former forester who edited *Ecology* magazine, Arthur Ringland, and Assistant Forester Leon F. Kneipp, none of whom evaluated the park proposal on its merits, proved conspiracy. Nusbaum also accused Ringland, Kneipp, and other agency representatives of trying to deceive Representative Temple.[19]

In actuality, both sides were guilty of excess during the Bandelier crisis. The conflict showed the Park Service at its most acquisitive; the 300,000-acre park it proposed took in so much of the western section of the Santa Fe National Forest that it would have precluded the need for Forest Service management in the Jemez Mountains. As a defensive response, the foresters engaged in hyperbole and slander, rallying local opposition. An impasse charged with tension and hard feelings resulted. Nusbaum's shrill response showed the level to which the situation had disintegrated. The stakes had risen so much that accusation replaced evaluation and merit, and politics superseded an important question of comparative resource management.

The issues at Bandelier typified the kind of battles over incommensurable values that separated the two agencies. Any evaluation of the Pajarito Plateau—the Bandelier–Jemez Mountains region—required the comparison of the recreational and cultural value of a large area of attractive mountain scenery dotted by archaeological ruins with its economic value. A national constituency of travelers, scholars, and others valued the aesthetic and cultural qualities of the area, while homesteaders and influential groups of northern New Mexicans valued its timber and pastureland. The dominant values did not lend themselves to direct comparison, and the battle degenerated into one of influence.

The resolution of the park proposal in northern New Mexico revealed much about the changing nature of the Park Service. It broke the solid front that characterized the Park Service before 1925. In a report that dampened enthusiasm for the park, Frank "Boss" Pinkley, the dynamic and outspoken superintendent of the southwestern national monuments group, remarked that he "would rather see [the ruins] left as a monument under [the Forest] Service than be transferred to ours as a park."[20] Like Pinkley, many others within NPS felt that new park areas that did not equal Yellowstone or Yosemite cheapened the system. That was how some responded to the proposed acquisition of Cedar Breaks in Utah. To counter this opposition, Albright used the specter of Forest Service recreation programs to build a groundswell of support from the same people who earlier had opposed the absorption of Cedar Breaks, which NPS ultimately acquired in 1933.[21]

Another Park Service tactic—incremental growth—boosted Park Service acquisitions. As early as 1919, Park Service officials would ask for a great deal of land—in many cases more than they really wanted—and settle for a portion of their request. After a number of years, they would renew their attempts, acquiring another sizable portion of the original request. In this manner, the Park Service could continue to grow and, more important, keep its acquisitive instincts honed and its morale high.

This policy was anathema to the Forest Service. Foresters referred to the Park Service as "inchers," an epithet that kept them vigilant in the face of NPS proposals. Yet in many ways, the Forest Service fought a losing battle, trying to protect a vast domain from seemingly random encroachment on all fronts. In a defensive posture as a result of NPS aggressiveness, it fell back on conventional techniques to resist a guerrilla war of acquisition.

Yet many within the Forest Service found ways to respond to the challenge that the Park Service presented. The ideas of Aldo Leopold, Arthur Carhart, and Robert Marshall regarding wilderness offered the agency an area into which to expand, staking a claim to a niche in recreational administration that the NPS neglected. The concept of primitive areas had gained a following within the agency, and the Forest Service castigated the Park Service for accommodating comfort-seeking travelers at the expense of the parklands. One reason the agency opposed the transfer of Bandelier, for example, was that the Park Service planned to replace the winding pack trail into Frijoles Canyon with a paved road. Foresters contended that the road would spoil the serenity of the canyon, and that their opposition stemmed from sensitivity to the "interests of the seriously-minded interested visitor." By 1928, the Forest Service declared a portion of the Bandelier area part of a wilderness preserve, much to the consternation of Jesse L. Nusbaum. Elsewhere, the foresters formalized designations for primitive and research areas, new responsibilities to which the Park Service had no existing claim. Chief Forester Greeley added forest campgrounds in the national forest system and rejected plans for a tramway at Mount Hood in Oregon, and throughout the West scenic strips to mask logging areas became increasingly common.[22]

But despite its importance in the battle with the Park Service, wilderness largely remained a side issue for the Forest Service. Compared with the commercial management of natural resources, wilderness, recreation, and other kinds of programs were distant contenders for attention. The leadership of the Forest Service generally relied on the doctrines and values of the utilitarian conservation espoused during the Progressive Era as the basis for their decisions. As a result, one of the best tools they had to combat the aggressiveness of the NPS went largely underutilized.

In contrast, the Park Service depended on innovation to move forward. An aggressive leader, Albright carried the Park Service forward during his tenure. He actually took over the agency in 1927, when Mather suffered a serious stroke, and officially became director in 1929. Albright developed a close rapport with Ray Lyman Wilbur, Herbert Hoover's secretary of the interior, and played an instrumental role in Hoover's proclamation of "lame-duck" national monuments after the 1932 election. The Park Service acquired five new national monuments as a result: Death Valley, White Sands, Saguaro, Black Canyon of the Gunnison, and the second Grand Canyon National Monument, later incorporated into the national park.[23]

Although Albright was closely identified with the Hoover administration, Roosevelt's secretary of the interior, Harold L. Ickes, kept Albright on. By all accounts an irascible man, Ickes brought his idiosyncratic brand of aggressive management to Washington. Although he terrorized nearly everyone else in the Department of the Interior, Ickes and Albright became close. Ickes liked the fortitude that Albright showed in their dealings. Ickes had come to Washington a devotee of utilitarian conservation; he once wrote to Pinchot that he had learned about conservation from the same source as Theodore Roosevelt—Pinchot. During the dramatic first hundred days of the administration of Franklin D. Roosevelt in 1933, Albright made Ickes into a staunch advocate of the national parks. Albright's ability to work with people like Ickes furthered the objectives of the Park Service.[24]

While the Park Service relied on this combination of personality and persistence, the Forest Service passed to lesser hands. When Major Robert Y. Stuart replaced Greeley in 1928, the Forest Service effectively passed to a new generation of leaders. Pinchot made the agency; Henry S. Graves and Greeley led for most of the following two decades. Stuart's ascendance inaugurated a new era in its leadership. At the worst possible moment, the charismatic and competent leaders who formed agency policy turned over the responsibilities of the agency to those who previously had only implemented policy.

The actions of Albright and Stuart revealed dramatic differences. Albright had been instrumental in shaping and implementing NPS policy. Stuart, by contrast, lacked the experience, tenacity, and confidence to thwart the ever-aggressive Albright. The situation built the growing confidence of the Park Service, while constraining the options of the Forest Service.

By the late 1920s, the Forest Service faced internal problems as well. The bust of the timber market had begun in earnest. Throughout the decade, but especially toward its close, Gifford Pinchot had attacked Greeley's timber management policies. Although the timber industry supported Greeley, an assault by the most prominent name in American forestry only compounded the problems of an agency already threatened from the outside. The Forest Service tried to respond by developing new timber management policies, but by 1930, in the words of one scholar, the agency's goals were "undefined and utterly up in the air."[25]

Stuart's mental health may also have contributed to the growing Park Service advantage in the dispute. He suffered a breakdown in 1932, and his leadership became erratic. In 1933, the agency did not respond to Executive Order 6166, which consolidated all the national monuments under the jurisdiction of the Park Service, until far too late to challenge the edict. Nor did Stuart put up effective resistance to Albright's expansion efforts. By late 1933, Stuart seemed to have lost control. In November of that year, he jumped or fell to his death from an office on the seventh floor of the Forest Service Building in Washington, D.C.[26]

The Park Service went through its own crisis of leadership the same year. In August 1933, Albright left the Park Service to enter private business, and Arno B. Cammerer, long an associate director, assumed the top position. Cammerer was in a position similar to that of Stuart when the latter took over the Forest Service. He had had little to do with forming the agenda and policies of a dynamic generation of leaders. As a result, the Park Service slipped into a mode similar to that of the Forest Service under Stuart.

Ickes's attitude toward Cammerer did not help matters. He quickly came to despise the genial Cammerer and frequently embarrassed him in public and in private. The secretary often overruled Cammerer's decisions, and nearly always criticized the choices of his subordinates. Ickes also controlled the federal relief programs, which played an important role in the development of the Park Service, and its leaders could not risk antagonizing Ickes. As a result, Park Service leadership, once innovative, became more interested in preserving the status quo and ducking beneath the sometimes capricious wrath of Harold Ickes.[27]

Ickes also antagonized others in Washington, and the position of the Park Service suffered as a result. Like others before him, he sought to combine the Park and Forest Services in a Department of Conservation, which he planned to head. The conquest mode of the 1910s had been reversed; now the secretary of the interior was after the secretary of agriculture. The relationship between Ickes and Henry Wallace, the secretary of agriculture, degenerated. As Ickes made plays for the Forest Service, the two departments found themselves in serious rivalry. Franklin D. Roosevelt did not want a fight between the two departments, but with Ickes at the helm, the struggle intensified.[28]

Ironically, Ickes's play for the agency galvanized supporters of the Forest Service in much the same way as Albright rebuilt support in cases like Cedar Breaks. The transfer posed an immense threat to the Forest Service and its constituency. After Stuart's death, Ferdinand Silcox became chief of the Forest Service. Despite his difficulties in dealing with the timber industry, Silcox was a strong leader who supported the ideas of the New Deal. As a result, the Forest Service began to regain the ground it had lost in the scrapes of the late 1920s and 1930s, and the friends of the agency banded together against Ickes's assaults. In 1937 and 1938, the Forest Service lobby, composed of such disparate elements as the Forest Service, the Izaak Walton League, timber- and grazing-industry support organizations, and the American Farm Bureau Federation, fought against the transfer of the Forest Service to Interior: "an avalanche of angry letters and resolutions and letters . . . brought unremitting pressure upon Congress." The support played a major role in influencing conservation policy, and by late 1938, the balance of power had begun to shift away from the Park Service.[29]

Ickes's aggressiveness, Cammerer's ineffectual leadership, and the solid response of the Forest Service and its supporters ended the decade-long advantage of the Park Service. The Jazz Age entity found itself operating in a new cultural arena, an era of massive government intervention that played more to the organizational strengths of the Forest Service than to those of the Park Service. With a powerful and patently vituperative enemy in Ickes, the foresters and their supporters were able to unite in self-defense. Their ability to do so changed the terms of the interagency dispute, moving it from a contest of charismatic styles to one based on the support of vocal constituencies.

Ironically, the characteristics that Mather and Albright had used to build the NPS contributed to the loss of its advantage when that agency became dominant. In an era of economic prosperity, the style of the NPS had considerable appeal; during the Depression, when business bashing again became sport, that flamboyance seemed inappropriate. Fear of Ickes certainly played a significant role; unlike Mather and Albright, Ickes inspired intense personal animosity, and the Park Service received many blows aimed at the secretary.

Perhaps even the successes of the NPS contributed to the loss of its advantage. As the smaller of the two agencies, the Park Service had had to utilize its resources carefully and focus on its objectives. As it succeeded, some of the vitality and vigor became submerged in additional layers of responsibility. The transition from its entrepreneurial stage to one of sustained growth was difficult. The clarity of mission diminished, and as the Park Service grew, it ceased to be the underdog. Its aggressiveness became threatening instead of endearing, ultimately engendering opposition from disparate elements.

The rivalry between the Park and Forest Services has continued in varying forms until the present. Since the 1930s, the agencies have had times of both cooperation and conflict, and at various junctures, both have held distinct advantages. But in many ways, the battle has been a standoff. Each time one side acquires too dramatic an advantage, the supporters of the other mount campaigns to promote their position, and the pendulum gradually swings the opposite way. When it swings too far in either direction, the corrective process again begins.

As the two agencies matured, the differences between them diminished. Their areas of overlapping concern also became smaller, and the direct engagements of earlier years became protracted political maneuvers involving subtlety to the point of obscurity. The dramatic flourishes of the 1920s and early 1930s disappeared along with the concerns and issues of that era.

NOTES

1. Thomas J. Allen, Jr., to Roger Toll, 11 November, 1932, Records of the National Park Service, Record Group 79, Series 7, Cedar Breaks National Monument file 12-5, pt. 1, National Archives, Washington, D.C. Many have discussed the relationship between the Park Service and the Forest Service. Richard Polenberg, *Reorganizing Roosevelt's Government: The Controversy over Executive Reorganization, 1936–1939* (Cambridge, Mass.: Harvard University Press, 1966), 100–122, addresses the relationship during the New Deal; Donald Swain, "Harold Ickes, Horace Albright, and the Hundred Days: A Study in Conservation Administration," *Pacific Historical Review,* November 1965, 455–65, and "The National Park Service and the New Deal, 1933–1940, *Pacific Historical Review,* August 1972, 312–32, discusses the inner workings of the Park Service; Harold K. Steen, *The U.S. Forest Service: A History* (Seattle: University of Washington Press, 1976), 152–61, 209, and Sally K. Fairfax and Samuel T. Dana, *Forest and Range Policy* (New York: McGraw-Hill, 1980), 131–34, 155–57, give the Forest Service view, while Ben W. Twight, *Organizational Values and Political Power: The Forest Service Versus the Olympic National Park* (University Park: Pennsylvania State University Press, 1983), offers ideas about the nature of interagency conflict.

2. Steen, *Forest Service,* 3–103; David A. Clary, *Timber and the Forest Service* (Lawrence: University Press of Kansas, 1986), 1–125, supports this idea by showing the degree to which the original values of the Forest Service permeated the agency as it grew and changed; Thomas G. Alexander, *The Rise of Multiple-Use Management in the Intermountain West: A History of Region 4 of the Forest Service* (Washington, D.C.: United States Department of Agriculture, Forest Service, 1987), 57–100, shows the priorities of the agency in one region.

3. Steen, *Forest Service,* 77.

4. Clary, *Timber and the Forest Service,* 22–26; Steen, *Forest Service,* 78–79.

5. Elers Koch, in *Early Days in the Forest Service* (Missoula, Mont.: Forest Service Northern Region, 1944), 1:109; Steen, *Forest Service,* 76–78, 83n, 98–99.

6. Clarence Swim, in *Early Days in the Forest Service,* 1:196; in *Forest Service,* Steen reveals the ascent of many of the men in question. Earle Clapp is recounted on 137–41, 157, 234–45; Ferdinand Silcox, 198–99; and Leon F. Kneipp, in numerous places. Alexander, *The Rise of Multiple-Use Management,* 57, traces Rutledge, who spent more than a decade in Region 4. Silcox's role as a peer and supporter of vaunted liberal forester Robert "Bob" Marshall is chronicled in James M. Glover and Regina B. Glover, "Robert Marshall: Portrait of a Liberal Forester," *Journal of Forest History,* July 1986, 112–19.

7. Edwin A. Tucker and George Fitzpatrick, *Men Who Matched the Mountains: The Forest Service in the Southwest* (Albuquerque: United States Department of Agriculture, Forest Service Southwestern Region, 1972), 25. The themes of self-reliance and self-sustenance appear repeatedly throughout the letters of early foresters. For countless examples, see *Early Days in the Forest Service.*

8. Clary, *Timber and the Forest Service,* xi.

9. Robert Shankland, *Steve Mather of the National Parks* (New York: Knopf, 1970), is a definitive study of Mather's career in the Park Service.

10. Ibid., 59–60, 95–99.

11. Clary, *Timber and the Forest Service,* 20–27. For an account of Pinchot's promotional activities, see Stephen Ponder, "Gifford Pinchot, Press Agent for Forestry," *Journal of Forest History,* January 1987, 26–35.

12. Horace M. Albright, as told to Robert Cahn, *The Birth of the National Park Service: The Founding Years, 1913–1933* (Salt Lake City: Howe Brothers, 1985), 1–93; Donald C. Swain, *Wilderness Defender* (Chicago: University of Chicago Press, 1970), also discusses the relationship between Mather and Albright; see also Shankland, *Mather,* 72–81, 103–4, 110–13.

13. Shankland, *Mather,* 83–84, 145–49, 157–59; Albright, *Birth of the National Park Service,* 19–21, 27–28, 103–4. John Ise, *Our National Park Policy: A Critical History* (Baltimore: Johns Hopkins University Press, 1961), discusses the achievements of the Mather–Albright team in numerous contexts, while Hal Rothman, "Protected by a Gold Fence with Diamond Tips: A Cultural History of the American National Monuments" (Ph.D diss., University of Texas–Austin, 1985), shows how their actions affected the national monuments.

14. Ise, *Our National Park Policy,* 296–97.

15. The question of who tried to take over whom and when remains largely unresolved. Shankland, *Mather,* 177–78, and Ise, *Our National Park Policy,* 279–82, present the Park Service side of the story—that the Forest Service resisted the establishment of the Park Service and as late as 1927 aggressively sought its acquisition—while Steen, *Forest Service,* 157–58 takes the Forest Service side. Clary, *Timber and the Forest Service,* 72–73, points to Secretary of the Interior Albert B. Fall as the initiator of these battles when he sought to take over the agency in the early 1920s.

16. Clary, *Timber and the Forest Service,* 71–93; Steen, *Forest Service,* 153–60.

17. Albright, *Birth of the National Park Service,* 174–75; Hal Rothman, "Conflict on the Pajarito Plateau: Frank Pinkley, the Forest Service, and the Bandelier National Monument Controversy, 1925–1932," *Journal of Forest History,* April 1985, 68–77;

Robert Righter, *Crucible for Conservation: The Creation of Grand Teton National Park* (Boulder: Colorado Associated University Press, 1982), 35–37.

18. Ise, *Our National Park Policy,* 271–85.

19. Rothman, "Conflict on the Pajarito Plateau." Many of the issues raised during the battle over the Bandelier would reemerge in the dispute over control over what became Olympic National Park; see Twight, *Organizational Values and Political Power.*

20. Frank Pinkley to Arthur E. Demaray, "Report on the Bandelier National Monument, 23 May 1927," Record Group 79, Bandelier National Monument file 12-5, National Archives.

21. Hal Rothman, "Shaping the Nature of a Controversy: The Park Service, the Forest Service, and the Cedar Breaks National Monument," *Utah Historical Quarterly,* Summer 1987, 213–35.

22. United States Forest Service, "Memorandum for the Members of the Coordinating Committee on National Parks and Forests," attached to Acting Forester L. F. Kneipp to Stephen T. Mather, 10 July 1925, Record Group 79, Proposed National Parks file O-32, Cliff Cities, National Archives. In fact, the foresters were correct. Pinkley's plans for a road into Frijoles Canyon predated 1925. Jesse L. Nusbaum to Horace M. Albright, 20 March 1928, Record Group 79, Bandelier National Monument file 12-5, National Archives, reveals the Park Service reaction to the plans of the Forest Service. The announcement came in the Santa Fe *New Mexican,* 3 March 1928. Steen, *Forest Service,* 155, 158–59, and Clary, *Timber and the Forest Service,* 150, support the primary-source documents.

23. Albright, *Birth of the National Park Service,* 232–33, 238–39, 265–68, 280–84.

24. Polenberg, *Reorganizing Roosevelt's Government,* 103–22; Swain, "Ickes, Albright, and the Hundred Days," 455–65.

25. Clary, *Timber and the Forest Service,* 84–89.

26. Steen, *Forest Service,* 196–97. For an account of Stuart under pressure from the Park Service, see Rothman, "Shaping the Nature of a Controversy."

27. Swain, "Ickes, Albright, and the Hundred Days," 455–65; see also Barry Mackintosh, "Harold L. Ickes and the National Park Service," *Journal of Forest History,* April 1985, 78–84. Others agreed with Ickes's assessment of Cammerer. In 1939, Kenneth Chorley, one of John D. Rockefeller, Jr.'s closest confidants and the man who directed Rockefeller's conservation and park work, remarked that he could not "recall seeing any organization decline . . . as much as the Park Service has since Mr. Albright left it"(Righter, *Crucible for Conservation,* 46–47, 104–5).

28. For Ickes's feelings about his attacks on the Department of Agriculture, see *The Secret Diary of Harold L. Ickes: The First Thousand Days, 1933–1936* (New York: Simon and Schuster, 1954), 522–23, 527, 576.

29. Polenberg, *Reorganizing Roosevelt's Government,* 103–22; Glover and Glover, "Robert Marshall," present Silcox's leadership, as does Clary, *Timber and the Forest Service,* 104-6.

Establishing Administrative "Standing": The Sierra Club and the Forest Service, 1897–1956

Susan R. Schrepfer

Because of the high ridges of the southern Sierra Nevada, the moist air off the Pacific Ocean is deposited on the western side, leaving the eastern slope a semiarid land of pumice soils and sagebrush. The forested aprons that spill out where the Sierra crest is low between Mammoth Lakes and Mono Craters are exceptions. They constitute high plateau, alpine country marked by hot springs, waterfalls, glacial moraines, volcanic cones, patches of rare red snow, floating pumice blocks, and glass-like obsidian flows. Irrigated by western rains and glacial waters, these areas, shadowed by the mountains, once held delicate stands of slow-growing lodgepole pine, red fir, and Jeffrey pine—some 400 years old—while the sunny meadows regularly bloomed with purple lupin, Indian paintbrush, blue iris, shooting stars, and an occasional snow plant. One of these oases was located along Deadman Creek in the Inyo National Forest.[1] In the 1950s the United States Forest Service began logging the Deadman area, sparking a controversy that came to involve the Sierra Club, a private, San Francisco–based group formed in 1892 to enjoy and protect California's Sierra Nevada. It may surprise readers familiar with the recent history of adversarial relations between the club and the Forest Service to learn that the federal agency had invited the group's involvement. Why this was so and what the consequences were are the subjects of this chapter.

Samuel P. Hays has argued that the members of such groups as the Sierra Club became attached to public lands by intimate acquaintance with them but were denied a role in devising the policy governing them by the centralizing tendency of modern resource management. To win a voice, according to Hays, they turned initially to legislative politics in the 1960s, only to learn that, because managers had such broad discretion, getting a law passed was merely the first step in achieving their goals. As a result, he noted, "environmental politics shifted in the 1970s from legislation to administration, from broader political debate to management," a development that "was not accepted by administrators with open arms."[2] With few exceptions, statutory

125

recognition of the public's right to a say in public-land-use decisions awaited, as Hays suggests, the demands of activists in the 1960s and 1970s. The significant role that environmentalists have played in public-resource decisions during recent decades, however, built in part upon the involvement of such wilderness groups as the Sierra Club in administrative politics dating back to the turn of the century. Their role also resulted from actions of the federal bureaucracy, which was far from a passive partner in the establishment of citizens' rights to be heard.

Indeed, in the first half of this century citizen activism was a complementary, rather than an antagonistic, development in the evolution of the administrative state. Federal land agencies formally and informally invited the advice of citizen groups. They did so in part because federal law barred them from using public funds to lobby Congress directly in their own behalf.[3] They were also often unable, for political reasons, to defend their own prerogatives. The Sierra Club's most immediate source of involvement in national forest management prior to 1960 was the Forest Service's use of the club as a friendly lobby to increase its congressional appropriations as well as its leverage in dealing with other federal agencies, commodity users, the state, and local interests. As a consequence, club leaders came to have informal, administrative "standing" in national forest management. Standing is traditionally understood to mean that a party has sufficient legal stake in a controversy to obtain judicial resolution of that controversy. It is used here to refer to a right established by custom and procedure and recognized administratively as well as legislatively and judicially. The Forest Service, then, extended to the club the equivalent of "standing" to speak and be heard as a representative of a specific constituency long before that right was provided by law. Evidence suggests this behavior was not unique to the Forest Service and the Sierra Club. Because of the central roles of both within the environmental movement, however, the precedent established by their early interaction—even were it singular—was of national significance.[4]

Faced with local opposition to logging along Deadman Creek, the Forest Service in 1953 asked the Sierra Club to endorse the operation. The service was moving, however, from a policy of custodial management to one of aggressive timber management, a shift that was straining the cooperative spirit on which the use of the club had been premised. The club was changing as well and began to see the service's courting of a clientele relationship as manipulative and dishonest. The Forest Service responded by attempting to limit the organization's role, but it had already established the precedents of public accountability and administrative "standing."

Precedents for the Sierra Club's "standing," solicited and unsolicited, in national forest affairs date back to the 1890s. The group played an informal, advisory role in passage of the 1897 Forest Management Act, establishing the federal Division of Forestry. The division's chief, Gifford Pinchot, asked for and received club support, including endorsement of the transfer of the forest reserves to his division, renamed the Forest Service. In the 1920s, when the agency began encouraging recreational use of the national forests and haltingly initiated a policy of designating areas that were to remain undeveloped, it again sought club support. In 1927 and 1928, Forest Service chief William Greeley directed his regional foresters to map out such areas. "Nothing was said about consulting with private people," S. B. Show, California's regional forester from 1926 to 1946, recalled, "but we felt Sierra Club leaders, with their deep and proper interest, should be consulted and could be helpful." Throughout his tenure, Show and his staff arranged meetings with club leaders. He was a skilled administrator who used such community groups to facilitate the execution of his duties. He also argued that the public had a right to know what federal agencies were doing and that saving wilderness areas was a sound policy, at least insofar as Greeley defined these areas as not including "large areas of presently or imminently commercially exploitable timber" and as compatible with controlled grazing.[5]

In the 1930s a small number of individuals within the service advocated a more vigorous policy of wilderness preservation, and they found in the club a good ally against both external and internal opposition. John Sieker, then with the service's Division of Recreation, later recalled that the club and other such organizations helped counter the antiwilderness pressure from lumber and mining interests and the United States Chamber of Commerce, so that the service had "groups that were for us as well as against us." Robert Marshall, chief of the Recreation Division in Washington and a founder of the Wilderness Society, met in 1937 with club president Joel Hildebrand to form a committee to study ways in which the service could better manage the Sierra Nevada; the club responded with a detailed report to the committee.[6]

With the encouragement of such individuals, the Forest Service refined and expanded its wilderness policies. In 1938 service officials attended a board meeting of the Sierra Club to explain use or "U-Regulations" that the agency planned to adopt for establishing sizes and designations for wilderness, wild, and primitive areas. In these areas, roads, settlement, and economic development would be restricted. There were some 1.7 million acres so designated. Wilderness and wild areas, although not primitive areas, could be modified or reclassified only after a ninety-day public notice, with a public hearing to be held if protests were registered. A service representative also asked the directors to appoint a standing committee to be available to discuss Sierra Nevada management. "We want to keep active," he said, "and current consultations with you in the picture and probably a small committee of your older and more experienced members would facilitate such contacts. We have in mind, too," he added, "that an annual meeting between your committee and the supervisors concerned is a very useful means of keeping in close touch with each other. I am sure you understand that what we

want is entire freedom on your part to initiate discussions on policies or practices at any time and to keep the way open for systematic re-examination at
relatively frequent intervals."[7] In discussing the U-Regulations before their
passage and inviting sustained club advice thereafter, the Forest Service established informal administrative precedents. When it adopted the regulations
in 1939, the agency formally offered citizens a voice, albeit only through
public hearings held at its discretion.

The Forest Service had a political goal in cultivating the Sierra Club's support at this time: to forestall attempts to transfer scenic areas under its jurisdiction to the National Park Service. The 1938 overtures to the club owed
much to the Gearhart bill, which called for transferring Kings Canyon from
the Forest to the Park Service. Secretary of Agriculture Henry Wallace, par-
tially in response to pressure from President Franklin D. Roosevelt, had
barred Forest Service personnel from publicly opposing this legislation.
Regional Forester Show and his staff violated at least the spirit of the ban by
appearing before any organization that sought their views on wilderness policies and the proposed transfer. According to Show, they were "aggressive,
adroit, and enormously successful in obtaining public support." No doubt
their solicitation of club advice on management of the Sierra Nevada, which
included the projected Kings Canyon Park, was part of this campaign. On
this occasion, they were successful, for the club voted to oppose the change
of jurisdiction.[8]

That same year, however, Park Service regional director Frank Kittredge
took some Sierra Club leaders to the Kings Canyon area and questioned them
about their opposition to the Gearhart bill. He asked them why they had
declined to support the park legislation. Secretary of the Interior Harold Ickes
then met with the club's directors and obtained their endorsement of the bill
by assuring them that Kings Canyon would remain wilderness. The club's
members lobbied Congress in support of the measure, spending $2,100 on
the campaign and circulating to the public a pamphlet entitled *The Kings
River Region Should Be a National Park*.[9] David Brower, in 1939 editor of
the *Sierra Club Bulletin* and chairman of the club's San Francisco Bay Chapter, came away with a distaste for the Forest Service's manipulation of public opinion, but in truth both agencies had used his organization for political
leverage in their battle, and with success. Although the club endorsed the
Kings Canyon National Park bill, which became law in 1940, the Forest Service's overtures strengthened relations with the club in general.[10]

During the interwar years, club members sat on Forest Service advisory
boards and the agency's national personnel acted as honorary vice presidents
of the club. Show joined the club during his first year in office, as did most
regional personnel; was appointed an honorary official in 1937; and used the
club's bulletin to explain forest-management plans and invite readers to contribute their opinions.[11] The service sponsored trips allowing members to see

firsthand how policies were applied in the field. Regional personnel also helped arrange and attended the conventions of the Federation of Western Outdoor Clubs, with which the club was affiliated. In 1939 the forester in charge of Tahoe National Forest and Robert Marshall participated in the federation's Lake Tahoe convention and successfully urged its affiliates to lobby Congress for increases in the service's budget, to endorse the U-Regulations, and to oppose the transfer of national forest recreational areas to the Park Service.[12]

Cooperative interaction between the Forest Service and the Sierra Club lessened during the war, but resumed upon its conclusion. In the mid-1940s, Bestor Robinson, club director and member of the service's advisory board, was among those supporting development of a ski resort in the San Gorgonio Primitive Area in southern California. The plan necessitated redrawing the area's boundaries, and in 1947 Forest Service personnel took club representatives on an inspection tour. Shortly thereafter, James Gilson from the regional office personally solicited the views of the club's board members. After debate, the board voted its opposition. The service then held hearings at which wilderness advocates outnumbered skiers. A few months later, Chief Lyle Watts abandoned the proposal.[13] The episode demonstrated strong, informal interaction between the agency and the club.

This cooperative spirit grew in the late 1940s. By 1948 Regional Forester Pat A. Thompson was not only attending club meetings regularly but participating in each gathering as well. He spoke often about the inadequacy of his agency's appropriations, which he said had declined 35 percent in purchasing power because of wartime inflation. The board responded by urging a vigorous campaign of support. In 1949 the club sent its president, Francis Farquhar, to Washington, D.C., to discuss with the secretary of agriculture and Chief Lyle Watts another matter: the loss of agricultural and forestlands in the national forests to dams. Farquhar reported back that such contacts increased club effectiveness. Because dams located on national forestlands were controlled by the Department of the Interior and Congress, such meetings also had the potential to increase the political effectiveness of the Forest Service, which could call on the Sierra Club to lobby against building dams on national forestlands.[14]

For the Forest Service, this cultivation of a clientele relationship resulted in not only such immediate objectives as Sierra Club testimony at specific hearings but also general support from the organization in the 1940s and early 1950s. Even the exceptions were handled carefully. In orchestrating opposition to the service's plans for San Gorgonio, Brower advised, "Let's be fair and logical in whatever protest we make." Moreover, to help the service find an alternative site to San Gorgonio, the club endorsed a ski resort in Mineral King, a less than totally pristine national forest area in the Sierra Nevada. Club leaders favored the Forest Service over the Park Service in nonwilderness recreational administration. They argued as well that the Forest Service protected wilderness more effectively than did the Park Service. Kings Canyon, the wild character of which Secretary Ickes had personally guaranteed, was the exception. In the case of the Oregon and Washington Cascades, they opposed proposals to transfer scenic national forest wildernesses to the Park Service.[15]

They did so despite awareness that the protection afforded these wild lands was limited. Since the first wilderness and primitive areas had been established, the Sierra Club had recognized that the Forest Service could reclassify them at will. More important, they knew that since the Department of the Interior administered all federal mining laws, the Forest Service could not stop mining on its own wilderness and primitive areas once claims had been recognized by Interior. For these reasons, through the 1940s and early 1950s the club endorsed the Wilderness Society's campaign for a national system of wilderness areas guaranteed by statute.[16]

Since Forest Service officials occasionally urged them to lobby for federal wilderness laws, club leaders did not see this endorsement as antagonistic to the agency. As he designated eight primitive areas in California in 1933, S. B. Show had told them that stronger laws were needed to protect these areas against mining authorized by Interior.[17] In 1950 the club tried to prevent a mining road in the very scenic Mount Dana–Minarets Wild Area by urging its inclusion in the National Park Service's Devils Postpile National Monument, but with the proviso that the Forest Service continue to administer the area. It was only the agency's lack of legal authority to restrict mineral claims, explained club members, that necessitated the transfer. The club's position on the Mount Dana–Minarets Wild Area is an example of why its members believed that wilderness legislation would strengthen the service's hand in dealing with commodity users.[18] It is also an example of the success of the Forest Service's efforts to court the club.

Through the first years of the 1950s, this pattern of cordial relations intensified. Service personnel continued to attend the Sierra Club's board meetings. They spoke of the need for an increased budget. In 1950 Thompson discussed with the board state and local proposals for trans-Sierra roads and a Mount San Jacinto tramway. In 1951 the board concurred with a suggestion by agency personnel that it sponsor the Institute of Forest Genetics to improve and restock the national forests. It also agreed to lobby against legislation that would strengthen the livestock interests in relation to the service.[19]

In the summer of 1952, Richard McArdle became the chief forester, replacing Lyle Watts. After America's entry into World War II, the Forest Service had begun increasing dramatically the timber yield from the western national forests. In the summer of 1950, the Korean War had further accelerated the demand for national forest lumber and roads, and McArdle continued the service's efforts to meet this growing demand. The agency began to reclassify its western primitive areas as wilderness areas. The reclassification promised greater protection, but it also held the potential for boundary changes that would release additional resources for development. The club endorsed the process but asked for a list of the boundaries that were not yet permanent so its members could familiarize themselves with them in advance of the final surveys.[20] The service provided the list in the hope that such cooperation would, as in the past, forestall opposition from the club as well as local political and economic interests.

The reclassification of the Middle Eel-Yolla Bolly Primitive Area in California's Trinity County proved the wisdom of the service's policy. The area encompassed private timber of sufficient value to justify construction of access roads for nearby mills. Late in 1952 service personnel explained to the club that creation of a consolidated wilderness area required turning the large timbered portion over to local companies in exchange for nontimbered private lands. In addition, they recommended selectively logging the remaining primitive area prior to reclassification. The club approved their plans, including the land exchange, which was opposed by a local state senator. The senator changed his mind at the club's behest, an act for which the service expressed its thanks. That same year, agency personnel also successfully solicited club approval to revise the boundaries of southern California's Devil Canyon–Bear Canyon Primitive Area to route a highway down its border. They later replicated this success when they invited club representatives to participate in the field surveys for changes in the boundaries of the Marble Mountain Primitive Area, a superb piece of low mountain country in the Klamath National Forest. When the regional office offered a ninety-day "publication period" during which objections could be made, a procedure not required for primitive area reclassifications, the club approved the procedure and the new boundaries.[21]

In a similarly cooperative vein the following year, Regional Forester Clare Hendee obtained the Sierra Club's support for several appropriation bills before Congress. He also described an application pending before the Department of the Interior for oil and gas exploration on national forest property near Santa Barbara. The service opposed the application, he explained, and noted that the Interior Department would soon hold local public hearings on the issue and encouraged club members to testify against the proposed drilling. He went on to describe legislation sponsored by Montana congressman Wesley D'Ewart to strengthen stockmen's rights in the national forests. Conservation groups nationally, including the club, opposed the bill, but for political reasons the service did so unofficially. Hendee asked club members to testify against the grazing interests at upcoming congressional hearings on the bill.[22]

At a club board meeting in Los Angeles later that same year, Forest Service representatives discussed the financial problems caused by the growing recreational use of California's national forests, thanked the club for efforts

to increase congressional funding, and explained the need for more appropriations. The supervisor of the Inyo National Forest, a club member, asked
the board to fight local opposition to a proposed White Mountain natural
area, which would protect a stand of ancient bristlecone pine, and urged it
to endorse a plan to enlarge the Hoover Wild Area near Tioga Pass. The club
voiced its encouragement of these and other service efforts to preserve wilderness and asked the service to initiate creation of an alpine Boundary Peak
wild area in the White Mountains.[23] This meeting in Los Angeles, then, evi-
denced the cooperative spirit that had characterized interaction between the
club and the service since the turn of the century. After 1952, however, this
relationship would become increasingly antagonistic.

One of the first occasions for hostility involved a pine forest along Highway 395 near Mammoth Lakes on the eastern slope of the Sierra Nevada.
Originally this forest, the trees of which were so neatly placed as to resem-
ble a park, extended through the watersheds of Dry, Glass, and Deadman
Creeks. These stands were part of Inyo National Forest multiuse lands and
within what the service called the Owens Cutting Circle. In 1952 logging had
begun along Glass Creek under a Forest Service–let contract. John Haddaway, who operated a small manufacturing business in Mammoth Lakes
making tiny pumps, protested, citing the area's scenic assets and the local
economy's dependence on revenue generated by outdoor recreation. He discussed with the National Park Service the establishment of an Inyo Craters
National Monument to protect the Inyo and Mono volcanic craters as well
as the nearby forested oases.[24]

Forest Service personnel conceded the area's recreational value but argued
that removal of dead or dying trees was necessary to control pine rust and
pine and fire beetles. Haddaway objected, insisting that the agency's own chief
pathologist had told him the infestation was mild, had always been present,
and represented no danger. To corroborate his assertion, Haddaway hired an
independent entomologist who concluded that the forest was "one of the
healthiest" he had ever seen. Haddaway also claimed to have photographs of
the area twenty years earlier showing that the condition of the forest was
unchanged. In addition, he argued that due to the pumice-type soil, high alti-
tudes, and dryness, regrowth would be very slow. The Glass Creek logging
operation, he observed, was far heavier than that which the agency had
promised. Moreover, he charged that the lumbermen's failure to clear up the
slash left behind after the logging had encouraged the spread of the pine
engraver beetle, fouled the stream, and destroyed recreational values.[25]

To quiet the controversy, the Forest Service held a public hearing near
Mammoth and sponsored a field trip to the sites that had been logged and
those scheduled for cutting. According to Haddaway, the hearing was
"stacked" with service "invitees, who made speeches for the Forest Service
plan." Agency officials, he noted, had not been able to show evidence of dis-

ease or infestations on the trip, and their "falsifications on rust and beetle were pretty well known." When the United States Bureau of Entomology reportedly detected abnormal insect activity, he accused the bureau and service of "collusion." When a district ranger told a local chamber of commerce that diseased trees had to be eliminated, Haddaway charged the service with "strategic deceit," claiming its officers "habitually infiltrate local service clubs, as well as conservation clubs," making "whitewashing speeches" and building up the public's confidence in their intentions. "They become," he continued, "club officers and attend meetings regularly, so that trouble for them can be averted at the start by a soothing word"; at campgrounds they "disseminate propaganda" and are the picture of a "benevolent bureau."[26]

A Forest Service official brought the Mammoth controversy to the attention of the Sierra Club's directors in May 1953. He assured them that the logging represented sound management and invited them to take a service-guided tour of the area. Six months before, the club had appointed David R. Brower, long associated with the organization, as its first executive director; his responsibilities included implementing board directives, preparing recommendations, supervising publications, administering the organization, and serving as its spokesman. Brower contacted Haddaway and in August 1953 submitted a report to the board that implied the club had been deceived. He said that the service had admitted to him it could not get a contract from commercial operators to cut only dying trees. He showed Haddaway's photographs of the heavily cut Glass Creek. The directors were mute on the implication of duplicity but had already suggested to the Forest and Park Services that disease, infestations, and fire be allowed to follow their natural courses in parks and wildernesses. They told Brower to accept the invitations to see the area.[27]

The service had found that such a "show-me" trip often resulted in Sierra Club support. In this case it did not. Brower arrived before the scheduled field trip for a tour by Haddaway of the cutting along Glass Creek, where he found extensive debris and slash left on the forest floor by the loggers. On the following day, service personnel showed him "some very modest little piles, very carefully worked over, and said, 'This is what John Haddaway is complaining about.'" Brower later exclaimed: "Of course it wasn't. It was something that had been tidied up for the little show-me tour. It had nothing to do with the destruction, which they were not showing me at all." Brower also visited Deadman Creek, the service having just announced it was going to allow a similar cutting operation there. The new Dwight D. Eisenhower administration had just charged the Forest Service with implementing fuller utilization of the nation's resources, perhaps encouraging the extension of logging in the Mammoth Lakes area. A few days after his tour, Brower joined Haddaway for a meeting with the regional forester in San Francisco, who emphasized that diseased or dying trees might fall on recreationists using the Deadman Creek area, who would then sue the agency.[28]

Brower related his experiences to the club's board and also described the "extraordinary" scenic and recreational values of the Deadman area, which if not of great size or quality was still a "jewel" along a major highway. In addition, he believed it held the finest stand of Jeffrey pine left on the Pacific coast, a stand nurtured only by the "lowness of the Sierra Crest" and the "moist air" flowing east. The American Museum of Natural History had studied these pines in order to create a $50,000 diorama for display in New York City. A 60 to 65 percent cut, such as he claimed the Glass Creek area had sustained, would destroy the rare natural, scenic, and recreational values.[29]

Meanwhile, having failed to dissuade regional officials from a course Brower and he now agreed would be a mistake, Haddaway appealed to the secretary of agriculture. In the fall of 1954, Chief Forester Richard McArdle ordered an investigation of the site. That December he announced it would be cut. He recognized its recreational value but noted that the area had only one modern band sawmill, built for private timber but now "dependent upon national forest timber." Lumbering was minor in the local economy but important for diversity. The pine stands along Deadman Creek were "over-mature and decadent," "degenerating rapidly," and filled with an "unusually large number of dead and dying trees." The public, he argued, needed a healthy and attractive forest such as the mature stands of Jeffrey pine that the Forest Service had set aside in the 1,000-acre Indian Summit Natural Area, a few miles east of Deadman Creek. Logging along Dry and Glass Creeks, McArdle conceded, had "not adequately protected its recreational values. In view of the recreational potential that we now see, it would have been better to cut more lightly and to have made more complete clean-up after cutting." He assured both Haddaway and the Sierra Club that recreation would be the primary use of the Deadman area and that the only trees cut would be those that were insect-infested, diseased, hazards to human safety, of poor thrift, overmature, or with a life expectancy of less than ten years. The service would ensure that logging would be done with care.[30]

Brower was not convinced. At his suggestion, Hal Roth of the Outdoor Writers Association of America in early 1955 submitted for publication in the *Sierra Club Bulletin* an article on the history of the controversy. The essay told of the service's supposed "misinformation" and "conflicting statements"; summarized its vacillation, "falsification of the facts and the well-known run around"; and described how mechanical equipment had torn up the loose pumice soil of Glass and Dry Creeks. Roth maintained that steep slopes had been logged, eliminating streamside camping and leaving ugly piles of slash to invite pests and fire. In addition, he drew attention to McArdle's concession that the operation had failed to protect recreational values, and he challenged the explanations given for the operation: disease and insect infestations were mild; the area held only 3,000 acres of commercially inferior wood that would be used for packing boxes; there would be no gain to the United States Treasury; and regrowth would be slow. The essay quoted Brower as claiming that the assistant United States attorney general had told him that minor changes in service regulations would end government liability for visitors injured by falling trees and limbs.[31]

Because the service was under "great pressures" to produce timber for revenue, argued Roth, the logging along Deadman Creek had produced "a major crisis." The Deadman area, he concluded, should be placed in a land-use category that excluded all logging. In the meantime, an "impartial umpire" should be appointed by the Forest Service to redefine recreation policies, and no cutting should be allowed near Mammoth until such action had been taken. Roth threatened that if the Forest Service did not respond to these demands, the Sierra Club would lobby for the transfer of the Deadman Creek area to National Park Service jurisdiction. Although Brower later claimed he had not intended to publish Roth's article, he circulated the page proofs among officers of the club and cooperating organizations "to get a reaction." Objections by the club's directors precluded the article's publication in the bulletin, but the essay came to the attention of the Forest Service. Brower claimed to be shocked to find the proofs "immediately on the Forest Service's desk" and identified the culprit as the American Forestry Association, confirming, he claimed, that foresters were "not going to help the Sierra Club." In his mind, the incident demonstrated the manipulative nature of the service.[32]

Four months later—in response, Brower claimed, to Roth's article—McArdle forwarded to his agency's regional foresters the draft of a new policy statement in which he cautioned that since local people "often build up a sentimental attachment" to heavily used recreation sites, "public opinion must be carefully considered" in the management of such areas. The public had to be educated about the need to remove trees that were diseased or not growing well. Damage to residual stands and soil must be minimized; the objective was not to be timber receipts. He warned against increasing beyond the level of sound management the timber allowed to the private company given the contract to do the logging, or what he called "sweetening the cut." "Many people," he wrote, "like big timber. . . . [T]o some a large, overmature, spiked-topped, catfaced, conky, old veteran is magnificent" and more desirable than "clear-boled trees" with high annual growth rates. Several months later, the regional forester in California forwarded to the club a copy of the draft. The Sierra Club's new conservation committee chairman, Edgar Wayburn, described it as "a major victory"—one that had resulted from the Deadman Creek controversy.[33]

That fall a Forest Service representative assured the Sierra Club's directors that only infected trees would be removed from the Deadman Creek area and that a timber sale was necessary. The director commended the service for its "enlightened policy in the preservation of aesthetic values in recreational areas." The agency responded by inviting board members on another show-me tour. The following June, several club leaders inspected the trees marked for cutting along Deadman Creek and toured the Glass Creek watershed. They reported that service personnel were "cordial and patient" and the plan was acceptable.[34]

Brower fired off indignant letters to the members of the board asserting that the number of trees marked were not commensurate with McArdle's proposed policy, which had suggested removal of hazardous trees only. The final plan indicated, he said, a 30 percent cut, little different from what the service had initially proposed and not significantly better than that which had taken place at Glass Creek. He claimed that those club leaders who had inspected the area had accepted a weak compromise in the hope of avoiding conflict. He maintained that the club had never discussed fully the issue of Deadman Creek and had no policy on logging in recreation areas largely because Forest Service officials had been present at all board meetings. The club should tell the service, he said, that experts disagreed on the risk from infestations, and while such infestations "have come and gone . . . the forest has remained, strengthened, conceivably, by its adversity, for all these thousands of years since the lava cooled over the moraines that lie half a mile beneath the Jeffreys." Deadman Creek was ideal for recreation, according to Brower, because of the availability of water, its proximity to southern California, flat camping sites, park-like forest, the Inyo craters, glass-like obsidian flows, and the "backdrop of the Sierra Crest." The area could provide an "everyman's wilderness experience . . . where indoctrination for big wilderness" could take place.[35]

Brower maintained that the need to remove diseased trees was a weak argument, since the foresters did not intend to touch infected areas near heavy recreation sites and on slopes. Indeed, he accused them "of blatant dishonesty" in using the presence of disease to justify their plans. He argued that figures on logging in the Owens Cutting Circle would demonstrate that the Deadman area was being cut merely to prolong the life of the Inyo Lumber Company, which would otherwise run out of timber in two or three years. He pointed out that infestations could be used to justify cutting in parks and wildernesses as well as recreation areas.[36]

The club members who had taken the tour of the Deadman area felt that Brower was being unfair in his criticism. One of them, Alex Hildebrand, acknowledged that the service had vacillated in the past, but foresters, he insisted, were "able, sincere, dedicated" and not "two-faced." They had drafted a policy the club had "applauded." Although he was skeptical of the effectiveness of their rust- and beetle-control methods, he believed the club had to accept logging in recreation areas. Art Blake, another member of the tour, argued that service personnel had admitted the "errors of their original cutting" and the club should now "allow them to make good." When the issue came before the club's executive committee in July, however, Brower prevailed. "Serious doubts [exist] as to the wisdom or the necessity of the degree of cutting proposed," concluded the committee.[37]

The club communicated its concern to Regional Forester Charles Connaughton, who responded somewhat obliquely that with "on-the-ground reviews," such as that on which the service had taken club leaders, all misunderstandings "melt away." Club secretary Lewis Clark shot back that Connaughton misunderstood the club's message; the group had expressed "serious doubts" about the logging and expected a response. "We were not trying to sell the policy on the ground," Connaughton retorted, "but rather showing you the application of the policy." The discourse ended in the summer of 1956 when the Deadman Creek watershed was logged. Both Forest Service officials and Sierra Club leaders would in retrospect view the first half century as a golden age in their relations. Until midcentury, the service did not see the club as powerful or adversarial. S. B. Show later told the club, "I felt that your leaders of those days took my word at face value and certainly I had no question regarding their integrity. We might and did disagree on issues but did so like gentlemen." Club leader Michael McCloskey recalled that foresters active between the 1920s and the early 1950s, as epitomized by Watts, came out of the Pinchot tradition of custodial management and were superior to their replacements, who had an "overwhelming commitment to manipulation and management." After 1956 the service continued its shift from a policy of custodial management to one of aggressive timber management. That and Brower's growing prominence within the Sierra Club would make the service's cultivation of the club as a friendly lobby increasingly difficult. As a result, there were controversies between the club and the service in the mid- and later 1950s over other sites—the Sierra Nevada's Kern Plateau, the Three Sisters and Waldo Lakes areas in the Oregon Cascades, and sites in the Washington Cascades. Brower would later say of Deadman Creek, however, "[T]hat's the place my disillusionment with the Forest Service began in earnest. I had been apprehensive in the Kings [Canyon] battle, but here I saw just out-and-out distortion and trickery."[38]

Although the Sierra Club and the Forest Service failed to harmonize their views about Deadman Creek, their interaction over the years had established a powerful precedent—a precedent in which the agency had played a major role. By 1956 the service's practice of soliciting the views of an activist organization such as the Sierra Club had become routine policy. Citizen groups now sought statutory recognition of their role in national forest management. At the request of the Wilderness Society, the Sierra Club, and the Natural Resources Council of America—the last comprised the nation's leading citizen groups in conservation—Senator Hubert Humphrey introduced in 1956 a bill to extend congressional protection to federal wilderness areas. At their request, he included a provision for a "council of interested outside parties" to advise the federal agencies in the administration of these areas.

That same year, Humphrey also sponsored, at the Forest Service's request, a bill officially recognizing that the service's authority had expanded from forest and watershed protection to management of grazing, mining, wildlife, and recreation on national forest lands. The Natural Resources Council—of which Brower was an officer and the Sierra Club a member—lobbied to include a clause providing for citizen advisory councils with authority to make policy recommendations to the secretary of agriculture.[39] Club leaders said little about precedents for such councils, suggesting theirs was less a theoretically justified claim than an assumed right.

Congress did not pass these first bills, and the final versions enacted in 1960 and 1964 did not provide for citizen councils. But the Wilderness Act of 1964, as well as other legislation in the 1960s and 1970s, guaranteed public access to policy makers through hearings. The 1956 bills, then, represented a coalescing of views linking the early informal voice of select, outside parties to statutorily guaranteed public participation. In turn, that statutory recognition served as precedent for citizen groups to obtain standing to sue, or the right to raise an issue in the courts. As Samuel P. Hays has shown, the use of the courts in the fight for environmental protection "was facilitated by provisions in environmental statutes . . . [whereby] citizens could bring legal action against administrators who failed to carry out the law." Moreover, in establishing judicial standing to sue in the 1970s, the Sierra Club and other citizen groups cited, in addition to legislative intent, their political, recreational, as well as administrative involvement in public land management dating back to the early twentieth century.[40]

Because many of those studying citizens' participation in environmental politics have looked only at statutorily and judicially recognized standing, they have seen this participation as solely a product of the 1960s and pressure from activists themselves. Hays has amply demonstrated that the achievement of effective standing required winning the cooperation of resource managers in the administration, but he argues this came only in the 1970s. The Sierra Club's involvement in public land management was, however, quite clearly not solely a phenomenon of the 1970s or even of the post–World War II period. Moreover, in the late nineteenth and first half of the twentieth century at least some sectors of the nation's developing bureaucracies promoted the interest and expertise of such citizens' groups. Individuals within the Forest Service turned to the Sierra Club for support in realizing stronger wilderness policies. For the most part, however, service personnel used the club to increase their leverage in dealing with other agencies, local and state interests, commodity users, and Congress. This administrative behavior illustrates the principle that in order to expand their responsibilities and budgets, public agencies must "depend upon mobilizing support from an attentive and vocal public."[41] But if citizen activism was in part the product of the emergence of the administrative state, there was a confusion inherent in the relationship between the activists and the state. The Sierra Club was promoted by (and itself promoted) a national, professional bureaucracy devoted to forest management. At the same time, it represented a tradition of voluntarism, localism, and wilderness protection. The paradox of the association between the federal agency and the citizens' group existed as early as the nineteenth century but became more apparent in the second half of this century, forcing the Sierra Club and similar organizations to fight for statutory and judicial guarantees of their voice.

NOTES

1. For descriptions of Deadman Creek, see David R. Brower, "Environmental Activist, Publicist, and Prophet," 84, interview with Susan Schrepfer, 1978, Sierra Club Papers, Bancroft Library, University of California, Berkeley; and Martin Litton [club activist and travel editor for *Sunset* magazine], "Deadman Creek" (n.d.), box 137, Martin Litton Papers, Bancroft Library.

2. Samuel P. Hays, *Beauty, Health, and Permanence: Environmental Politics in the United States, 1955–1985* (Cambridge, Mass.: Harvard University Press, 1987), 393, 473; Samuel P. Hays, "Human Choice in Great Lakes Wildlands," in *The Great Lakes Forest*, ed. Susan Flader (Minneapolis: University of Minnesota Press, 1983), 301. Roderick Nash similarly suggested that the activists, having begun by defending areas they loved, moved in the 1950s to protect wilderness in the abstract. See Nash, *Wilderness and the American Mind*, rev. ed. (New Haven, Conn.: Yale University Press, 1973), 222.

3. 18 U.S.C. 1913.

4. On standing, see *Black's Law Dictionary*, 5th ed. (St. Paul, Minn.: West, 1979), 1260–61. The Forest Service and the National Park Service also cultivated clientele relationships with the Wilderness Society, the Federation of Outdoors Clubs, the Save-the-Redwoods League, the National Parks Association, and the New Mexico Game Protective Association (NMGPA).

5. S. Bevier Show, "National Forests in California," 159–60, 162, 163–64, 198, interview with Amelia Roberts Fry, 1965, Sierra Club Papers.

6. John H. Sieker, "Recreation Policy and Administration in the U.S. Forest Service," 19, interview with Amelia Roberts Fry, 1968, Sierra Club Papers; James M. Glover, *A Wilderness Original: The Life of Bob Marshall* (Seattle: Mountaineers Press, 1986), 145–46, 191, 204, 220–21, 232–33, 253–54, 264; Sierra Club, Board of Directors, minutes, 7 May 1938, Sierra Club Papers.

7. Sierra Club, Board of Directors, minutes, 7 May and 8 October 1938.

8. On Forest Service–Park Service rivalry, see Glover, *Wilderness Original*, 94–95; Hal K. Rothman, " 'A Regular Ding-Dong Fight': The Dynamics of Park Service–Forest Service Controversy During the 1920s and 1930s" [this volume]; Show, "National Forests in California," 200; and *Sierra Club Bulletin*, August 1938, 88–89. For the club's position, see *Sierra Club Bulletin*, February 1939, i–vi.

9. Sierra Club, Board of Directors, minutes, 14 October 1938, reported in *Sierra Club Bulletin*, October 1939, xxxv; Brower, "Environmental Activist," 19; Frank A.

Kittredge, "The Campaign for Kings Canyon National Park," *Sierra Club Bulletin,* December 1960, 32–46; William Colby, "Status of Kings Canyon National Park," August 1939, *Sierra Club Bulletin,* 11; Douglas Strong, *Trees or Timber? The Story of Sequoia and Kings Canyon National Parks* (Three Rivers, Calif.: Sequoia National History Association, in cooperation with National Park Service, 1968); Glover, *Wilderness Original,* 234.

10. Brower, "Environmental Activist," 43; Sierra Club, Board of Directors, minutes, 7 May 1938, 6 May 1939; *Sierra Club Bulletin,* April 1939, xvi; 3 June 1938, ix; April 1940, 11.

11. S. B. Show, "Primitive Areas in the National Forests of California," *Sierra Club Bulletin,* Februrary 1933, 24–30.

12. Federation of Western Outdoor Clubs, minutes, 2–3 September 1939, in *Sierra Club Bulletin,* October 1939, xxxvii–xl; Federation of Western Outdoor Clubs, minutes, 1 September 1945, Minute Books, folder 45, Sierra Club Office, San Francisco.

13. *Sierra Club Bulletin,* January 1947, 10; February 1947, 3–4; July 1947, 3–4; Sierra Club, Board of Directors, minutes, 6 May 1950. In 1956 the service reclassified San Gorgonio as a wild area.

14. Sierra Club, Board of Directors, minutes, 27 November 1948, 5 February 1949.

15. *Sierra Club Bulletin,* February 1947, 3; Susan R. Schrepfer, "Perspectives on Conservation: Sierra Club Strategies in Mineral King," *Journal of Forest History* 20 (1976): 176–91. In 1947 the club endorsed legislation to transfer the Shasta Dam Recreation Area from the Park to the Forest Service. See Sierra Club, Board of Directors, minutes, 31 August 1947; Richard M. Leonard, "Mountaineer, Lawyer, Environmentalist," 2:251–52, interview with Susan R. Schrepfer, 1975, Sierra Club Papers.

16. Art Blake to Robert Sterling Yard, 25 February 1942; Blake to Howard Zahniser, 29 December 1950, box 112, Art Blake Papers, Bancroft Library.

17. Show, "Primitive Areas in the National Forests of California."

18. Sierra Club, Board of Directors, minutes, 4 February 1950; Blake to Zahniser, 29 December 1950.

19. Sierra Club, Board of Directors, minutes, 31 August 1952; 2 September 1951; 3 May 1952; 4 February 1950; 5 May 1951; for San Jacinto, see Sierra Club, Board of Directors, minutes, 4 February 1950; 5 May and 10 November 1951.

20. David A. Clary, *Timber and the Forest Service* (Lawrence: University Press of Kansas, 1986), 119; Harold K. Steen, *The U.S Forest Service: A History* (Seattle: University of Washington Press, 1976), 283–284; Sierra Club, Board of Directors, minutes, 8 November 1952.

21. Sierra Club Board of Directors, minutes, 8 November 1952; 17 October 1953; 31 August 1952; 8 November 1952.

22. Sierra Club, Board of Directors, minutes, 2 May 1953. For background on the Uniform Federal Grazing Bill, see Steen, *Forest Service,* 275–76.

23. Sierra Club, Board of Directors, minutes, 17 October 1953.

24. Litton, "Deadman Creek"; Brower, "Environmentalist Activist," 84. Dry Creek had been logged in 1946 without protest from the club. See Peggy Wayburn and Edgar Wayburn, "The Fate of Deadman Creek," *Sierra Club Bulletin,* October 1956, 5–9.

25. John Haddaway to District Ranger Barney Sweatt, 16 August 1952; Haddaway, "Chronology of Statements on Rust and Beetles by Forest Service" (n.d.), box 137, Litton Papers; "Sierra Club—Confidential Draft Only," 16 February 1955; Haddaway to Sweatt, 16 August 1952; Richard McArdle to John Haddaway, 20 December 1954.

26. *Inyo Register* [Bishop, Calif.], 8 October 1953; Haddaway, "Chronology of Statements on Rust and Beetles."

27. Sierra Club, Board of Directors, minutes, 2 May 1953; *Sierra Club Bulletin,* January 1953, 3–4; Sierra Club, Board of Directors, minutes, 5 December 1952; 16 August 1953.

28. Brower, "Environmental Activist," 84. On Eisenhower's partnership policies, see George Van Dusen, "The Politics of 'Partnership': The Eisenhower Administration and Conservation, 1952–1960" (Ph.D. diss., Loyola University, 1974), 253, 285–91; Haddaway, "Chronology of Statements on Rust and Beetles"; "Sierra Club— Confidential Draft Only," 10.

29. Sierra Club, Board of Directors, minutes, 20 June 1954; 2 February and 20 November 1955; Brower, "Environmental Activist," 84; "Sierra Club—Confidential Draft Only."

30. Richard McArdle to John Haddaway; McArdle to Sierra Club, 20 December 1954, box 137, Litton Papers.

31. "Sierra Club—Confidential Draft Only," and cover letter from Brower, 16 February 1955, box 5, David Brower Papers, Bancroft Library. The page proofs did not indicate authorship. Brower, "Environmental Activist," 85.

32. "'Sierra Club—Confidential Draft Only," and Brower cover letter; Brower, "Environmental Activist," 85.

33. Richard McArdle to regional foresters, 21 June 1955, box 175; comments, 17 October 1955, attached to McArdle to regional foresters, 21 June 1955; Edgar Wayburn to Charles Connaughton, 21 December 1955, Sierra Club Papers.

34. Sierra Club, Board of Directors, minutes, 15 October 1955; 20 November 1955; Alex Hildebrand, "Memorandum Dead Man Creek Recreation Area," 18 June 1956, box 114, Harold Bradley Papers, Bancroft Library.

35. David Brower to Alex Hildebrand, Harold Bradley, and Edgar Wayburn, 27 June 1956, and Brower to Bradley, 5 July 1956; Brower to Edgar Wayburn, 28 June 1956, box 175, Sierra Club Papers.

36. Brower to Wayburn, 28 June 1956; Brower, "Environmental Activist," 84, 93, 84, 86; see also Sierra Club, Board of Directors, minutes, 20 November 1955; Sierra Club, Conservation Committee Report, 13 September 1955; David Brower, "Logging Operations Mammoth Lakes Area," 16 February 1955, Minute Books, folder 1319, Sierra Club Office; David Brower to Bestor Robinson, 11 April 1956, 16 September 1957; Brower to Ervin Peterson, 12 April 1957; Brower to Richard McArdle, 9 November 1956, box 175, Sierra Club Papers.

37. Alex Hildebrand to David Brower, 2 July 1956, box 175, Sierra Club Papers; Art Blake to Edgar Wayburn, 6 July 1956, box 112, Blake Papers; Sierra Club, Executive Committee, Board of Directors, minutes, 11 July 1956.

38. Lewis Clark to Charles Connaughton, 18 July 1956; Connaughton to Clark, 1 August 1956, box 114, Bradley Papers; Connaughton to Clark, 20 August 1956, box 175, Sierra Club Papers; Brower, "Environmental Activist," 83–85; Sierra Club,

Outdoor Newsletter, 22 August 1960, 7–8; S. B. Show to H. Bradley, 22 March 1957, quoted in Bradley to Sierra Club, Board of Directors, minutes, 28 March 1957; Michael McCloskey, "Sierra Club Executive Director: The Evolving Club and the Environmental Movement, 1961–1981," 13, interview with Susan R. Schrepfer, 1983, Sierra Club Papers. See also Joel Hildebrand, "Sierra Club Leader and Ski Mountaineer," 24–25, 31, interview with Ann Lage and Ray Lage, 1974, Sierra Club Office. For a discussion of the impact of Brower's militant leadership, see Susan R. Schrepfer, *The Fight to Save the Redwoods: A History of Environmental Reform, 1917–1978* (Madison: University of Wisconsin Press, 1983), 103–29, 163–85.

39. After 1956 the Forest Service would continue, albeit less frequently, to solicit Sierra Club views and support. See, for example, Sierra Club, Board of Directors, minutes, 6–7 February 1960; Steen, *Forest Service,* 304.

40. Hays, *Beauty, Health, and Permanence,* 481, 280, 482–84. Hays argues that standing in court owed much in its origins to legislative precedents. See also Thomas More Hoban and Richard Oliver Brooks, *Green Justice: The Environment and the Courts* (Boulder, Colo., Westview, 1987), 143–54; Schrepfer, *Fight to Save the Redwoods,* 190–92.

41. Sally Fairfax, "NEPA: A Disaster in the Environmental Movement," *Science,* 17 February 1979, 743–47; Stan L. Albrecht, "Legacy of the Environmental Movement," *Environment and Behavior* 8 (1976): 149, 155; D. L. Sills, "The Environmental Movement and Its Critics," *Human Ecology,* January 1975, 1–41; Jeanne Nienaber Clarke and Daniel McCool, *Staking Out the Terrain: Power Differentials Among Natural Resource Management Agencies* (Albany: State University of New York Press, 1985), 5, 10–11, 139. See Hays acknowledges that other agencies established clientele relationships with user groups. See Hays, *Beauty, Health, and Permanence,* 469–79.

Economic Development and Indian Land Rights in Modern Alaska: The 1947 Tongass Timber Act

Stephen W. Haycox

Between 1933 and 1945, Interior Secretary Harold Ickes and Indian Commissioner John Collier attempted to extend the Indian Reorganization Act of 1934, the Indian New Deal, to Alaska. With other administration officials, Ickes was determined to protect Native land title and help Natives defend their fishing and hunting rights. He also hoped the act would provide Natives with desperately needed financial help. But although the IRA was amended to apply to Alaska in 1936 (Alaska Reorganization Act), its implementation largely failed due to poor administration by the Office of Indian Affairs, inadequate funding by Congress, confusion and inconsistency in defining policy, and the strength of the regional Native brotherhood, which opposed some aspects of the act.[1]

By 1945 the attempt to establish the Indian New Deal in Alaska had ended. Over the next several years, as the direction of national Indian policy changed, Congress debated several measures dealing with Alaska's Indians. One of these, the Tongass Timber Act, which authorized the secretary of agriculture to sell timber leases in Alaska's vast Tongass National Forest, passed the Congress, and was signed by President Harry S. Truman on August 8, 1947.[2]

The Tongass act authorized timber lease sales in Alaska despite protests by the Tlingit and Haida Indians living there, by the Indians' Washington, D.C., attorneys, and by the last proponents of the Indian New Deal in the Interior Department. Debate turned principally on the question of Indian land rights and whether the economic development of Alaska should take precedence over protection of Indian rights and land title.[3] Sharp debate divided departments within the government, and in part disagreement over the bill represented the clash between the last remaining support for the Indian New Deal and its rejection by new proponents of Indian assimilation and termination to whom federal protection represented dictatorial guardianship.[4]

Though conceived by allies of Secretary Ickes and supporters of his policies as a way to protect Indian rights in Alaska, the Tongass bill became law in a form so different from its original version as to be angrily denounced by Ickes and New Deal advocates, and by the Indians themselves, as a betrayal. Some called it Alaska's "Teapot Dome," claiming that the act was the result of collusion between the Forest Service and private investors, intended mainly to benefit developers who sought to establish a pulp industry in Alaska utilizing land and timber that belonged to the Indians by aboriginal title.[5] At the same time, supporters of the final legislation, most particularly the Forest Service and Alaska's territorial officials, hailed its passage as a victory for land and resource development. In Congress, Senator Elton Watkins proclaimed the act actually protected the rights of Alaska's Indians.[6] Such widely opposing interpretations suggest the differences within the government over how to approach not only Alaska Indian matters, but national Indian policy as well.

The genesis of the Tongass Timber Act was a severe newsprint shortage that followed World War II. Industry analysts searched the continent for untapped pulp timber, and spokesmen expressed considerable interest in Alaska's Tongass National Forest, where there were suitable stands of western hemlock and Sitka spruce. Established in the first decade of the twentieth century, the forest comprised 16 million of the 18 million acres of Alaska's southeastern panhandle. Interest reached a high pitch in 1946 when the Senate established a special subcommittee to investigate the newsprint shortage and dispatched Chairman Homer E. Capehart to survey Alaska resources.[7]

Capehart reported favorably on the Tongass Forest and encouraged investors to conclude negotiations already under way with the Forest Service. The regional forester, B. Frank Heintzleman, had found three companies that were particularly anxious to establish pulp facilities in Alaska: Puget Sound Pulp and Timber, the D. & F. Company of New York City, and American Viscose Corporation.[8] An enthusiastic advocate of Alaskan economic development, Heintzleman assured the potential investors that the Forest Service was just as prepared as the pulp industry to see the effort move ahead. With them he worked out a comprehensive pulp-development program. The plan projected five mills to be built in the Tongass Forest, each with a fifty-year life span and each producing 500 tons of pulp or paper daily, an annual level of production that would supply a significant amount of the nation's demand for newsprint.[9]

The project would have a dramatic economic impact on Alaska. Heintzleman estimated that 2.5 persons would be employed in the forest and mills (combined) per ton of daily production—that is, 1,250 persons per mill. There would also be a need for 1.5 service persons per ton for each mill, an additional 625. Adding wives, children, and other nonworking dependents of employees, Heintzleman said, the total would be 6,500 persons dependent on each mill, needing housing and servicing within commuting distance of the sites.

This was a remarkable projection. The total population of Alaska in 1947 was approximately 120,000, but the population in the southeast approached only 30,000, of which about 6,500 were Tlingit, Haida, and Tsimshian Indians. The primary economic resource in the region was the salmon fishery, which dominated all other factors, but was seasonal and utilized a sizable imported labor force.[10] By Heintzleman's calculations, the establishment of the pulp industry in Alaska would provide significant economic livelihood for the entire population of the panhandle region, including the Natives, on a year-round basis.

The question of Indian land title clouded the implementation of these ambitious plans, for there were fourteen Tlingit and Haida Indian villages within the external boundaries of the Tongass National Forest. Moreover, much of the best timber was situated on lands near the Native villages. One of Secretary Ickes's objectives in extending the IRA to Alaska had been to protect forestlands in the vicinity of the Indian villages. He thought Forest Service policies threatened such lands, and in 1944 he had invited Indians in the Tlingit and Haida villages of southeastern Alaska to prepare claims on lands they had traditionally used in the forest. He promised that the Interior Department would protect Indian lands once they were appropriately identified.[11]

Interior Department attorneys helped the Indians prepare their claims. In doing so, they relied on a new interpretation of the theory of aboriginal Indian title. Before 1941, it had been assumed that lands once used by Indians but subsequently abandoned, the title to which had not been formally recognized by the federal government, came under the jurisdiction of the United States to dispose of as it might desire. However, in an important decision of the U.S. Supreme Court in 1941 involving the Santa Fe Railroad and the Walapai (Hualpai) Indians of Arizona, Indians were still held to retain aboriginal title over formerly used but abandoned lands.[12] This decision meant even if the United States had taken and disposed of lands formerly used by Indians, if the Indians could prove their former use of the land and its resources, they could sue the government for damages.

This new departure in Indian land law was seized upon by the brilliant Indian rights attorney Felix Cohen, who served in the Interior Department Solicitor's Office from 1933 to 1948. Cohen saw the *Hualpai* decision as providing the basis for protection of Indian lands in Alaska. Unlike the practice in other western territories, the United States had never signed treaties with any of Alaska's Natives and had not established traditional reservations. Nor, with the exception of a few town sites and some very small school reserves, had the government recognized Indian land titles in Alaska. For the most part, the Tlingit and Haida Indians congregated in their fourteen southeastern Alaska villages, also utilizing some traditional salmon-fishing and berry-gathering sites. While some Tlingit and Haida were well assimilated, many others were not, and pursued a subsistence lifestyle heavily dependent on fishing and hunting.[13] Non-Native encroachment threatened the resources on which they depended. Yet, for all practical intents and purposes, the Indians had abandoned most of the 18 million acres of southeastern Alaska. Thus while they had a possessory right to the locations they actually occupied and used, it was assumed they had lost any rights to the rest of the land.

On the basis of the *Hualpai* decision, Cohen and Ickes challenged that assumption, choosing to regard most of southeastern Alaska as Indian land, subject to aboriginal title. This was a highly controversial decision. But the Indian Reorganization Act of 1934 authorized the secretary of the interior to create new Indian reservations to protect Indian lands, and soon after the *Hualpai* case, Secretary Ickes relied on it to establish seven new Indian reservations in Alaska.[14] He relied on it also in assuring the Tlingit and Haida Indians that he could protect their aboriginal lands in the Tongass National Forest.

In making his promise, Ickes put the Interior Department and Alaska's Indians on a collision course with the Forest Service, for Indian or Interior Department control of forestlands might jeopardize the sale of timber leases on lands near the villages and pulp-mill development might be severely curtailed, if not rendered financially unfeasible. Predictably, the Forest Service reacted negatively. Heintzleman accused Ickes of "introducing a new, wholly impractical, unnecessary and harmful element" into the development of Alaska.[15] As in other national forests, the Forest Service treated all undeveloped land within the external boundaries of the Tongass Forest as under its jurisdiction, a practice affirmed by the courts.[16] Particularly, the agency claimed ownership of the forest trees and all forest resources, regardless of any land rights. The legislation establishing the Tongass Forest provided that "existing property rights" would be "respected and safeguarded."[17] But along with the General Land Office and most non-Native Alaskans, the Forest Service had never regarded the use of land by Indians on a shifting, infrequent basis for hunting and berry gathering as any evidence of Indian possession. If there was visual evidence of active Native use, the land would be considered occupied. Otherwise, it was considered abandoned, and available.[18]

Alaska's leading territorial officials, Governor Ernest Gruening and Congressional Delegate E. L. "Bob" Bartlett, also reacted negatively. Both were ardent supporters of Alaska's economic development and its eventual statehood. A referendum held in the territory on the issue of statehood in October 1946 passed handily, and was viewed widely as the beginning of the final statehood campaign. Bartlett and Gruening thought that economic development was critical to statehood.[19] New industry would attract additional population and would increase the tax base needed to finance state government. Gruening thought that the newsprint shortage would be short-lived, and therefore believed that the readiness of the pulp industry to establish mills in Alaska must be seized upon quickly. Failure to implement Heintzleman's plan, he wrote at one point, would "shut off perhaps for all time, or at least for many years to come, the first important year-round industry that has ever been available to Alaska and which is ready to begin immediately."[20]

With Gruening's support, Heintzleman was prepared to move ahead. The Forest Service had sold some limited timber leases before the Indian New Deal was extended to Alaska, and Heintzleman assured the pulp investors that the agency was ready to auction sufficient stumpage to meet the long-term need projected by the industry, a fifty-year supply. But unlike Alaska's chief forester, the investors were unwilling to go ahead unless they could be assured there would be no litigation over Indian land rights. The capital investment needed to start the industry was too great to justify such a risk.[21]

Before leaving the department in 1946, Secretary Ickes arranged for hearings on Indian land claims to be held in three of the Tlingit and Haida villages—Kake, Klawock, and Hydaburg—to determine the extent of traditional-use land beyond the physical village sites (that is, land to which they might have aboriginal title). The hearing officer, Richard A. Hanna, a former chief justice of the New Mexico Supreme Court, found the evidence presented by the Indians to support most of their claims to prior use to be inadequate, and he confirmed Indian title only to very small areas in immediate proximity to the villages. He recommended that Congress investigate the evidence for title to greater acreage and provide compensation for any lands taken for which Indian title could be proven. Ickes thought Hanna's finding too narrow and overruled it. Instead, he recommended the withdrawal of several hundred thousand acres in separate, new reservations around the three communities. Under IRA provisions, village residents needed to vote on whether or not to accept the reservations. There was considerable ambivalence about reservations among the Indians in Alaska, however, and the votes had not been completed when Ickes left office. The Tongass situation remained unresolved.[22]

Ickes's replacement, Julius A. Krug, was uncertain whether to proceed on the basis of the validity of aboriginal title. He decided that the administration should gather more information on Indian land use before he could recommend any solution to the Alaska problem. In June he asked Theodore Haas, the chief counsel in the Office of Indian Affairs, to travel to Alaska in the company of Walter Goldschmidt, an anthropologist attached to the Department of Agriculture, the Forest Service's parent agency. In their joint report, Haas and Goldschmidt applied former Secretary Ickes's recommendation for reservations for Kake, Klawock, and Hydaburg to all fourteen Indian villages, proposing boundaries that would protect traditional lands adjacent to and beyond each village. But the total land area recommended for all villages combined was less than 2 million acres, or about 10 percent of the Tongass National Forest, far less than the 18 million acres to which Cohen thought the Indians had aboriginal title.[23]

Krug, much to the dismay of Cohen and other proponents of aboriginal title, endorsed the Haas–Goldschmidt recommendation as a working proposal for solving the Alaska lands problem. He concluded that the acreage it projected as Indian land was the most land to which the Indians could expect to gain any title.[24] He directed a new assistant secretary in the Interior Department, Warner W. Gardner, to determine the acceptability of this proposal to the Forest Service, other interested agencies, attorneys for the Alaska Indians, and the absentee-owned Alaska canned-salmon industry, whose right to certain fishing sites might be affected by confirmation of Indian land title.[25]

Gardner found that the Forest Service was adamantly opposed to the Haas–Goldschmidt recommendation. Protesting that the validity of aboriginal title would not stand the test of time, the Forest Service recommended that the government, by administrative or congressional action, extinguish any Indian title that might exist beyond actual village sites and advise the Indians to sue for damages, if any.[26] Attorneys for the Agriculture Department also adopted this position. It was a method of appropriating Indian land that had been used often in the development of the West. Interior Department solicitor Maston G. White acknowledged that technically the procedure was legal; Congress could extinguish any Indian title by simple legislation. But White and other Interior Department officials objected that for the government to solve the problem that way would violate the American sense of fair play. It was now "too late in the history of the country," White said, to act in such a cavalier manner toward its Indian citizens.[27] But the Agriculture Department and the Forest Service appeared unyielding. Agriculture Undersecretary W. E. Dodd pointedly warned Gardner that if the Interior Department was to reserve 10 percent of the land in southeastern Alaska to protect Indian title, such action would create "competing jurisdictions" and would make pulp development "very uncertain."[28] Seeking a way out of the impasse, and skeptical that an administrative solution was likely, Interior Secretary Krug recommended in January 1947 that Gardner draft legislation for Congress. But the positions of the departments were so far apart that Gardner told the secretary that "no agreement is possible just now." There would need to be more cooperation before anything could be recommended to Congress.[29]

Delegate Bartlett already had proposed that the government mandate an administrative settlement. At the beginning of 1945, he introduced a bill modeled on Judge Hanna's recommendation, authorizing the Interior Department to negotiate with the Indians for relinquishment of any potential title to most of their claims in return for cash compensation and clear title to the remainder. The Indians debated this proposal at several annual conventions of their powerful political body, the Alaska Native Brotherhood (ANB).[30] A sophisticated organization, the brotherhood had acted as a focal point and forum for Native interests in Alaska since 1912.[31] Although ANB leaders were usually elected from among the well-assimilated minority, the organization spoke for all Natives, including those in other parts of Alaska, and was well known to officers in the Bureau of Indian Affairs and the Interior Department.

The ANB had supported action on Alaska land claims for many years. Its members had worked with the Office of Indian Affairs toward passage in 1935 of the Tlingit–Haida Jurisdictional Act, which authorized a case in the United States Court of Claims. As of 1947, however, no suit had been filed because of questions associated with the implementation of the Indian Reorganization Act in Alaska and repeated difficulties securing approval by the bureau of Indian Affairs of an appropriate attorney. In 1947 the Indians requested bureau approval for a highly experienced lawyer to advise them on land claims and on other matters relating to the federal government. He was James Curry, general counsel of the National Congress of American Indians (NCAI). Curry had worked in the Office of Indian Affairs and in the Interior Department before going into private practice in 1945. Like Gardner, he was a good friend of Felix Cohen, and like Cohen, he accepted the validity of aboriginal title. Curry began working with the Indians even before he received government approval of his contract.[32]

ANB leaders were divided on Bartlett's suggestion of a negotiated settlement. Some argued that the Indians should stake everything on Secretary Ickes's promise of protection of their ancestral lands. Others, however, argued for the expediency of negotiations if extinguishing title to some land would result in quick cash payment that could be used to secure title to the remainder. After prolonged debate, the ANB approved Bartlett's proposal, with that provision.[33]

In 1947, however, Curry advised the Indians not to relinquish any potential land title through administrative proceedings, as proposed by Delegate Bartlett. They should wait, he counseled, for the courts to rule specifically on their claims, and he proposed to prepare the suit authorized by the 1935 act. In the meantime, the Indians might consider a legislative settlement as a more secure alternative, should they judge its terms to be advantageous. The ANB accepted Curry's advice, overturning its earlier endorsement of Bartlett's proposal.[34]

Bartlett agreed that a legislative solution was preferable, if an acceptable one could be drafted quickly. Legislation might settle the matter of land titles conclusively, he thought, but, he told Secretary Krug, to accommodate the pulp industry, Congress must act before recessing for the summer.[35] Gardner also supported a legislative solution. So did Felix Cohen, and he proceeded to provide one in a proposal that he forwarded to Gardner and to the Agriculture Department in March 1947. Fearful that the Forest Service might go ahead on its own, Cohen suggested that Congress pass legislation neither confirming nor denying the Indian land claims, but authorizing the Forest Service to sell timber leases free and clear of such claims. At the same time, the agency would give the Indians 10 percent of the receipts from all leases sold. The Indians would then use the cash to finance their suit at the Court of Claims, testing the validity of aboriginal title in Alaska.[36]

Initially, most of the interested parties found the proposal attractive. The solicitor in the Agriculture Department, Edward Mynatt, apparently persuaded the Forest Service to help facilitate the Cohen proposal by informally recognizing the Indians' right to an amount of land in the forest equal to 160 acres for each Native, just over 1 million acres, or 6.5 percent of the forestland. This was the minimum that Mynatt thought the courts would award the Indians in a final disposition of the forestlands. During April, the other agencies involved also indicated their approval of the proposal, and Gardner agreed to have Mynatt draft a bill to take to the appropriate committees in Congress.[37]

Curry also accepted Cohen's proposal and the Forest Service's 160-acre provision, though he cautioned Gardner that he was not sure of the Indians' support and could not bind them. Gardner was concerned about Indian approval, for he doubted that any bill could be passed without it. Curry told Gardner he would send a representative to Alaska to explain the implications of the plan to the Indians. Ten percent of Tongass timber receipts would adequately finance a comprehensive land suit, Curry thought. Recognition of 6.5 percent of the land area as clearly Indian-owned, though not the 10 percent recommended in the Haas–Goldschmidt report, offered protection of vital hunting areas in the vicinity of the villages. Confident that the claim of aboriginal title to the remainder of the forest would be upheld in the courts, Curry predicted a sizable future damage or compensatory award for the Indians. He assigned Ruth Muskrat Bronson, executive secretary of the NCAI and also an associate in his Washington, D.C., office, to go to Alaska to work with a Native attorney there, William Paul, Jr. Bronson and Paul would attempt to persuade the Indians to accept the proposal.[38]

Even as Bronson was leaving Washington for Alaska on May 1, however, agreement on the plan began to unravel. Attorneys for the canned-salmon industry vigorously objected to it. The chief spokesman for the salmon industry, W. C. Arnold, thought that Indians had no right to land other than the actual sites on which their villages were situated. Payment of 10 percent of timber sales receipts to the Indians might imply legal acknowledgment of their ownership of the timber sold to generate those receipts, he asserted. This would open the door to recognition of Indian ownership of any and all timber in the Tongass Forest and fishing sites within the forest where the industry operated salmon traps and cannery operations.[39]

The swiftness with which other critics of the proposal responded with their own objections manifested the power of the salmon industry. Almost immediately, members of the Washington State congressional delegation told Gardner they would oppose the legislation.[40] In addition to shipping a significant amount of the annual salmon pack through Seattle, industry investors had worked with Washington legislators for years to guarantee stability in Alaska's economy, a stability that benefited Seattle shippers and merchants. They would accept the legislation, the Washingtonians said, only if a provision were included in it guaranteeing access to the salmon industry's present number and location of trap sites in perpetuity. Gardner knew that the Indians, who had objected to salmon trap sites since 1920, would never support such a provision.[41]

Delegate Bartlett also withdrew his support for the 10 percent proposal. Upon learning of Arnold's opposition, he immediately telephoned Gardner to tell him that "the deal is off." No bill that was objected to by the salmon industry, he said, would ever get through Congress.[42] At the same time, the Justice Department also notified Gardner it could no longer support the legislation, echoing Arnold's argument that it might imply legal recognition of Indian claims.[43] Governor Gruening, unenthusiastic about the plan before, now notified Gardner that he, too, was opposed. Cohen, who was in close touch with Gardner, considered this the "death blow" for the plan, for Gruening made clear his intention never to allow any "crack in the door" that might doom industrial development in Alaska and the statehood movement.[44]

With time running out on the legislative session, Gardner desperately tried to salvage something from the proposal, that would allow pulp development while protecting the Indians' rights. Conceding the strength of the salmon industry, he arranged for Bartlett and Cohen to meet with him in Secretary Krug's office, where, in a tense session with Krug, they hammered out the bill that would pass Congress as the Tongass Timber Act of 1947.[45] In this version, the 10 percent provision was dropped entirely. Instead, the secretary of agriculture was authorized to sell timber on any "vacant, unappropriated or unpatented land" within the forest, and all receipts from such sales would be put into escrow, "maintained in a special account in the Treasury," pending final determination of the extent of Indians' claims. In the meantime, nothing in the act was to be construed "as recognizing or denying" the validity of such claims. This new version of the bill, in other words, simply ignored the question of aboriginal title, and left the Indians to sue in court. In addition, the bill authorized the secretary of the interior to sell small tracts of lands, "notwithstanding any claim of possessory rights," for mill sites and other processing needs.[46]

Although this legislation developed out of concern for Indian land rights, very little protection of those rights survived in the final version of the bill; while the act did not expressly appropriate much Indian land, by effectively ignoring aboriginal claims, it left the Indians with a protracted, costly, and uncertain judicial appeal as their only recourse for determining the extent of their claims to the land or financial compensation for its loss. In the meantime, the Forest Service could sell timber that might belong to the Indians, the cutting of which would irrevocably alter the character of the land on which the timber grew and the uses to which it might be put; the secretary of the interior could sell lands that might later be found to be owned by Indians, but that would be used by non-Indians for nontraditional purposes. The Indians were made dependent on the secretary of the interior to protect their villages, on the secretary of agriculture to get a fair price for the timber, and on the courts of the United States to determine what, if anything, they were entitled to as compensation.[47]

When Curry learned the provisions of the new bill he told Bartlett, Cohen, and Gardner that the Indians would never support the new proposal.[48] In Alaska, Bronson learned this firsthand. At every village she and Paul visited, the Indians articulated their objections to the new measure. It did not answer their protest about land claims, they said, but instead left them facing endless litigation with no way to pay for it. Some argued that pulp was not the best use for much Tongass timber. But even if it was, it was Indian timber and should be sold by Indians, not by the Forest Service. And the Indians were "cynical," Bronson wrote, about work opportunities. The canners did not employ them if they could do otherwise, and the pulp industry would do the same. Moreover, the Indians feared destruction of their fishery. When the pulp mills come in, they said, "they will destroy the fish, shrimp and other seafood resources because of the poison that is generated." Not only would the Indians lose what little income they had from selling small amounts of fish to canneries, but they would be forced to move great distances away from the mill sites in order to continue their fishing. The new bill was a "blow" to the Indians, Paul wrote, and they made plans to send a delegation to Washington to protest the legislation.[49]

Determined to have the matter settled, however, Secretary Krug sent the new bill to Congress on May 16.[50] In the Senate, it was assigned to the Committee on Public Lands, which held brief, perfunctory hearings, which were not published. In the House, it went to the Committee on Agriculture, where Chairman Clifford Hope of Kansas scheduled immediate hearings.[51] Most of the principals testified in the last week of May and the first week of June. Gruening repeated his assertion of the necessity to capitalize on the present willingness of the investors in the pulp industry. C. M. Granger, assistant chief of the Forest Service, seconded that assertion, and went on to say that the service needed the lands that Interior had identified in the Haas–Goldschmidt recommendation because they contained the best timber. Assistant Secretary of Agriculture Charles Brannon argued that the proposed bill carried out former Interior Secretary Ickes's desires by implicitly inviting the courts to make a final disposition of Alaska Indian claims, an assertion that Ickes would hotly deny in several news columns. Interior Solicitor Maston White assured the congressmen that the Forest Service had the right to the timber and could cut if it liked, but that the Indians would certainly seek an injunction if the government did so without Indian approval, perhaps tying up pulp development indefinitely. Whatever plan was worked out would need their approval. James Curry used extensive testimony to make a passionate case for the Indians' rights not only to timber and land, but also to the government's need to respect their right to a settlement prior to any lease sales, not after. He seemed to raise serious doubts with the congressmen as to the constitutionality of the legislation.[52]

Members of the Indian delegation were able to make brief statements on the next to the last day of the hearings. They said that the bill violated the promise made by Secretary Ickes to implement a just and definite determination of their land rights and the Haas–Goldschmidt recommendation for reservation boundaries. They also argued that the bill violated the United States Constitution by taking property that belonged to others without adequate judicial procedure. The resulting sale of timber leases by the Forest Service would pauperize the Natives, they said, and violated the American sense of justice. Shrewdly, they suggested that the bill would not protect the investors, for the Indians were sure to sue the government and the pulp companies, and the litigation would probably hold up pulp development.[53]

Regardless of the opposition's testimony, the committee seemed determined to get the bill out for a congressional vote before the summer recess. The newsprint shortage loomed large in their questions and discussions, as did the need to develop Alaska.[54] There was considerable discussion of how much land was appropriate for the Indians, and how such a determination should be made. They were not in a position to make a judgment on that question, the congressmen agreed, leaving the matter to be settled by the courts. Facilitating economic development was the critical factor, the committee determined, and should not be jeopardized by the theory of aboriginal title. Judging that their colleagues would agree, they sent the bill forward with a recommendation for passage.[55]

There was little interest in the bill in the full House. In the last days of the session, Chairman Hope called it up one morning immediately after the daily invocation, when the floor was nearly empty. It passed with no comment, though Hope noted the objections of the Indians.[56]

Interest in the Senate was nearly as desultory. Senator Hugh Butler of Nebraska, an outspoken advocate of Alaska development, brought the bill up three days before the scheduled adjournment date and succeeded in having it placed on the unanimous consent calendar. Senator Warren G. Magnuson of Washington spoke for the bill and quickly summarized its intent as he understood it. Speaking proprietarily, he said that what "we" seek to do "is to sell the timber, protect the Indians, and give Alaska a needed pulp and paper industry. That is all it amounts to." Taking aim at James Curry, he added that some "Indian lawyers downtown" wanted to justify their existence and continue to make their living "off the Indians" by telling their clients that they were protecting their rights in objecting to the bill. But everyone in the Pacific Northwest and Alaska, Magnuson asserted, "including the Indians themselves, wants to get this industry established." The senator seemed unaware of the Indian protest.[57]

While the bill was before the Senate, former Secretary Ickes criticized it vigorously in a regular newspaper column he wrote on government affairs, excoriating both the secretary of agriculture, Clinton Anderson, and the Interior Department. Ickes called the bill a "timber grab." Indian ownership of "great stretches" of the Tongass Forest had been confirmed by the Interior Department, Ickes wrote, but the Agriculture Department "arrogantly" proposed to overrule Interior without even taking the matter to court. Recognizing the urgent need for pulp wood, Ickes continued, did not justify the Forest Service in conducting a "raid on privately owned property." Perhaps the "shadiest side" of the matter, he said, was that the Interior Department, the supposed "guardian" of the Indians, was equally guilty, refusing to fight any further for the Indians' rights. Ickes suggested that the Indians erect totem poles to Anderson and to the Interior Department. This old Indian custom was supposed to yield one of two results when someone took something that did not belong to him: either the property would be returned, or the person or persons to whom the pole was dedicated would have "an early demise."[58]

But Ickes's remarks had no effect, for the bill passed the Senate on a voice vote on July 26 during the last fifteen minutes of the session. Elton Watkins, chairman of the Indian Affairs committee and a former judge, said that the question of land claims should be left to the courts. He confessed that he was not sure of the act's constitutionality. But he said he would vote for it and leave that question to the future. In the meantime, economic development in Alaska would benefit both Natives and whites.[59]

President Truman did not sign the bill at once, and Curry and his associates launched a last-minute effort to persuade him to veto it. Curry published an article in which he argued that the measure was inconsistent with the defense of the rights of "little people" by the United States. That Indian ownership of resources was blocking "the road of progress" was, Curry wrote, "an old, old excuse." All the Indians were being offered, he said, was "the right to sue the Federal Government for the value of what is taken from them." But when the timber of the Chippewa Indians of Minnesota had been taken in 1908, he pointed out, adjudication had taken thirty-one years, and then the court ruled that the timber had not been marketable in 1908, even though it had been sold for millions of dollars later. So the Chippewas were denied any compensation. California Indians had waited ninety-one years in a similar case, Curry wrote, and then had been awarded far less in compensation than the true value of the land and resources that had been taken from them.[60]

The day Truman signed the bill—August 8—Bronson published an article in which she charged that the act had been rushed through Congress in the last "hectic" days of the session to hide a "sickening" timber theft from the American public. She compared the government's action with the infamous "Teapot Dome" scandal of the 1920s, when Interior Secretary Albert

Fall set aside Wyoming Indian lands as a petroleum reserve and then allowed Sinclair Oil Company to pump and market the oil on the commercial market, paying Fall a percentage of the profits. Bronson did not charge that any government officials were being paid by pulp developers for their support of the Tongass bill, and the comparison with the oil scandal was, at best, inflammatory. But Bronson apparently judged that it made "good press," as others would also. As Ickes had, Bronson also argued that the right to sue the government was of little use to the Indians. Such suits, she said, were of value "only to their grandchildren."[61]

Unpersuaded, President Truman signed the bill. He made no public announcement upon doing so. But in a major statement on Alaska the preceding May, Truman had urged industrial and economic development in Alaska, and had pledged his support. Governor Gruening was much relieved by the bill's passage, writing to Secretary Krug that the territory had "had a narrow escape."[62]

Passage of the Tongass timber bill cleared the way for pulp development, as Gruening and others hoped it would, and while the industry's ambitious plans for Alaska were not realized on the grand scale imagined, eventually two pulp mills were constructed in Alaska, although little of the pulp they produced was suitable for use as newsprint.[63]

It is more difficult to determine the significance of the act for Alaska's Tlingit and Haida Indians. For a time, passage of the act fueled more protest by opponents. Secretary Ickes wrote more columns, adding Gruening and Heintzleman to his list of villains, and at least one newspaper editor called for the act's repeal. The Alaska Native Brotherhood collected a number of such protests and, with the NCAI, published them in a pamphlet entitled *Alaska's Teapot Dome*. A photograph of former Secretary Fall was printed opposite the title page. Other bills in Congress that affected Alaska Indians were under active debate, and the protests were directed more toward these bills than toward repeal of the Tongass Timber Act. Secretary Krug retired in November 1949. Still uncomfortable about unprotected Indian lands in Alaska, on his last day in office he executed an order creating three new Indian reservations there. The continuing protests of the advocates of aboriginal title and the rights of the Tlingit and Haida people may have helped to convince Krug that Alaska Indian lands needed administrative protection, considering Congress's action on the Tongass bill.[64]

Reaction to the Tongass Timber Act continued for many months after its passage. Early in 1948, Felix Cohen, recently retired from government service, published an article he called "Open Season on Alaska Natives" in which he charged that the actions of the Forest Service in assisting the pulp industry were an example of capitalist colonialism that denied the Indians their legitimate rights and condemned them "to die of diseases of malnutrition." Employment opportunities for Alaska's Indians, only some of whom were well assimilated, were poor; health care was not adequate; and educational attainment was low. Governor Gruening estimated that 10 percent of the receipts from timber sales for pulp development would have amounted to hundreds of thousands of dollars annually, which might have helped to alleviate Indian suffering. And while he could not approve an implied congressional recognition of Indian land title by the provision that they be paid for the timber, he was concerned about the Indians' plight. Not long after passage of the Tongass act, he recommended to Secretary Krug that it be amended to allow the government simply to use 50 percent of the sales receipts to aid the Indians "until some sum such as twenty-five or thirty million dollars has been expended." Although Krug responded positively, the Forest Service objected to the proposal.[65]

As Curry's associate C. M. Wright had written to the Tlingit and Haida people before the Tongass bill passed, the New Deal in Alaska was over for the Indians. Gruening's and Heintzleman's ideas for the economic development of Alaska had found broad support in Congress and in the federal bureaucracy. These ideas took precedence in Alaska over protection of Indian land title and over the question of justice for Alaska's Indians. The Tlingit and Haida Indians, in turn, did not ask the courts to enjoin the Forest Service from auctioning Tongass timber. Instead, with Curry approved as their attorney by the Interior Department, they began earnestly to pursue their aboriginal claims suit to the whole Tongass National Forest. Eventually, they would win that suit in the United States Court of Claims, in 1959, but they would be awarded only $7.5 million in damages. The Indians considered the amount of the award inadequate. In 1971, in the comprehensive Alaska Native Claims Settlement Act, the Tlingit and Haida would obtain clear title to their villages and certain lands surrounding them. But the total acreage would be far less than either the 10 percent of the Tongass Forest recommended in the Haas–Goldschmidt recommendation in 1946, or the 6.5 percent the Forest Service had been persuaded to concede in early 1947.[66]

That outcome could not be anticipated in 1947, however, and the story of the Tongass Timber Act is one of a conflict of values and the policies that embodied them. For the Forest Service and advocates of Alaska statehood, the primacy of modern capitalist development in the Tongass National Forest was more important than the protection and safeguard of potential Indian land rights and resources, which they interpreted as a threat to that development. Assimilation of Indians into the mainstream of white culture in Alaska seemed both necessary and appropriate to those who held this view, a position doubtless reinforced by the fact that the most articulate Indian spokesmen were themselves well assimilated. This fact likely obscured the negative effects of the curtailing of federal services. Supporters of the Indians, however, argued for the primacy of aboriginal title and protection of Indian rights. To secure Indian lands, and Indian culture and identity, they placed the sanctity of Indian land title above the value of economic development. In the Tongass Timber Act of 1947, the advocates of Indian rights lost an important, early contest over these values to the proponents of development and assimilation.

NOTES

1. Francis Paul Prucha, *The Great Father: The United States and the American Indians* (Lincoln: University of Nebraska Press, 1984), 2:957–63; Felix Cohen, *Handbook of Federal Indian Law* (Charlottesville, Va.: Michie Bobbs Merrill, 1982), 750–52.

2. U.S. Congress, House, Committee on Agriculture, *Hearings on H.J. Resolution 205, Tongass National Forest,* 80th Cong., 1st sess., 1947, passim; 61 *United States Statutes* 920–21; the bill was in the form of a joint resolution: 80th Cong., 1st sess., H.J. Res. 205, and S.J. Res. 118; U.S. Congress, House, Committee on Agriculture, *Authorizing the Secretary of Agriculture to Sell Timber Within the Tongass National Forest,* H. Rpt. 873, 80th Cong., 1st sess., 1947; U.S. Congress, Senate, Committee on Public Lands, *Authorizing the Secretary of Agriculture to Sell Timber Within the Tongass National Forest,* S. Rpt. 874, 80th Cong., 1st sess., 1947.

3. House Committee on Agriculture, *Hearings on H.J. Resolution 205,* 3–6, 7–10, 37–40.

4. Susan M. Hartmann, *Truman and the 80th Congress* (Columbia: University of Missouri Press, 1971), 7–8, 37–38, 143–45; Senator Hugh Butler to Senator Arthur H. Vandenberg, file S.J. Res. 118, box 262, Hugh Butler Papers, Nebraska Historical Society, Lincoln.

5. Alaska Native Brotherhood, October 1947, Alaska Timber, box 62, James Curry Papers, National Anthropological Archive, Smithsonian Institution, Washington, D.C.

6. Governor Ernest Gruening to Secretary of the Interior J. A. Krug, 18 September 1947, file 40-04, reel 274, Records of the Office of the Governor of Alaska, Record Group 348 [hereafter cited as RG 348] (National Archives Record Microcopy 939); *Congressional Record,* 80th Cong., 1st sess., 26 July 1947, 10407.

7. House Committee on Agriculture, *Hearings on H.J. Resolution 205,* 2–3; David C. Smith, "Pulp, Paper, and Alaska," *Pacific Northwest Quarterly,* April 1975, 61–70; Ernest Gruening, *The State of Alaska* (New York: Random House, 1954), 370–71; U.S. Congress, House, Committee on Agriculture, *Disposition of Revenues from Tongass National Forest, Alaska,* H. Rept. 2568, 84th Cong., 2nd sess, 2.

8. B. Frank Heintzleman to Ernest Gruening, 14 April 1947, file 41-01, reel 280, RG 348; House Committee on Agriculture, *Hearings on H.J. Resolution 205,* 23; Lawrence W. Rakestraw, *A History of the United States Forest Service in Alaska* (Anchorage: Alaska Historical Commission, 1981), 125–26.

9. B. Frank Heintzleman to Ernest Gruening, 4 March 1947, file R-10, box 1500, Records of the Forest Service, Division of Timber Management, Record Group 95, National Archives [hereafter cited as RG, NA].

10. House Committee on Agriculture, *Hearings on H.J. Resolution 205,* 7, 47.

11. Claude Wickard to Secretary of the Interior Harold Ickes, 5 February 1945,

file, Alaska, Office files of Oscar L. Chapman, 1933–53, Records of the Office of the Secretary of the Interior, RG 48, NA; Felix S. Cohen, "Report to the Commissioner of Indian Affairs," 10 July 1944, and Interior Solicitor Maston G. White to Assistant Secretary of the Interior William E. Warne, 5 December 1947, file Territories, Alaska: Indian claims, box 68, Office of the Solicitor, RG 48, NA.

12. *United States, as Guardian of the Hualpai Indians of Arizona*, v. *Santa Fe Pacific Railroad*, 314 U.S. 339; Cohen, *Handbook*, 488, 490, 521–22; Lucy Kramer Cohen, ed., *The Legal Conscience: Selected Papers of Felix S. Cohen* (New Haven, Conn.: Yale University Press, 1960), 273–304.

13. House Committee on Agriculture, *Hearings on H.J. Resolution 205*, 5–6; Cohen, *Handbook*, 743–46; David S. Case, *Alaska Natives and American Laws* (Anchorage: University of Alaska Press, 1984), 86; Gruening to Krug, 18 September 1947.

14. U.S. Congress, Senate, Subcommittee of the Committee of Interior and Insular Affairs, *Hearings on S. 2037, Repeal Act Authorizing the Secretary of Interior to Create Indian Reservations in Alaska*, 80th Cong., 2nd sess., 1948, 53–56; Case, *Alaska Natives*, 101–4.

15. B. Frank Heintzleman to Assistant Secretary of the Interior Warner W. Gardner, 15 March 1947, file R-10, box 1500, RG 95, NA.

16. Memorandum, Bureau of Indian Affairs to Secretary of the Interior, through Maston G. White and William E. Warne, 26 September 1947, file Alaska Salmon Trap & Timber Bill, box 56, Office of the Solicitor, RG 48, NA.

17. Maston G. White to Warner Gardner, 4 March 1947, file Alaska Salmon Trap & Timber Bill, box 58, Records of the Office of the Secretary of the Interior, Office of the Solicitor, RG 48, NA; House Committee on Agriculture, *Hearings on H.J. Resolution 205*, 3; 36 U.S. *Statutes* 847.

18. White to Gardner, 4 March 1947.

19. Clause-M. Naske, *An Interpretive History of Alaskan Statehood* (Anchorage: Alaska Northwest, 1973), 67, 73; E. L. Bartlett to Felix Cohen, 15 April 1948, file 14.8, box C1B, Curry–Weissbrodt Papers, Alaska Historical Library, Juneau.

20. Ernest Gruening to Frank Peratrovich, Andrew Hope, Frank Johnson, and Fred Grant [Tlingit Indians], 1 July 1947, in House Committee on Agriculture, *Hearings on H.J. Resolution 205*, 186–87; *Alaska Daily Empire*, 25 March 1948, 4.

21. Warner Gardner to J. A. Krug, 12 March 1947, file Alaska, box 73, Krug Papers, Library of Congress; Senator Hugh Butler to Secretary of Agriculture Clinton Anderson, 12 March 1947, file Alaska, box 219, Butler Papers.

22. Editorial, *Journal of Forestry*, June, 1945, 391–92; Kenneth Philp, "The New Deal and Alaskan Natives, 1936–1945," *Pacific Historical Review*, August 1981, 320–21.

23. Haas–Goldschmidt Report, 10 December 1946; Acting Secretary William Zimmerman to Assistant Secretary William Warne, 4 February 1947, file Records Concerning Claims of Natives of Southeast Alaska, box 56, Office of the Solicitor, RG 48, NA; House Committee on Agriculture, *Hearings on H.J. Resolution 205*, 8–9.

24. Department of the Interior Statement of Policy on Aboriginal Claims and Native Reservations in Alaska, 20 November 1946, file General Correspondence, 1930–58, box 60, Office of the Solicitor, RG 48, NA.

25. Warner Gardner to W. C. Arnold, 5 June 1946, file Alaska—Fisheries, box 3,

Warner Gardner Papers, Harry S. Truman Library, Independence, Mo.; Philp, "New Deal and Alaskan Natives," 321–22.

26. Memorandum, Bureau of Indian Affairs to Secretary of the Interior, through White and Warne, 26 September 1947.

27. White to Gardner, 4 March 1947.

28. W. E. Dodd to R. Welch, House Committee on Public Lands, 24 February 1947, file 17.2, box C1B, Curry–Weissbrodt Papers.

29. Warner Gardner to J. A. Krug, 27 January 1947, file Alaska—Native Land Claims, box 3, Gardner Papers.

30. Alaska Native Brotherhood, minutes, and Resolution No. 2, Angoon convention (1945), 87–99, file 26.2, box C3A; minutes, Wrangell convention (1946), file 26.2, box C3A; Elizabeth Peratrovich to James Curry, 27 January 1950, file 11.4, box C1, Curry–Weissbrodt Papers.

31. Philip Drucker, *The Native Brotherhoods: Modern Intertribal Organizations on the Northwest Coast* (Washington, D.C.: Bureau of Ethnology, 1956), passim.

32. *The Alaskan* [ANB newspaper, Petersburg, Alaska), 29 November 1929; David Morgan to William Paul, Sr., 1 June 1940, file 23, box C3A, Curry–Weissbrodt Papers; William Paul, Sr., to Office of Indian Affairs, 27 May 1941, file Alaska—S, Office File of John Collier, RG 75, NA; Report of Land Suit Attorney, William Paul, Jr., 3 October 1941, file 6, box C3, Curry–Weissbrodt Papers; Stanley James Underdall, "On the Road Toward Termination: The Pyramid Lake Paiutes and the Indian Attorney Controversy of the 1950s" (Ph.D. diss., Columbia University, 1977), 120–21; Joaqlin Estus and Glenda Choate, *Curry–Weissbrodt Papers of the Tlingit and Haida Indian Tribes of Alaska: An Inventory* (Juneau: Central Council of Tlingit and Haida Indian Tribes of Alaska, 1983), 10; Acting Commissioner of Indian Affairs William Zimmerman to Don Foster, chief, Office of Indian Affairs, Juneau, 22 March 1947, file 26.2, box C3A, Curry–Weissbrodt Papers.

33. William Paul to William Baker [editor, *Ketchikan Chronicle*], 21 May 1945; Paul to James Curry, 18 March 1947, file 19, box C1B, Curry–Weissbrodt Papers.

34. James Curry to William Paul, Jr., 22 March 1947, file 3.4, box C3, Curry–Weissbrodt Papers; Gruening, *State of Alaska*, 373–74; Ernest Gruening to E. L. Bartlett, 15 April 1947, file 40-04, reel 274, RG 348.

35. C. M. Wright [Curry associate] to file, 21 March 1947, file 19, box C1B, Curry–Weissbrodt Papers.

36. Felix Cohen to Edward F. Mynatt [associate solicitor, Department of Agriculture], 17 March 1947, file Alaska—Territories, box 69, Office of the Solicitor, RG 48, NA.

37. Warner Gardner to James Curry, 21 March 1947, file 3.3, box C3, Curry–Weissbrodt Papers; Gardner to White, 21 March 1947, file Alaska Salmon Trap & Timber Bill, box 56, Office of the Solicitor, RG 48, NA; C. M. Wright to file, 3 April 1947, file 19, box C1B, Curry–Weissbrodt Papers.

38. James Curry to Warner Gardner, 7 April 1947, file 19, box C1B; Ruth Bronson to file, 8 May 1947, file 19, box C1B, Curry–Weissbrodt Papers.

39. Warner Gardner to Felix Cohen, 23 April 1947, file Alaska Lands, box 143, Records of the Office of Territories, RG 126, NA.

40. C. M. Wright to file, 18 April 1947; Bronson to file, 8 May 1947, file 19, box C1B, Curry–Weissbrodt Papers; Gruening, *State of Alaska*, 393–405.

41. Warner Gardner to Maston White, 5 May 1947, file Alaska Native Land Claims, box 3, Gardner Papers.

42. Frances Lopinsky [Curry associate] to James Curry, 13 May 1947, file 17.2, box C1B, Curry–Weissbrodt Papers.

43. Gardner to White, 5 May 1947.

44. Lopinsky to Curry, 13 May 1947; Ernest Gruening to Oscar Chapman, 15 February 1949, file GRI-GRY, box 46, Papers of Oscar L. Chapman, HST Library.

45. Warner Gardner to Maston White, 18 May 1947, file Alaska Native Land Claims, box 3, Gardner Papers; Lopinsky to Curry, 19 May 1947, file 17.2, box C1B, Curry–Weissbrodt Papers.

46. 61 *U.S. Statutes* 920-21.

47. Curry's associates labeled it "Gov. Gruening and the Sec. of Agriculture's Bill"; Lopinsky to Curry, 13 May 1947.

48. James Curry to file, 19 May 1947, file 17.2, box C1B, Curry–Weissbrodt Papers; Lopinsky to Curry, 19 May 1947.

49. Ruth Bronson to James Curry, 19 May 1947, file 17.2, box C1B; William Paul, Jr. to Johnson, 21 May 1947, file 2, box C3, Curry–Weissbrodt Papers.

50. House Committee on Agriculture, *Hearings on H.J. Resolution 205,* 2–3.

51. Hugh Butler to Senator Arthur Watkins, 12 August 1947, file Alaska, box 219, Butler Papers. Watkins was chairman of the Senate Indian Affairs Committee.

52. House Committee on Agriculture, *Hearings on H.J. Resolution 205,* 37–40 (Gruening), 25–26 (Granger), 175, 190–92 (Brannon), 185 (White), 51–150 (Curry).

53. Ibid., 151–67. The Alaska Native Brotherhood did not take an official position on the bill until its November 1947 annual convention, when it condemned the measure; clipping [unidentified], 15 November 1947, file Alaska Native Brotherhood, box 1, Paul Papers, University of Washington Library, Seattle; 17 November 1947, file 6 (resolutions), box C2, Curry–Weissbrodt Papers.

54. House Committee on Agriculture, *Hearings on H.J. Resolution 205,* 9, 12, 38, 40–41.

55. Ibid., 16–17, 32–33, 43, 84–90.

56. *Congressional Record,* 80th Cong., 1st sess., 10 July 1947, 5524; Harold Ickes, *Washington Post,* 21 August 1947, 8.

57. *Congressional Record,* 80th Cong., 1st sess., 23 July 1947, 9809.

58. Harold Ickes, *Washington Evening Star,* 23 July 1947, 9.

59. *Congressional Record,* 80th Cong., 1st sess., 26 July 1947, 10407.

60. James Curry, *Commonweal,* 1 August 1947, 4–5.

61. Ruth Bronson, *New York Herald Tribune,* 8 August 1947, 2.

62. Alaska Development Plan, 22 May 1947, Administrative Correspondence Files, Office of the Solicitor, RG 48, NA; Gruening to Krug, 18 September 1947.

63. Smith, "Pulp, Paper, and Alaska," 68–70; U.S. Congress, Senate, Special Committee to Study Problems of American Small Business, *Survey of Alaskan Newsprint Resources,* S. Rept. 852, 80th Cong., 2nd sess., 3.

64. *New York Post,* 21 August 1947, 8; *Richmond Times-Dispatch,* 1 September 1947, 6; Alaska Native Brotherhood, October 1947, Alaska Timber, box 62, James Curry Papers; Oliver La Farge to Philleo Nash, 17 August 1949, file Alaska Native Land Claims, box 76, Philleo Nash files, HST Library; Information Bulletin, Department of the Interior, 3 November 1949, Central Office File, box 90, RG 48, NA;

Memorandum for the President, David Niles, 6 February 1950, file Alaska Native Claims, box 76, Philleo Nash files.

65. Institute of Ethnic Affairs, *Newsletter,* February 1948, 4–8, copy in file S.J. Res. 118, box 262, Butler Papers; Gruening to Krug, 18 September 1947; Warne to J. A. Krug, 2 February 1948, file Alaska Field Staff, 1948–53, box 77, Office of the Solicitor, RG 48, NA.

66. C. M. Wright to the Tlingit and Haida Indians of Southeastern Alaska, 11 April 1947, file 19, box C1B, Curry–Weissbrodt Papers; William Paul, Sr., to James Curry, 2 November 1947, file 6 (Hydaburg convention), box C3, Curry–Weissbrodt Papers; *Tlingit and Haida Indians of Alaska et al. v. U.S.,* 177 F. Supp. 452 (Ct. Cl., 1959); 79 *U.S. Statutes* 543; *Tlingit and Haida Indians of Alaska et al. v. U.S.,* 389 F.2d 778 (Ct. Cl., 1968); Robert Arnold, *Alaska Native Land Claims* (Anchorage: Alaska Native Foundation, 1976), 150–51.

The Bitterroot Revisited: "A University [Re]View of the Forest Service"

Arnold W. Bolle

In 1970, the United States Senate ordered the printing of a report entitled *A University View of the Forest Service.*[1] Senator Lee Metcalf requested this report, and a University of Montana faculty committee, of which I was chairman, prepared it. We called it the "Bitterroot Report." It was sometimes called the "Bolle Report," but credit for the work goes to all the other committee members as well.[2]

Reports usually enjoy very short lives. Some are stillborn, but the Bitterroot Report lives on because it continues to have significance in the management of our public lands. To understand some of why this is so, let me describe as best I can the situation that existed in the late 1960s, the conflicts that arose, the various actions emanating from these conflicts, and especially how our report came into being.

The postwar housing boom created a market for timber from the national forests of the Rocky Mountains. The Forest Service suddenly faced an opportunity to expand national forest timber production, and it did so. Without implementing the vital concept of sustained yield, the Forest Service pushed timber sales. It changed from a custodial agency to one aimed at commodity production. This was a massive change from what the agency had been doing, and some people were upset. Local at first, the unhappiness grew and spread until it became a national sentiment. In the minds of many people, the Forest Service had become the enemy. The watchers of the national forests had sold out to those whom it was established to watch, the timber industry. It now appeared to be advocating the "cut out and get out" policy that it had been established to oppose.

From its creation in 1905, the Forest Service was almost entirely a custodial agency guided by the Forest Service Organic Act of 1897,[3] which called for the government to "protect and improve"[4] those areas set aside as national forests. Before the 1940s in what was referred to as the "Stetson Hat Period," Forest Service officials were highly respected guardians of the public forests. During this period, some timber was sold in accessible areas containing high-quality timber. In the northern Rockies, western white pine was the choice

163

species, and ponderosa pine was the staple species of the lower elevations. Some Douglas fir was taken, and western larch was also finding its way into the market. But the lodgepole pine, spruce, and fir were rated as weed species. Most of Montana's commercial timber came from private lands in and around valley bottoms. Very little of it came from the national forests.

Ranchers grazed some of their livestock in national forests, and irrigators drew their water from streams originating in national forests. In addition, much of the local public as well as visitors from farther away looked to the national forests for hunting, fishing, backcountry recreation, and to provide the scenic and aesthetic surroundings of daily life. These various users deeply resented change, especially sudden change that they did not understand and over which they had no control.

After World War II, new family formation by returning veterans and the forced savings of war workers (whose earnings had been held in check by wartime rationing) produced a large national demand for timber. Higher prices for timber and new road-building technologies made most forestlands economically as well as physically accessible.

In the 1940s, a bark-beetle epidemic in the central Rockies killed several billion board feet of spruce. A salvage program was not mobilized in time to save much of the timber, but the epidemic did generate ideas.[5]

In the 1950s, the Forest Service saw an opportunity to salvage large amounts of alleged waste timber killed in a beetle epidemic in the northern Rockies. In the Flathead National Forest, a massive blowdown occurred and provided the conditions for an outbreak of beetles in the trees weakened by the blowdown. The beetles then spread to healthy trees. The first major spruce sale took place in the North Fork of the Flathead River. The Forest Service constructed a minimum road, and Plum Creek Lumber Company bid $1 per 1,000 board feet over the objections of other companies, which hoped to have the government pay them to get the timber out. Spruce was sold in solid blocks, with some green timber included to sweeten the sale. Clear-cutting was the standard harvest method, and the new pattern was set.

This spruce salvage program was heralded as a great success, but the Forest Service never analyzed whether it was a success for the taxpayer. Spruce timber substitutes well for western white pine, which was becoming scarce and had nearly priced itself out of the market. Spruce is also lighter, and freight costs were less, so profits soared and the industry expanded, as did Forest Service work. The beetle infestation and consequent spruce salvage program spread throughout the region. Ranger stations became busy production centers, and their walls were adorned with special awards for meeting and surpassing production goals. The Forest Service had moved on to its "Hard Hat" era, and timber was king.

The system that developed for harvesting spruce was applicable to other species, and the housing market accepted whatever could be produced. Consequently, the system spread to all species and all national forests through-out the region. Clear-cutting became the method used throughout; it became a crusade based on the Forest Service belief that it was good for the nation, the land, and the forests. The Forest Service seized the chance to get rid of those low-quality old forests and replace them with desirable stands of high genetic quality planted in neat, orderly rows to produce the maximum amount of lumber for America's lumber-hungry people.

In 1956, Congress adopted a Forest Service proposal to greatly expand timber production in Montana's national forests entitled "Full Use and Development of Montana's Timber Resources."[6] This plan, which grew from the spruce salvage program, was intended to expand the program of clear-cutting to all the national forests of Montana. Also planned was a consider-able increase in Forest Service funding, activity, and manpower. As a brainchild of the Region 1 Office timber staff, the program was widely her-alded in Montana as the great chance for national forests to take their true place in the national economy.

The idea met with favor in Washington, D.C.—so much so that other parts of the country demanded equal treatment, and Montana's program became a national program. Both the Forest Service and the timber industry sold the idea to Congress as a great money-making opportunity because the additional timber could be sold for far more than it would cost to arrange the sales. In turn, it promised to greatly enrich the national treasury. Hence, a series of deals was initiated with Congress: more money to cut more tim-ber to bring more profit to the treasury.

Timber became the main activity of the Forest Service, which grew and grew until it became the biggest and richest agency in the Department of Agriculture. Although Congress continued to demand more timber produc-tion from the Forest Service, appropriations did not continue to grow apace. In fact, under the Nixon administration, the requested increase in timber came with a decrease in appropriation. The outcome, of course, was that management of the national forests became directly tied to timber produc-tion because "that's where the money was." At first there was considerable public acceptance of this activity. The Forest Service's tremendous expansion provided many jobs. Harvests increased many times—by ten times on the Flathead National Forest, for example. Between 1945 and 1969, the annual allowable harvest officially rose from 40 million board feet to 200 million.[7]

The timber industry also expanded. Existing mills grew, new mills were established, and many new jobs appeared. The timber expansion gained momentum in the 1950s and on into the 1960s. But problems began to sur-face. With the increasing environmental awareness of the mid-1960s, a grow-ing unhappiness with Forest Service activity became evident.

The "environmental movement" reflected a national concern, and had gained limited visibility in the 1950s. Later, Stewart Udall's *Quiet Crisis*,[8] written while he was secretary of the interior, was widely acclaimed. This growing national sentiment was directly at odds with the Forest Service's timber activity.

On the local level, some of the protest was directed to Forest Service officials, but it did not find sympathetic ears. In fact, it met with outrage, or at least bureaucratic unhappiness. Most forest officials were deeply committed to the timber mission. They considered the criticism uninformed and totally unfair. They ignored it and tended to withdraw from the public and close off the corridors of communication. To many observers, it seemed that they deemed their mission too big and too important for local criticism. After all, they were serving important national goals.

In 1962, the Resources Conservation and Development Project (RC&D) was established in the Bitterroot Valley.[9] It involved and drew together a group of valley citizens to identify, encourage, and promote their many interests. One focus of public concern was the accelerated timber harvest on national forests, particularly the clear-cut areas that were so clearly evident on mountain slopes around the valley. The group first sought to involve Forest Service people in its discussions, but this did not work out. However, three retired Forest Service officials—Guy "Brandy" Brandborg, former supervisor of the Bitterroot National Forest; Charles McDonald, former district ranger at Stevensville; and Champ Hannon—agreed with the locals and thoroughly and openly disagreed with the new timber-harvesting activity of the Forest Service. They became identified as the ringleaders of the opposition, and Forest Service employees were forbidden to have any association with them, especially with Brandborg.

Local dissatisfaction with the new Forest Service activities became focused in the Recreation Committee organized by the RC&D program, and Brandborg became the leader. Their dissatisfaction centered on the effects of clearcuts as they appeared on the mountainsides, including soil erosion, water runoff, and wildlife damage. Irrigators feared for their water supplies, and real-estate agents clearly identified the effects on scenic values as devaluing private property. At the center of all local criticism was a genuine feeling that the rate of timber harvest was too high, that forests were being overcut. The Forest Service ignored the valley's future economy, and the mess being left by clear-cutting showed utter contempt for the concerns of the local citizens.

While at first the public at large was not well informed, the Recreation Committee's activity soon developed a solid core of various officials, interest groups, and individuals who were knowledgeable and strongly motivated. Instinctively at first perhaps, their actions became more deliberate as knowledge and support increased. They set out to build the necessary strength to change the outcome of the policy struggle.

With growing support throughout the valley, the group moved forward on several fronts. They continued to seek a response from the Forest Service.

When communication with local offices of the service was cut off, they went to the regional office in Missoula. They also went to the newspapers, at first in Hamilton and then in Missoula, and aroused support in both places. They wrote to Senator Mike Mansfield and Senator Lee Metcalf, a native of the Bitterroot Valley. At first, letters came from individuals simply asking for help with various problems. But as the movement gathered force and organization, the group requested a full-scale congressional investigation.[10]

The group, headed by Brandborg and the Recreation Committee, also expanded citizen support through various state and national organizations that had members in the valley. Both the Farmers' Union and the National Grange were active locally and statewide. This increased the letters to the Forest Service, senators, and local newspapers. The Montana Wildlife Federation and National Wildlife Federation also responded sympathetically. Public awareness of environmental issues was expanding statewide and nationally and creating a more receptive audience to such forest-management issues.

By the mid-1960s, Recreation Committee activity began to bear tangible fruit. The regional forester in Missoula, Neal Rahm, saw to it that Bitterroot citizens' complaints were recognized. By 1968, discussions and correspondence led to a field trip of Recreation Committee and Forest Service officials to look over perceived problems on the land. The *Missoulian* assigned reporter Dale Burk to the case, and he started to meet with local people to gather material for stories.[11]

On May 19, 1969, the RC&D committee sent Neal Rahm a letter detailing its concern with forest practices on the Bitterroot National Forest. This letter came after some period of committee communication with the Regional Office that led to a request by Rahm for a detailed statement of complaint. Rahm also heard from Senator Metcalf and decided that he needed to investigate the matter. He appointed a Forest Service Task Force, which was reviewing the problem by June 1969.

Well aware of citizen complaints in the Bitterroot Valley, Senator Metcalf knew many of these people personally. Rather than a full congressional investigation, he proposed a smaller look at the problem and asked me to consider examining it to give him an understanding of the situation. He had a file of personal letters from his friends and neighbors complaining about Forest Service activity. "I don't know how to answer these people," he said. "I would like to have you look into it and provide me with what I need to know."

Previously, the University of Montana's School of Forestry and university interests generally had created a continuing relationship with the Montana congressional delegation. There was regular communication with the senators on other forestry matters, such as proposed legislation and Forest Service budgets. It was therefore natural for Metcalf to discuss the Bitterroot problems with me, first in Washington in mid-1967, and then again in January 1968, conversations that continued by phone and later meetings in

Washington. At first, our discussions were rather informal, but they grew more serious as the problem became more serious.

When the RC&D group came to the point of asking for a full-scale congressional investigation, Metcalf proposed something on a lesser and more personal level. Several faculty members took a tour of the Bitterroot National Forest in the fall of 1968 to examine the problems firsthand. Meanwhile, a faculty committee was formed. We were not sure that we really could have a constructive role. We needed to understand the situation well enough to identify the various aspects of the controversy and to decide what the problem was and whether a positive solution might be conceivable.

We decided to undertake the project at Senator Metcalf's request with the understanding that we would need to look into things carefully before making a final commitment. We wanted it understood that if we got into it and saw that our efforts might be utterly futile, or the complaints unsupportable, we were free to bow out.

Serious discussions with Senator Metcalf regarding the university's involvement started in May 1969, about the time that the Forest Service Task Force was established. Metcalf saw no reason to hold off our investigation because of the Forest Service action. He respected the Forest Service study and had encouraged it. He did not assume that it would be a "whitewash," as some locals immediately labeled it. But because of the local criticism, he thought that there was even more reason for the university committee to give another view—perhaps even some corroboration of the Forest Service report.

I drew in a team of faculty who had been involved with the School for Administrative Leadership (SAL), conducting a special course for resource administrators from federal and state resource agencies throughout the country for more than twenty years. Metcalf wrote his formal letter of request addressed to Dean Colle on December 2, 1969.

In approaching its study, the faculty committee recognized that it had to determine what the Forest Service ought to be doing, what it was doing, and whether its actions indeed departed from what it ought to be doing. We recognized three levels of policy. The original policy was the law of the nation as passed by Congress and signed by the president. The second was the written policy of the agency, which had responsibility for carrying out the law as enacted by Congress. The third level—actual agency action—was more difficult to identify. John D. Black identified it as "a more or less consistent pattern of behavior."

The committee began by studying Forest Service behavior. We learned from a diverse group of citizens what the Forest Service was doing and how this policy departed from what the service should have been doing. In the final analysis, we took these many ideas and viewpoints and distilled the information as the basis for our own judgments. We sought to contrast Forest Service actions with its own written policies and the laws of the land.

On April 15, 1970, the United States Forest Service's Forest Task Force released its report.[12] Despite certain shortcomings, the report strongly criticized some program weaknesses, including the overemphasis on timber. In this respect, the Task Force members were courageous. But they gave short shrift to range, watershed, wildlife, and recreation issues. Moreover, theirs was an internal report; since it could not criticize Congress or take a broader look at the problem, it discussed only Forest Service operations. Senator Metcalf assured us that our probe was still necessary. "And don't confine your report to just a review of the Forest Service report," he advised.

During 1969, our committee met with segments of the timber industry, wildlife representatives, Bill Worf of the Forest Service team, reporter Dale Burk, and many people from the Bitterroot Valley. We held regular weekly meetings to become well acquainted with all viewpoints. Following Senator Metcalf's visit to the campus, during which he met with the committee, we met with the Forest Service personnel in regional and field offices. As summer 1970 approached, we took field trips into the Bitterroot area and directly observed Forest Service harvesting practices. We flew the area with the Forest Service and met with groups of ranchers, with a group of realtors, and, as always, with various interested parties.

Our skepticism slowly dissolved. By the late summer of 1970, we concluded that we could and should proceed to complete our study and issue our report. We began to write the report in late September, and had pretty well completed it by the end of October. With the election coming up, Metcalf insisted that we release it after the November election date in order to keep it free from politics.

Senator Metcalf came to the university, where the committee verbally presented the report to him to help him answer the people in his hometown of Stevensville, and then we mailed him the written report on about November 10; he released our report in Missoula on November 18. When he returned to Washington, Senator Metcalf called a national press conference with results that were startling to the committee. Stories appeared in the *New York Times,* the *Los Angeles Times,* and the *Washington Post;* it seemed as if every newspaper in the nation and beyond our borders, even in Europe and Africa, carried the news. The super headline in the *Missoulian* proclaimed, "University Condemns the Forest Service."[13] The committee members were shocked. That was not what we thought we had done. We considered our report a constructive treatise. We had been restrained. There were things that we left out because they would inflame the situation. If we had set out to condemn the Forest Service, we could have very well done so, but we had no such intention.

Metcalf had our report printed as a Senate document, and on December 1, 20,000 copies appeared and were quickly distributed throughout the nation. To our surprise, the report became a hot local and national issue. The central focus was on the practice of clear-cutting. Although the problem was much deeper and broader, clear-cuts were the symbol that drew the criticism. The real problem was timber primacy, which now dominated and controlled Forest Service activity. This marked a clear departure from the broader congressional policy of multiple use as earlier conceived. Nonetheless, clearcutting itself was an important issue. An accepted practice under certain circumstances, it had been adopted as the principal method of harvest on all sites. In the Bitterroot, we learned from the chief Forest Service silvicultural researcher that the agency's recommendation for clear-cutting throughout was not based on sound silvicultural knowledge. His research recommended clearcutting under some conditions, but certainly not under all, or even most. When he objected to the practices there, he was told to be quiet. We did not include this inflammatory item in our report, nor did we press it further.

The response to our report came from individuals, private and official, from citizens' groups, and from organizations of many kinds. It came by word of mouth, telephone, and mail, and it covered the spectrum from hostile to extremely favorable. Neal Rahm, the regional forester, responded with documented comments from his staff that agreed with much of our report, for it was consistent with his Task Force's report. As a result, Rahm took a sound professional stance and adopted many of our recommendations. But he was not unanimously supported by his staff. The Forest Service timber people were furious, almost in shock.

We had many comments from Forest Service employees. It was interesting to note the strong support from older employees and retirees and also from young foresters with just a few years of experience. The older ones were unhappy with the agency's changes; the young ones had their ideals of good forestry offended by the heavy timber cutting.

The Bitterroot citizens felt vindicated, of course. And so did citizens throughout the country. Heartwarming letters arrived that merely said "thank you."

The local forest industry took a while to respond. No industries had been mentioned directly, but of course they were directly concerned. They took strong action by writing to the university president and the governor to arouse alumni support to suppress or oust me and the whole committee, thereby discrediting the report.

Local foresters were divided, but most were deeply interested. Committee members became the main attraction at Society of American Foresters meetings throughout the region, and attendance at meetings jumped from a desultory 20 to 200 or more. The first was held in Missoula on January 20, 1971, before a wild overflow audience. Committee members had a great time responding to questions, attack, and vituperation. We had an advantage: our committee had done its work carefully and was ready to be tested in any fair examination. We earned support in the audience, though it tended to be rather quiet at first. But as we stood up to the vocal opposition, supporters came forward to our defense. This was often the pattern at other meetings in neighboring states and even farther afield.

As faculty, the committee members were perhaps most interested in word from their peers in other universities. That response was slow in coming. A few early letters were more or less neutral, but the real message did not come through until we had been to professional meetings around the country. Then it came through loud and clear—they were green with envy.[14]

The publicity kept growing. It moved from newspapers into magazines. *American Forests* featured our report, and *Washington Magazine* carried an excellent piece on it. Justice William O. Douglas quoted it in a Supreme Court case. And then Jim Miller from *Reader's Digest* came out and interviewed us and wrote a most favorable account. When this appeared, University of Montana president Robert T. Pantzer, who had taken lots of heat on the matter and staunchly supported us all the way, laughed and said, "Now we're respectable!" And so we were.

The report continues to have a life of its own. It is a standard reference in forest history and policy and keeps reappearing in recent writings such as Charles F. Wilkinson and H. Michael Anderson's *Land Resource and Planning in the National Forests*.[15] The report was one of several items that influenced the Senate to look further into Forest Service timber-harvesting practices. Senator Metcalf, of course, made certain that the report was thoroughly studied by Congress, especially those portions of it that indicated that much of the problem was directly influenced by Congress in its support of the Forest Service. The Senate hearings on clear-cutting under the chairmanship of Idaho senator Frank Church followed.[16] I was invited to testify. These hearings, printed in three volumes, brought in a vast array of foresters and other professionals from throughout the land. Interestingly, clear-cutting was defended by almost everyone, but the "misuse" of clear-cutting was just as universally condemned. There appeared to be a consensus that the Forest Service was guilty of some of this misuse.

Following Senator Church's hearings, Congress urged the president to issue a directive to the Forest Service. When President Nixon failed to do so, Congress issued the Church Guidelines, which placed clear limitations on the use of clear-cutting.[17] Their concern was with the prevention of damage to the land and related resources, and also with regeneration of cutover areas. They identified the lands on which clear-cutting should not be practiced, one of which was where regeneration could not be ensured within five years of cutting. The guidelines repeatedly stressed that the Forest Service's mission and responsibility was to protect the health of the resource and not commodity production and income. The Church Guidelines were later incorporated almost without change into the National Forest Management Act of 1976.[18]

The Senate went on from there and enacted the Forest and Rangeland Renewable Resources Planning Act (RPA) of 1974[19] under the chairmanship of Senator Hubert Humphrey. This was done in-house without much conflict. RPA appeared to establish a new program for national forests, one that could provide for sound management of those controversial public forests indefinitely.

And then came the Monongahela case.[20] The committee became involved rather early, starting with a telephone call. I answered the phone, and a voice said, "This is Gifford Pinchot." I gasped and thought, "Oh, my God! Now I've done it." (After all, he had been dead for some years.) I managed to respond, "Well, hello," and after a short pause I felt it appropriate to ask, "And where are you these days?" "I'm in Baltimore," the voice responded. I thought, "The poor fellow, he deserved better than that." It quickly became clear, of course, that this was Gifford Pinchot, Jr., a faculty member at Johns Hopkins. He was calling out of personal interest, but also as a member of the Natural Resources Defense Council (NRDC) board of directors, who wanted to come out and see the Bitterroot for themselves. John Adams and Pinchot arrived not long after. We invited Dale Burk to go with us. It was while examining some of the Bitterroot clear-cuts that Pinchot remarked, "If my father had seen this, he would have cried." Quoted by Burk in a story soon after, it raised all kinds of fuss. The headline for an article in *Journal of Forestry,* which repudiated Pinchot's claim, read "Gifford Pinchot would have laughed."[21]

The NRDC was looking for a suitable forest to initiate a lawsuit on clearcutting. Its workers had examined a number, and the Bitterroot was a candidate. But they chose the Monongahela. In the Monongahela case, the court found that the Forest Service had been breaking the law for seventy-plus years, and the length of this transgression did not make its actions legal.[22] The court held that the 1897 act allowed the Forest Service to harvest only old, large, or dead trees, each individually marked.[23] The opinion went on to say that if the law was indeed out-of-date, then it was the duty of Congress to write a new law, not the courts. That, of course, was an open invitation for Congress to act. And since the Monongahela is in West Virginia, that state's senator, Jennings Randolph, had the first crack at it. He put together a committee of people from throughout the country, as well as representatives from West Virginia organizations, to draft a new law. I was invited to participate, and I spent my weekends in 1975 commuting to Washington.

During the writing of the Forest and Rangeland Renewable Resources Planning Act, Bob Wolf of the Library of Congress's Research Service had written a brief paragraph that would have amended the 1897 act and taken care of the problems. The "inside" story is that his paragraph was left out at the urging of the timber industry and the Forest Service, because it would have slightly reduced Forest Service discretionary power and was considered unnecessary. When Monongahela blew up, the service and the timber industry asked Humphrey to introduce this little paragraph as an amendment to RPA. Humphrey sent them to Senator Herman Talmadge, who bluntly advised them to stay in court.

Monongahela led to the National Forest Management Act (NFMA) of 1976,[24] the most complete forestry legislation ever passed. From Randolph's committee, the bill went to the Senate Interior Committee, chaired by Senator Lee Metcalf in the absence of Chairman Henry M. Jackson, who was running for president.

Strains of the Bitterroot Report carry through into the NFMA of 1976, and the University of Montana faculty committee is still involved after twenty years. The questions that still stand before us are simply these: Did we accomplish what we sought to accomplish? Where are we now? Did we make any difference?

What we sought with our report was *change*. When we pointed out the difference between what the Forest Service was doing and what it ought to be doing, our goal was to change the agency's behavior to reflect congressional policy. As a result, Congress enacted a series of land laws that attempted to define more clearly what the Forest Service ought to be doing. The question now is: Has that been done?

When the NFMA was enacted in 1976, I had a great feeling of accomplishment. I felt that the law clearly stated what must and must not be done. A key battle during the writing of the NFMA was the extent to which forest practices should be included in the bill. There was considerable pressure to be very detailed. I opposed this on principle and argued for the requirement that the Forest Service provide these details in a set of regulations clearly and specifically defining what it considered good forestry for the various conditions on the land. This argument prevailed, but the results have not lived up to our expectations. The Forest Service had one goal, it seemed, and that was to maintain maximum discretion by saying as little as possible in the regulations. There is, to my knowledge, still no official definition of good forestry.

The land laws dealing with forestry are in excellent condition. They clearly stipulate the changes in policy that are needed. But changing the behavior, the actual policy, of the Forest Service to conform to those policies has not yet been accomplished. Resource-management plans required by the National Forest Management Act have been completed for nearly all of the 156 national forests administered by the Forest Service. These plans call for a careful analysis of physical conditions as well as economic and social conditions, and for the development of a program of full public participation to foster understanding and support among the public. While many benefits have been derived from the development of these plans, full agreement is not one of them. Much of the public is more convinced than ever that national forests are managed almost entirely for timber production.

Forest supervisors at the beginning of the planning process believed that the process would be a "bottom-up" approach, and they were delighted with the idea. They had not gone far with this, however, before John Crowell was appointed assistant secretary of agriculture by President Ronald Reagan and announced at his confirmation hearings that while national forests were capable of producing three times the volume they had been producing, he would insist on only doubling production. The Forest Service was not ready to go that far and used various bureaucratic devices to at least reduce this demand, but they could not defeat it.

Forest supervisors who wrote the first plans had them returned by Crowell's office with the brutal demand that proposed timber production be doubled or at least greatly expanded. The choice was "do it or else." And most of them did it. Greatly out-of-balance plans appeared that brought protest from all sides, but especially from conservationists. Foresters have told me that because of the timber goals, which were excessive and imposed from above and which they could not support, they were forced to put together plans that were contrary to their scientific knowledge and their sense of integrity to the public and the forestry profession.

One of the greatest benefits from the NFMA and related legislation is that they require, and cause to be generated and used, a far higher level of scientific knowledge in the planning and management of the national forests. Another benefit is the requirement for a far higher level of public involvement in forest planning and management.

These two build on each other. Public interest has increased, and the level of public understanding has also increased to new and often highly constructive levels. Our hope, and certainly my conviction, is that sound forestry and resource stewardship generally have their best chances for success when they are based on the sound convictions of the intelligent majority.

The founding of the Association of Forest Service Employees for Environmental Ethics is clear evidence of dissatisfaction within the Forest Service.[25] Its charter closely parallels some of the language in our Bitterroot Report of twenty years ago and confirms that timber production is still the primary function of the Forest Service. The major breakthroughs in the law have not effectively changed Forest Service policy and behavior. Some change has taken place in the agency's stated policy, though generally it has tended to weaken the law. However, there are indications that rank-and-file behavior is moving in the right direction. There is one massive roadblock to getting the change as stated in the laws into the agency's regular behavior, and that is the simple fact that the Forest Service is saddled with an annual output goal for timber that makes sound management of our national forests impossible. The change will not come until the management of forests is based on the land's capability to produce within recognized and honored natural limits.

The Forest Service decision on Annual Sale Quantity (ASQ) is not based on land capability or economic feasibility. It is political. The congressional

Budget Committees and the Office of Management and Budget have a great deal to do with these decisions and can effectively frustrate the will of Congress and the public.[26] But even more, when an agency dislikes a congressional law and has the administration's support, it can effectively defeat the law by just not carrying it out. "Business as usual" can make the law totally, or at least essentially, ineffective.

Politics have kept RPA, NFMA, and other laws ineffective. But politics may some day have the opposite effect. We can look to the day when the political change will occur. When it does, sound, intelligent forestry will succeed in this country, in spite of the power and ingenuity of private greed.

NOTES

1. S. Doc. 115, 91st Cong., 2nd sess., 1970.

2. Bolle's collaborators included Richard W. Behan, then associate professor of natural resource policy and administration at the University of Montana School of Forestry; Gordon Browder, professor of sociology at the University of Montana and director of its Institute for Social Science Research; Thomas Payne, professor of political science at the University of Montana; W. Leslie Pengelly, professor of wildlife management at the University of Montana School of Forestry; Richard E. Shannon, professor of forest policy and administration and chairman of the University of Montana School for Administrative Leadership; and Robert F. Wambach, associate professor of forest economics at the University of Montana School of Forestry.

3. 16 U.S.C. §§471–75, 478, 479–82, 551 (1982).

4. 16 U.S.C. § 475 (1982).

5. For example, the Forest Products Laboratory in Madison, Wisconsin, carried on research in milling and manufacturing spruce lumber that was available when the 1950s epidemic hit the northern Rockies.

6. *Full Use and Development of Montana's Timber Resources,* S. Doc. 9, 86th Cong., 1st sess., 1956, 6.

7. Compare United States Department of Agriculture, Forest Service, Region 1 internal annual reports for 1945 and 1969.

8. Stewart Udall, *The Quiet Crisis* (New York: Holt, Rinehart and Winston, 1963).

9. Resource Conservation and Development Act of 1962; 16 U.S.C. §§ 3441–51 (1982). The act established the Bitterroot Conservation and Development District.

10. Harold Maus of Hamilton, a lifelong resident of the Bitterroot, wrote to Metcalf about the controversy: "I am the witness to another innovation, one that is destroying the scenic beauty, recreational value and last but not least, the very soil itself. This innovation is the clear-cutting method used to harvest timber from our national forest lands. . . . The people of this area . . . absolutely do not like what they see happening but efforts to communicate these feelings to local Forest Service personnel have been of no avail. Therefore, the only hope the citizens of this area have to correct this situation is through you, the people's representative in Congress. Won't you please *help?*"

11. C. Ransick, "The Bitterroot Controversy: Dale Burk's Role as Journalist and Activist" (M.A. thesis, School of Journalism, University of Montana, 1988).

12. United States Department of Agriculture, Forest Service, "Management Practices on the Bitterroot: A Task Force Appraisal, May 1969–April 1970," files 1500 and 2470 (available from the Forest Service Region 1 office).

13. *Missoulian,* 18 November 1970, 1.

14. About the report, Herb Borman of Yale wrote: "That's the kind of thing a private university like Yale should be doing, but here you, a state university, did it. We could never have done it. It would have cut off our private funding. Or threatened to. Our president or dean wouldn't have allowed it. You could now hire the best half of our faculty if you had the money."

15. Charles F. Wilkinson and H. Michael Anderson, *Land and Resource Planning in the National Forests* (Washington, D.C.: Island Press, 1987), 22.

16. *"Clearcutting" Practices on National Timberlands: Hearings Before the Subcommittee on Public Lands of the Senate Committee on Interior and Insular Affairs,* 92nd Cong., 1st sess., 1972.

17. *Report of Subcommittee on Public Lands, Senate Interior and Insular Affairs Committee, Clearcutting on Federal Timberlands,* 92nd Cong., 2nd sess., 1972, 8–9. The Church Guidelines were actually written by Leon Cambre, a Forest Service employee who was on assignment to Senator Lee Metcalf.

18. 16 U.S.C. §§ 1604(g) (3) (E); (F) (1976).

19. 16 U.S.C. §§ 1600–1614 (1982).

20. *West Virginia Division of the Izaak Walton League, Inc. v. Butz,* 522 F.2d 945 (4th Cir. 1975).

21. Al Wiener, "Gifford Pinchot Would Have Laughed," *Journal of Forestry,* November 1973, 13, 34–37.

22. *Izaak Walton League* v. *Butz,* 952.

23. Ibid., 955.

24. 16 U.S.C. §§ 1600–1687 (1982).

25. *High Country News,* 5 June 1989, 30.

26. V.A. Sample, "Implementation of National Forest Planning: The Impact of the Federal Budget Process" (Ph.D. diss., Yale University, 1989), 31.

Part Four

MULTIPLE USES

From Rule-of-Thumb to Scientific Range Management: The Case of the Intermountain Region of the Forest Service

Thomas G. Alexander

In a major reorganization in 1908, the Forest Service began the decentralization of its operations on a scale unmatched by any other federal agency. Chief Forester Gifford Pinchot sent personnel from the Washington office to staff six newly created multistate regions. In the process, the Washington office delegated considerable autonomy to the regional foresters who headed these units.[1] At that time, Region 4 (the Intermountain Region) consisted roughly of all of Utah and Nevada, Idaho south of the Salmon River, Wyoming west of the Continental Divide, and Arizona north of the Grand Canyon. Subordinate to the regional foresters were forest supervisors, who directed the work within the national forests. Under their direction, the district rangers worked as line managers on the ground. Various assistants, specialists, and research organizations provided staff support.[2]

During the period between 1905 and 1930, the Forest Service shifted away from the values and practices of what might be called a rule-of-thumb management, which emphasized traditional organization, friendship and political preference in hiring, competence and diligence for retaining employees, and the practical application of conventional wisdom in range and timber management. In its place, the Forest Service, under Gifford Pinchot and his successors, Henry S. Graves and William B. Greeley, instituted what might be called a bureaucratic-scientific system of management. The service based this system in part on European forestry traditions and in part on the managerial and scientific revolution taking place in the United States.[3] Within the Forest Service, the first step in the transition was the adoption of a bureaucratic system; requirements for hiring included minimum educational ability such as reading, writing, and mathematics; a civil service examination of the applicant's outdoor skills; and a rudimentary knowledge of the practical aspects of range management and forestry.

Between 1910 and 1930, Region 4 began to adopt scientific and professional techniques of range management. The region established two units—the Caribou National Forest and the Great Basin Experiment station—as models for the implementation of research-validated methods. While in the narrow sense the adoption of scientific and professional techniques on these units may be seen as an example of forest and range management, more fundamentally it can be seen as study of change within a large organization.[4] After reviewing employee records from Region 4, it seems clear that environmental factors, genetic factors, and personal capacity influenced the adoption of concepts associated with scientific methods of range management. Moreover, range managers learned to adopt scientific methods because they realized that they must do so in order to operate successfully within the system.

On a conceptual level, though not in practice, the Forest Service had fully completed the transition to the bureaucratic-scientific system by the late 1920s. By then, its hiring requirements included an education in the scientific aspects of forest and range management and a civil service examination testing those skills and knowledge. The service based retention and promotion principally on performance inspections designed to test the application of the education, diligence, and competence of the employee.

The lag between adoption of the bureaucratic-scientific theory and its implementation came about for a number of reasons. One was an overly optimistic estimate of the capacity of the land to regenerate itself. A second was pressure from stockmen, politicians, and others who feared the loss of grazing permits, and who refused to concede that livestock had overgrazed the land. A third reason was resistance on the part of the stockmen and others who remained unconvinced by the results of scientific investigations. And a final cause grew from the fact that many of the initial generation of foresters came from livestock families and both sympathized with their families' position and applied rule-of-thumb outlooks and procedures learned from them.[5]

As a result, many early forest officers had to confront not only their personal inclinations favoring stockmen but also enormous external pressures when they tried to reduce livestock numbers to the carrying capacity of badly overgrazed ranges. The reduction of livestock required such measures as cooperation with stockmen's associations and individual permittees, monitoring the condition of the range and of animals leaving it, subjecting the operations and the forest officers themselves to periodic inspections and critiques, and providing support and training through rangers' and supervisors' meetings.

The lag between conceptualization and practice contributed to the failure of the employees of Region 4 to immediately establish proper stocking limits. Some reductions in numbers did take place during the 1920s, but, in general, forest officers were unable to reduce livestock numbers to the carrying capacity of most ranges in Region 4 until the late 1950s and afterward.

In adopting the new system, the Forest Service sought to apply scientifically based techniques to range management. The service set up a number of research centers, including the Great Basin Experiment station, which it established in 1912 in Ephraim Canyon on the Manti National Forest in central Utah. The men working at these centers endeavored to establish a scientific basis for management policy. Though the Great Basin Station was not the first established, by 1913 the Forest Service had chosen it as the center for experiments in range management.[6]

From the outset, things went well at the Great Basin Station, with Arthur W. Sampson as its first director. Already noted for his range and forest research, Sampson and his successors recruited a number of bright and creative scientists who laid the groundwork for and promulgated the science of range management. For example, Sampson and his colleague Frederick S. Baker later joined the faculty of the University of California and spread their enthusiasm and knowledge of range and forest research to their students. W. R. Chapline, who started his career as a student researcher at the station, became chief of range research for the Forest Service. Clarence L. Forsling, who succeeded Sampson as director in 1922, became head of the Forest Service's Division of Forest Research and later of the Interior Department's Grazing Service. Later, Sampson authored the standard texts on range management.

In line with the bureaucratic-scientific model, the Washington office of the Forest Service established an administrative structure designed to ensure that its research arm addressed its most pressing needs. In 1912 Chief Forester Henry S. Graves set up a central investigating committee, and each region established similar committees, which were to function in cooperation with the regional foresters. The original committee for Region 4—which consisted of O. M. Butler, assistant regional forester for silviculture; Homer E. Fenn, assistant regional forester for grazing; and Clinton G. Smith, Cache National Forest supervisor—was closely tied to regional administration. By the 1920s the regional investigating committee consisted of representatives from the regional administration, the Great Basin Experiment Station, forest supervisors, and Utah State Agricultural College. The committee planned the agenda of research, and guaranteed that the region's most pressing problems received the highest priority.[7]

By the 1930s, the Great Basin Station's most important work was in watershed and range research. Sampson began his first studies on two watersheds, designated A and B, of eleven and nine acres. By manipulating the extent of grazing on the watersheds, the researchers demonstrated that they could control water and sedimentary runoff. They also established that proper management of vegetative cover could preserve the land from excessive erosion. Other aspects of these studies included artificial revegetation, range readiness (when animals should be allowed on the range), plant vigor studies (to determine how often and extensively the range could be grazed),[8] poisonous plant research (to determine methods of eradication), the relation of grazing to aspen reproduction, and the relationship between weather and plant development.[9]

Significantly, the range and watershed studies had immediate application to range management in Region 4. The sample plots and quadrats that Sampson established at the station, beginning in 1913, became models for range reconnaissance and carrying-capacity studies.[10] Studies at the station showed the fragility of arid intermountain grazing land. Among other things, it was evident that overgrazed vegetation recovered very slowly.[11] Studies showed that the removal of vegetation more than once or twice a year was detrimental to the plant community.[12] Although preliminary findings suggested that forest officers could achieve good results in revegetation with hardy native species grown under conditions similar to those in the area to be reseeded, further research indicated a lack of success with artificial revegetation, and Region 4 curtailed its revegetation activities until after World War II.[13]

If the Great Basin Station provided the laboratory for conceiving methods of range management, the Caribou National Forest in southeastern Idaho provided an actual situation in which the Forest Service could test theoretical findings. Range conditions on the Caribou at the time of the establishment of the Great Basin Station approximated the average condition of the various forests of Region 4, and the regional administration conceived of grazing management on the Caribou as a model that other forests might follow.[14]

Forest officers in the Intermountain Region had difficulty in managing the range in part because the demand for grazing land far exceeded the supply. Region 4 managed more range and more animals than any region in the national forest system. In 1927 the land under forest supervision in Region 4 was 28 percent greater than in any other region, and the net range area, at 31.8 million acres, was 21 percent greater. Though lower in animal unit months for cattle and horses than Regions 2 (Colorado and Wyoming) and 3 (Arizona and New Mexico), Region 4 grazed more head of the two species than any other region except Region 2. No other region even came close to the number of sheep grazed in Region 4.[15]

Between 1910 and America's entry into World War I in 1917, the Forest Service began to make systematic evaluations of range conditions and tried new techniques to improve rangelands, such as rotation, deferred grazing, and bedding sheep out. Following the war, a number of changes took place in the kinds of scientific evaluations employed, including the inauguration of period studies, designed to determine the date at which stock should be allowed to enter the range, and palatability studies, to catalogue plants that animals preferred to eat. Range-management strategies also changed: the service revised fee schedules to place them in line with the actual value of the range. In response, western range interests mounted the first of a number of attempts to gain control over forest grazing lands and thus to avoid reductions in stock numbers and increased fees.

Forest supervisors themselves held widely divergent views on proper management prescriptions. Such diverse attitudes were clear in meetings supervisors held with the region administrators in Boise and Ogden in January 1911. Especially important at these meetings were two factions that championed divergent views of proper stocking. One emphasized attention to the condition of the land, and the other concerned itself with the needs of stockmen.[16] Several supervisors, led by Clarence N. Woods, of the Sawtooth National Forest, believed that managers ought to give priority to the condition of the grazing land itself. To protect the land, Woods insisted, supervisors ought to consider that the range was fully stocked when it had reached three-fourths of the presumed carrying capacity.

The most vocal opposition to Woods came from David Barnett, of the Targhee National Forest, and N. E. Snell, of the Caribou National Forest, who were more concerned with making grazing lands available to stockmen than they were with the condition of the land itself. These men argued that forest officers ought to stock to the range's presumed capacity, and they should modify this policy only in the event of potential damage to timber reproduction and watershed. Under this conception, if animals ate all the forage early in the season, herders would have to pull them off the range. For Barnett and Snell, stockmen's demands would take first priority in management decisions. When put to a vote, Woods's proposition lost 8 to 9.[17]

In spite of the vote, research played a most important role in shaping management policy. Woods and his supporters rode the wave of the bureaucratic-scientific future and were rewarded for their prescience. Woods himself rose rapidly within the ranks of Region 4 officers and finished his career as regional forester, and his supporters, such as Guy B. Mains, J. B. Lafferty, and Dan Pack, have become legendary figures. By contrast, Barnett and Snell have been almost forgotten.

Although before 1940 the secretary of agriculture nominally granted permission for the numbers of stock grazed on each forest, he based his decision on the recommendation of the supervisors, approval of the regional forester, and information gathered by previous inspections. But until the supervisors had access to the results of reconnaissance and carrying-capacity studies to formulate research-validated grazing plans, they based most recommendations on tradition, user pressure, and eyeball estimates.

That was as true for the Caribou as for any other unit; precedent and user pressure usually decided levels of stocking. Early in the 1911 grazing season, for example, Forest Supervisor George G. Bentz asked special approval to graze 322,000 sheep on the forest—since three former permittees had failed to submit their requests on time. Regional Forester Edward A. Sherman disapproved the request, and later Bentz admitted that even "320,000 head is considerably in excess of the number the range will support without injury."[18] Nevertheless, he said, "It is not deemed advisable . . . to recommend a reduction in the allotment at this time because of the 50,000 cut made last year, and because of the adverse [economic] conditions surrounding the sheep business today." He proposed instead to take "advantage" of "forfeitures, lapses of permits, and reductions made on transfers," where the reduced numbers were not needed for qualified permittees. Still, he believed that in addition to the 7,000 head of cattle permitted on the forestland, others trespassed on it. Apparently in response to user pressure, he recommended that if that proved to be the case, "an increase in the allowance of cattle will be necessary."[19] Under these conditions, user pressure, economic conditions, and tradition dictated stocking levels.

Increasingly, research findings were expected to take precedence over other considerations in allocating numbers to permittees. Range reconnaissance studies—designed to determine the condition and carrying capacity of the range—began in the Forest Service in 1910; in Region 4 they started on the Targhee National Forest in 1911, the Manti National Forest in 1912, and the Caribou National Forest in 1913. Since these studies could proceed only with the available, limited funds, by 1915 carrying-capacity studies had been completed on only five forests in Region 4. Many national forests did not complete the studies until the 1920s, and some not then.[20]

Range reconnaissance, like timber reconnaissance, consisted basically of a survey of the area to gather information for future planning and management. The grazing examiners who conducted the surveys followed the United States Geological Survey maps where possible, but where maps were unavailable, they often made form line maps using control points established by the regional engineering division. After the control points had been established, they created maps, using standard methods with a plane table, alidade, and Abney level. The examiners plotted various species of plants, land configuration, and the health of the land and plants on the maps. In addition, they collected plants for a forest herbarium, estimated the percentage of each plant in the total plant community, and undertook to establish the palatability of various species.[21]

Carrying-capacity studies began in 1913 on the Caribou range. They succeeded range reconnaissance and were based on the theory that range research could produce a rule for optimum stocking through empirical measurement of use, forage volume and vigor, and animal weights. Carrying capacity was defined as "the minimum acreage required to maintain a foraging animal in good, thrifty condition through the grazing season stipulated." These studies proceeded in two phases, one of which involved the development of long-range sample plots; the other consisted of gathering immediate data by measuring the weight gain of animals.[22]

On the Caribou, examiners intended "to conduct tests on every distinctly different and representative unit of the range." Such tests required the cooperation of sheepmen to a greater extent than before, since they now had to graze in "accordance with a definite plan" established under research-derived principles. Expecting each study to last over a three- to five-year period, Homer E. Fenn, assistant regional forester for grazing, said the studies would "be considered complete when sufficient data [had] been collected to serve, together with the reconnaissance data, as a basis of an intensive plan of grazing management for every part of the Caribou Forest and as much range on neighboring forests as similarity of conditions will permit."[23]

In general, the method of determining carrying capacity had been worked out by Arthur Sampson, James T. Jardine, of the Washington office, and Mark Anderson, a grazing examiner, and they published the data gathered on the Caribou and other forests. But this early work was supplanted by carrying-capacity studies Clarence E. Favre and W. Vincent Evans conducted in the 1910s. These studies included animal weight measurements and the establishment and careful control of sample plots consisting of eight quadrats and two seasonal variation enclosures on each of five allotments; in addition, the scientists harvested the plants on the ten enclosures twice during the year and weighed them, both green and dried. Favre and Evans sought two results: they tried to determine a standard forage area required for sheep and sought the method of grazing best adapted to Caribou conditions. In evaluating Favre and Evans's work, Homer Fenn considered the "reconnaissance and supplemental range [carrying-capacity] studies conducted on the Caribou . . . [to be] the most intensive and systematic range inspection that has ever been made of a forest." By World War I, C. H. Shattuck cited the Caribou as a model of range management. By the mid-1920s, rangers were brought to the Caribou to "see how other rangers were handling problems similar to those . . . on [their] own districts."[24]

The data from reconnaissance and carrying-capacity studies led foresters to propose a standard forage acre as the determinant of proper stocking. This measure took the total land area multiplied by the fraction of the surface supporting vegetation, the fractional density of cover, and the percentage of palatable forage. Thus an area of eighty acres covered with 70 percent vegetation, with a density of 80 percent, and with 80 percent of the area covered with palatable vegetation would equal thirty-six forage acres.[25] The researchers also tried to determine grazing practices that forest officers ought to adopt in utilizing available forage. To determine grazing patterns best suited to the Caribou, Evans and Favre tested suggestions Sampson had made following his experiments in Oregon and Utah. Sampson had proposed that stockmen defer grazing until the seed crop had ripened, on the theory that such practices would then produce a greater volume of feed and more vigorous plants. He also proposed that when stockmen rotated animals from one portion of the allotment to another in different annual cycles, the plants grew better.[26]

Evans and Favre believed the Caribou ranges were unsuited for deferred and rotation grazing. "Where there is an extreme diversity of types and a considerable range of altitude on each allotment," they said, "it is particularly difficult to secure a division of allotments into rotation areas that will conform to the best use of the range and that will provide a uniform amount of forage per allotment each year." With regard to deferring, they agreed that "with grasses it appears to be true that there is no very rapid deterioration in food value for some time after physiological maturity, . . . the same was not true of most palatable weeds." On weed range like the Caribou, there occurred "a rapid decay in food value after maturity, so much so that sheep will prefer" living browse, which was "much inferior in mutton-producing qualities" to the dry weeds. On a practical level, Evans and Favre found the deferred and rotation systems difficult to implement since they required "an extra large amount of supervision," which neither the forest nor the ranchers could supply. Nevertheless, they recommended deferring grazing "in those cases where through internal mismanagement of the range, areas are overgrazed."[27]

Even though many more sheep than cattle grazed the ranges of Region 4, sheep carried a negative image—many argued they injured tree growth. Some forest officers, however, believed that with scientifically designed grazing systems and control, land managers could develop proper prescriptions for sheep as well as cattle. Bryant S. Martineau reported studies on the Old Payette National Forest between 1912 and 1914 that ought to have laid to rest the prejudice against grazing sheep among trees. In conducting this investigation, Martineau used methods of bedding-out that Arthur Sampson had pioneered. Under this system, instead of bringing the sheep back to a central camp each evening, the stockmen allowed the animals to bed down wherever they happened to be grazing. Moreover, they used dogs only to protect the flocks against predators, and particularly not to force the stock over the same ground. Martineau found that with the bedding-out method "these areas may be fully stocked, provided they are properly handled, without injury to the reproduction of yellow pine or other conifers." By 1926, 93 percent (the highest in the service) of all sheepmen in Region 4 used the bedding-out system.[28]

Those familiar with the livestock industry recognized that inadequate herd supervision and the grazing habits of cattle made them a potentially more serious threat than sheep to forest ranges. C. N. Woods pointed out that in spite of sufficient feed on the allotments cattle tended to "remain too much on the lower, less steep country and along the water and among the willows." The remedy, he said, was driving and holding cattle "in rougher country and in putting salt higher in the mountains." Sheep, he indicated, "graze the range more evenly than either cattle or horses." Since stockmen generally turned cattle onto the range and allowed them to graze at will, some areas of a cattle allotment could be badly overgrazed while others were hardly used at all. Thus the adoption of scientifically regulated grazing practices for cattle was much more difficult to implement than for sheep.[29]

These difficulties increased due to the impact of World War I on stocking levels. Between 1910 and 1917, there had been an increase of 59 percent—from 376,000 to 597,000—in the number of cattle and horses on the range. At the same time, there had been an increase in sheep from 3.9 million in 1910 to 4.4 million in 1912, followed by a decrease to 3.5 million in 1917, a net decrease of 10 percent. However, in 1918 the number of cattle and horses, at 620,000, reached their highest point since the Forest Service began administering the lands, and the number of sheep increased to about the 1913 level.[30]

These numbers exacerbated an already hazardous situation, and Regional Forester Leon F. Kneipp was well aware of the reasons for and impact of this overgrazing. In 1919, he wrote to Weiser supervisor J. B. Lafferty that the "economic conditions and the labor situation incident to the war have led us, during the past couple of years, to tolerate conditions which obviously are not in accord with the purpose for which a particular forest was created, and the result has been in many instances detrimental to the interests of the Service and the purposes for which it stands." Justification for excessive stocking had disappeared by 1919, and he urged the "vigorous application of proper principles of forest administration, including grazing management, to enable us to regain lost ground and to make the progress in the improvement of the forest lands which may reasonably be expected as a result of our expenditures of funds and effort."[31]

During the war, an increased volume of meat and wool seemed patriotic.[32] Afterward, concern for the condition of grazing lands began to weigh more heavily on forest officers. In 1919, the number of permitted sheep was lower than in any year since 1917, and in 1920, the numbers were lower than in any year since 1906, when the number of forests and extent of acreage in the Intermountain Region was far lower. By 1921 even the level of cattle permitted had dipped to approximately the 1916 level, and it continued to decline during the decade.

These reductions were largely the result of the application of data gathered from reinaugurated range reconnaissance and other scientific studies that had been curtailed during the wartime emergency. In Region 4, which led the service in reconnaissance and carrying-capacity studies during the 1920s,[33] it became clear that a major part of the overgrazing problem was due to the early dates at which livestock was allowed to enter the allotments. On the LaSal National Forest, rancher Charles Redd said that cattle would move onto the forest in "a free-for-all" over the "snow and mud," as early as April 1, to "get there before someone else did." Following a drought in 1919, some of the cattlemen's associations agreed to change the opening date on the Caribou Ranges to May 5 because of overgrazing in particular areas. By that time, Supervisor Earl C. Sanford argued the need for additional tests to "arrive at proper grazing seasons and generally to secure a proper adjustment of the grazing on these allotments."[34]

To accomplish this, specialists began period studies on the Caribou in 1921. After a survey of four allotments, consisting of twelve cattle units, on which the season began between April 20 and May 1, H. E. Malmsten recommended deferring grazing by ten to fifteen days during an average year. On years with particularly severe winters, like 1920/1921, snow still covered some north slopes, and vegetation was not ready for grazing until May 20. In line with general service policy, Ernest Winkler, staff assistant for range management in the regional office, recommended that Sanford phase in the new dates over a period of time to prevent economic dislocations.[35]

In 1928 James O. Stewart, grazing inspector from the regional office, returned to the original Caribou quadrats to remap those that time and the elements had not obliterated. The results were mixed, but generally negative; of twelve sample plots located by Stewart, grasses had decreased on eight, increased on two, and changed but little on two. Less palatable species had tended to increase.[36]

These and other long-term examples of continued deterioration led range managers to question and then reject the standard forage acre. In 1927, at a meeting of the Society of American Foresters, Charles DeMoisy of Region 4 argued that problems had resulted from the application of standard monthly forage acre figures (0.8 and 0.3) to fallacious palatability estimates. He said further that only through intensive study of individual ranges could examiners determine the proper stocking. In a report of 1927, Dean Phinney, then on the range staff of the Caribou, said that "the old forage acre estimates continue to be high. Palatability percentages used on the old reconnaissance are, in the main, responsible for the high forage acre figures."[37]

More recent research in certain areas has shown other standards to have been faulty, something that range managers in the 1920s could not have known. During the 1920s, forest officers based forage volume estimates on the assumption that animals could eat 75 to 85 percent of the vegetation without damage to reproduction. More recent studies have shown that there "should have been closer to 50 percent forage left at the end of the grazing season." In carrying-capacity weight-gain estimates, lamb weights of sixty-five to seventy pounds were considered acceptable, while by the late 1960s, weights of more than ninety pounds were not unusual. Even the seventy-pound animals from the 1920s must have looked good to sheepmen used to the forty-pound lambs produced in 1909 on forests like the Humboldt.[38]

Thus even conscientious managers who stocked their ranges conservatively, on the basis of the research-produced and generally accepted standards, could cause overgrazing. This did not invalidate the new bureaucratic-scientific conception since the questions raised about the previous, forage-acre estimates came through additional research. It does, however, indicate that managers would have done well to have asked some hard questions about the considerable difference—ranging to 89 percent— between the forage estimates based on range reconnaissance and the higher estimates based on rules of thumb from the old conception.[39]

In most instances, however, it seems obvious that the new bureaucratic-scientific ideas produced more satisfactory results than the old. Reports from the forests indicate that supervisors' rule-of-thumb carrying-capacity estimates generally followed closely ideological trends and economic pressures. On the Boise National Forest, for instance, one notes an upward swing in carrying-capacity estimates for both cattle and sheep during World War I, then a considerable decline in the late 1920s, as the forests came under pressure to improve ranges.[40]

By 1929, though results were not satisfactory and did not become so until recently, some improvement did take place. As a result of reconnaissance figures, period studies, and an understanding of "conditions on the ground as a result of use," there were reductions in the numbers of animals grazed and the length of grazing seasons.[41] On the Caribou, the number of cattle and horses allowed declined from 22,900 in 1921 to 18,000 in 1929, and the number of sheep from 265,000 to 235,000. In the four states comprising the Intermountain Region, permits for cattle and horses declined from 558,333 to 389,337 head, and those for sheep from 3,165,015 to 3,101,914. The reductions in numbers were accompanied by reductions in the length of the grazing season. By 1927 the longest grazing season on the Caribou was May 1 to October 31 in the lower country along the Snake River. Most seasons began on May 16 or 20, and one started as late as June 1. In 1929 the starting date for the Snake River allotment was set back to May 15. As might be expected, stockmen voiced considerable "opposition and vigorous criticism" of the reductions in numbers of stock and length of seasons.[42]

At the beginning of the 1930s, then, a number of important changes had taken place in Forest Service management. The training of range managers to accept the bureaucratic-scientific conception of range management was virtually completed, so that few, if any, would have argued that the Forest Service ought to base management decisions on any other system than one derived from research. By the same token, a degree in forestry or range management from a recognized college or university and successful completion of the civil service examination was a requirement for employment. Moreover, while overgrazing and erosion continued on many ranges, forest officers had accepted the new bureaucratic-scientific system to such a great degree that no one seems to have suggested an alternative.

A great deal had to be done before the ranges could be said to be in optimum condition. Scientists had to perfect, and managers had to implement, techniques to more precisely measure the trend of range improvement and deterioration. Rangers and supervisors had to continue to develop public-relations skills in dealing with stockmen and their political allies, which was particularly necessary in order to sidetrack both the movement for user control of federal grazing lands and those proposals that substituted traditional methods for scientifically validated measures of proper stocking. And researchers and forest officers had to develop management plans and techniques that they could implement in the face of practical range conditions and user resistance. In practice, these efforts did not succeed until the late 1950s and early 1960s.

It should be pointed out, however, that in the long run, given the bureaucratic-scientific conceptions adopted in the period between 1910 and 1930, Region 4 developed what is arguably the best range research organization in the Forest Service. Close cooperation between the scientists and range managers allowed rapid implementation of the results of research. The cooperative work of management and research within the bureaucratic and inspection systems allowed rapid critiques of both management techniques and the results of research. Moreover, acquiring the culture of the organization under the traditions of technical professionalism and experimentation that had grown during the 1910s and 1920s helped Region 4 to develop the capacity to adopt changing techniques and eventually to implement effective range management in most portions of the Intermountain West in the 1950s and early 1960s.

NOTES

1. I am using the term "region" throughout this chapter, since that is the current designation. The term "district" was used early in the period.

2. See Harold K. Steen, The U.S. Forest Service: A History (Seattle: University of Washington Press, 1976); William D. Rowley, U.S. Forest Service Grazing and Rangelands: A History (College Station: Texas A & M University Press, 1985); Ben W. Twight, Organizational Values and Political Power: The Forest Service Versus the Olympic National Park (University Park: Pennsylvania State University Pres, 1983); Herbert Kaufman, The Forest Ranger: A Study in Administrative Behavior (Baltimore: Johns Hopkins University Press, 1960), which should be supplemented, however, by Christopher K. Leman, "The Forest Ranger Revisited: Administrative Behavior in the U.S. Forest Service in the 1980s" (Paper presented at the 1981 annual meeting of the American Political Science Association, New York, 3–6 September 1981).

3. Samuel P. Hays, Conservation and the Gospel of Efficiency: The Progressive Conservation Movement, 1890–1920 (Cambridge, Mass.: Harvard University Press, 1959).

4. Among the theoretical works most useful in conceptualizing this study of organizational change were Max Weber, From Max Weber: Essays in Sociology, trans. and ed. H. H. Gerth and C. Wright Mills (New York: Oxford University Press, 1946), 240–50; and Max Weber, The Theory of Social and Economic Organization, trans. A. M. Henderson and Talcott Parsons (New York: Oxford University Press, 1947), 341–45 363–73; Robert L. Heilbroner, The Nature and Logic of Capitalism (New York: Norton, 1985), 20–25; Alfred D. Chandler, Jr., The Visible Hand: The Managerial Revolution in American Business (Cambridge, Mass.: Harvard University

Press, 1977), 7–10, 498–500; Thomas S. Kuhn, *The Structure of Scientific Revolutions*, 2nd ed. (Chicago: University of Chicago Press, 1970), esp. 43–51; and Anthony Giddens, *Central Problems in Social Theory: Action, Structure and Contradiction in Social Analysis* (Berkeley: University of California Press, 1979), 120.

    5. Rowley, *Forest Service Grazing and Rangelands;* William Voit, Jr., *Public Grazing Lands: Use and Misuse by Industry and Government* (New Brunswick, N.J.: Rutgers University Press, 1976); Michael Frome, *The Forest Service,* 2nd ed., rev. (Boulder, Colo.: Westview Press, 1984).

    6. Wendell M. Keck, *Great Basin Station: Sixty Years of Progress in Range and Watershed Research,* Forest Service Research Paper INT-118 (Ogden, Utah: Intermountain Forest and Range Experiment Station, 1972), 1; Lawrence Rakestraw, *A History of Forest Conservation in the Pacific Northwest, 1891–1913* (New York: Arno Press, 1979), 254; Jenks Cameron, *The Development of Governmental Forest Control in the United States* (Baltimore: Johns Hopkins University Press, 1928), 256–57; *Annual Reports of the Department of Agriculture, 1913* (Washington, D.C.: Government Printing Office, 1914), 185.

    7. See Herbert A. Smith, ed., *Review of Forest Service Investigations,* 2 vols. (Washington, D.C.: Government Printing Office, 1913); Steen, *Forest Service,* 136–37; Investigative Program, D-4, 1926, file 1680, History, National Forests of the Intermountain Region, Historical Files, Regional Office [hereafter cited by the name of the file and Historical Files, Regional Office].

    8. Arthur W. Sampson, memorandum to district forester, 7 November 1919, file Grazing, Manti, FD 17, Historical Files, Supervisor's Headquarters, Manti-LaSal National Forest, Price, Utah [hereafter, historical records from the national forests in Region 4 cited with the name of the file and the name of the forest].

    9. For a summary of activities in research, see Annual Program, District Investigative Committee, District 4, FY 1917, file 1680, History, National Forests of the Intermountain Region, Historical Files, Regional Office, Ogden, Utah. On grazing in ponderosa pine, see C. B. Morse, memorandum to district forester, 5 December 1925, file RS-Regeneration Seed Studies, 1912–1928, Regional Office Records, RG 95, Denver Federal Records Center, Denver, Colorado [hereafter, federal records centers cited by the location followed by the letters FRC].

    10. *Annual Reports of the Department of Agriculture, 1914* (Washington, D.C.: Government Printing Office, 1914), 158–59. See also Elbert H. Reid and Raymond Price, "Progress in Forest-Range Management," in *American Forestry: Six Decades of Growth,* ed. Henry Clepper and Arthur B. Meyer (Washington, D.C.: Society of American Foresters, 1960), 116; C. L. Forsling, "Why the Range Should Not Be Grazed Too Early in the Spring," attached to Ernest Winkler to forest supervisor, 26 April 1926, file: 1650, Historical Library, Range Allowances, 1935–38, Bridger-Teton; *Annual Reports of the Department of Agriculture, 1916* (Washington, D.C.: Government Printing Office, 1917), 183.

    11. *Report of the Forester, 1928* (Washington, D.C.: Government Printing Office, 1928), 56.

    12. *Annual Reports of the Department of Agriculture, 1920* (Washington, D.C.: Government Printing Office, 1921), 254.

    13. Ibid., 253. The major problem in implementing these findings was in securing a reasonably extensive and economical seed supply. See *Annual Reports of the*

Department of Agriculture, 1917 (Washington, D.C.: Government Printing Office, 1918), 192. Homer E. Fenn to forest supervisor, 10 February 1917, file G-Studies, Caribou, Natural Reseeding, 1927, Caribou.

14. In 1910 the Caribou ranges were in worse shape than forests of western and central Idaho such as the Payette, Boise, and Salmon; those in Nevada; and the Teton in Wyoming. They were not, however, in as bad a condition as some of the forests of Utah, like the Manti and Dixie, or the Kaibab in Arizona. Caribou range conditions may have approximated those of the Cache, Wasatch, and Uinta in Utah and the Bridger in Wyoming.

15. Ernest Winkler to forest officer, 25 November 1927, Targhee National Forest Records, RG 95, Seattle FRC.

16. See District 4, "Minutes of Supervisors' Meeting, Idaho and Wyoming Forests, Boise, Idaho, 2–4 January 1910 [1911]" (n.p., 1911); and District 4, "Minutes of Supervisors' Meeting, Utah and Nevada Forests, Ogden, Utah, 23–25 January 1911" (n.p., 1911), copies, Historical Files, Boise.

17. "Minutes of Supervisors' Meeting, Idaho and Wyoming Forests," 30–45. The vote was recorded on 45.

18. George G. Bentz to district forester, 10 June 1911, and E. A. Sherman to forest supervisor, 14 June 1911, file G-Management, Allowances, 1907–1916, Caribou National Forest Records, RG 95, Seattle FRC.

19. Grazing Chapter Annual Forest Plan, Caribou National Forest, 1911, file G-Management, Allowances, 1907–1916, box 32115, Caribou National Forest Records, RG 95, Seattle FRC. On the Sawtooth National Forest in 1911, it was usual to require a 20 percent transfer reduction. See Ray Ivie, "Grazing on the Sawtooth National Forest and Some Forage Plants Thereon," file O-Supervision, General, Historical Files, Sawtooth.

20. *Annual Reports of the Department of Agriculture, 1910* (Washington, D.C.: Government Printing Office, 1911), 402; *Annual Reports of the Department of Agriculture, 1911* (Washington, D.C.: Government Printing Office, 1912), 397; *Annual Reports of the Department of Agriculture, 1913,* 185; A. C. McCain to S. B. Arthur, 12 February 1915, file G-Plans, Humboldt, General, 1912–1919, Grazing Records, Humboldt.

21. I am particularly indebted to Mont E. Lewis and Irwin H. "Hap" Johnson for information on systems of range investigation. See Arnold R. Standing, memorandum on work in the Forest Service, 4 January 1962, Historical Files, Fishlake. Milo H. Deming, "Minidoka Grazing Reconnaissance," 1923, file G-Management Inventory, Sawtooth (Minidoka), 1922–23, Grazing Records, Sawtooth; United States Department of Agriculture, Forest Service, "Grazing Reconnaissance Section Plat, Form 765, Revised 28 December 1911 [and February 1913]," manuscript, files of Mont E. Lewis, Regional Office; Albert F. Potter, ed., "Grazing Reconnaissance," manuscript, 1913, Historical Files, Regional Office. For a discussion of the method, see Arthur W. Sampson, *Range and Pasture Management* (New York: John Wiley and Sons, 1923), 307–26; E. C. Sanford, "Caribou Grazing Reconnaissance Report for Field Season of 1915," manuscript, Caribou, 1916, file GS-Studies, Reconnaissance, Caribou, 1916–1917, Caribou.

22. Sampson, *Range and Pasture Management,* 330; for a discussion of carrying capacity, see 328–33.

23. Homer E. Fenn to George G. Bentz, 10 February 1915, file G-Studies, Carrying Capacity, 1914 and 1915, Historical Files, Caribou.

24. Mark Anderson, "Carrying Capacity Tests for Caribou National Forest, 1914," manuscript, 1914, file G-Studies, Carrying Capacity, 1915 and 1914, Caribou; "Carrying Capacity Working Plan," manuscript, 1915, file G-Studies, Carrying Capacity, 1914 and 1915, Caribou; "Report on Sawtooth Carrying Capacity Test, 1914," file G-Studies, Carrying Capacity, Sawtooth, 1914, Grazing Records, Sawtooth. For a description of the method, see Sampson, *Range and Pasture Management*, 339–55; Clarence E. Favre, memorandum for grazing, 3 August 1916, file Grazing History, Range History Files, Caribou. W. Vincent Evans, "Progress Report, Caribou Carrying Capacity, 1916," manuscript, 1916, 56, file G-Studies, Carrying Capacity, 1916, Caribou; C. H. Shattuck, "Value of Grazing Management on the Caribou National Forest," *American Forester* 23 (1917): 536–38; Sterling R. Justice, *The Forest Ranger on Horseback* (n.p., 1967), 82.

25. Sampson, *Range and Pasture Management*, 325.

26. Ibid., 60–83.

27. Evans, "Progress Report, 1916," 46–48; see also Homer E. Fenn to forest supervisor, 20 December 1916, file G-Studies, Carrying Capacity, 1916, Caribou. Clarence Favre had arrived at the conclusion in regard to dry feed in 1915. Albert F. Potter to district forester, 18 February 1916, file G-Studies, Carrying Capacity, 1916, Caribou. See James T. Jardine's critique of the Evans report in Jardine to district forester, 22 February 1917, file G-Studies, Carrying Capacity, Caribou, 1917, Caribou.

28. Noel C. Heath, "Sheep Grazing and Its Effects on the Reproduction of Yellow Pine on the Sawtooth National Forest," file D-Supervision, General, Historical Files, Sawtooth. Forest Examiner William Spearhawk made intensive studies of the effect of sheep grazing on forest reproduction on the Boise from 1912 through 1914. See Elizabeth M. Smith, *History of the Boise National Forest, 1905–1976* (Boise: Idaho State Historical Society, 1983), 85; Bryant S. Martineau, "A Résumé of the Grazing Studies Conducted on the Payette National Forest, 1914," file G-Studies: Payette, Management of Grazing in Yellow Pine, 1911–1914, grazing files in the possession of Walter W. "Pete" Pierson. See also Smith, *Boise National Forest*, 95. Smith may not have had access to Martineau's report, since her version of it is much more negative than Martineau's narrative; Ernest Winkler to forest officer, 25 November 1927, file 1, 1650, Historical Library, Range Allowances, 1925–38, Bridger-Teton.

29. C. N. Woods, "Grazing Chapter—Supervisor's Annual Working Plan, Sawtooth National Forest," 1913, 2, file D-Supervision, General, Historical Files, Sawtooth. Woods found this problem also on the Old Payette in 1925, where in spite of fine grazing plans, the cattle did not always go where the plans indicated they ought to and overgrazing of certain areas resulted. C. N. Woods, memorandum to district forester, 16 September 1925, file G-Inspection, Boise (Payette), 1904–1929, Lands and Recreation Library, Regional Office; W. E. Tangren, memorandum to forest supervisor, 10 November 1927, file 1658 Historical Information, 7, Range Management, Uinta; C. N. Woods to Charles DeMoisy, 26 January 1921, and 17 February 1921, file G-Supervision, General LaSal, 1906–1926, Manti-LaSal.

30. The relationship between sheep and cattle at the time is derived from Charles DeMoisy, "The Value of Range Reconnaissance in Grazing Administration" (Paper presented to the Intermountain Section of the Society of American Foresters, 1 January 1927, Ogden, Utah), file GS-Reconnaissance 1924 to 1927, Caribou.

31. Leon F. Kneipp to J. B. Lafferty, 30 July 1919, folder G-Inspection: Payette (Weiser), 1909–1919, Pierson Collection, Payette.

32. For an analysis of this situation, see Rowley, *Forest Service Grazing and Rangelands,* 112–14.

33. Winkler to forest officer, 25 November 1927.

34. Charles Redd, interview with James Jacobs, March 1968, 4, Historical Files, Regional Office; "Annual Grazing Report of the Forest Supervisor, Caribou National Forest, 1920," file G-Management, Allowances, 1916–1921, Caribou National Forest Records, RG 95, Seattle FRC.

35. D. A. Shoemaker, memorandum for Messrs. Deming and Cronemiller, 29 March 1922, file Period Studies of 1921, Grazing Studies and Salting, 22, Caribou; H. E. Malmsten, memorandum for grazing, 26 October 1921, and Ernest Winkler to Earl Sanford, 1 November 1921, file Period Studies of 1921, Grazing Studies and Salting, 22, Caribou.

36. James O. Stewart, memorandum to forest supervisor, 6 April 1928, file RG-Carrying Capacity—Caribou, 1928, Caribou.

37. E. C. Sanford to district forester, 1 March 1921, and D. E. Shoemaker, memorandum for grazing, 11 March 1921, file GS-Carrying Capacity—Caribou, 1921, Caribou; Charles DeMoisy, "The Value of Range Reconnaissance in Grazing Administration," file GS-Reconnaissance 1924 to 1927, Caribou; T. Dean Phinney, "Progress Report, Caribou National Forest, 1927," file GS-Reconnaissance 1924 to 1927, Caribou.

38. Charles DeMoisy, interview with Arnold R. Standing, April 1965, 8, Historical Files, Regional Office. See Sampson, *Range and Pasture Management,* 62–66; Delbert Chipman and Ora Chipman, interview with James Jacobs, 3, Historical Files, Regional Office; John Yelland to Chester J. Olson, 8 February 1933, file Range Management, Timber Management, Wildlife Management, Engineering, Humboldt.

39. Sanford to district forester, 1 March 1921; Shoemaker, memorandum for grazing, 11 March 1921; see the estimates of C. N. Woods and Mark Anderson on 423.

40. "Twenty-four Years of Range Conditions on the Boise National Forest, Extracts from Annual Grazing Reports, 1906–1929, [inclusive]," file G-Inspection, Boise, 1927–1945, Lands and Recreation Library, Regional Office.

41. Dana Parkinson to forest supervisor, 13 April 1926, file Results of the Grazing Investigative Studies of 1925, Caribou.

42. Figures based on the annual allowance letters, file G-Allowances, 1921–1930, Caribou. Ernest Winkler to Earl Sanford, 5 February 1927, and Winkler to forest supervisor, 11 January 1929, file G-Allowances, 1921–1930, Caribou.

The Social Context of Forestry: The Pacific Northwest in the Twentieth Century

William G. Robbins

In the timber-rich Pacific coast country stretching from California's Humboldt Bay north into British Columbia and the Alaskan panhandle, the forest resource has always been the centerpiece of the area's economic culture. Although other forms of activity have shaped the region—fishing, shipbuilding, mining, and farming—the men and women who toiled in the logging camps and in the mills have been the mainstay of the economy. It was their labor that made the Pacific edge of North America the leading center of forest products manufacturing for much of the twentieth century.[1]

The north Pacific slope was also the last frontier for a migrating logging and lumbering industry that had its beginnings in the extensive white pine and hardwood forests of northeastern North America. For more than 300 years, the timbered wealth of the continent was important to westward expansion and to the commercial and industrial development of the United States and Canada. The expansive and turbulent dynamics of late-nineteenth- and twentiethth-century resource capitalism produced a mercurial and destructively competitive economic environment and brought cycles of instability and unemployment to resource-dependent communities. Those insecurities and hardships visited every center of lumbering activity—the river-born mill towns of Maine and New Brunswick, sawdust towns like Saginaw and Muskegon in the Great Lakes states, the numerous longleaf pine–manufacturing centers along the Gulf plain, and finally the communities that evolved along the last forest frontier in the Pacific Northwest.[2]

At one time the forest bounty, especially along the Douglas fir strip of the northwest coast, seemed endless. Indeed, it was the great timbered wealth of the region that attracted the likes of Andrew Jackson Pope and William H. Talbot to Puget Sound in the early 1850s, Edward Stamp to Alberni Inlet and Sewell Prescott Moody to New Westminster in the early 1860s, and finally Frederick Weyerhaeuser and a host of others at the turn of the century.[3] This was an environment lush with promise, requiring only the capital, technical expertise, and labor power to mill the lumber for sale in distant markets. Whether they were lumber entrepreneurs, local businesspeople, millworkers, or loggers, they were part of a cultural system that knew few limits in their quest to turn nature's bounty to market advantage.

By the beginning of the twentieth century, the northwest coast had taken on the aura of an investor's frontier as lumber capitalists from eastern North America and the Great Lakes states turned their energies to exploiting the region's timber bounty. Long after he left the United States Forest Service, William Greeley remarked that the people in the state of Washington were "in the lumber business in the same way that the citizens of Iowa are dependent upon corn, and the folks of the South are subjects of King Cotton."[4] Greeley's analogy also fit the neighboring state of Oregon and, to a lesser extent, the province of British Columbia. Because of the increasing timber harvests in the two states after the turn of the century, Oregon and Washington soon led the nation in the production of lumber. At the same time, the rapid liquidation of the forests in the more accessible locations became a growing concern. Although there were no reliable estimates of the resource until the Forest Service began making extensive surveys of timberland in the 1930s, some professional foresters feared that the old pattern of a gutted forest environment was being repeated.

Oregon's timberlands, although relatively untouched by comparison with those in Washington in the first decade of the twentieth century, were part of that concern. In his report for 1912, Oregon's state forester, Francis A. Elliott, pointed to the experience of states like Michigan and Wisconsin, which, he said, "proves the fallacy" that forests are inexhaustible. The "almost total depletion of those great pine forests," he said, should teach Oregon to harvest its stands "in such a way as to insure future crops." In 1919 Elliott again warned that large acreages of private timber were "being rapidly mined . . . and then left unproductive."[5]

In truth, there was cause for concern about depleted timber supplies in some sections of the Northwest. For many years, the major log-producing districts in the region were the magnificent old-growth forests in the Puget Sound, Grays Harbor, and Willapa Bay areas. The high quality of the timber, less difficult terrain, and easy access to water transportation attracted lumbermen in the late nineteenth century and partly explains the early emergence of western Washington as a major timber producer. Although Washington reached its peak in lumber manufacture in 1929 and continued to lead the nation in timber production until the 1940s, the center of lumbering activity was gradually shifting south to the Columbia River.[6]

By the time of the Great Depression, several communities in western Washington were beginning to reap the social costs inherent in the rapid liquidation of the forest resource. Although there was a drastic decline in output in both states beginning in 1929 and continuing until 1933, Washington continued to produce more logs than its southern neighbor until 1938.[7] Increased log production in the great expanse of ponderosa pine country east of Oregon's Cascade Range explains part of the reason for the emergence of Oregon as the leading lumbering state in the nation. But massive harvests in the Douglas fir area of western Washington had taken their toll.

The experiences of Tacoma, smaller manufacturing towns on Puget Sound, and the Grays Harbor settlements suggest that little had changed in the long history of boom-and-bust cycles for forest-dependent communities. There was no economic incentive for lumbermen to conserve, to harvest on a sustained-yield basis, and to reforest cutover lands. The big profits were in cutting, stripping, and then moving on to the next stand. The dynamics and logic of a social system in which profit and loss were the major criteria for human decisions both created and impoverished the lumber towns in western Washington. As Norman Clark stated so well in his classic study of Everett, Washington, this "was not and could not be a humane system."[8] This was a cultural world that encouraged plunder of both humans and the environment.

Under different social and economic arrangements, the Grays Harbor area might have served as a cautionary example for timber-harvesting practices elsewhere after World War II. When western Washington timber production peaked in 1929, Grays Harbor County was the leading log producer in the Pacific Northwest. Yet, only ten years later Forest Service Region 6 forester H. J. Andrews described Grays Harbor as "vast expanses of cutover land largely barren of conifer growth."[9] In effect, two market-related disasters struck the area simultaneously—the Great Depression and a drastically depleted timber supply.

In 1935 I. J. Mason of the Forest Service conducted a study of Grays Harbor to determine the causes of the sudden collapse in the area's economy. The sawmills in the district, he learned, were obsolete—lumbermen had constructed plants "with no consideration of permanent timber supplies, but only as to a timber supply adequate to depreciate them." The "excessive sawmill installations" had brought the end of the present industry "in sight." Those dynamics, according to Mason, were market oriented. Although the Grays Harbor sawmill industry lasted for sixty years, that was "not due to any planning on the part of the timber industry but rather to the huge . . . original timber supply and the restrictions on production imposed by general market conditions."[10]

In 1941 the Washington State Planning Council published a study of the small timber-dependent town of Elma, located on the eastern fringe of Grays Harbor County. The planning council chose the Elma area for an extensive survey because it "had been denuded of its principal economic asset, timber." The "sobering and grave problem" for those communities, according to the Elma report, was "how to maintain and perpetuate a community which had depended largely on the logging of timber and the manufacturing of lumber products."[11] For timber-dependent settlements elsewhere, the Elma survey provided a harrowing preview of mill closures, population decline, and the inability of a community to meet its social obligations.

Forest Service officials led the struggle in the 1930s to attack the social problems associated with excessive timber harvests. At the urging of Chief Forester Ferdinand A. Silcox, who insisted that forestry questions be considered in their broader social context, the agency showed special concern for the stability of timber-dependent communities. When he spoke in Portland, Oregon, in 1934, Silcox warned that "quick liquidation instead of sustained yield" was bringing distress to timber-growing states like Oregon and Washington. One year later, in an address to the Society of American Foresters, Silcox accused foresters of placing too much emphasis on timber production without considering its effects on nearby towns. Lumbermen, he said, did not give appropriate attention to the "social consequences of timber depletion."[12]

Forest Service Region 6 chief C. J. Buck told the Northwest Regional Planning Council in 1934 that sustained-yield management was the only way Oregon and Washington could avoid "a day of social and economic reckoning." Buck pointed to conditions in Clatsop County, Oregon, and Gray's Harbor County, Washington, to show "the effect of our present 'cut-out and get-out' policy upon families and communities." The remedy, he told the planning council, was a sustained yield of timber that would protect both the region's economic structure and its cultural and civic life.[13] In the absence of effective controls over the rate of timber harvests on private land, however, stable forest communities would remain largely the dream of state planning boards and a few progressives in the forestry profession.

The establishment of planning councils in Oregon and Washington in the 1930s gave some legitimacy to sustained-yield proposals. In 1936 the Oregon State Planning Board outlined a sustained-yield program for the state that would provide existing sawmills with a continual supply of timber. "The present 'cut-out and get-out' policy of forest cutting," the report stated, "will result in a brief period of industrial activity, followed by inevitable economic and social disaster." The study also indicated that Oregon, because of its large virgin timber stands, was one of the few states where a sustained-yield program could be put in operation without curtailing production.[14] Although those proposals may have been appealing in the abstract, they did not move anyone to action.

The Northwest Regional Planning Council published a brief informational pamphlet in 1940 that outlined "the basic facts concerning Forest Depletion in the Pacific Northwest." Despite their significance to the region's economy, the council pointed out that forests were "being depleted at a dangerous rate." Annual harvests in the Northwest were more than twice the annual growth rate, and the "numerous ghost towns" in the region were "grim indicators of what happens when the timber supply gives out." Unless the rapid depletion of the forests was checked, the council warned, "serious economic and social dislocation is inevitable." The answer to the problem, it indicated, was placing forests "under sustained yield management."[15] But public discussion of sustained-yield proposals and concern for "disorderly liquidation" were soon lost amid the furor to increase lumber production during World War II.

The resurgence of patriotism, in fact, gave industry leaders the opportunity to pursue wartime production goals unhampered by moral appeals to community stability. George Harris Collingwood, a forester with the National Lumber Manufacturer's Association, told Forest Service acting chief Earle Clapp that trees were less important than human lives and that the country would "have to sacrifice future needs for immediate demands."[16] Production and profit making, therefore, would dominate politics during the war, not appeals to forestry and community welfare.

In the midst of the wartime effort to increase production, the warnings continued. The Forest Service again singled out the Pacific Northwest, where "concentrated and unnecessarily destructive cutting" was jeopardizing "opportunities for sustained-yield operations." Under those conditions, the service warned, "many communities are bound to suffer."[17] Words of caution, however, meant little to lumbermen who were operating on cost-plus contracts during the war. For those districts in the region with large stands of old-growth timber, the supply problem lay somewhere in the future.

With the ending of the war, both the technology and the markets were suddenly available to dramatically increase the rate of timber harvesting on the Pacific coast. The development of the gasoline-powered chain saw and the widespread use of diesel- powered donkeys vastly stepped up the speed of production in the woods. It also meant that logging companies required fewer workers to accomplish the task of getting logs to the mills. As a symbol of the increased productiveness of woods operations after the war, a retired forest worker cited the example of a lone gyppo (i.e., independent) logger: "Just one guy goes out, he cuts the trees down, he cuts it up in logs, loads it on his truck, and takes it to town all by himself."[18] The combined production of the small operators, however, did not match that of the large companies where the availability of more sophisticated equipment made possible the rapid cutting and hauling of timber.

At the end of World War II, southwestern Oregon had the largest remaining stand of old-growth timber in the United States. Covering a vast four-county area, much of the timber was tributary to Coos Bay, the best shipping port along the Oregon coast. The timber was also close to the California market, soon to be the center of a booming home-building industry. Unlike western Washington, which had large areas that had been completely cut over, private timber holders in the Coos country confronted great marketing opportunities immediately after the war. Within two years of the Japanese surrender, newspapers were heralding the Coos Bay region as the "lumber capital of the world."

The burgeoning California and foreign export lumber market placed heavy demands on both labor and the timber resources in southwestern Oregon. The communities in the Coos country literally hummed with activity in the postwar era as new mills opened, gyppo operations multiplied, and immigrants flocked to the area. Coos County's population grew more than 30 percent in the 1940s and 1950s, a percentage increase that compares with that of many areas in California during those two decades.[19]

Because of the excellent growing conditions and the fact that the largest timber holders in the Coos Bay district were treating timber like a crop, the *Portland Oregonian* predicted bright prospects for the long-range economy of southwestern Oregon. Forecasters, it said, "look for no end to the song of axe and saw." It was on Oregon's south coast, the newspaper continued, that the lumberman "must prove up as either an ogre" or a "basic economic contributor to a community."[20] If the region was less than a worker's paradise, it seemed, on the surface at least, to offer enough opportunity for a person to make a decent living.

Permanence of operation and sustained-yield production, however, were not the center of attention in the postwar period. Rather, the building of new Weyerhaeuser mills, the opening of virgin timber stands, the construction of all-weather roads, and the monthly production figures of the sawmills made headlines in Oregon newspapers. Boosters of southwestern Oregon enjoyed the flattery and attention showered on Coos Bay as the "world's largest lumber port." And the major companies in the area buttressed that optimism with assurances that they were operating on a permanent basis.[21] The future seemed bright and full with promise.

And who could doubt that hope? Certainly one could not after reading the assessment of Harrison Hornish, an editor of the *Coos Bay Times,* who flew over the southwestern Oregon backcountry in the summer of 1949. He reported "looking down on mile after mile of treetops, a vast green blanket that seemed from the Coos–Douglas county line to stretch in an almost unbroken series of waves of green clear to the ocean." Hornish concluded that the area "would seem [to] . . . have an inexhaustible supply of trees."[22] Still, increased output began to take their toll on the Coos area timberlands.

By the mid-1950s, southwestern Oregon mills were beginning to scramble for access to timber. Inventories on private lands were diminishing rapidly in some areas, and lumbermen were increasingly looking to public timberlands—state, Bureau of Land Management, and Forest Service—to satisfy their needs.[23] For operators in southwestern Oregon who were already cutting great swaths into "the last great stand" of private timber in the United States, that meant more competition for government timber. Market forces were alive and well in western Oregon.

There were other developments that had a great impact on the volume of timber harvesting in the Douglas fir region after the war. One of those was the emergence of the Georgia-Pacific Corporation and its large purchases in the region, including the huge Coos Bay Lumber Company manufacturing plants and 120,000 acres of timberland in 1956. The primary attraction of the purchase, according to the *Portland Oregonian,* was the large acreage of old-growth forest—the "timber-rich jewel" in the Coos Bay Lumber Company's holdings.[24] The Georgia-Pacific "buyout," as it is called on the southern Oregon coast, was a momentous development. Suddenly the most aggressive of the expanding forest products empires occupied a central place in the area's economy.

What happened to the "last great stand" in the Coos country is a story common to corporate practice in market-oriented resource economies. Because the company had expanded so rapidly during the early 1950s, Georgia-Pacific found it necessary to create a "cash-flow" and sell part of its standing timber in southwestern Oregon to swing the purchase. Thus with a booming lumber market in California, there began what Jerry Phillips, a veteran of more than thirty years with the Oregon Department of Forestry, calls the "rapid liquidation phase" of the old Coos Bay Lumber Company timberlands. Ross Youngblood, the district BLM forester at the time, also remarked about the quick sale of timber that followed the buyout: "That's private enterprise, and . . . that's the way the cards turn."[25] Georgia-Pacific's vastly increased cutting rate and the large timber sales to other mills marked a dramatic shift in the harvesting policy on those lands. Corporate profit needs and the availability of markets, not a social commitment to sustained-yield forestry and community stability, guided the Georgia-Pacific liquidation program.

Georgia-Pacific's timber management decisions created a great deal of concern in southwestern Oregon. The company's dramatically increased harvests were common gossip among loggers and union people who were well aware of the lumber industry's propensity to "cut and run." The sizable timber sales "raised eyebrows" in the industry, according to the *Portland Oregonian,* because most companies were seeking to acquire, not dispose of, old-growth timber. To refurbish its tarnished image, the corporation purchased a series of advertisements in the Coos Bay newspaper.[26] But a strong lumber market and rising timber prices were the only factors that guided the firm's harvesting policy after the buyout. Although the rapid liquidation of the old-growth stands in southwestern Oregon created a multitude of jobs at the outset, and the region's economy remained strong even after the decline of the small sawmill operators in the late 1950s, the long-range consequences for southwestern Oregon communities were fraught with danger.

Georgia-Pacific was not the only large timber holder to increase its cut during those years. Through the 1950s, the Weyerhaeuser company harvested timber from its own lands only to satisfy the needs of its new plant on Coos Bay. According to the respected Phillips, the company "could have sustained that cut, if they had chosen to, forever." But the company's executives decided otherwise. In the early 1960s, Weyerhaeuser elected to increase the volume of its annual harvests—they sold timber to firms in Eugene, and they began a major log export program, primarily to Japan. Phillips notes that many people on the bay became aware that Weyerhaeuser was "cutting a great deal faster than they could sustain."[27]

Raw statistics support the increasing concern in southwestern Oregon and elsewhere about depleted timber inventories and declining employment in the forest products industry. In an important study of log production in Oregon and Washington published in 1972, Forest Service economist Brian Wall underscored the significance of private timber harvests in the 1950s and 1960s. By 1952 the "Oregon timber industry was in high gear in southwestern Oregon," and harvesting rates remained high in Lane, Douglas, Coos, Curry, and Jackson Counties through the 1960s. But, he warned, the rapid "inventory depletion" and inadequate reforestation indicated "that the extremely high rates of log production in parts of western Oregon have a limited future." Although the total output of logs in Oregon remained fairly constant during the 1950s and 1960s, public harvests were making up an increasingly larger share of production.[28] Those words of caution pointed especially to southwestern Oregon, where the liquidation of private timber was still in full swing.

There were other warnings. In the year of the Georgia-Pacific purchase, a study estimated that private ownerships in the area tributary to Coos Bay "will be reduced to minor value in about 30 years" and the "experience of other areas in this regard should not be ignored." Charles Stanton of the *Roseburg News-Review,* in neighboring Douglas County, told his readers that southwestern Oregon counties should not be "flattered" by production statistics showing their leadership in national lumber production. Other counties had held that distinction in the past, he noted, and "some of the former champions" were not doing so well.[29]

The heavy drain on the timber inventory in southwestern Oregon began to take its toll in the 1960s. The closure of an Evans Products plant on Coos Bay in 1961 was the standard-bearer for the future of southwestern Oregon. The company cited inadequate timber supplies and a soft market as the reason for its decision.[30] Twenty years hence when mill closures hit the Pacific Northwest in epidemic proportions, corporation public-relations managers made similar references.

At the onset of the 1970s, evidence pointed to a growing shortage of timber supplies in southwestern Oregon. The BLM and the Forest Service were adopting rules that reduced the annual harvests on federal timberlands. Georgia-Pacific's liquidation program, Weyerhaeuser's expanded cutting rate, and indications that smaller mills in the district were coming to the end of their merchantable timber brought matters to a head. The convergence of those factors, according to Phillips, showed "that there was a greater installed capacity in the mills than there was a permanent timber supply."[31] The concern about depleted timber stands in southwestern Oregon and in other lumbering districts led to legislative hearings and a study of timber inventories in the state. But market conditions, not the future stability of timber-dependent communities, continued to guide harvest decisions.

Next to Gifford Pinchot, William Greeley is the most prominent forestry figure in the first half of the twentieth century. In a revealing letter in 1946, the aging forester warned that western states were "rapidly approaching the end of their virgin forests." He urged Northwesterners to organize their forest industries on a "crop that is maintained steadily, without violent fluctuations from one decade to another." Otherwise, the region would experience the "same sort of migratory forest industries" and "ghost towns" that characterized earlier forest frontiers.[32]

To Jerry Phillips, sustained yield was "a rather naive, elementary, oversimplified concept," and the forestry profession has "disavowed it." Each timberland owner, he believes, "should choose responsible goals for himself and the community." It is important to understand, Phillips points out, "that every area of the world has had its turn in the bucket in going through from the old growth to the young growth cover-type stage." Although the process can "destabilize employment in a community," it is necessary to liquidate the old growth to convert to a tree-farming regime. As for southwestern Oregon, Phillips notes that the conversion stage "has taken us a hundred years, 1880 through 1980." The Coos country, the Oregon forester indicates, is "one of the last places in the world to complete that conversion."[33] Corporate timber supplies rather than human social needs defined forestry practice.

The extraordinary harvests of the postwar years in southwestern Oregon repeated a pattern played out on other forest frontiers. In the mid-1970s, a state forestry board–commissioned study forecast a sharp decline in timber harvests for the rest of this century. That decrease, it predicted, would be especially stressful for the timber-dependent south coast, where harvests were expected to fall by 35 percent.[34] Southwestern Oregon, once hailed as the lumber capital of the world, would now take "its turn in the bucket."

But the once-booming lumber district was merely a microcosm of forest-dependent communities everywhere in the Northwest. The excessive harvests of the postwar years, the resurgence of the southeastern forest products industry, and upward-spiraling interest rates combined to bring economic disaster to many of those communities in the early 1980s. Mill closures abounded—the Georgia-Pacific Corporation, which had harvested the remaining timber on the old Coos Bay Lumber Company lands in twenty-five years, led the list of mill closures in southwestern Oregon. And the company has continued to close other mills—citing increased labor costs, lack of timber, and shipping expenses to eastern markets.[35] The corporation was behaving like most multinational resource units of the modern age.

By the 1980s, lumbering towns throughout Oregon and Washington were suffering severe economic depression. Federal deficits, a strong United States dollar, and the importation of Canadian lumber exacerbated those conditions. Citing lumber price declines and a reduced volume of harvestable timber, the Weyerhaeuser company closed mills in Raymond and Everett, Washington, and Klamath Falls, Oregon, in 1984 and in the early months of 1985. When Champion International Corporation announced in January 1985 the closure of eight mills affecting more than 2,000 jobs, most of them in Oregon, the social tragedy of widespread unemployment spread even further. The economic dislocations that struck Coos County in 1979 and 1980 were by then affecting virtually every timber-dependent district in the Pacific Northwest.[36]

Meanwhile, the giant Weyerhaeuser firm was diversifying its investments into fields far removed from forest products—aquaculture, the construction of resorts and condominiums, and an experimental hydroponic vegetable facility in the Northeast. In the words of Louisiana-Pacific executive Harry Merlo, forest products investment capital was "going where the opportunity seems better." In many instances, that meant the eastern United States.[37] This points to a fundamental truth—the movement of resource capital has become more sophisticated in the last half of the twentieth century. This has brought suffering to the timber-dependent communities in the region and to the men and women who harvested and milled the old-growth forests and created that surplus capital.

Market economies tend to perpetuate certain historic features. In this case, a migratory forest products industry continues to wreak social costs on dependent communities in a region once billed as the last great forest frontier. Meanwhile, many of the forest products giants are looking to the eastern United States as the center of the industry's growth for the duration of this century. That shift, according to a Seattle newspaper, "is an ironic retreat to the nation's early days when the lumber industry was concentrated in the Northeast and Midwest."[38] The great hopes that some entertained of the socially oriented exploitation of the forest resource on the Pacific forest frontier has never materialized.

NOTES

1. The more important accounts of lumber-industry activity in the Pacific Northwest include Edmund S. Meany, Jr., "History of the Lumber Industry of the Pacific Northwest 1917" (Ph.D. diss., Harvard University, 1935); Stewart Hall Holbrook, *Holy Old Mackinaw: A Natural History of the American Lumberjack* (New York: Macmillan, 1938); Lawrence W. Rakestraw, "A History of Forest Conservation in the

Pacific Northwest, 1891–1913" (Ph.D. diss., University of Washington, 1953); George T. Morgan, Jr., "The Fight Against Fire: Development of Cooperation in the Pacific Northwest, 1900–1950" (Ph.D. diss., University of Oregon, 1964); Harold K. Steen, "Forestry in Washington to 1925" (Ph.D. diss., University of Washington, 1969); and Norman Clark, *Mill Town: A Social History of Everett, Washington* (Seattle: University of Washington Press, 1970). For a sampling of company history and biography, see Edwin T. Coman and Helen M. Gibbs, *Time, Tide and Timber: A Century of Pope and Talbot* (Palo Alto, Calif.: Stanford University Press, 1949); Stewart Holbrook, *Green Commonwealth: A Narrative of the Past and a Look at the Future of One Forest Products Community* (Seattle: University of Washington Press, 1945); Robert E. Ficken, *Lumber and Politics: The Career of Mark E. Reed* (Seattle: University of Washington Press, 1979); Murray Morgan, *Mill on the Boot: A History of the St. Paul and Tacoma Lumber Company* (Seattle: University of Washington Press, 1982); and Donald MacKay, *Empire of Wood: The MacMillan Bloedel Story* (Vancouver: Douglas & McIntyre, 1982).

2. On the migrating lumber industry, see Nelson Courtlandt Brown, *The American Lumber Industry: Embracing the Principal Features of the Resources, Production, Distribution, and Utilization of Lumber in the United States* (New York: Wiley, 1923); Ralph Clement Bryant, *Lumber: Its Manufacture and Distribution* (New York: Wiley, 1923); Henry Clepper, *Professional Forestry in the United States* (Baltimore: Johns Hopkins University Press, 1971); Thomas R. Cox, *Mills and Markets: A History of the Pacific Coast Lumber Industry to 1900* (Seattle: University of Washington Press, 1974); Samuel Trask Dana and Sally Fairfax, *Forest and Range Policy: Its Development in the United States,* rev. ed. (New York: McGraw-Hill, 1980); William Buckhout Greeley, *Forests and Men* (Garden City, N.Y.: Doubleday, 1951); Ralph W. Hidy, Frank Ernest Hill, and Allan Nevins, *Timber and Men: The Weyerhaeuser Story* (New York: Macmillan, 1963); Holbrook, *Holy Old Mackinaw;* and Harold K. Steen, *The U.S. Forest Service: A History* (Seattle: University of Washington Press, 1976). For the revisionist view, see Charlotte Todes, *Labor and Lumber* (New York: International, 1931); Vernon H. Jensen, *Lumber and Labor* (New York: Farrar and Rinehart, 1945); Roderick Nash, *Wilderness and the American Mind,* rev. ed. (New Haven, Conn.: Yale University Press, 1973); William G. Robbins, *Lumberjacks and Legislators: Political Economy of the U.S. Lumber Industry, 1890–1941* (College Station: Texas A&M University Press, 1982); and Jamie Swift, *Cut and Run: The Assault on Canada's Forests* (Toronto: Between the Lines, 1983).

3. Holbrook, *Holy Old Mackinaw,* 160–62; MacKay, *Empire of Wood,* 2, 6–7; Robert E. Ficken, "Weyerhaeuser and the Pacific Northwest Timber Industry, 1899–1903," *Pacific Northwest Quarterly,* October 1979, 146–54; Clark, *Mill Town,* 58–63.

4. W. B. Greeley, "Washington and Her Forest Industries," undated manuscript, box 16, William B. Greeley Papers, University of Oregon Library, Eugene.

5. *Report of the State Forester* (Salem, Ore., 1912), 19–21, and (1919), 33–35. Voicing similar concerns were Henry S. Graves, dean of the Yale Forestry School and Greeley's predecessor as Forest Service chief, who in 1925 warned of "a feverish haste to cut the choicest of the last remaining bodies of timber" in the Northwest; in 1929, Greeley's successor, Robert Y. Stuart, remarked that the rapid cut in the Northwest was troubling and might require federal attention. See Henry S. Graves, "Federal and

State Responsibilities in Forestry," *American Forests and Forest Life,* November 1925, 677; United States Forest Service, *Annual Report* (Washington, D.C.: Government Printing Office, 1929), 2, 6.

6. Brian Wall, *Log Production in Washington and Oregon, an Historical Perspective,* United States Forest Service, Resource Bulletin PNW-42, Pacific Northwest Forest and Range Experiment Station (Portland, 1972), 5–6; Thomas R. Cox, "Trade, Development, and Environmental Change: The Utilization of North America's Pacific Coast Forests to 1914 and Its Consequences," in *Global Deforestation and the Nineteenth-Century World Economy,* ed. Richard P. Tucker and J. F. Richards (Durham, N.C.: Duke University Press Policy Studies, 1983), 21–25.

7. F. L. Moravets, *Production of Logs in Oregon and Washington, 1925–1948,* United States Department of Agriculture, Forest Service, Forest Survey Report No. 101, Pacific Northwest Forest and Range Experiment Station (Portland, 1950), 7.

8. Clark, *Mill Town,* 234.

9. Quoted in Wall, *Log Production in Washington and Oregon,* 6.

10. I. J. Mason, "Grays Harbor Study," 4 April 1935, in S Plans, Timber Management, Olympic, 1927–35, box 54139, Federal Records Center, Seattle, Wash.

11. Washington State Planning Council, *The Elma Survey* (Olympia: Washington State Planning Council, 1941), 1, 35–39.

12. Quoted in *Coos Bay Times,* 18 August 1934; Ferdinand A. Silcox, "Foresters Must Choose," copy in box 7, Greeley Papers; Steen, *Forest Service,* 199, 229–34.

13. Quoted in *Coos Bay Times,* 20 December 1934.

14. Oregon State Planning Board, *Oregon's Forest Problems* (Portland, 1936), 1–2, 4.

15. Northwest Regional Council, *Forest Depletion in Outline* (Portland, 1940), iii–iv.

16. G. H. Collingwood to Earle Clapp, 19 March 1942, box 54, National Forest Products Association Records, Forest History Society, Durham, N.C.

17. United States Forest Service, *Annual Report* (Washington, D.C.: Government Printing Office, 1942), 4.

18. Dow Beckham, interview with author, 28 March 1984.

19. Bureau of Municipal Research and Service, University of Oregon, *Population of Oregon Cities, Counties and Metropolitan Areas, 1850–1957,* Information Bulletin No. 106 (Eugene, 1958), 19; Bureau of Governmental Research and Service, University of Oregon, *Population and Housing Trends, Cities and Counties of Oregon* (Eugene, 1982), 26.

20. *Portland Oregonian,* 8 June 1947.

21. *Coos Bay Times,* 2 November 1944, and 1 May 1951.

22. Harrison Hornish, in *Coos Bay Times,* 25 July 1949.

23. *Coos Bay Times,* 31 March 1956; Elmo Richardson, *BLM's Billion-Dollar Checkerboard: Managing the O&C Lands* (Santa Cruz, Calif.: Forest History Society, 1980), 145–47.

24. Dennis C. LeMaster, *Mergers Among the Largest Forest Products Firms, 1950–1970,* Washington State University, College of Agriculture Research Bulletin No. 854 (Pullman, 1977), 1; *Portland Oregonian,* 27 May 1956.

25. Wylie Smith, interview with author, 16 April 1984; Jerry Phillips, interview with author, 6 April 1984; Ross Youngblood, interview with author, 27 April 1984.

26. *Portland Oregonian,* 29 August 1958; *Coos Bay Times,* 8 April 1959.

27. Jerry Phillips, interview with author, 6 April 1984.

28. Wall, *Log Production in Washington and Oregon,* 7–8, 29.

29. Alan H. Muir and Richard A. Searle, *A Study of Industrial Development Possibilities for the Coos Bay Port District* (Menlo Park, Calif.: Stanford Research Institute, 1956), 17–20. Stanton's editorial was reprinted in the *Coos Bay Times,* 27 August 1955.

30. Oregon Coastal Development Commission, *Economic Survey and Analysis of the Oregon Coastal Zone* (Salem, 1974), E5, E11; *Portland Oregonian,* 17 January 1959.

31. Jerry Phillips, interview with author, 6 April 1984.

32. William Greeley to Roderic Olzendam, 7 May 1946, box 7, Greeley Papers.

33. Jerry Phillips, interview with author, 6 April 1984.

34. John K. Beuter, K. Norman Johnson, and H. Lynn Scheurman, "Timber for Oregon's Tomorrow," *Research Bulletin 19,* Forest Research Laboratory, School of Forestry, Oregon State University (Corvallis, 1976), 1, 18, 43; Russell Sadler, "John Beuter Reckons with Timber," *Willamette Week,* 26 December 1977.

35. *Eugene Register-Guard,* 29 November 1981; *Portland Oregonian,* 29 November 1981, and 13 November 1984; *Corvallis Gazette-Times,* 6 October 1982.

36. *Oregonian,* 9 October and 13 November 1984, 21 February and 10 March 1985.

37. Russell Sadler, "Adaptable Timber Firms Can Survive Shakeout," *Portland Oregonian,* undated news clipping in author's possession; *Seattle Times,* 8 April 1984; *Seattle Post-Intelligencer,* 8 April 1984; *Salem Statesman-Journal,* 10 April 1983.

38. *Seattle Times,* 8 April 1984; *Seattle Post-Intelligencer,* 8 April 1984.

What Price Sustained Yield?
The Forest Service, Community Stability, and Timber Monopoly Under the 1944 Sustained-Yield Act

David A. Clary

The Sustained-Yield Forest Management Act became law on March 29, 1944. Largely the work of David T. Mason and Edward T. Allen of the Western Forestry and Conservation Association, the act expressed Mason's vision of sustained yield as a system of forest management designed to stabilize forest industries so that they could harvest continually in a given locality rather than exhaust the resource in one area and move on to the next. This interpretation of sustained yield differed from that of the Forest Service, which aimed at sustaining the productive capacity of the forests rather than the well-being of the forest user, although in practice the two philosophies were not incompatible. Nevertheless, the Sustained-Yield Act was the fruit of industrial support in Congress with little encouragement from the Forest Service.

The 1944 legislation, recognizing that public and private timberlands were intermingled in the West and that a number of timber companies needed new sources of raw material, authorized two types of sustained-yield units, cooperative and federal. Cooperative units would merge the management of national forests and adjacent private timberlands to form "catchment areas" large enough to allow continual harvesting of timber. The federal units would achieve the same end by reserving national forest timber in a given area for exclusive use by local operators. The objective of both kinds of units was community stability—permanent communities of forest workers who would not have to move on when the local timber supply gave out. Both kinds of units stabilized local economies by giving favored private companies a monopoly over the national forest timber in their area.[1]

The Forest Service had multiple reactions to this law. On the one hand, cooperative management offered federal foresters new powers to require conservation on lands bordering national forests. On the other hand, the service's top leaders were bent on regulation, not cooperation, and doubted that the industry would ever adopt the service's principles of sustained yield.

Cooperative units might backfire, giving private companies as much or more of a voice in national forest management as the Forest Service would acquire in decisions about the private lands. Finally, both types of sustained-yield units sanctioned monopolies, a kind of economic organization that the Forest Service had historically opposed. The service's first reaction was, accordingly, cautious.[2]

Most federal foresters, moreover, favored management by short-term sales rather than long-term agreements with the private sector. It was not even clear that the cooperative units would necessarily reward only operators who practiced good forestry. When Watts said that cooperative agreements would favor and perpetuate "responsible private ownership," one regional official, Charles L. Tebbe, ventured that "a number of applicants for cooperative sustained yield units definitely had in mind to eventually turn their holdings over to Government."[3]

Officials in the Forest Service's Washington office were also concerned over the local impact of the law. Assistant Chief E. E. Carter, for example, wondered "whether we mean it when we talk about the stabilization of communities within or close to a National Forest." The proposed Big Valley federal unit in California would protect a nearby town, but "it would also block other possible purchasers who might wish to reach into this working circle [the basic Forest Service planning unit] or become established in it." Cooperation with the largest timber owner in the area, he thought, was impossible.[4]

The war complicated matters further. When a group including a congressman approached Chief Forester Lyle Watts with a proposal for a cooperative unit in the Rogue River area of Oregon, he showed some favor to the proposition, but advised that even an acceptable application would require time to prepare for public hearings, and he had no intention of holding such hearings while the war was still on.[5]

The world war was not a lame excuse for delayed implementation of the Sustained-Yield Act. Manpower shortages in the Forest Service were a genuine obstacle to new initiatives. Yet Watts felt called upon to make some effort at establishing sustained-yield units, despite this problem. He selected one—the application of Simpson Logging Company for lands around Shelton, Washington, submitted two days after the law was passed. The Shelton proposal appeared to offer the best possibility of meeting the purposes of the act because Simpson Logging had already "demonstrated a sincere interest in working out arrangements for cooperative sustained yield forest management."[6] A year of negotiations and drafts produced a cooperative agreement and management and operating plans for the linked federal and private lands. The two parties entered a 100-year contract, planning to harvest 100 million board feet per year until 1956, after which the cut would be reduced to the "allowable sustained yield of the combined ownerships." The objects were better utilization of the forest, higher local employment, manufacturing capacity matched to the available resources, and an end to fluctuations in population and payrolls.[7]

When the proposal was presented to a public hearing in September 1946 it unleashed a storm of controversy. People in the communities immediately affected by the proposed unit generally supported the idea. Those elsewhere did not. In granting Simpson a monopoly on federal timber, the Forest Service closed the area to others. Farmers, organized labor, small logging operators, and competing companies and communities howled in pain. The competitive free market would be destroyed, timber would be diverted from the Puget Sound market, and land uses other than timbering would be restricted. The Grays Harbor communities believed themselves especially ill-used, on the grounds that their economy was imperiled by unfair competition from Simpson and its newly protected resource base around Shelton—a resource now closed to Grays Harbor enterprises. Nearly all opponents asked for a reduction in the proposed annual cut. The local grange objected bitterly to the federal government's establishing monopolistic power.[8]

With some minor revisions, the Shelton Cooperative Sustained-Yield Unit became active on December 12, 1946. The Grays Harbor region would not be won over, however. When its representatives prevailed upon Senator Warren G. Magnuson to ask for an adjustment in the unit boundary to leave timber for Grays Harbor, Watts refused to budge, insisting that the boundaries as established were "needed to insure sufficient annual cut under sustained yield to stabilize Shelton and McCleary." As for landowners and operators outside the unit boundaries, Watts said that Simpson Logging Company was free to purchase timber outside the unit "if it so desires."[9]

The Forest Service hierarchy maintained before the public its dedication to stabilizing communities dependent on national forests. As Watts put it in 1947:

> In establishing the boundaries of national forest working circles, whether or not subject to cooperative sustained yield management, we are emphasizing consideration of community aspects wherever it is possible to do so. We hope to have milling or logging communities so located with respect to the merchantable timber . . . that woodworkers will have an opportunity to live at home in permanent communities and to commute to and from work.[10]

To Watts, support from the immediate community was enough to justify a cooperative unit. Having decided that opponents could be ignored or dismissed as favoring their own interests over the public interests, he advised regional foresters to enlist local support for cooperative units. It was not to be, however. The Forest Service attempted to form additional units at Libby, Montana, and Quincy, California, but quickly ran into a storm of opposition from small operators, organized labor, and communities adversely affected. Overriding everything were objections, from self-interest and on legal and ethical principles, to the monopolistic nature of cooperative units, favoring one to the exclusion of all others. In the end, the Shelton Unit was the only cooperative program established under the 1944 legislation. Local opposition scuttled even the Department of the Interior's attempt at cooperative sustained yield on its lands in Oregon.[11]

Frustrated in its attempts to establish more cooperative units, the Forest Service turned to establishing units involving only national forestland.[12] Federal units were not to come easily either. They involved intervention in local economies that troubled some people in the Forest Service. Worse, in many minds, were the possible enemies who could be generated for the whole sustained-yield-unit program. Reviewing a plan for the Sitgreaves National Forest in Arizona, even C. M. Granger worried about how the service could stabilize any community without destabilizing its neighbors:

> In addition to considering whether such an obligation would be worth the additional community benefits, we should also consider whether the additional benefits to Heber would more [than] offset the disruption of established community values at Safford, where the Company's finishing facilities are now located. If Safford is a better place to live than Heber, should we force the Company to move its employees now residing at Safford?[13]

The line between promoting community stability and high-handed manipulation of private affairs was indeed a fine one, and that made development of sustained-yield units more difficult. The Forest Service managed to create only five federal sustained-yield units—each a continued source of frustration and complaint—reserving 1.7 million acres of national forestland in Arizona, California, New Mexico, Oregon, and Washington.[14]

The Vallecitos Sustained-Yield Unit, on 65,000 acres of the Carson National Forest in northern New Mexico, reflected the service's problems. This unit began as a social-engineering project with some peculiarly scattered purposes—range improvement, community stabilization, and timber sales. The cutting level on the forest was low after World War II, and the regional forester wanted to raise it starting in 1947. The Forest Service came up with a plan to support a sawmill and a box and stock factory near the town of Vallecitos to use the timber and "raise the economic well-being of these small farm-stock owners." Its main purpose, however, was to provide compensating employment income to subsistence-level graziers whose federal grazing allotments were about to be reduced. Sustained-yield forestry, in other words, masked a plan to improve grazing lands.[15]

In assuming charge of the national forests of northern New Mexico, the Forest Service brought technically trained resource managers face to face with an entrenched, deeply traditional, and extremely poor rural population that depended on its herds of livestock for subsistence. Peonage had not been abolished in New Mexico until 1867, and even in the mid-twentieth century the economy and social arrangements in some rural areas were almost medieval. Foresters interested in restoring overused rangeland inevitably threatened the very survival of people in the region. The Forest Service was not insensitive to the problems, but was determined to have its way.[16]

When the Forest Service reduced grazing allotments in 1947, Pedro Martinez told the regional forester that the agency did not have the interests of the "poor people" at heart. Nor did he have any confidence in the proposed sustained-yield unit. "Strangers" would come from other states, he predicted. They would say, "The hell with the poor people of Vallecitos, Petaca, and Cañon Plaza. We got the money and we are going to drive them out." He predicted the end of his people's way of life, "as you have taken away from us the rights of our predecessors who were permitted 25 head on a free permit and 60 free sticks of wood for our own use. And where are they? Dead."[17]

It remained to be seen whether technicians trained to manage timber and grass could manage people adeptly, especially people who were so different from the technicians themselves. It also remained to be seen whether a federal sustained-yield unit would be an effective tool of community stabilization. The process did not start smoothly. Shortly before the unit was activated, the firm that was to develop the sawmill and stock plant pulled out, and the Forest Service had to search for a replacement.

On January 21, 1948, Chief Watts established the Vallecitos Federal Sustained-Yield Unit, amending it to include the communities of Petaca and Cañon Plaza along with Vallecitos. The policy provided that local people could purchase the locally produced lumber, "but we have no basis for requiring that such sales be made at any specified price."[18] Thus the service could not guarantee that Martinez and his neighbors could afford to buy the lumber, even if they had a legal right to do so.

Vallecitos was the first federal sustained-yield unit established under the 1944 legislation, and the smallest, with an average annual cut of 1.5 million feet. The management plan called for selling unit timber to provide steady employment for local residents and lumber for local requirements. The Vallecitos Lumber Company was established and designated as the "approved responsible operator," charged with installing, maintaining, and operating a "primary manufacturing plant including planer" at or within a mile of the village of Vallecitos. Ninety percent of the employees were to live within ten miles of the plant. The company's designation soon was terminated for "noncooperation" with this clause of the agreement, and in 1952 the designation went to Jackson Lumber Company of Vallecitos.[19]

Operations in the unit suffered from labor–management difficulties arising from cultural conflicts, divergent priorities, and poor relations between the designated operator and the Forest Service. Only five men showed up to operate the mill in the fall of 1952, and the Carson National Forest's timber staff officer investigated. Two storekeepers told him that "the fault was probably with the employees not wishing to work in cold weather, wanting to cut wood for their homes, and possibly wishing to be released to go on relief." Another added that the crews believed that they were not being paid properly for the volume harvested. In addition, the employees preferred to cut only pine, but the company wanted mixed conifer production. A year later, however, the regional office's curiously flat and terse response was that "the advantages to the community are clearly evident."[20]

Meanwhile, relations between the operator and the Forest Service deteriorated. In 1955 Jackson Lumber Company engaged a former Forest Service man as "consulting forester" to work with the Forest Service in "planning and supervising the woods operation." He soon complained about the "feeling of continual antagonism and bickering which prevails between the Forest Service and Jackson Lumber Company at Vallecitos." He accused Forest Service personnel of finagling on the scaling of logs and thus cheating the firm, "inciting unrest or dissatisfaction among the workmen," meeting with the people of Vallecitos "to stir up dissent against the Company," and arbitrarily threatening to shut down operations. The Forest Service dismissed his complaints as merely the spite of a disgruntled former employee.[21]

The company failed to meet its quota of 90 percent local employment; about half the labor was imported, and local people complained. The Forest Service proposed new guidelines, extending the labor pool to eight communities and "adjacent rural areas."[22] Jackson Lumber appealed, and the Department of Agriculture held public hearings. Testimony revealed that the ten-mile radius for the labor pool ran through the middle of the community of Ojo Caliente, many of whose residents worked for Jackson. Furthermore, Jackson and its employees fell out over piecework versus hourly payment for work in nonfederal timber, and the workers tried to establish a union to demand an hourly wage. The company fired some of them and brought in workers from Texas.[23]

The main point of dispute was whether Ojo Caliente was a community that ought to be included within the labor-pool boundary; if it was, the company would have no difficulty in reaching the 90 percent local-employment level. Ojo Caliente was an old colonial land grant that had evolved into a succession of small holdings extending ten miles down a valley. The Anglo foresters saw it not as a community but as a rural area. The company and the Forest Service fell into a series of arguments and appeals over the drawing of the ten-mile boundary. Finally, in 1956 the Forest Service agreed to "consider persons residing within the Ojo Caliente Land Grant to qualify as local laborers for purposes of complying with the terms of the two noncompetitive timber sale contracts."[24]

That did not end matters. The sustained-yield exercise in people management was going nowhere, so the Forest Service held hearings on whether to discontinue the unit. Residents of six villages asked that if the unit was to be continued, the 90 percent local-employment policy (that is, exclusion of Ojo Caliente) be enforced.[25] The hearings became so tense that Jackson Lumber Company chose to make no presentation and, instead, later submitted a statement for the record. Early in January 1957, the chief of the Forest Service noted that the people generally favored continuing the sustained-yield unit, but not with Jackson Lumber Company. So he appointed an advisory board to offer recommendations on the labor question.[26]

The Carpenters and Joiners Union bombarded the Forest Service with complaints that Jackson Lumber imported workers from elsewhere. Senator Dennis Chavez tried to work out a compromise formula, but the union claimed that the company would not conform even to that. The Forest Service developed a clause for timber sale contracts requiring local employment on the agency's terms, but the company insisted that it must have the right to say whether sufficient local labor was "available." On May 2, 1957, a Forest Service delegation went to Vallecitos to tell J. L. Jackson, owner of Jackson Lumber, that the clause would stand. Jackson "said that if it had to be that way he was through—that he could not sign a contract with that clause in it." Jackson's mill burned to the ground that night. Three days later, the company refused to work under the labor restrictions, and on May 23 the Forest Service revoked Jackson Lumber's designation for the sustained-yield unit.[27]

The Vallecitos Federal Sustained-Yield Unit managed to stay on the books, with little effect on the ground. Another operator was eventually located, but its mill burned down in 1963. In 1966 an inspection report said that the unit had "failed conspicuously to meet its objective" and recommended termination, with a caution about the "delicate public relations situation involved." The question became critical the next year when a fire on the Carson National Forest left a lot of timber to be salvaged. The timber had to be put on open sale because the unit was not functioning.[28]

The Washington office wondered "what to do about an inoperative unit which is obstructing use of National Forest land for benefit of local communities." It was known that the people of Vallecitos would not take termination of the unit lightly. Another local operator, Duke City Lumber Company, was pleading by 1969 for the government to modify or terminate the unit to make the timber available to other firms.[29] Duke City Lumber had a mill operating in Vallecitos, and had been buying national forest timber in regular sales since 1962. It needed access to the unit's timber, but the people of Vallecitos would not budge. The answer was to bring them together. Duke City Lumber applied for designation as the "approved responsible operator." A public meeting in Vallecitos consented, and on April 4, 1972, Duke City

Lumber became the sustained-yield unit's operator. Yet this solution too was short-lived—the Duke City sawmill burned down in 1977.[30]

The Vallecitos unit was a dismal failure. By the time the Forest Service acknowledged the fact, it proved impossible to correct it; local people simply would not go along with termination, for whatever reason. As an exercise in sustained-yield timber management, the unit dedicated to oft-burning, usually idle mills actually inhibited systematic management of the timber on the national forest.

Much of the error lay in the unit's vague and conflicting purposes. The national forest's immediate concern was reduction of livestock grazing by people who could not afford to give up a single calf. The federal managers of the forest were unhappy because of its low timber sales. Superficially, the postwar sustained-yield-unit movement appeared to offer an answer to both concerns. It did not because sustained-yield management turned less on matters of economics or forestry than on the sentiments of people. People can be cantankerous, and they certainly were at Vallecitos. The problems to be solved there were not the sort that foresters were trained to handle. Even the ageless magic of "sustained yield" proved wanting in the real world. Slogans and labels could not force national forests to be managed the way foresters thought they should be rather than the way the public wanted them managed. The original conceivers of the sustained-yield unit walked into northern New Mexico with their eyes shut to this reality, and as a result their unit never stood a chance.

The last federal unit established under the 1944 legislation—the Flagstaff unit on the Coconino National Forest in Arizona, created in 1949—came to a better end than the Vallecitos unit. It was terminated.

The Forest Service estimated in 1939 that half the population of Flagstaff depended on the two sawmills drawing on the Flagstaff working circle: Southwest Lumber Mills and the Saginaw-Manistee Lumber Company. As early as 1943, Assistant Chief E. E. Carter suggested that the Flagstaff region might be a good candidate for a sustained-yield unit. An application had been received, and a study was under way by 1946. The locally stationed federal foresters favored the proposal as the best way to defeat two basic threats to Flagstaff's economic stability: competition among local mills, and competition between local mills and companies based elsewhere. The first threat arose when previously close cooperation between the two largest local firms—collusion promoted by the Forest Service for several years—threatened to come apart. Forest Service officials saw a sustained-yield unit as a way to stabilize the community and regulate industrial harvesting. Mostly, it appears that Acting Forest Supervisor Roland Rotty was thoroughly enamored of the idea for a sustained-yield unit. The regional forester, in contrast, regarded the whole thing as an unwarranted gift to the two local companies.[31]

The staff of the national forest wanted to stabilize the two firms by giving them a 100-year exclusive contract for timber from the Coconino

National Forest. The foresters hoped that their own management plan would allow them to divert the companies from railroad to highway logging, and above all to avoid the introduction of seasonal logging camps by smaller operators that could undercut the established firms' bids. However, the regional office turned down the proposed 100-year lease, and the Washington office decided that Flagstaff did not qualify under the Sustained-Yield Act. By 1947, the applicants had enlisted political assistance, and the Forest Service was discovering that the true degree of the community's dependence on timber could not easily be measured. The locally stationed federal foresters kept promoting the idea, but the Washington office was increasingly sensitive to its monopolistic aspects.[32]

Suddenly in 1948 the Washington office turned around and told the region to go ahead with public hearings on a sustained-yield unit, offering suggestions on how to load the hearings with favorable witnesses. Meanwhile, Forest Service arbitration had produced a formal and approximately equal division of the unit's timber between the two large concerns. The service's twenty-year plan covered the two large companies and one small sash-and-door mill (the owner of which was soon eager to sell out to the large combine for a good price). This plan gave the big industries a nearly permanent resource that they could exploit over the counter in a number of imaginative ways. Roland Rotty was not worried. "Once I was much concerned about this," he said,

> because I did not see why any private citizen should profit by dealing in something that belongs to all the people. Since then I have come to realize that this is the case throughout the entire business world. . . . I see no reason to get excited about this. We should go ahead and conduct our timber management business without trying to prevent somebody making a profit by selling out.[33]

The Washington office was very concerned about public opposition to the proposed unit, however. C. M. Granger gave the regional office advice on how to handle possible opposition at the hearings. He warned the regional staff to "anticipate" the appearance of opponents at the hearing "and be prepared so far as possible to have them counteracted." It is our "responsibility to make sure that everyone has a good understanding of the proposal but not to engage in public debate at the meeting." The solution was to line up supporting witnesses in advance.[34]

Public sentiment favoring open competition was one major threat to the service's plans for Flagstaff. The current timber plan called for competitive bidding, and the regional office feared that high bidders might take federal timber to mills elsewhere. Establishment of the sustained-yield unit would prevent that. In the interim, the region promised its industrial clients in Flagstaff that "we will continue to supply stumpage to established plants dependent on national-forest timber such as those at Flagstaff. This can be done under war power acts, as long as prospective purchasers bid the OPA [Office of Price Administration] ceiling prices"[35]

During the more than a year that the Flagstaff sustained-yield unit had been under discussion, high-level enthusiasm for the program had swept away any misgivings in the Forest Service. On October 25, 1948, Chief Watts approved the proposed unit. His only real concern was public opposition, which he directed the regional forester to defuse. "When you are convinced," he said, "that the proposal will be actively supported locally, you are authorized to proceed" with public hearings.[36] Watts feared the public's "strong sentiment for making all Federal Units competitive." He underscored his belief that the two mills at Flagstaff could not operate year-round if they had to face competitors. He wanted it clearly explained, however, that 15 percent of the allowable annual cut would be set aside for competitive bidding by other purchasers.[37] Charges that the Forest Service was promoting monopolies clearly worried Watts, and he grasped for responses. "One of the strongest arguments," he said, "is that the two large sawmills offer an opportunity for local laborers to have a choice of employer. Flagstaff is not at all a one company town." Considering that the two mills operated essentially as a combine, and that the Forest Service plan required them to do so, that was a remarkable suggestion. Watts believed that "community stability" depended on "maintaining the equivalent of the manufacturing facilities now in operation." That meant no more as well as no less.[38] As Watts was coming to support the Flagstaff unit in Washington, the southwestern regional office prepared an elaborate booklet justifying the sustained-yield unit, sent officials out to make speeches, and obtained favorable comment in the press. But the Forest Service did not win everyone over. The Western Forest Industries Association, a group of small operators opposed to the unit, noted that "government agencies should be concerned only with the stability of wood using communities and not with that of individual operators." Nine small operators banded together as the Coconino Small Mills Association—belying the assumption that the timber industry of Flagstaff was represented by two large firms and one small—and bought a full-page advertisement in the Flagstaff newspaper under the headline, "Sustained Yield or Sustained Grab?" The stage was set for the public hearing.[39]

The meeting finally took place in Flagstaff on February 2, 1949. A parade of civic leaders, bankers, organized labor, and others came forward to promote the sustained-yield unit. Their chief argument was that stabilizing the two large mills by guaranteeing their timber supply and protecting them from competition would attract development capital and permit them to grow. Small operators, understandably, bemoaned the plans to shut them out of the national forest and predicted the death of their businesses. Afterward, the regional forester suggested increasing the amount of the annual cut to be set aside for competitive sale, but Watts turned that down. Small operators were told that they would receive somewhat more timber than they had taken in recent years and should console themselves with the thought that the two big Flagstaff concerns would not be allowed to bid against them. When one of the two giants tried to buy out a small operator, the Forest Service stopped the action as violating the unit plan.[40]

It did nothing, however, when in 1954 Southwest Lumber Mills bought out Saginaw-Manistee, and the Forest Service made the new giant the sole "approved responsible operator" for the Flagstaff unit. The Flagstaff Federal Sustained-Yield Unit had become a monopoly whose economic benefits the service could not quantify: it was "impossible to demonstrate" that the Flagstaff unit had produced "any effect upon community developments or expansion," a 1956 report noted. "Improvements have occurred but no basis exists for attributing them to the existence of the Federal Unit." Yet there seemed to be no reason to discontinue it, despite the fact that the unit had affected the structure of the local economy: by 1957, the number of small operators in the area had dwindled from nine to four.[41]

Southwest Lumber Mills was certainly doing well. In 1957 it received a thirty-year pulpwood contract involving about 6 million cords, to be harvested beginning in 1962. By 1960, the company had attracted $40 million in capital to finance its expansion, the financial commitments contingent on the continued availability of the sustained-yield unit. Meanwhile, the Forest Service tried to attract a newsprint plant to Flagstaff to support "community stability" further by providing a customer for Southwest's pulpwood.[42]

In 1962 the Forest Service granted its burgeoning "approved operator," by then renamed Southwest Forest Industries, authority to bid on all competitive sales offered within or without the Flagstaff Federal Sustained-Yield Unit, until further notice. Thus ended the reservation of 15 percent of the annual cut for smaller competitors, which thereafter faced direct competition from a very profitable giant, which could now gobble them up.[43]

Southwest Forest Industries clearly enjoyed significant advantages from its monopoly on the sustained-yield unit's future timber. Its profits guaranteed, it dominated the forest industry in a region extending beyond the Flagstaff unit (the corporate headquarters, in fact, were in Phoenix). Relations with the Forest Service were very close. Southwest bought out the Kaibab Lumber Company, one of the few remaining small companies, in 1965 and received permission to transfer that company's national forest timber purchases to itself.[44] The Coconino National Forest staff met with corporation officials to map out how to break the news to the public. The foresters advised explaining that the purchase of Kaibab had been approved "in order to bring local mill capacity in line with available timber."[45]

Throughout the early 1960s, the Flagstaff Federal Sustained-Yield Unit helped Southwest Forest Industries to build a veritable economic empire. By the later years of that decade, however, the political times and Forest Service personnel in the region had changed. The approved operator, jealous of its prerogatives, began to face more serious competition. In 1968 the C. T. Bunger Lumber Company reconstructed an old sawmill, and Passalacqua Lumber Company erected a new facility (both in or near Flagstaff). When these two firms petitioned for exclusion of Southwest from the 15 percent of annual cut formerly reserved for small operators, Regional Forester William D. Hurst agreed. Southwest hit the roof. It claimed that it had "paid dearly" for Kaibab Lumber in order to institute two shifts at its main plant. It was also building a large particleboard plant at Flagstaff to increase timber utilization, and claimed that loss of even 15 percent of the sustained-yield unit's annual cut would be "economically disastrous." To Southwest, its new competitors were "a haphazard and inefficient operation capable of cutting only three to four million feet per year."[46]

The regional forester denied Southwest's appeal on the grounds that the company had never been told it could count on maintaining two shifts indefinitely. Allowable cuts might rise or fall in future years, Hurst said. "For this reason we have not encouraged industry to build beyond the capacity of the Unit to sustain. In past years members of your company have discussed overcutting on the Unit to permit two full-time shifts in the mill with the realization that after a few years the allowable cut would drop to a one shift basis," he told the firm's vice president. Hurst apparently believed that the Forest Service had created a monster he could no longer control. He hinted that a complete review of the sustained-yield unit could be required if the company insisted—a veiled threat that Flagstaff might no longer qualify under the original legislation.[47]

The extent to which forest officers had previously assisted the designated operator in the name of community stabilization came to light in 1969 after a public complaint led to an internal audit. At Flagstaff, the Forest Service had consistently adjusted destination calculations in timber appraisals to keep those in the sustained-yield unit lower than those in competitive sales. The Washington office expressed a "strong belief that there is nothing in the Sustained Yield Forest Management Act which either requires or permits timber in the Sustained Yield Units, either Federal or Cooperative, to be appraised any differently than if it were not in a unit." Furthermore, it was a "false premise" that community stability was to be promoted "by assuring a supply of timber to dependent communities but by a price concession as well. This . . . simply can't be read into the Act." Competing timber industries had justifiably complained about the lower appraisals in the sustained-yield unit. "The effect of appraising this timber to Flagstaff is to give Southwest . . . a price concession as well as providing protection against competition," conceded the regional office. "Our job is to establish fair market value, not sell at reduced prices." Advising Washington on corrective measures, the region admitted that it had "drifted into [its] present position without considering all of the complications." The Coconino National Forest was ordered to correct its appraisal concessions in the sustained-yield unit, but accusations of unfair pricing continued.[48]

The national forest also had to reevaluate its policy on sales to small operators. The regional office declared that the intent of the original 15 percent set-aside "was to afford protection of the small operators who were operating on the Coconino in 1949." However, by 1969 all such operators had "passed out of the picture with one exception" because the Forest Service had refused to allocate timber to small operators. Nevertheless, as it had in the past the region decided to allow operators of all sizes to bid for the timber on the 15 percent.[49]

When the Forest Service restudied the Flagstaff unit in 1970, it concluded only that "it is difficult to assess what competition would be if the Unit did not exist." Certainly there was little competition visible at the time; only three small competitors of Southwest were working the reopened 15 percent set-aside in 1970. Moreover, the justification for the unit as protecting Flagstaff's economy had also dwindled; Flagstaff was by this time only about one-fifth dependent on forest products industries. Nonetheless, the report recommended continuing the unit because it "has been successful in fulfilling all of its objectives and the purpose for which it exists." F. Leroy Bond in the regional office disagreed, however, pointing out that the timber industry was no longer the "key to economic stability" in Flagstaff.[50]

The unit continued for several more years, despite periodic revisions of the management plan and growing public complaints. When critics again proposed closing the unit down in 1977, Supervisor Michael A. Kerrick of the Coconino National Forest directed the preparation of a "white paper" on the Flagstaff unit. The paper concluded that "it might be that eliminating the designated operator would serve to promote open and fair competition" and suggested that alternatives should be submitted to the public. Opponents of the unit went to work, and the Forest Service began to hear from members of Congress in 1978. The resulting review concluded that "the Unit discriminates against other communities, businesses, and citizens of adjacent communities," and ought to be abolished. Public response to the review included such phrases as "enough is enough" and "Fidelity to SFI [Southwest Forest Industries] is like 'DCS' (Damned Chrysler Syndrome)," the latter a reference to the contemporary public bailout of the failing Chrysler Corporation. The unit's days were numbered.[51]

Public hearings on the future of the Flagstaff unit were held in January 1980. Southwest Forest Industries and its friends tried their best to guard its privileges.[52] It was to no avail, however, for public sentiment would no longer tolerate unseemly governmental interest in the care and feeding of a thoroughly prosperous firm, especially when such federal action disadvantaged others. In

May 1980, Forest Service chief Max Peterson told the region, "We concur with your recommendation that the Unit be dissolved." The region's press release said that opinion at the public hearing on this had been about "equally divided," but as Flagstaff was no longer "primarily dependent on the sale of national forest timber," Southwest's monopoly could not be justified.[53]

The Flagstaff unit's peculiarities—along with those of all the sustained-yield units created under the 1944 law—reflected national as well as local considerations. Certainly, the Arizona Forest Service staff hopped onto the sustained-yield bandwagon because they saw the new unit as equivalent to their own earlier proposal for a 100-year sales contract with the two combined large companies (a contract that would have constituted a sustained-yield unit by another name). Nevertheless, the real creators of the unit were the Forest Service's leaders in Washington. C. M. Granger was a great booster of sustained-yield units, which were his special charge, but it was Lyle Watts, more than anyone else, who saw the Flagstaff unit—questionable origins, conceptual warts, and all—into existence.

Despite initial misgivings, Watts and the Forest Service wagered much of their public credibility on the sustained-yield program because it appeared to serve a number of cherished Forest Service objectives—to promote community stability, justify the existence of the national forests, and force operators to harvest conservatively on private lands. Watts was able to achieve only one cooperative unit, however, and the federal units fared little better. In response to these unaccustomed defeats, Watts quit urging the establishment of more units, yet could not bring himself to admit that the program was dead. He told a newspaper in 1950 that there was "some difficulty with sustained yield units but my mind was not changed one iota. That was one of the finest pieces of legislation passed." In 1953, after Watts had retired, the Department of Agriculture effectively buried the program by requiring communities, rather than the Forest Service, to initiate proposals, reserving the right of final approval for the secretary of agriculture. The secretary announced four years later that it was departmental policy to establish no new sustained-yield units of either type, although established units would be "continued for the present."[54]

The sustained-yield-unit program was the Forest Service's grandest and most systematic attempt to promote community stability through management of national forest resources. It was doomed by a complex mixture of faulty conception, compromise with monopoly, human nature, and questionable intervention into local and private affairs. The program provoked unexpectedly strong and often highly emotional opposition—not just from the timber industry, but from conservation groups, organized labor, civic organizations, and other traditional supporters of the Forest Service. Coalitions of these groups rose up in outrage, and defeated the proposals one by one. There were doubtless some bruised feelings among those federal foresters leading the campaign for unit establishment, as they heard themselves castigated as enemies of small business, disrupters of communities, friends of monopoly, and bedfellows of certain industries. The Forest Service had never heard such things from its friends before. Its political enemies previously had been well defined and rather easy to dismiss as self-serving—large industry, mostly, especially during the Progressive and New Deal eras, when large industry was a national whipping boy.

Such opposition from unexpected sources should have given the agency pause, causing it to reexamine its objectives and redefine its vision of the public interest. The wreck of the sustained-yield-unit program might have been good preparation for an approaching era of increasingly vocal but not necessarily consistent attacks on the Forest Service by groups that once had supported it. Instead of taking the lessons of the sustained-yield program to heart, however, the service more often failed to consider whether the objections were valid, or really even to listen to what opponents had to say, and in the process did itself a disservice.

NOTES

Abbreviations
The National Archives and Records Service regional depositories are cited as NARS-D for Denver, NARS-LN for Laguna Niguel, and NARS-FW for Fort Worth. Record numbers for these regional collections are cited as accession number/record number (e.g., 54-A-111/59858). Records held in the National Archives in Washington, D.C., are identified by NA record group and box number (e.g., RG95/1369). Abbreviations for frequently cited individual files are explained in the first citations to such files.

1. Sustained-Yield Forest Management Act of 1944, 58 Stat. 132; Harold K. Steen, *The U.S. Forest Service: A History* (Seattle: University of Washington Press, 1976), 251–52; Roy O. Hoover, "Public Law 273 Comes to Shelton: Implementing the Sustained-Yield Forest Management Act of 1944," *Journal of Forest History,* April 1978, 86–101.

2. Hoover, "Public Law 273," 88; "Policy and Instructions Governing the Establishment of Sustained Yield Units," 21 July 1944, "S, Plans, TM, Federal Units 1936–1949," Region 2, 56-A-144/62230, NARS-D.

3. Charles L. Tebbe to the files, 12 August 1944, "S, Plans, TM, Federal Units 1936–1949," Region 2, 56-A-144/62230, NARS-D.

4. E. E. Carter to the files, 11 April 1945; Christopher Granger to regional forester, Atlanta, 10 May 1945, both in Division of Timber Management, RG95/1369.

5. Ira J. Mason to regional forester, Portland, 23 June 1945, DTM, RG95/1369.

6. "Hearing Record, Shelton Cooperative Sustained Unit, Hearing, 19 September 1946," Timber Management Office Permanent Files, Pacific Northwest Region [hereafter cited as TMO and listed with the Forest Service regional office that holds

them]. Except as otherwise indicated, the account of the establishment of the Shelton unit follows Hoover, "Public Law 273."

7. "Hearing Record."

8. Besides Hoover's excellent summary of the hundreds of pages of testimony and statements of the record, see the extensive file in TMO, Pacific Northwest Region. See also Lyle Watts to the record, 10 December 1946; Watts to Representative Walt Noran, 11 December 1946, all in DTM, RG95/1368.

9. Lyle Watts to Warren Magnuson, DTM, RG95/1368.

10. Lyle Watts to George H. Cecil, 16 January 1947, DTM, RG95/1368.

11. Lyle Watts to Region 1, 13 March 1947, DTM, RG95/1367; Hoover, "Public Law 273," 101; Steen, Forest Service, 252. There is a lot of correspondence in RG95/1367 and RG95/1368 related to the futile attempts to establish cooperative sustained-yield units, most of which indicates utter lack of support in the communities to be blessed, as well as opposition from almost every conceivable type of person and organization. The Forest Service response was almost uniformly to blame opposition on "a lot of misinformation" (a frequent phrase). The Washington office repeatedly urged the regions to beat the bushes in the affected communities for support. The Department of the Interior received authority to institute cooperative sustained-yield units on lands under its jurisdiction in the late 1930s, but was never able to establish any. See Elmo Richardson, BLM's Billion-Dollar Checkerboard: Managing the O&C Lands (Santa Cruz, Calif.: Forest History Society, 1980).

12. Lyle Watts to regional foresters, 11 April 1946, DTM, RG95/1368.

13. Christopher Granger to regional forester, Albuquerque, 15 May 1946, DTM, RG95/1369.

14. Steen, Forest Service, 252.

15. David Q. Scott to regional forester, 18 September 1946; Duncan M. Lang to forest supervisor, Carson National Forest, 26 September 1946; Scott, "Sustained Yield Case Study: Vallecitos Working Circle," 20 March 1947; L. W. Darby to the chief, 20 November 1953, all in File 2410, "Plans," TMO, Vallecitos Federal Sustained Yield Unit, Southwest Region [hereafter cited as Vallecitos File 2410].

16. See, for example, Ronald B. Hartzer, Half a Century in Forest Conservation: A Biography and Oral History of Edward P. Cliff (Bloomington, Ind.: David A. Clary & Associates, 1981), 147. In the 1960s, northern New Mexico saw an uprising of Spanish Americans resentful about several things, among them attitudes and activities of Forest Service personnel.

17. Pedro Martinez to regional forester, 21 November 1947, Vallecitos File 2410.

18. D.J.K. [Dahl J. Kirkpatrick] to [C.] Otto [Lindh], n.d. [1948], Vallecitos File 2410; Ira J. Mason to Region 3, 21 January 1948; Lyle Watts to Region 3, 21 January 1948, both in DTM, RG95/1367. In explaining why the Vallecitos unit was established, the Forest Service told a senator, "This unit . . . is for the purpose of improving living conditions of a small and remote community of Spanish Americans" (E. I. Kotok to Senator Henry C. Dworshak, 10 August 1948, DTM, RG95/1366).

19. Plan submitted by P. V. Woodhead to the chief, 26 January 1948, with revisions and amendments; Richard E. McArdle to O. D. Connery, Vallecitos Lumber Company, 17 September 1948; McCardle to Jackson Lumber Company, 8 October 1952, all in Vallecitos File 2410. Lyle Watts to Connery, 31 March 1948; McArdle to Connery, 17 September 1948, both in DTM, RG95/1366 and RG95/1367.

20. L. A. Wall to the files, 23 November 1952; L. W. Darby to the chief, 20 November 1953, both in Vallecitos File 2410.

21. J. L. Jackson to C. Otto Lindh, 14 January 1955; Dahl J. Kirkpatrick to the files, 1 April 1955; Vernon Bostick to Walter L. Graves [supervisor, Carson National Forest], 25 April 1955, all in Vallecitos File 2410.

22. Buford H. Starky to Jackson Lumber Company, 2 April 1955; Walter L. Graves to Jackson Lumber Company, 30 March and 18 August 1955; Fred H. Kennedy to the chief, 5 April 1956; Dahl J. Kirkpatrick, "Guide Lines to be Used in Determining Compliance with Local Labor Requirements Imposed in the Harvest and Manufacture of National Forest Timber from the Vallecitos Federal Sustained Yield Unit," 22 April 1955, all in Vallecitos File 2410.

23. Thomas M. Smith to Fred H. Kennedy, 9 December 1955, Vallecitos File 2410.

24. Dahl J. Kirkpatrick to Carson National Forest, 9 February 1956; Kirkpatrick to J. L. Jackson, 9 February 1956; Kennedy to the chief, 17 February and 5 April 1956; L. A. Wall to the files, 23 February 1956; Senator Dennis Chavez to Ezra Taft Benson, 27 March 1956; Kennedy to the chief, 6 April 1956; Richard E. McArdle to Jackson Lumber Company, 20 April 1956, all in Vallecitos File 2410.

25. "Vallecitos Sustained-Yield Unit Hearing Record," petitions, 20 August 1956, Vallecitos File 2410.

26. Catron & Catron to Sidney Williams, USDA, 18 October 1956; Richard E. McArdle, "Decision on Continuation of Vallecitos Federal Sustained Yield Unit, Carson NF, N. Mex.," 3 January 1957, both in Vallecitos File 2410.

27. Dahl J. Kirkpatrick to the files, 1 May 1957; Edward C. Groesbeck to the files, 21 May 1957; Kirkpatrick to the files, 7 May 1957; Richard E. McArdle to J. L. Jackson, 23 May 1957, all in Vallecitos File 2410.

28. M. M. Nelson to R-3, 29 July 1966, "1440 Inspection; GFI Timber Management, Mason Bruce, 11–29 October 1965," 75-135/231179, NARS-LN; William D. Hurst to the files, 9 August 1967, "2410-Plans," C-07-073-3-6, NARS-FW.

29. B. H. Payne to regional forester, Albuquerque, 10 August 1967; Don D. Seaman to regional forester, Albuquerque, 13 March 1968; T. W. Koskella to forest supervisor, Carson National Forest, 27 May 1969; M. J. Hassell to regional forester, Albuquerque, 15 May 1969; Koskella to William D. Hurst, 31 October 1968; Yale Weinstein, Duke City Lumber Company, to Hassell, 18 April 1969, all in file "2400-Plans," C-07-0733-6, and "2400-Timber, FY 69," E-27-036-2-4, NARS-FW.

30. William D. Hurst to the chief, 14 February 1972; Edward P. Cliff to Yale Weinstein, Duke City Lumber Company, 4 April 1972; Weinstein to M. J. Hassell, 22 July 1977, all in Vallecitos File 2410.

31. United States Department of Agriculture, Forest Service, *Coconino National Forest, Arizona,* 12; A. A. McCutchen to the chief, 9 September 1947 (citing, E. E. Carter of 12 May 1943); Duncan M. Lang to the files, 9 July 1946; James G. McNary to regional forester, Albuquerque, 16 September 1946 (application for sustained-yield unit); C. Otto Lindh to regional forester, Albuquerque, 23 October 1946; "A Case Study of the Flagstaff Federal Sustained Yield Unit," approved 9 September 1947; Roland Rotty to regional forester, Albuquerque, 17 February 1947, all in File 2410, "Plans," TMO, Southwest Region.

32. C. Otto Lindh to Roland Rotty, 19 February 1947; R. W. Hussey to Timber Management, 8 August 1947; "A Case Study of the Flagstaff Federal Sustained Yield

Unit," approved 9 September 1947; James G. McNary to Clinton P. Anderson, secretary of agriculture, 18 September 1947; Anderson to McNary, 26 September 1947; Lyle Watts to secretary of agriculture, 17 October 1947; Christopher Granger to Region 3, 20 October 1947; Rotty to regional forester, Albuquerque, 29 October 1947, all in File 2410, "Plans," TMO Southwest Region. L. S. Gross to Ira J. Mason, 30 October 1947 [quotation], DTM, RG95/1367.

33. H. E. Ochsner to Region 3, 1 January 1948; Lyle Watts to Region 3, 5 April 1948; L. S. Gross to the record, 23 April 1948, all in DTM, RG95/1366. Forest Service, "In the Matter of Federal Sustained Yield Unit, Coconino National Forest, Memorandum of Southwest Lumber Mills, re: Allocation of Timber Resources," received 10 February 1948; James G. McNary, "Memorandum of Southwest Lumber Mills, Inc., re: Allocation of Timber Resources," received 10 February 1948; P. V. Woodhead to the chief, 5 April 1948; Christopher Granger to Region 3, 5 April 1948; Woodhead to G. R. Birklund, 7 April 1948; Woodhead to McNary, 7 April 1948; Roland Rotty to regional forester, Albuquerque, 7 April 1948; Woodhead to the chief, 8 April 1948; Gross to the record, 23 April 1948; Granger to Region 3, 29 April 1948; Rotty to regional forester, Albuquerque, 7 May 1948; Woodhead to the chief, 10 May 1948; Granger to Region 3, 4 June 1948; Birklund to Woodhead, 29 June 1948; Rotty to regional forester, Albuquerque, 7 May 1948 [quotation], all in File 2410, "Plans," TMO, Southwest Region.

34. Christopher Granger to Region 3, 26 July 1948, DTM, RG95/95.

35. Duncan M. Lang, "Flagstaff Sustained Yield Unit Under Public Law 273," 23 October 1946; P. V. Woodhead to the files, 25 October 1946, both in File 2410 "Plans," TMO, Southwest Region.

36. Lyle Watts to regional forester, Albuquerque, 25 October 1948, DTM, RG95/1366.

37. Lyle Watts to regional foresters, 1 November 1948, DTM, RG95/1366.

38. Lyle Watts to Region 6, 23 November 1948, File 2410, "Plans," TMO, Flagstaff Federal Sustained Yield Unit, Southwest Region [hereafter cited as Flagstaff File 2410].

39. "Résumé of the Arguments for the Establishment of the Federal Sustained Yield Unit at Flagstaff," received 14 December 1948; *Arizona Daily Sun* [Flagstaff], 1 December 1948; *Arizona Labor Journal,* 6 January 1949; *Arizona Farmer,* 8 January 1949; R. T. Titus, Western Forest Industries Association, to P. V. Woodhead, 24 January 1949; C. J. Warren, Southwest Lumber Mills, to C. Otto Lindh, 26 January 1949; *Arizona Daily Sun,* 27 January 1949; *Winslow [Arizona] Mail,* 20 January 1949, all in File 2410, "Plans," TMO, Southwest Region.

40. "Transcript of Proceedings, In re: Flagstaff Sustained Yield Unit, Public Hearing, Flagstaff, Arizona, February 2, 1949"; P. V. Woodhead by C. Otto Lindh to the chief, 22 March 1949; Lyle Watts to Region 3, 11 April 1949; Woodhead by George W. Kimball to R. T. Titus, 17 January 1949; Kenneth A. Keeney to regional forester, Albuquerque, 24 May 1950; Dahl J. Kirkpatrick by Duncan M. Lang to Coconino National Forest, 29 May 1950, Flagstaff File 2410.

41. J. B. Edens, Southwest Lumber Mills [drafted by Kirkpatrick], to forest supervisor, Coconino National Forest, 11 January 1954; C. Otto Lindh by Dahl J. Kirkpatrick to Edens, 16 February 1954; Ira J. Mason to Region 3, 11 February 1954; *Arizona Daily Sun* [Flagstaff], 2 June 1954; James M. Porter, Coconino Pulp and

Paper, to Kenneth A. Keeney, 26 March 1956; Richard McArdle to Coconino Pulp and Paper, 30 March 1956; Irving A. Jennings, Arizona Pulp and Paper, to McArdle, 22 June 1956; McArdle to Arizona Pulp and Paper, 22 June 1956; Clare Hendee for Edward P. Cliff to E. H. Weig, Ponderosa Paper Products, 14 October 1964; Art Greeley to Ponderosa Paper Products, 5 August 1968; Kirkpatrick to the chief, 9 November 1956, letter and enclosures; Fred H. Kennedy by Kirkpatrick to the chief, 14 February 1957; Kirkpatrick to the files, 24 July 1957, all in Flagstaff File 2410.

42. Southwest Lumber Mills, *Annual Report for the Year Ended April 30, 1957;* Fred H. Kennedy by Dahl J. Kirkpatrick to the chief, to attention of Ira J. Mason, 22 October 1957; R. W. Crawford to James M. Porter, 15 January 1960; Kennedy by Kirkpatrick to M. E. Halfley, Arizona Development Board, 2 February 1960; Kennedy by Kirkpatrick to the chief, 15 and 29 February 1960; Richard E. McArdle by Edward P. Cliff to regional forester, Albuquerque, 15 March 1960; Yale Weinstein to John T. Utley [correspondence to this individual was addressed variously to John T. Utley, Jack Uttley, and Jack T. Udey; citations use the exact form that appears on the correspondence], 9 November 1977, all in Flagstaff File 2410.

43. J. Morgan Smith to Southwest Forest Industries, 13 August 1962, Flagstaff File 2410.

44. M. C. Galbraith to Kaibab Lumber Company, 15 July 1965; E. L. Quirk, vice president, Southwest Forest Industries, statement, 30 September 1965, both in Flagstaff File 2410.

45. R. M. Honsley to regional forester, 19 July 1965, Flagstaff File 2410.

46. C. T. Bunger to Forest Service, 18 April 1968; Phil Passalaqua Lumber Company to Forest Service, received 16 April 1968; W. B. Finley to regional forester, Albuquerque, 7 June 1968; A. T. Hildman, Southwest Forest Industries, to William D. Hurst, 10 April 1969; Hurst to Hildman, 22 April 1969, all in Flagstaff File 2410.

47. Hurst to Hildman, 22 April 1969.

48. T. W. Koskella for William D. Hurst to forest supervisor, Flagstaff National Forest, 10 March 1969; Rawleigh L. Tremain, Department of Agriculture, Office of General Counsel, to the chief, 23 October 1963; Ralph F. Koebel, assistant general counsel, to the chief, 3 May 1962; Washington office of the U.S. Forest Service [no date or signature] to Region 3, 10 March 1969; Don D. Seaman to regional forester, 21 March 1969; F. Leroy Bond to chief, 28 March 1969; Homer J. Hixon to M. M. Nelson, 29 April 1969; B. H. Payne to Greeley and Edward P. Cliff, 9 May 1969; M.M.N. [Nelson] to Cliff and Greeley, 12 May 1969; J. D. Porter, Western Pine Industries, to Richard Worthington, 26 March 1975; D. D. Westbury for Worthington to Porter, 4 April 1975; W. L. Evans to Porter, 20 February 1975; Worthington to Joseph D. Cummings, Office of General Counsel, 18 July 1975; Division of Timber Management to regional foresters, Region 1 through Region 10; Porter to Jack Uttley, n.d. [December 1975]; William L. Holmes to Porter, 6 February 1976, all in Flagstaff File 2410.

49. F. Leroy Bond to the files, 17 September 1969, citing memoranda from Region 3 to the chief, 22 March 1949, and the chief to the region, 11 April 1949; William D. Hurst to the chief, 22 September 1969; Homer J. Hixon to regional forester, Albuquerque, 5 November 1969, all in Flagstaff File 2410.

50. "Periodic Reanalysis, Flagstaff Federal Sustained Yield Unit," 19 November 1970; Bond to the files, 17 September 1969, both in Flagstaff File 2410.

51. Michael A. Barton for John R. McGuire to Congressman Bob Stump, House

of Representatives, 15 August 1978; Stump to McGuire, 28 July 1978, both in Flagstaff File 2410; "Periodic Reanalysis, Flagstaff Federal Sustained Yield Unit, 1979"; "Summary of the Flagstaff Federal Sustained Yield Unit, 1979"; Not for Public Distribution Summary of Public Response Relating to the Periodic Reanalysis of the Flagstaff Fed. Sus Yield unit, n.d. [ca. 1980], all in Timber Sales Office files, Coconino National Forest.

52. Record of public hearing, 9 January 1980, Timber Sales Office Files, Coconino National Forest.

53. Max Peterson to regional forester, Albuquerque, 20 May 1980; press releases 28 May 1980, both in Flagstaff File 2410.

54. "Forester Acts on War Peril," *Portland Oregonian*, 15 August 1950; Steen, *Forest Service,* 252. Barton for McGuire to Stump, 15 August 1978; "Briefing for Chief Peterson Regarding Flagstaff Federal Sustained Yield Unit," n.d., both in Flagstaff File 2410.

The National Forests and the Campaign for Wilderness Legislation

Dennis Roth

The Wilderness Act, signed by President Lyndon B. Johnson on September 3, 1964, is a landmark in conservation history. The act provided statutory protection for more than 9 million acres of recreational wilderness and charged three federal agencies—the Forest Service, the Park Service, and the Fish and Wildlife Service—with the enormous task of reviewing potential wilderness areas in their jurisdictions. Confrontations between preservationists and commercial interests commanded the lion's share of public attention during the dramatic eight-year congressional battle that resulted in the Wilderness Act. However, the federal agencies that were to assume responsibility for implementing the new national wilderness preservation system also played a crucial part in shaping the bill's history.

Long before the legislative battle for wilderness began, the Forest Service had designated more than seventy areas within the western national forests for special wilderness management. As the federal agency with the largest percentage of potential wilderness in its jurisdiction, the Forest Service played a key role in forging the federal response to wilderness management. Moreover, the agency carried a broad multiple-use mandate, and its growing commitment to wilderness was subject to strong and varied interest-group pressures. Unlike the Park Service and the Fish and Wildlife Service, whose priorities were closely linked to traditional nonutilitarian preservation concepts, the Forest Service was involved in profound and controversial reassessments of its forest management philosophy throughout the various stages of the wilderness movement. Thus the history of the Wilderness Act is largely a history of national forest wilderness politics.

Until the early twentieth century, wilderness conditions had existed as a by-product of the movement to preserve scenic wonders in national parks and to reserve from the public domain some forests and rangeland so that watershed and future supplies of timber could be protected. Not a specific land classification, wilderness was embedded in other land management categories.[1] In the late nineteenth century, national park advocates had shifted their interests from "natural wonders" to broader notions of preserving scenic and primeval landscapes, and passage of the National Park Act in 1916 was in part a tribute to that impulse. Yet the act was as much a mandate for development as it was for preservation. It called on the newly created Park Service to protect the natural integrity of the parks but at the same time make them accessible for public use.[2] This contradiction was latent, for automobiles were still a novelty in 1916 and park tourism was only a fraction of what it would become a few decades later. But the promotional zeal that would become so characteristic of national park administration as a result of the 1916 act curbed the service's role as a pioneer in wilderness management planning.

Ironically, it was the Forest Service that initiated experiments in federal wilderness management. In keeping with its concept of multiple-use planning, the service recognized recreational activities in its jurisdiction as early as 1905, although they ranked well below commercial use in the agency's priorities. In 1917 some 3 million recreationists visited the national forests, and in that year the Forest Service commissioned a landscape architect, Frank Waugh, to survey the forests for their recreational potential.

The shift from recreational to wilderness concerns came shortly thereafter; the Forest Service's growing attention to wilderness in the 1920s and 1930s was a response to a number of pressures from public and industrial interests and to competition with the Park Service for recreational budgets and land. But in large part, the call for wilderness designation came from within the agency itself. In the first half of the twentieth century, Aldo Leopold, Arthur H. Carhart, and Robert Marshall designed and helped implement a wilderness policy for the Forest Service. Doing so, they forged a defense of wilderness that would figure prominently in the creation of the national wilderness preservation system in 1964.

Aldo Leopold was a young forest supervisor on the Carson National Forest in New Mexico who at the end of World War I had become apprehensive about the expansion of Forest Service road systems into the backcountry.[3] Wilderness, he felt, was the forge on which the American national character had been created, and loss of wilderness regions deprived the country of a source of renewing this heritage. Leopold had also been inspired by the new science of ecology, which considered wilderness an ideal laboratory for the study of natural processes.[4] In 1918 the Ecological Society of America was formed, and in 1920 Francis B. Sumner, an eminent student of ecology and genetics, urged the society to back the setting aside of untouched areas. A year later, Leopold seconded this call in a *Journal of Forestry* article that suggested a wilderness of at least 500,000 acres for each of the eleven states west of the Great Plains.[5]

In May 1922, Leopold, now assistant district forester in Albuquerque, made an inspection trip into the headwaters of the Gila River. When he returned, he wrote a wilderness plan for the area that excluded roads and additional use permits, except for grazing. Only trails and telephone lines, to be used in case of forest fires, were to be permitted. Leopold's plan encountered opposition from some of his own colleagues in the district office who thought that development should take precedence over preservation. However, on June 3, 1924, District Forester Frank Pooler approved Leopold's concept. The Gila area was to be placed under a ten-year wilderness recreation policy; grazing and waterpower development were not to be impeded, but roads were to be limited and efforts were to be made to acquire private inholdings through land exchanges. Pooler's action did not carry immediate national significance because the Forest Service's Washington office was not involved in the decision, but the 500,000-acre Gila Wilderness would serve as a precedent for wilderness designation in other areas in the coming decades.[6]

Leopold looked at wilderness through the eyes of a hunter and budding ecologist. Arthur Carhart, a landscape architect the Forest Service hired in 1919, emphasized the aesthetic and recreational benefits of a policy of non-development. Carhart was assigned to the district office in Denver and was asked to survey the Trappers Lake area in Colorado's White River National Forest for summer-home sites. While laying out his survey lines, he came upon two wealthy hunters, Paul J. Rainey and William McFadden, who convinced him that the area should remain wild and that houses and roads should be excluded from the vicinity of the lake. As a result, Carhart developed a recreational plan to preserve the area's pristine conditions and convinced his superiors to halt plans to develop the region, marking, in the words of Donald Baldwin, "an unprecedented step in Forest Service history."[7]

Carhart followed his success at Trappers Lake with a memo to Leopold after a meeting between the two men in the Denver district office. "The Forest Service," Carhart admitted, "is obligated to make the greatest return from the total Forests to the people . . . that is possible." But, he concluded, there is "a great wealth of recreational facilities and scenic values within the Forests, which have not been so utilized and at the present time the Service is face to face with a question of big policies, big plans, and big utilization for these values and areas."

Carhart later surveyed the lake region of the Superior National Forest in Minnesota and repeated his recommendation that development be minimized and that the area be preserved as much as possible for primitive travel by canoe. On September 9, 1926, Secretary of Agriculture William H. Jardine signed a plan to protect the area, providing a wilderness policy decision at the highest departmental level.[8]

Carhart resigned from the Forest Service at the end of 1922, and Leopold's departure two years later for the Forest Products Laboratory left the agency's evolving wilderness policy in others' hands. The strongest impulse behind the movement continued to be growing pressure for recreational use of the national forests, as Forest Service annual reports from 1921 to 1929 reflect.

Beginning in 1926, wilderness too was singled out for separate discussion. According to Chief William B. Greeley, the wilderness idea had "merit and deserves careful study, but its correlation with the other obligations and requirements of National Forest administration must be carefully worked out before definite steps are taken to give any areas a wilderness status."[9] With that, Greeley and Assistant Forester for Lands Leon F. Kneipp ordered an inventory of all undeveloped national forest areas larger than 230,400 acres (ten townships). Three years later, wilderness policy assumed national scope with the promulgation of the L-20 Regulations covering so-called national forest primitive areas. Management priorities were defined "to maintain primitive conditions of transportation, subsistence, habitation, and environment to the fullest degree compatible with their highest public use with a view to conserving the values of such areas for purposes of public education and recreation." A management plan was to be prepared that would show the conditions under which timber, forage, or water resources would be utilized, permanent improvements constructed, and special-use occupancy allowed.[10]

According to James P. Gilligan, whose 1953 doctoral dissertation was to play an important role in the development of the wilderness bill, these regulations were simply strong recommendations to Forest Service field personnel suggesting limitations on unplanned development in untouched areas. They did not categorically prohibit any form of development or use, and, consistent with the agency's decentralized style of administration, they gave a great deal of discretion to field personnel. By 1939, for example, some 14 million acres of national forestland had been designated "primitive," yet as late as 1953 logging, grazing, and roads had been totally excluded from only four primitive areas.[11]

Historians have suggested that the Forest Service had two primary reasons for recommending the L-20 Regulations. First, they were to discourage personnel from rushing into unnecessary development projects. Second, they were to stem the transfer of more land to Park Service units. Most of the national parks since 1916 had been carved out of national forest acreage.[12] Designating primitive areas showed that the Forest Service too was interested in preserving wild regions and that land transfers to the Park Service were unnecessary.

Some Forest officials have denied the importance of interagency rivalry in explaining the L-20 Regulations, since they proved to be no guarantee that land would not be transferred to the Park Service.[13] Nevertheless, it is possible that primitive designations forestalled creation of even more parks. For example, despite vigorous campaigning the Park Service never convinced Congress to convert portions of the Idaho national forests to park status, perhaps because the Forest Service had previously designated large sections of this area—now part of its Frank Church River-of-No-Return Wilderness— as primitive. The Forest Service's reluctance to place an acreage minimum on primitive areas also suggests an intent to discourage parks. Leopold had suggested 500,000 acres, and Kneipp had asked for an inventory of areas exceeding 230,400 acres, but the L-20 Regulations permitted instead many smaller designations. Although this may have been an early recognition that wilderness can be protected in relatively small areas, the suspicion persists that it was an attempt to encompass any area that might have national park potential.[14] This interagency rivalry was clearly reflected in bureaucratic terminology. In the 1920s, the Forest Service called its undeveloped areas "wilderness," while the Park Service called its backcountry "primitive." When the Forest Service published its L-20 Regulations covering "primitive areas," the Park Service switched to "wilderness."[15]

Preservation organizations, such as the Sierra Club and the Wilderness Society, were later able to take advantage of this rivalry. Given its legislative mandate to preserve scenic landscapes, the Park Service naturally received strong support from wilderness advocates, but the Forest Service too found it expedient to court this growing element in the public lands constituency. Moreover, the Forest Service could press its advantage by asserting that it would not clutter its primitive areas with recreational developments, which many wilderness advocates were finding disturbingly prevalent in the national parks by the 1930s.[16]

Few were more skilled at exploiting this situation than Robert Marshall. The son of a wealthy New York attorney, Marshall dreamed of wilderness exploration while growing up on Park Avenue and hiking in the Adirondacks. Afraid that he had been born too late to emulate his boyhood heroes, Lewis and Clark, he felt compelled to climb every peak and explore every wilderness possible. After a short stint in the Forest Service (1925–1928), he earned a Ph.D. in plant physiology and became chief forester for the Office (now Bureau) of Indian Affairs, where he established a system of Indian wilderness. From his position with the Department of the Interior, he exhorted the Forest Service to increase its primitive acreage. In 1933 he wrote the recreation section of *A National Plan for American Forestry* (the Copeland Report), thereby gaining broader public exposure for his wilderness ideas.

While working within the BIA, Marshall pressed his conservation-minded boss and friend, Secretary of the Interior Harold L. Ickes, for a stronger Park Service commitment to wilderness preservation. An astute and ambitious administrator, Ickes hoped to expand his domain by enlarging the national parks at the expense of the national forests. Thus Ickes was disposed to listen to Marshall, and in 1939 he proposed legislative protection for park wilderness. Ickes's plan died, however, primarily because the National Parks Association, the service's main support organization, feared that special protection for park wilderness would result in the degradation of heavily used areas of the parks.[17]

Marshall left the Interior Department in 1937, disappointed by what he saw as the Park Service's growing attachment to recreational development. He was recruited to head the Forest Service's Lands Division, which had recently been renamed Recreation and Lands. From this new position within the Forest Service, Marshall spoke out for stronger wilderness protection, focusing his advice particularly upon Forest Service chief Ferdinand A. Silcox.

In 1939 the U Regulations, drafted by Marshall and approved by Silcox, supplanted L-20. The new regulations afforded much greater protection to wilderness areas, prohibiting timbering, road construction, and special-use permits for hotels, stores, resorts, summer homes, organizational camps, and hunting and fishing camps. The use of motorboats or the landing of aircraft, except where such practices were well established or were needed in emergencies or for administration, was also prohibited. Livestock grazing was permitted, as it had been under L-20, because stockmen would have vigorously opposed any ban. Water-storage projects were also allowed if they did not involve road construction, as were improvements necessary for fire protection, "subject to such restrictions as the Chief deems desirable." Forest Service wilderness areas, like the rest of the national forest system, remained subject to existing mining and leasing laws and to the possibility of reservoir and dam construction. The Forest Service could insist under the U Regulations only that such developments be undertaken with a minimum of damage to the wilderness environment.[18]

In two and a half years with the Forest Service, Marshall had succeeded in strengthening its wilderness policies, but he became disenchanted by the slow pace of reclassification and the failure to enlarge the potential bank of wilderness areas beyond 14 million acres. Before his death in 1939, he was considering leaving the Forest Service in order to apply pressure from outside the government.[19]

Shortly after Marshall's death, the Forest Service entered a new phase of timber management. Timber had replaced grazing as the service's largest source of income by the mid-1920s, but the annual cut was insignificant compared with the potential harvest; many roadless areas were preserved in their pristine state simply because there was no demand for their resources. Rapid expansion of the wood products industry at the end of World War II, however, compelled it to turn its attention to national forest timber resources. The Forest Service thus entered an era of intensive management and became involved in the market economy.

The revived postwar economy also brought more people to the national forests and increased the demand for recreational facilities. This, plus the clamor for wood-based commodities, gave preservationists a growing sense of unease over the long-term security of the wilderness areas. They especially feared policy changes by new Forest Service leaders, who seemed willing to interpret the concept of "wise use" flexibly to meet increased demands for timber in the postwar world. Moreover, preservationists distrusted the agency's decentralized organization, which worked admirably in allowing personnel to adjust to local social and economic conditions, but which, they felt, militated against the application of uniform standards for the protection of fragile wilderness resources. Finally, preservationists sensed a crucial difference in the foresters' "mental image" of wilderness, which considered environmental changes as subject to the recuperative powers of nature, and their own, which abhorred such changes as a threat to the idea of wilderness purity.[20] Congressional protection, they hoped, would ensure the survival of wilderness.

All the structural criticisms that the preservationists raised regarding wilderness management in the 1940s and early 1950s became focused on the issue of Forest Service primitive area reclassification. Perhaps the best-known example of the anger reclassification generated occurred on the Willamette National Forest in the mid-1950s. The Forest Service removed 53,000 acres of timbered land at lower elevations in the Three Sisters Primitive Area. This action aroused the ire of Oregon's junior senator, Richard L. Neuberger, who soon after became a co-sponsor of the wilderness bill. Neuberger remained the bill's most ardent congressional advocate until his death in 1960.[21]

Wilderness advocates were aware that the Forest Service was under pressure from local communities to increase the amount of land available for timber harvesting. Ever since the creation of the national forests in the late nineteenth century, administrators had been criticized by Westerners for "locking up" resources. Sensitive to these pressures, preservationists began to explore ways in which the Forest Service and Park Service could successfully resist development and give free rein to their best wilderness intentions. In addition, preservationists felt that they had to combat what they perceived as a deterministic attitude among foresters who felt that however worthwhile wilderness preservation might be, it must give way to economic development.[22]

Wilderness areas not covered by the U Regulations were disappearing at a rapid rate. At least 35 million acres of "de facto wilderness" in the national forests had been developed between the Kneipp survey of 1926 and 1960. Continued development seemed certain, but the preservationists differed with the determinists in that they believed that many such de facto areas could be preserved by congressional action.[23] This conviction later became the philosophical preamble of the Wilderness Act, which was to ensure that "an increasing population, accompanied by expanding settlement and growing mechanization, does not occupy and modify, all areas within the United States and its possessions, leaving no lands designated for preservation and protection in their natural condition."[24]

In 1946 Howard C. Zahniser of the Wilderness Society drew together these concerns in his criticism of an American Forestry Association conference report presented at Higgins Lake, Michigan. To Zahniser, the conference recommendations appeared only to rationalize—"with . . . up-to-date terminology"—increased commercial use of America's forests. If this assumption proved correct, he intimated, he and his fellow conservationists would be compelled to "charge our expectations up to disillusionment and enter a prolonged period of fighting for wilderness preservation with our guard up whenever 'good forestry' is mentioned." Zahniser responded with a call for wilderness zoning for certain areas of "primitive America."[25] He was probably thinking of some form of legislation to compel zoning, although he did not say as much to the foresters. It was indeed such a statutory mandate that Aldo Leopold had suggested when Zahniser was hired as executive secretary of the Wilderness Society and editor of its publication, *Living Wilderness*.[26]

Zahniser was born in Franklin, Pennsylvania, in 1906, the son of a Free Methodist minister to whom Zahniser attributed the evangelical fervor of his own crusade for wilderness. He joined the United States Biological Service in 1930 and from 1931 to 1945 served as a writer, an editor, and a broadcaster for several conservation agencies. In 1945 he accepted a position as executive secretary (later executive director) of the Wilderness Society. With Aldo Leopold's death in 1948, Zahniser became the nation's foremost wilderness advocate and assumed most of the burden of articulating a philosophy and program of wilderness protection until his own death at fifty-eight, a few months before passage of the Wilderness Act.[27]

Zahniser's enthusiasm corresponded with the concerns of a growing number of people who were discovering the attractions of wilderness after World War II. Although he derived great inspiration from nature, he was not a backcountry adventurer like Marshall and Leopold, and, anyway, he seldom found the opportunity to get away from work. When he suffered a heart attack in 1952, he blamed himself for not taking his own advice on the therapeutic value of wilderness.[28]

In a 1947 exchange of letters with a Berkeley forestry professor, Frederick S. Baker, Zahniser expressed several of the philosophical themes that he would repeat over the next seventeen years. He accepted neither Baker's fatalistic assumption that wilderness would inevitably disappear nor his solipsism that wilderness is "within us" and need not depend on a pristine physical reality. For Zahniser, wilderness was indeed "within us," but the mental image itself was "dependent on the perpetuation of wilderness." He likened wilderness areas to art museums that also contained national treasures; even people not destined to see them firsthand could appreciate the effort to protect them.[29]

To Baker's argument that wilderness enthusiasts were interested only in self-gratification and escape, Zahniser countered that wilderness was also morally uplifting.

Love of solitude, eagerness for adventure, and indulgence in romantic experience are, as you point out, the most common motives for "fleeing to the wilderness" for recreation. Once there, however, many, I believe, experience a better understanding of themselves in relation to the whole community of life on earth and rather earnestly compare their civilized living with natural realities—to the improvement of their civilization.[30]

This moral view of wilderness, hardly evident before World War II, may have been accentuated by the implications of living in a nuclear age.[31] Nature must uplift man lest he destroy it along with himself.

Zahniser's letters reveal two personality traits that would serve his cause admirably. He was patient but determined, and he was pragmatic, and although he adamantly defended the moral value of wilderness, he recognized that the concept meant different things to different people. Flexibility and persistence enabled him to follow the wilderness bill doggedly for seven years through sixty-six rewrites and many compromises. Even then, he wore himself out and, like Marshall and Leopold, died at a relatively young age.[32]

One of Zahniser's first successful efforts occurred in 1949 when he persuaded Congressman Raymond H. Burke, chairman of the Subcommittee on Wildlife Resources of the House Committee on Merchant Marine and Fisheries, to commission the Library of Congress to complete a study of America's wilderness needs. The study was assigned to C. Frank Keyser, an economist with the Legislative Reference Service, who sent questionnaires to federal and state agencies and conservation organizations. The Forest Service's response pointed to mining and reservoir construction as the largest threats to its wilderness areas, but it recommended further study before any legislative action. The more sanguine Park Service said it managed parks as units and kept recreational developments to a minimum: it suggested only that more wilderness land be transferred to its jurisdiction. The Fish and Wildlife Service, which managed the nation's wildlife refuges under authorities less clearly defined than those governing the Park Service and the Forest Service, favored some kind of national wilderness policy. After analyzing the responses, including a forty-six-page report from Zahniser, Keyser concluded that majority opinion favored national legislation for wilderness. The report was published as a House committee print, and a limited number of copies were given to the Wilderness Society for distribution to those interested.

Keyser's report set the stage for Zahniser's first detailed proposal for federal wilderness legislation. His plan, offered at the Sierra Club's Second Biennial Wilderness Conference, included several points he would later incorporate into the initial wilderness bill. Congress, he suggested, should establish a national wilderness system; it should define the proper uses of areas within the system and prohibit incompatible uses; it should identify appropriate areas and list areas qualified for possible inclusion later; it should specify that additions could be made by executive order, but that removal of areas from the system could be effected only by Congress; it should make clear that no changes in jurisdiction over wilderness areas would be involved, that the agency administering a designated wilderness area would simply be charged with responsibility for preserving its wilderness character; and finally it should authorize a commission to recommend to Congress any necessary adjustments in the program. Zahniser's choice of the term "system" emphasized his preference for comprehensive wilderness legislation.

The unveiling of Zahniser's plan coincided with the beginnings of a controversy that would fundamentally alter the campaign for wilderness—in the late 1940s, in response to proposals from the Bureau of Reclamation and Army Corps of Engineers for dams in several western national park units, water users suggested a dam at Echo Park in Dinosaur National Monument as part of the ambitious Upper Colorado River Storage Project. Located in northwestern Colorado and eastern Utah in an isolated and starkly beautiful region known primarily for its valuable paleontological remains, Dinosaur National Monument had been proclaimed a national monument in 1915 and considerably enlarged by President Franklin Roosevelt in 1938. This threat to inundate it rekindled memories of the bitter Hetch Hetchy defeat and the loss of that beautiful valley in Yosemite National Park some forty years earlier, and preservationists launched what would become a five-year campaign to thwart it. By the time the proposal had been deleted from the storage project in 1955, it had provoked more public opposition than any issue in recent conservation history. Preservationist organizations and the public, skillfully mobilized by advocates such as David R. Brower of the Sierra Club and Zahniser, responded not only to the Echo Park proposal but to what they perceived as a threat to the entire national park system.

The Echo Park controversy clearly demonstrated that in the absence of an aroused public opinion the national park system was ultimately unable to protect wilderness values, and that a new, more comprehensive system was needed. The campaign had great educational value as well; although focused on a national park unit as little known as many of the Forest Service primitive areas, the Echo Park campaign had succeeded in rallying massive public support for wilderness values. The very anonymity of Echo Park had special significance; had the dispute involved a better-known park unit, it may not have highlighted the need for comprehensive wilderness legislation.

Conservation organizations came away from the Echo Park controversy greatly encouraged and more united than ever. The time was ripe for a wilderness bill. In May 1955, Zahniser, in a speech to the American Planning and Civic Association, presented the philosophical arguments for wilderness preservation and repeated the specific proposals he had made in 1951. Senator Hubert H. Humphrey, who had been involved in the fight to preserve Echo Park, inserted the speech in the *Congressional Record*. The Wilderness Society mailed reprints of the speech to its members and those in other conservation organizations under the franks of cooperative legislators.

Humphrey was so impressed with the strength of the wilderness sentiment that he asked Zahniser to develop a bill, and he began work on the first draft in February 1956. Within weeks, the document was circulating among leaders in the conservation movement.

Zahniser and his collaborators expressed three main concerns. They wanted a clear, unambiguous bill, free of loopholes; they wanted to maintain the coalition that had formed earlier to protect Dinosaur National Monument; and they hoped to minimize opposition. Tactical considerations aside, the bill's drafters hoped to provide clear statutory authority for the maintenance of wilderness areas, to remove Forest Service authority for declassifying or decreasing the size of wilderness-type areas, to protect national forest wilderness against mining and water projects (both of which were authorized by Congress), and to require designation of wilderness zones in units of the national park system, in the federal wildlife refuge and range system, and within Indian reservations.[33]

To gain support from federal land-managing agencies, Zahniser specified that existing jurisdictions would be respected and that the bill would not supersede the purposes for which the land was being administered, except to require that its wilderness character be preserved. Moreover, as Senator Humphrey later pointed out, it was not to be a "reform" measure but a bill that merely encouraged and sanctioned the good practices of the country's land-managing agencies.

Zahniser attempted to blunt opposition from commodity interests by assuring them that existing uses would be respected. This, however, was of little comfort to stockmen or operators of motorboats or airplanes because their uses of wilderness were considered "nonconforming" and were to be terminated in a manner "equitable" to them. The bill contained language that could be used to enforce condemnations if the agencies were unable to reach voluntary agreements with the nonconforming users.

The bill's supporters gave much thought to two provisions that would be hotly contested in the ensuing national debate and that would be primarily responsible for delaying passage for more than eight years. These concerned mining and the manner in which Forest Service primitive areas could be added to the wilderness system. (The wilderness and wild areas were to go immediately into the system.) Zahniser's first draft had prohibited mining and prospecting except on claims already established. In a later draft, he liberalized this section by allowing the president to open wilderness areas to prospecting and mining if necessary for the common defense and security of the nation. (National park wilderness, most of which had never been open to mining, remained under the categorical ban.) This was done to disarm critics who charged that the wilderness system endangered national security. However, on the advice of Lyle F. Watts, former Forest Service chief, this provision was deleted and Zahniser reverted to his original position. Needless to say, mining interests emerged as the most vigorous opponents of the wilderness bill.

In his first draft, Zahniser gave congressional imprimatur to the Forest Service U Regulations as they applied to wilderness and wild areas. The Forest Service was given until January 1, 1965, to reclassify all its primitive areas. Previous practice was altered only in that congressional authority was necessary to modify or eliminate wilderness areas. In a later draft, this procedure was dropped in favor of a "legislative veto." Under this scheme, proposals from the executive branch that would modify, eliminate, or create a wilderness area could be stopped by a majority vote of either house. The procedure was consistent with the preservationists' view of the federal agencies: they usually did the right thing, but had to be stopped when they went astray. It had the effect of increasing the initiative of the executive branch and placing Congress in the role of a somewhat passive reviewer, but as far as the preservationists were concerned, it combined the best of both worlds. On the one hand, it provided fast and professional administrative action, unencumbered by legislative logjams or a committee chairman's power to delay legislation. On the other hand, Congress retained the authority to react quickly to public dissatisfaction should the executive branch attempt an unpopular decision.

At the end of February 1956, copies of the draft bill were informally given to the Park Service and the Forest Service. Conrad L. Wirth, director of the Park Service, replied that such a bill was not necessary and might even endanger national park wilderness areas by lumping them together with those of other agencies. The Forest Service opposed the provision establishing a wilderness commission (later changed to "council") to monitor the land-managing agencies. Administrators also feared that other special interests would seek similar legislative guarantees for their uses of the national forests. In the late 1940s and early 1950s, stockmen had attempted precisely that. Their push for virtual proprietary rights over national forest rangelands had been blocked by 1956, but the nearly successful effort was still fresh in the minds of Forest Service leaders. Ironically, Arthur Carhart, a citizen of Colorado where the "range war" had been most intense, at first opposed the wilderness bill for that reason.[34]

The Wilderness bill, with Senators Humphrey and Neuberger as co-sponsors, was introduced on the Senate floor on June 7. By then, support for and opposition to S. 4013 had already begun to coalesce. Because it was late in the legislative season and the presidential election was only five months off, Humphrey introduced the measure only as a study bill. The full legislative process did not begin until February 1957, when Humphrey reintroduced the bill as S. 1176.[35]

The legislative history of the bill can be summarized as a process of drawing together support for the wilderness system and chipping away opposition through a series of compromises aimed primarily at commercial users of the national forestlands. Regulations regarding grazing best illustrate this process. Grazing is the oldest and best-established commercial use of national forest areas. Until the 1920s, grazing fees were the largest source of income from all national forest system lands. Stockmen were a potent political force in the West and exerted their power whenever the Forest Service threatened to raise grazing fees or cut back on overgrazing. Under these circumstances, the service had allowed controlled grazing in wilderness areas under the L-20 and U Regulations.

In his 1949 report to the Library of Congress, Zahniser had called grazing a "nonconforming" use that should be terminated. In 1956 he incorporated this language into the wilderness bill, with the proviso that terminations be made "equitably." In 1957 the bill was amended to state that grazing "may" continue under such "restrictions" as the secretary of agriculture deemed desirable. Finally, in 1963 "may" was changed to "shall" and "restrictions" to "regulations."[36]

But even with grazing recognized as a valid use of national forest wilderness, stockmen feared that they would be denied the money-saving advantages of roads and motorized equipment. Moreover, they, like other commodity groups, had an amorphous fear that wilderness legislation somehow contained a hidden gremlin or that it could be used to expand the wilderness system. A 1958 colloquy between Senator Richard Neuberger and George D. Zahn of the Washington State Cattlemen's Association exemplifies that attitude.

> SENATOR NEUBERGER. Mr. Zahn, I just want to read you one sentence in the bill, because you particularly mentioned grazing because that is the interest of the Washington State Cattlemen's Association. One sentence in the bill reads as follows: "Within national forest areas included in the wilderness system, grazing of domestic livestock . . . may be permitted to continue subject to such restrictions as the Secretary of Agriculture deems desirable." Now, do you believe that that is substantial protection for the economic interest in which you are interested?
>
> MR. ZAHN. Senator Neuberger, I believe that it is no protection at all. The word "may," if it was "shall," it would he excellent, but the bill in other places says "existing rights if any." I believe the whole tenor of the bill is a mandate to the administering agencies of the Federal domain to place wilderness use paramount above all others.[37]

Like stockmen, water users formed a potentially formidable source of opposition to the bill. Many national forests owed their existence to pressure from western farmers and urbanites who wanted to protect their watersheds from damage by overgrazing or excessive timber cutting. Zahniser was undoubtedly deferring to this fact when he proclaimed watershed protection the dominant use of wilderness. But protecting a watershed and developing it so that it will yield more water in the right ways are different matters. Not surprisingly, reservoirs and waterworks were prohibited in the first wilderness bill. However, the bill's sponsors quickly realized that the water issue alone could kill the bill. For instance, Senator Thomas H. Kuchel of California, who was a co-sponsor of the first bill, dropped out in the next round because of his concern over California's need for water. This problem was largely solved in 1957 when Zahniser accepted the Forest Service's suggestion that the president be allowed to authorize such projects, including the building of roads and transmission lines, when he deemed them in the national interest.[38]

Miners, too, enjoyed a long tradition of free entry on the nation's public lands that the wilderness bill seemed to threaten. Under the Mining Act of 1872 and the Mineral Leasing Act of 1920, mining and energy concerns were given license to explore, stake claims, and apply for leases on the public domain. The miners argued that to exclude them from wilderness areas flouted American legal and cultural traditions and would damage the national interest by restricting the extraction of important metals. Although somewhat ambivalent initially, Zahniser had prohibited mining in the first wilderness bill. At the urging of the Forest Service, the bill's advocates later introduced a provision allowing mining, like water projects, when the president found it to be in the national interest. But the mining factions were not satisfied. Clearly, it would be more difficult for an individual miner or mining concern to obtain such permission than it would be for an entire community to get permission for a reservoir. Presidential authorization, as Senator Gordon Allott of Colorado put it in 1961, was "just another piece of sugar held out to make people believe that we are not going to suffer under the bill."[39]

For the next three years, the bill was stalled in the House Committee on Interior and Insular Affairs as its chairman, Wayne N. Aspinall, successfully maneuvered to incorporate congressional affirmative action, which allowed only Congress to create and enlarge wilderness areas, and the continuation of mining. The Senate was finally forced to accept the House committee's provision that opened the national forest wilderness areas to the mining and leasing laws until January 1, 1984. This was a bitter pill for the preservationists, but many who would not have sympathized with the miners' position were placated by the compromise language in the bill's final form.[40]

The Wilderness Act, signed by President Lyndon Johnson in September 1964, has had a profound effect on the Forest Service—the federal agency most involved in the formulation of the act's basic principles. Because the act involved fundamental questions of definition, its passage was a welcome opportunity to clarify policy regarding uses of national forest wilderness areas. Next to the question of congressional affirmative action, in fact, the complex of issues relating to national forest wilderness was paramount in the bill's legislative history.[41]

Casualties of language litter the battlefields of public policy, and in the case of the wilderness bill, the expression "multiple use" (in foresters' parlance, that combination of uses yielding the greatest public benefit) came close to linguistic extinction. Because it had been coined by practical foresters interested in using commercial forest resources, the term usually put preservationists on the defensive. When they did care to pronounce it, they meant only those uses that were consistent with maintaining the forest's wilderness character—scientific research, recreational and scenic enjoyment, educational enrichment, and watershed protection. In fact, Zahniser maintained that watershed protection was the dominant use of any wilderness area; if recreationists threatened this purpose, their numbers and activities should be restricted.[42] The term was rescued from semantic muddle only with the passage of the Multiple Use–Sustained Yield Act of 1960, which recognized that "the establishment and maintenance of areas of wilderness are consistent with the purposes and provisions" of the act.[43]

In the national forests, the debate over multiple use and wilderness restrictions had focused on timber cutting and grazing. The Wilderness Act clarified Forest Service policy in both areas, although prescribing different approaches to each activity. A wilderness bill that allowed timber harvesting would have been no wilderness bill at all, for it would have licensed the largest possible alteration of wilderness environments; commercial timbering was completely prohibited under the Wilderness Act, except that wilderness miners could cut timber for their operations if it was not otherwise available and if the cutting was done under good forest management practices defined under national forest rules and regulations.[44]

Grazing restrictions were somewhat more complex. The secretary of agriculture can regulate established wilderness grazing but not abolish it. Grazing is a permanent, legitimate use of national forest wilderness. However, the drafters intended to freeze the status quo in wilderness grazing. For instance, grazing cannot be introduced into a wilderness area that has not previously known it. Structures and improvements used for grazing can be maintained, but no new facilities can be built unless, like drift fences, they are needed to protect the wilderness environment. Moreover, the Forest Service can promulgate reasonable grazing regulations, as it does in other national forest areas, and reduce stocking in areas that it finds to be overgrazed. Grazing in wilderness areas is a "privilege," just as it is elsewhere in the national forests.[45]

Zahniser once said that wilderness, like chastity, is defined by that which it negates.[46] The history of the wilderness bill is essentially the history of how much the preservationists could compromise before themselves being compromised. When it was all over, some felt that they had given too much.[47]

But as a soap-opera character might say, since the preservationists accepted the violation of their principles only under duress, they were never really violated. More important, those who championed the wilderness concept, from Aldo Leopold to Howard Zahniser, created a strong popular movement that has been able to vitiate some of what advocates perceived as compromising provisions.[48] While creating legislative sanction for the wilderness system, they also generated tremendous public support for their cause. Consequently, it has been possible to preserve and enlarge the wilderness system despite what seemed to be disabling provisions in the act. Thus the evolution of the wilderness concept did not stop with the signing of the Wilderness Act; it has but moved to a somewhat more secure and elevated plane.

NOTES

1. Joel Gottlieb, "The Preservation of Wilderness Values: The Politics and Administration of Conservation Policy" (Ph.D. diss., University of California, Riverside, 1972), 121–32.

2. Stephen Fox, *John Muir and His Legacy: The American Conservation Movement* (Boston: Little, Brown, 1981), offers a good general history of the conservation movement.

3. Elliott Barker to Senator Clinton B. Anderson, 12 August 1959, box 619, Clinton B. Anderson Papers, Manuscript Reading Room, Library of Congress.

4. Susan L. Flader, *Thinking Like a Mountain: Aldo Leopold and the Evolution of an Ecological Attitude Toward Deer, Wolves, and Forests* (Columbia: University of Missouri Press, 1974), 15–17.

5. James P. Gilligan, "The Development of Policy and Administration of Forest Service Primitive and Wilderness Areas in the Western United States" (Ph.D. diss., University of Michigan, 1953), 77.

6 Ibid., 83; Donald Nicholas Baldwin, *The Quiet Revolution: Grass Roots of Today's Wilderness Preservation Movement* (Boulder, Colo.: Pruett, 1972), 153–65.

7. Baldwin, *Quiet Revolution,* 34.

8. Quoted in Walter Gallacher, *The White River National Forest, 1891–1981* (Glenwood Springs, Colo.: White River National Forest, 1981), 45; R. Newell Searle, *Saving Quetic-Superior: A Land Set Apart* (St. Paul: Minnesota Historical Society, 1979).

9. United States Forest Service, *Report of the Forester* (Washington, D.C.: Government Printing Office, 1926), 36; United States Forest Service, *Report of the Forester* (Washington, D.C.: Government Printing Office, 1927), 13.

10. Regulation L-20, October 1930.

11. Gilligan, "Development of Policy," 191–97.

12. Gottlieb, "Preservation of Wilderness Values," 141–53.

13. Richard E. McArdle, "Wilderness Politics: Legislation and Forest Service Policy," *Journal of Forest History,* October 1975, 166–79.

14. Gilligan, "Development of Policy," 118–98.

15. Ibid., 157.

16. Scott, "Origins and Development of the Wilderness Bill," chap. 4, 10–21.

17. Ibid., chap. 3, 28–35.

18. Gilligan, "Development of Policy," 197.

19. Jack M. Hession, "The Legislative History of the Wilderness Act" (M.A. thesis, San Diego State University, 1967), 27.

20. Scott, "Origins and Development of the Wilderness Bill," chap. 2, 16–22; Michael McCloskey. "The Wilderness Act of 1964: Its Background and Meaning," *Oregon Law Review* 45, no. 4 (1966): 294.

21. Hession, "Legislative History of the Wilderness Act," 31.

22. *Living Wilderness*, Winter 1947–1948, 1.

23. Albert Dixon, "The Conservation of Wilderness: A Study in Politics" (Ph.D. diss., University of California, Berkeley, 1968), 61.

24. United States Department of Agriculture, *The Principal Laws Relating to Forest Service Activities*, Agricultural Handbook No. 453 (Washington, D.C.: Government Printing Office, 1978), 201.

25. Howard C. Zahniser, *Living Wilderness*, December 1946, 28.

26. Zahniser to Clinton B. Anderson, August 6, 1959, box 619, Anderson Papers.

27. *Living Wilderness*, Winter 1947–1948, 1; Fox, *John Muir*, 269–71.

28. Fox, *John Muir*, 267, 269; *Living Wilderness*, Autumn 1947, 7–16.

29. *Living Wilderness*, Winter 1947–1948, 1–4; *Living Wilderness*, Autumn 1947, 12.

30. *Living Wilderness*, Winter 1947–1948, 4.

31. Fox, *John Muir*, 287.

32. Ibid.; *Living Wilderness*, Winter 1947–1948, 4; for details on the drafting of the wilderness bill, see Scott, "Origins and Development of the Wilderness Bill," chaps. 5–7.

33. McCloskey, "Wilderness Act of 1964," 298.

34. Harold K. Steen, *The U.S. Forest Service: A History* (Seattle: University of Washington Press, 1976), 301–7.

35. Hession, "Legislative History of the Wilderness Act," 72.

36. *Living Wilderness*, Winter–Spring 1956–1957, 34; U.S. Congress, Senate, *Establishing a National Wilderness Preservation System*, 88th Cong., 1st sess., S.R. 109, 1963, 10; U.S. Congress, Senate, *Hearings Before the Committee on Interior and Insular Affairs*, 85th Cong., 1st sess., 19, 20 June 1957, 181–82 [hereafter cited as *Hearings*].

37. U.S. Congress, Senate, Committee on Interior and Insular Affairs, *National Wilderness Preservation Act, Hearings*, 85th Cong., 2nd sess., 1959, 310.

38. *Hearings*, 394; *Living Wilderness*, Autumn 1957, 31.

39. *Congressional Record*, 87th Cong., 1st sess., 5 September 1961, 18089.

40. *Congressional Record*, 88th Cong., 2nd sess., 20 August 1964, 20601.

41. Hession, "Legislative History of the Wilderness Act"; Roderick Nash, *Wilderness and the American Mind*, 3rd ed. (New Haven, Conn.: Yale University Press, 1982); Dixon, "Conservation of Wilderness."

42. U.S. Congress, House of Representatives, *Hearings Before the Subcommittee on Public Lands*, 88th Cong., 2nd sess., 27–30 April, 1 May 1964, 1227.

43. *Principal Laws Relating to Forest Service Activities*, 197.

44. Ibid., 303.

45. McCloskey, "Wilderness Act of 1964," 311; Senate Committee on Interior and Insular Affairs, *National Wilderness Preservation Act, Hearings,* 257; Michael McCloskey, "What the Wilderness Act Means," in *Action for Wilderness,* ed. Elizabeth R. Gillette (San Francisco: Sierra Club Books, 1972), 14–21.

46. *Hearings,* 158.

47. Gottlieb, "Preservation of Wilderness Values," 184.

48. Ibid., 190; Ronald Gibson Strickland, "Ten Years of Congressional Review Under the Wilderness Act of 1964: Wilderness Classification Through 'Affirmative Action' " (Ph.D. diss., Georgetown University, 1976), 226–27.

Forest Dreams, Forest Nightmares: An Environmental History of a Forest Health Crisis

Nancy Langston

When whites first came to the Blue Mountains of eastern Oregon and Washington in the early nineteenth century, they found a land of lovely open forests full of yellow-boled ponderosa pines five feet across. These were stately giants the settlers could trot their ponies between, forests so promising that people thought they had stumbled into paradise. But they were nothing like the humid forests to which Easterners were accustomed. Most of the forest communities across the inland West were semiarid and fire-adapted, and whites had little idea what to make of those fires.

After a century of trying to manage the forests, what had seemed like paradise was irrevocably lost. The great ponderosa pines were gone, and in their place were thickets of fir and lodgepole. The ponderosa pines had resisted most insect attacks, but the trees that replaced them were the favored hosts for defoliating insects such as spruce budworm and Douglas fir tussock moth. As firs invaded the old ponderosa forests, insect epidemics swept the dry western forests. By 1991, on the 5.5 million acres of Forest Service lands in the Blue Mountains, insects had attacked half the stands, and in some stands nearly 70 percent of the trees were infested.[1]

Even worse, in the view of foresters and many locals, was the threat of catastrophic fires. Although light fires had burned through the open pines every ten years or so, few exploded into infernos that killed entire stands of trees. But as firs grew underneath the pines and succumbed to insect damage, far more fuel became available to sustain major fires. Each year, the fires seemed to get worse and worse. By the beginning of the 1990s, one major fire after another swept the inland West, until it seemed as if the forests might entirely go up in smoke. The Forest Service responded by declaring that the region faced a crisis in forest health.

What happened in the Blue Mountains happened across the American West, from Washington south to Arizona and from the Dakotas west to the Pacific—wherever there were relatively dry forests dominated by ponderosa pine. In this chapter, I analyze the environmental history of the forest management practices that led to forest health problems in the Blue Mountains, summarizing the arguments I developed at greater length in *Forest Dreams, Forest Nightmares*.[2] Although I restrict my analysis to a 5.5-million-acre region, similar environmental problems have developed from American transformations of forests throughout the West.

In an unusual admission of guilt and confusion, the Forest Service stated in the 1991 *Blue Mountain Forest Health Report* that the forest health crisis was caused by its own past management practices—and so therefore it would have to change those practices.[3] But no one could agree exactly which management practices caused the problems, much less how to restore the forests. On one level, the landscape changes resulted from a series of ecological changes. Heavy grazing removed the grasses that earlier had suppressed tree germination, allowing dense thickets of young trees to spring up beneath the older trees. When the federal foresters suppressed fires, the young firs grew faster than pines in the resultant shade, soon coming to dominate the forest understories. High-grading—removal of the valuable ponderosa pine from a mixed-conifer forest—helped change species composition as well. But the story is much more complex than this. Changes in the land are never just ecological changes: people made the decisions that led to ecological changes, and they made those decisions for a complex set of motives.

There are two basic perspectives on the causes of forest decline in the Blues—both of them inadequate. Many environmentalists argue that to feed the demands of the timber companies, federal foresters promoted excessive harvests, and these harvests led to soil compaction, removal of valuable pines, and even-aged management, creating a simplified ecosystem that is increasingly susceptible to epidemics.

Many other people believe exactly the opposite: they argue that the Forest Service bowed to the demands of sentimental preservationists, and refused to harvest the forests intensively enough to save them from disaster. These people put the blame on past decades of light, selective cutting, arguing that only intensive management can save the forests. Since ponderosa pine is shade intolerant, they reason that clear-cutting, even-aged harvests, and intensive management are the only ways to ensure that fir stands do not replace pine stands. In their view, the best way to eliminate insects, disease, and fire from a stand is to manage it as intensively as possible.

These two perspectives on the history of forest health problems obviously lead to radically different management prescriptions. It is probably obvious that these two stories of what went wrong are, at least in part, shaped by the different ideologies of their proponents. A traditional forester who sees an old-growth forest as a place of decay, waste, and decadence tends to believe that the human role in forestry is to prevent waste and promote a clean, productive, growing stand. Conversely, someone trained in an ecosystem perspective will tend to see insects and disease as having value in a forest, and will value old-growth stands more than single-species stands under even-aged management.

Ideology is not everything, however, even though it certainly shapes one's view of who is to blame. The story is more complicated than either perspective suggests. The training of early foresters was heavily influenced by European silviculture, which had as its ideal a waste-free, productive stand: nature perfected by human efficiency. Early Blue Mountains foresters all agreed that their goal was to transform decadent old growth into vigorous, regulated stands for sustained-yield forestry. Yet until World War I, they never tried to implement these ideals, largely because there were few markets for the trees. It was neither economically nor technologically feasible to cut the forests heavily enough to bring about intensive sustained-yield forestry. After World War I, however, the Forest Service established extremely high rates of ponderosa pine harvests, creating the ecological and economic conditions that directly led to the forest health crisis of the 1990s.

Why did the Forest Service promote such high harvests? Desire for profit, power struggles, bureaucratic empire building—all of these played an institutional role, but none of them can explain motivations of individual foresters. To understand their decisions, we need to examine the links between ideals and material reality in American forestry. Federal foresters shaped the western landscapes according to a complex set of ideals about what the perfect forest ought to be. In turn, these visions were shaped by available logging technology, developing markets for forest products, the costs of silvicultural practices, and what Rich Harmon called "the unrelenting pressures . . . aimed at government officials to make public resources available for private profit."[4]

Ultimately, landscape changes resulted from attempts to manage, perfect, and simplify the forests: to transform what in 1913 the forester George Bright called "the general riot of the natural forest"—by which he meant the old growth—into a regulated, productive, sustained-yield forest.[5] In other words, this is not just an ecology story; it is a story about the complex metaphors people use to mediate their relationship with nature—and the ways these metaphors have led to millions of acres of dying trees.

Federal foresters came to the Blues with a vision of working with wild nature to make it perfect—efficient, orderly, and useful. They wanted to be good land stewards, to make everything just right, to clean out every timber stand so it would be free of decadence and full of elk. Yet in trying to make the land green and productive, they ended up making it sterile. This is not a story with a villain (the greedy timberman) and a hero (the brave environmentalist). Instead, it is a tragedy, in which decent people with the best of intentions ended up destroying what they cared for most. Foresters destroyed the forests, not in spite of their best intentions, but *because* of them—precisely because foresters' ideas of what was good for the forest were based on an ideal of deliberately transforming nature to serve industrial capitalism.

Forest change comes about not just because people cut down trees, but because they cut down trees in a world where nature and culture, ideas and markets, tangle together in complex ways. To understand forest history, we need to pay attention to at least three interwoven categories.

Cultural: How did cultural ideals affect the ways different groups of people changed the forests? What kinds of visions of the relationship between humans and nature did foresters bring to the forests? How did these visions shape the land? In particular, what scientific visions of the forest shaped the foresters' work? In which political and cultural contexts did these scientific theories develop? How did foresters' scientific ideas and technology shape the forests?

Ecological: What were the biotic and abiotic factors that shaped forests? Plant communities; disturbance processes such as fires, floods, insect epidemics, and soil processes; and hydrological processes are major (but often overlooked) players in forest history. How did ecological constraints affect the land's response to management? How did management change the paths of forest history?

Political: Over the course of a century, forest communities in the Blues were transformed into a collection of resources exported out of the region to feed the demands of distant markets. How did different groups negotiate conflicts over who should determine the rate and extent of logging? How did government officials respond to congressional, corporate, and local pressures to make public resources available for private profit? Whose vision of the land determined how the land was shaped?

Most forest histories have focused on this final category of political, administrative, and institutional relationships, treating ecological factors as unchanging givens, rather than as dynamic players in the story.[6] In this analysis, I pay less attention to political forces, focusing instead the links between categories.

To understand what went wrong in the Blues, we first need to consider the complexity of the Blues forests, particularly the ways that these forests differed from humid eastern forests. These were disturbance-prone landscapes, marked by varying patterns of change. Fire, wind, insect epidemics, and droughts shaped a shifting mosaic, where patterns of forest types and grassland and sagebrush were anything but stable.

Water and fire—and the changes that water and fire brought—were at the heart of these differences. Much of what went wrong in the Blues was a failure to pay attention to the land's signs. Trees made the Blues appear a fertile, promising, easy place to the first whites who came, but those perceptions proved to be illusions. The forests' fertility was based on ash soils that were quite different from eastern soils, and when managers tried to apply forestry techniques based on eastern forests, those techniques decimated the soils. The constraints that aridity imposed were unfamiliar to people who knew only forests that grew in moister places.

The critical resource in the Blues—the resource on which the rest depended—was not trees or grass, or even soil, but water. Water—the lack of water, the distribution of water, the storage of water—affected every aspect of forest and grassland ecology in the Blues. Because most of the Blues' precipitation came in the form of winter snows, the water that trees needed to grow came not from rains that fell during that period of growth, but instead from stored water.[7] Any activities that decreased the ability of the forest soils to hold snowfall had magnified effects on the forests.

Whites who first arrived in the Blues found a land completely unlike the humid forests of home. What seemed familiar at first glance proved to be different, and this was unsettling. People expected forests to be moist and fertile, but these forests seemed too dry, too open, and not very fertile. Fires burned much more often than people thought was normal or desirable, and no one understood how forests could survive these constant fires. Sagebrush typically indicated poor soil, but the soil under this sagebrush seemed better than much of the forest soil. Rivers normally drained to the sea, but many of these rivers drained into the Great Basin and never flowed out. The canyons were far too steep; people could not believe the evidence their eyes gave them. Trees grew on top of these steep canyons but not down by the water, where trees were supposed to grow. It seemed like someone had turned the world upside down.

Part of what seemed strange to Easterners, especially to those used to the vast stretches of climax forests in Maine and the Midwest, was the diversity of vegetation types within the Blues. When the government forest inspectors came to classify the Blues forests at the turn of the century, the variety of trees, habitats, and forest types astonished them. The inspectors walked through steep treeless grasslands covered with sagebrush and bunchgrass, and then crossed into juniper woodlands. These gave way to stately ponderosa forests spaced in as open and pleasing a pattern as any that the inspectors knew from the landscaped parks in eastern cities. Along the creeks, strips of lush cottonwood forests shadowed the waters, and these cool riparian zones offered shelter from the brutal summer sun. When the inspectors crossed from the south face of a canyon to the north face, they moved out of the ponderosa forests into much denser forests dominated by Douglas fir, grand fir, and larch—communities they called the north-slope type or fir–larch forests. At first glance, these north-slope forests appeared uniform, but when the foresters looked more closely, they realized that there were many small patches of larch, fir, spruce, and pine jostled together. The inspectors climbed higher into the hills, finding themselves in thickets of lodgepole pine. Their way became nearly impassable as piles of dead wood and tangles of wind-thrown lodgepole blocked the route. If the men kept climbing, they would enter high, eerie forests filled with the stumps of subalpine fir and contorted, wind-twisted whitebark pines. Where fires had burned in small, hot patches, lush meadows interrupted the high forests, and finally the forests gave way to mats of wind-cropped fir and then rock and snow.[8]

Out of all these forests, it was the ponderosa pines that caught men's eyes. These were trees to warm a lumberman's heart: the largest ponderosa recorded on the Wallowa Forest was seventy-four inches across at breast height, a granddaddy of a tree. Even the averages were impressive. In 1912, the average-size ponderosa pine on the Wallowa was thirty-three inches across; eighty years later, the averages had shrunk to nineteen inches, not because ponderosa had stopped growing, but because loggers had cut most of the oldest trees.[9]

Ponderosas were sturdy, sun-loving trees that seemed as if they could take anything. They had very long taproots, which gave them the edge over Douglas firs on the hot, dry south slopes. With their taproots, ponderosas could reach water deep in the soil, thriving where Douglas firs could barely survive. Thick furrowed bark made the older trees extremely fire resistant. Even the young trees were quite resistant to fires, for once they were about ten years old and two inches across, they put on a layer of dead bark that protected them from damage.[10] In sum, they were long-lived trees: they resisted drought, fire, winds, storms, and most insect attacks. All they needed was sun and space and time to grow.

Walking today in one of the few remaining forests of big ponderosa pines gives you a strong sense of déjà vu. "Where have I seen this before?" you wonder. You saw it in a thousand Westerns, where the cowboys loped their ponies between the trees, and a glimpse of granite peaks broke the upper-right-hand corner of the frame. These forests feel like the real West, or at least like the real Western. "Charming" is a good word for them. The grass lies green and lush and lovely in the spaces between the trees, which are huge and many. People call these forests parklands—a perfect name for the open, easy feeling they evoke. There is just enough shade to keep the sun off your forehead, just enough breeze filtering through the trees to keep the flies away. The parklands appeal even to people who do not much like forests—they are forests on the edge of forestedness, forests that claim grandeur and awe among their forest-like attributes, without being claustrophobic. This is not a tangled, terrifying wilderness of nasty beasts and wicked woodcutters; this is the land of butterscotch and ponies and Westerns.

Ever since whites first came to these forests in 1811, they were struck by nostalgia. Time and again, journals of explorers and travelers recorded that the pinelands gave rise to sweet memories of an imagined childhood home. As Narcissa Whitman wrote in 1836 when she was making her way across the Blues to help establish a mission among the Cayuse Indians: